LOVE STORIES NOW AND THEN

LOVE STORIES NOW AND THEN

A History of *Les romans d'amour*

Translated by Carmen Ruschiensky

Marie-Pier Luneau and Jean-Philippe Warren

Baraka Books

Montréal

Originally published as *L'amour comme un roman.* (Presses de l'Université de Montréal)

ISBN 978-1-77186-364-3 pbk 978-1-77186-375-9; epub 978-1-77186-376-6 pdf

Cover by Gianni Caccia
Book Design by Folio Infographie
Editing and proofreading: Robin Philpot, Anne Marie Marko

Legal Deposit, 4th quarter 2024
Bibliothèque et Archives nationales du Québec
Library and Archives Canada

Published by Baraka Books of Montreal
Printed and bound in Quebec

TRADE DISTRIBUTION & RETURNS

Canada – UTP Distribution: UTPdistribution.com

United States
Independent Publishers Group: IPGbook.com

We acknowledge the support from the Société de développement des entreprises culturelles (SODEC) and the Government of Quebec tax credit for book publishing administered by SODEC.

Société de développement des entreprises culturelles Québec

Funded by the Government of Canada
Financé par le gouvernement du Canada
Canada

Contents

Preface to English Edition

This book represents the first study of the French-language Quebec romance novel, from its beginnings in the early nineteenth century to its most contemporary expressions.

The translation of this work is of interest to English-speaking readers because it introduces them to a little-known literature that is often scorned by cultural gatekeepers. Three other factors, however, highlight its relevance to an English readership. First, the rise of the sentimental novel in Quebec followed a laborious path—more so than in the United States or the United Kingdom. French Canada's classic novel, *Maria Chapdelaine* (1913), written by a visiting Breton named Louis Hémon, ends with the heroine mourning her one true love and marrying a good but unremarkable man. The novel teaches that a woman must wait for "the encounter with some young man, like other young men" and accept a marriage "dreary and chill as an autumn field," rather than aspire to be lifted by desire and passion. Similarly, in Gabrielle Roy's celebrated *The Tin Flute* (1945), Florentine Lacasse's dreams of escaping her impoverished milieu through a loving marriage are ultimately shattered, and she must resign herself to becoming engaged to a man for whom she feels only lukewarm affection.

The reason for such mistrust was that a burning passion between two people threatened long-standing, traditional French-Canadian codes. The elites accepted love of nation, love of land and, above all, love of God as honourable goals of a patriotic and Christian life. But they could not tolerate a carnal love that took the form of a fever, a delirium, and that risked jeopardizing the social norms of the time. They feared that if everyone were free to listen only to their hearts, it would become acceptable for a Catholic to marry a Protestant, a French-speaking man to marry an English-speaking woman, a farmer's son to marry a socialite! Indeed, this is what some novels hinted at, daring to defy the prohibitions of conservative elites. *Les fiancés de 1812* (1844), for example, proclaims the primacy of feelings in the moral realm. In this novel by the very liberal Joseph Doutre, Louise explains to her father and mother why she has chosen to follow her heart and disown her parents, without fear of the scandal she is about to provoke. "In spite of the sacred bonds that nature had imposed on me, [...] shall I hide from you that it is still with a kind of happiness that I distance myself from you! Am I not following in the footsteps of the husband whom heaven and my heart have chosen for me!"

It is therefore interesting to analyze the conditions that enabled the emergence of the romance novel in Quebec, and how a few works, first rare, then more frequent, attempted to show that love could blossom within the French-Canadian community without posing a threat to it. To do this, the authors of these novels sought to describe how love, however "mad," could respect endogamous imperatives. The example of incest, which we discuss in our book in its specific literary form, is particularly interesting in this respect: morally reprehensible from the point of view of societal norms, its representation served to reinforce the reproduction of family heritage and frame passionate attraction as an ideal fusion (which translates into a desire to marry one's "better half"). This is undoubtedly why it exerts such a fascination in nineteenth-century works, where metaphors of incestuous love abound. The dime novels of the 1940s and 1950s are just as captivating, since, curiously enough, they lack the insistence on escape (historical or geographical) so characteristic of the productions of Mills & Boon and, later, Harlequin. The heroine is never seen in the arms of an oil millionaire on a Midwestern ranch or an aristocrat in a remote corner of Edwardian Scotland. Everything takes place in the present and in Quebec, between white, heterosexual, Catholic and French-speaking characters. Exoticism is sometimes used to discredit the secondary characters, when not otherwise quickly erased to restore respectability to the heroines and heroes. The eponymous heroine of *Jarna la créole* (1951), a creation of Éditions Police-Journal, was born in New Orleans, but her parents were Québécois and she grew up in Montreal under the care of Catholic nuns: she would make a suitable wife.

The history of the Quebec romance novel shows how difficult it is to build a national literature of romance, except in countries that have made exoticism an essential part of their national identity, such as the United States, where the English language already presents itself as an international language and American culture as a world culture. The materialism and sexuality of romance novels are anchored in a globalized universe, insofar as this materialism is part of a borderless consumerism (only the external characteristics of the house, the car, the evening dress, the venues change from one title to the next). At the same time, sexuality is conceived as instinctual, wild and impulsive, independent of any moral "restrictions." When love is turned towards material and physical pleasure, and when absolute love is also the ideal (those who measure their love betray their inability to truly love), an overly local and context-specific romance market is inevitably weakened, and this is in fact what we see almost everywhere. Quebec thus offers a fascinating field of study for analyzing the factors that contribute to Harlequin's easy absorption into so many national cultures and national regional cultures' incapacity to produce

Harlequin-type romance novels in turn. Attempts to compete with Harlequin in French-speaking markets, for example, have so far met with limited success at best.

Second, the history of Quebec sentimental literature also appeals to an English-speaking audience because, in the late twentieth and early twenty-first centuries, it integrated many feminist values (without necessarily accepting their most radical consequences). This trait is particularly noticeable in teen literature. The novel *The Big Loser* (1986), by Raymond Plante, is exemplary in this respect. It features sixteen-year-old François Gougeon, who falls in love with classmate Anik Vincent. Not very good-looking (he has a big nose and wears glasses), shy, awkward and insecure, François knows he cannot compete with Anik's boyfriend, Patrick Ferland, who is older, fitter, stronger, richer, and more attractive. During a brawl, Patrick beats him up. Anik, a real tomboy, seems to do everything better than François: she excels at sports as much as she does at school. François only succeeds in seducing Anik when he agrees to make fun of himself and become a "pink man"—a Québecois term for a progressive man (when Anik discovers that he wears pink boxers, she tells him that she loves it).

In Quebec chick lit, there is a similar will to establish more egalitarian relationships between women and men. Still socially and professionally deficient, the chick lit heroine lives a life fraught with tension: she feels she needs a man around her, and yet realizes that this admission infantilizes her and make her less autonomous. To resolve the contradiction of having to fulfill herself both alone and with a man, she does not hesitate to play the game of love with a certain detachment, when she is not indefinitely postponing a happy ending with an ideal partner. Chick lit's portrayal of love can be explained by a disenchantment with the promise of happiness that a loving marriage once held. Nowadays, the heroine knows that even the most ardent attraction can wither and that she needs to be lucid and persevere in a relationship that is constantly beset by the worries of everyday life. As singer Lisa Leblanc put it in 2012: "I'm fed up with Disney fairy tales / Prince Charming's a moron, / and the princess is a bitch / Nothing will come easy."

Quebec chick lit thus favours "satisfying endings," i.e., denouements in which the female character accepts being in a relationship with a nice, simple guy, whose many flaws she does not try to hide. In *La mort d'une princesse* (2017), by India Desjardins, the heroine, having realized that the romantic comedies she devoured as a teenager were entirely unrealistic reaches the conclusion that love is made up of compromises and that even the greatest love cannot escape the hassles of a contemporary household. In the final pages of the novel, she rings the doorbell of a man she finds attractive, introduces herself to him as a girl who just wants to enjoy spending some time with someone nice, and kisses him. "How long," she wonders, "will it be before I move on? I decide to chase these thoughts away and simply live in the moment. There will always be time to deal with the rest later." The absence of a Mr. Right (a handsome, rich and domineering man, like the one Candace Bushnell's heroines constantly dream of in *Sex and the City* [1996]) forces the Quebec chick lit heroine to depend more on herself and seek out relationships in which she will be treated with respect, as an equal, instead of being at the mercy of a man she passionately loves.

Third, the history of Quebec sentimental literature is of interest to an English-speaking audience because it tells us about the different place sexuality holds in English and French narratives. Until the 1960s, in the Quebec literary tradition, a woman had to attract a suitor by playing with a more or less subdued eroticism, while denying her own sexuality: the more a man loved, the more he tried to preserve the "virtue" of his chosen one. According to a hypothesis formulated by Anne-

Marie Lugan-Dardigna,* this attitude is rooted in a French romance tradition in which the woman is more likely to love before she desires, whereas in the English romance tradition, the woman is more likely to desire before she loves. In the former case, she must expiate her future sins and purify herself through sacrifice and suffering (as illustrated by *The Princess of Cleves* [1678], the classic novel in which the heroine refuses to give herself to the Duc de Nemours, even after her husband's death), while in the latter, she has to live out her desire outside of love, which she can only do by sublimating her fantasies or describing scenes of rape (as in the illustrious *Pamela, or Virtue Rewarded* [1740], a novel in which the heroine accepts an offer of marriage after many men take advantage of her).

Even today, there is a division between the English-speaking and French-speaking publishing worlds. Harlequin's famous clinch is frowned upon by many French-language publishers, who dare not go too far in marketing their catalogues, eschewing embossing and the use of glossy paper and garish colours, as can be seen on any given day by visiting two Montreal bookstores, one francophone and the other anglophone, and comparing the French and English versions of the same novels. The more or less crude nature of the English book covers reflects a more explicit content, while the French marketing and visuals betray a way of telling love stories that calls for more ethereal, stylized and poetic descriptions. Indeed, studies on French translations of Harlequin novels have shown that passages that are too bold have been omitted or reworked to respect an approach to love that favours eroticism over overt sexuality. For instance, in Harlequin novels the term "fuck" has no equivalent in French translations. It is in this sense that we can argue that the paths of love are generally different in the French and English literary

* Anne-Marie Lugan-Dardigna, "Presse du cœur et roman rose: la quête de l'amour vrai ou comment trouver un maître," in Didier Coste and Michel Zéraffa (ed.), *Le récit amoureux*, Seyssel, Champ Vallon, 1984, p. 284-296.

traditions: the former goes from love to desire (without which love is nothing), and the latter goes from desire to love (without which desire is vain).

Although notable differences remain, things began to change in the 1960s. In *Love Stories Now and Then*, we hypothesize that the market for sentimental novels suffered between 1960 and 1980 due to the new popularity of other media, including the rise of photonovels, the craze for the new crooners of the 1950s (including the "King of Cool," Dean Martin), the arrival of soap operas featuring more sensual romance (with the broadcast of Montreal's first private French-language television channel, Télé-Métropole, in 1961), and the end of film censorship. In the late 1970s, the romance novel enjoyed a renaissance because it offered something the other mediums could not: a genuine sexualization—not just eroticization—of lovemaking, leading to the famous "rape sagas" popularized by Kathleen E. Woodiwiss's *The Flame and the Flower* (1972). The romance novel was able to say what other mediums could not (in much the same way that the arrival of soap operas signalled the end of radio dramas). Interestingly, the film based on *Fifty Shades of Grey* (2011), released in 2015, closely follows the novel, except for the sex scenes, some of which have been removed from the film adaptation altogether.

For all the above-mentioned reasons, we believe that *Love as Romance* is sure to be of interest to English-speaking readers, introducing them to a little-known literature that is the heir to two great traditions, French and English. As a school of sentimental fiction, the romance novel teaches what to do and, perhaps above all, what not to do. The tribulations of heroines and heroes reveal the *pride* and *prejudices*, as well as the *senses* and *sensibility* that cause the characters' momentary downfall, before reversals occur that are as unforeseen (by their implausible twists and turns) as they are predictable (by their conformity to the inevitable happy ending). As a result, the romance novel is always set in a social and historical context. While the Quebec romance novel shares a common core with other works in the genre, it also brings its own nuances to the game of love and reflects a certain originality within the much broader context of the global romance publishing industry.

Jean-Philippe Warren, Concordia University (Montreal)
Marie-Pier Luneau, Université de Sherbrooke (Sherbrooke)

INTRODUCTION

All your fine words

Love is generally held to be an absolute and universal aspiration, all individuals being subject to its power. Presented as a natural and irresistible phenomenon, the feeling of love is thought to spring forth mysteriously, as though people fall in love (especially and ideally in the case of "love at first sight") without any forethought or purpose. A popular French-Canadian saying translates its perceived indomitability well. If, as is often said, "one cannot prevent a heart from loving," (*On ne peut pas empêcher un coeur d'aimer*) it is because the social institutions, the rules of common sense, and the self-interest and will of lovers—who sometimes desperately fight their own inclinations—cannot resist this devouring, irrational passion, which often arises unexpectedly and at the unlikeliest moments.

This book is based on the premise that love is not as spontaneous and free as one would have us believe. While it is true that love exists in all human communities, not all communities love in the same way. One has only to open an anthropology or history book to see that different societies attribute a precise place to the impulses of love, codifying its manifestations, structuring its relations, and determining its outcomes in different ways. The words used to speak of love, which simultaneously reveal and censor, inform and sublimate, channel and repress the stirrings of the heart, are chosen according to norms that must be understood in their specific contexts.[1]

The history of intimacy is often viewed against the backdrop of a gradual liberation of mores. Modern societies have gone from a repressed or discreet intimacy to an outwardly exhibited one.[2] While our analysis does not deny this general evolution, we do not take it as confirmation of the fundamental emancipation of the place of intimacy in society. The latter is best understood in terms of the evolution of intimacy itself, which implies both acceptance and constraint. Modern societies have slowly embraced the feeling of love, accepted its new forms of expression, and freed it from former moral constraints. But, at the same time, they have devoted, and continue to devote, a colossal amount of energy to defining what love is and what it is not. They are incessantly formulating a grammar of love.

This grammar of love is found in multiple forms of cultural production (cinema, television, music, etc.) which determine, in more or less restrictive ways, the rules of encounter, declaration, and courtship. To examine the different forms of passion in French-Canadian and Québécois society,[3] we have chosen to study the history of the romance novel. This literary genre lends itself particularly well to a historical analysis of regulatory discourses and fantasized representations, since it can be read as a narrative that is both heavily codified (to the point of adopting the serial format) and potentially subversive (to the point of being banned from libraries).[4] Far from corresponding to a simple leisure activity or innocent distraction, romantic fiction facilitates the internalization of models that mark out the stages from courtship to marriage. By providing details on letter writing, urban outings, the etiquette of physical intimacy, or recipes for a successful marriage, romance novels reveal the "codes of love."[5] They uniquely combine escape (as a leisure activity), education (as a school of feelings), and alienation (as an instrument of social control), and are, consequently, best apprehended through these three dimensions.

As a product of popular culture, the Quebec romance novel has received little scholarly attention and has never been the subject of a comprehensive survey. While the genre rarely displays the qualities that make for "great" literature, its status has been doubly downgraded since the nineteenth century: associated with mass culture and targeting a primarily female readership, it is considered to be a mediocre, puerile and even intoxicating product.[6] Although it does not necessarily belong to the realm of paraliterature (think only of *The Princess of Cleves*, classic among the classics), it is has often inspired more contempt than methodical research. This lack of interest is regrettable. By adopting facile prejudices against romance literature, critics have neglected to grasp its foundations and explore its themes. Filling this important gap, the present work provides a retrospective look at a popular literature that has been largely devalued. In doing so, it aims to promote a better understanding of the metamorphoses of love in the romance novel from the nineteenth century to the present day.[7]

This historical overview generally limits analysis to the representation of love in romance novels, but we have allowed ourselves, when relevant, to refer to events or facts that shed light on the social and cultural mutations recorded in the fiction over time. Although most studies addressing this subject have done so in an indirect way, notably through monographs on marriage[8] or sexuality,[9] they provide useful historical and sociological background to our own research.[10] Birth, marriage, and divorce rates, for example, can offer insight into the evolution of the romantic imagination. Without entering the complex debate on the relationship between reality and fiction, which has received ample attention,[11] suffice it to say that we believe the romance novel, while linked to the context in which it was produced, has evolved according to its own logic. The claim that love as passion escapes reason (expressed in the idea of blind love, mad love or love as disease and fever) and only answers to itself (being a law unto itself) is reinforced by a literature that offers both objective description and dreamlike fantasy, oscillating between real life and utopia. This confusion reaches its paroxysm in the passages of certain stories where the characters, transported by the joy of love, confess to living a "true love story," in an interesting *mise en abyme.*

Our focus on the representation of love has also guided our approach to the study of the works themselves. It is the expression of passion that constitutes the core of our subject. Clearly, even the simplest romance novel includes digressions, parallel stories, or other peripheral considerations that could have found their way into our analysis but would have obliged us to spend far too much time on each work. We have limited our analysis to the central sentimental narrative of each novel, rather than exploring the full range of possible interpretations. In particular, we do not consider the characters' physical appearance, clothing, occupation, and profession, except where necessary to understand the dynamics of the novel. For example, while it may be instructive to note that the nineteenth-century black-eyed heroine is replaced by a blue-eyed heroine a century later, this information does not affect the romantic relationships based, in both cases, on the immeasurable beauty of the dulcinea.

Finally, it is important to point out that the context in which the works were received is given some, but limited, consideration here. On the one hand, we include some general observations on the market in which the romance novel is situated. The romance genre has known in French Canada (1830-1960), then in Quebec (1960-present), periods of waxing and waning popularity and sales over nearly two hundred years. On the other hand, in the spirit of focusing on the expression of the sentiment of love itself, we do not examine the precise effects of romance literature on those who consume it. Without avoiding the question of readership altogether, which, since Janice Radway's classic, *Reading the Romance*,[12] has refined our appreciation of how the works were received, we chose to not dwell on this aspect, as it would lead us astray from our primary object of study.

What is a romance novel?

If our definition of the romance or sentimental novel (the two expressions are used synonymously here)[13] were to include any novel that speaks of love, our corpus would exclude very few works. In order to keep the genre of the romance novel as circumscribed as possible and avoid getting lost in a maze of literary texts, we have adopted a strict definition based, in part, on the one put forward by Ellen Constans in her work *Parlez-moi d'amour*.[14] Constans highlights three "invariants" that must be present in a story in order for it to qualify as a "romance novel."

First, the "fable must consist of a single love story whose unfolding structures the entire narrative."[15] This means that there is, in the traditional novel, a HER and a HIM, who are identified by the reader from the first pages, and whose tribulations we follow until the end.[16] Secondary plots can be grafted onto the main story, but they remain subordinate. It is the actions of the heroine and the hero, directed towards the search (conscious or not) for happiness in love, that structure the narrative framework, until its outcome. The erotic novel, whose quest is primarily focused on the sexual pleasure of the protagonists, is thus absent from our corpus. We will see that, up to a certain point, the romance novel and erotic novel exclude each other, since, in the traditional literary imagination, love must sublimate the impulses of sexuality, to triumph, so to speak, over the flesh and rise to a purer and more sublime level. An often-encountered cliché in our corpus from the nineteenth and twentieth centuries hammers home the same point: the more the hero loves the heroine, the more willing he is to delay physical intercourse (including kissing). This hierarchy, in which the heroine's sexual initiation rests on the man's shoulders, remained prevalent even after the cultural revolution of the 1960s.

The second invariant follows from the first: "the two protagonists of this fable are designated as elements of a couple from the very first pages and we find the same couple at the denouement."[17] The heroine and the hero are placed in a relationship of superiority to the other characters, which relegates the secondary figures (confidant, rival, etc.) to the shadows, once they have fulfilled their narrative function. In an exemplary manner, at the end of Jane Austen's *Pride and Prejudice* (1813), Elizabeth Bennet lists the characters in the novel, indicating how each of them has been useful to her happiness, i.e., to her union with Mr. Darcy, a character whose appearances, nevertheless, constitute only a small part of the overall narrative. It is at that point that we understand that the whole novel, from beginning to end, was to culminate in this single outcome.

The heroine and hero are distinguished by physical and psychological features that set them apart and form an integral part of the genre. The traditional heroine, often present from the first page, has a strong character, but is also reserved, fragile, and sensitive. The traditional hero, entering the scene soon thereafter, displays, in contrast to her, characteristics of virility and power. The heroine and hero are symmetrical, being defined in relation to one another, which does not mean that they are equal—far from it. Moreover, we can say that these two characters who are made "for each other" are constructed as opposites, creating a tension that leads them to both attraction and repulsion, a tension based on gendered universes defined in and by their opposition. When, from the moment of their meeting, the heroine and the hero are convinced they hate each other, we know beyond any doubt that we are in the presence of a future couple. "I had not known you a month, and already I felt that you were the last man in the world that I would consent to marry," Elizabeth of *Pride and Prejudice* exclaims. Seen in this perspective, love is a war, a duel, a bullfight.[18] According to these enduring stereotypes, the woman is on the defensive and the man is inclined to attack. In our corpus, many conquering heroes enter the intimate space of the heroine without knocking, try to steal a kiss from her, or threaten her with abuse. But the heroine is also capable of wounding, of insult and injury. The important thing is that, despite the conflict between the woman and the man, love emerges victorious, each protagonist eventually laying down their arms and surrendering to the other, admitting their mistakes, their errors, their blindness. This element, which is very important in the romance novel, explains why a society that has gone through a feminist revolution could still later create love stories featuring career-driven, determined women and discreet and sensitive men, the opposition between the sexes being infinitely more important than the sex of the oppositions, a point unfortunately obscured by Western Civilization's patriarchal influence on the genre.

Finally, the last invariant specifically concerns the unfolding of the narrative, which always includes the following sequence of three moments: meeting, disjunction, and final conjunction in happiness or misfortune.[19] Revisiting the Greek novels, Ellen Constans recounts a scene involving a glance exchanged between the heroine and the hero, where the future lovers, without having met before, spot each other in the crowd. As soon as the emotional tension is established, the protagonists part ways, which announces the disjunction, a stage extending over most of the novel: from that point on, the readers are led to wonder how the two lovers will end up being reunited. Because, reunion, there must be. She and he, whether they know it or not at the outset, are an essential half (the "better half") of each other. The insistence on the opposition between the characters serves not only to obscure their homophily (of class, religion, ethnicity, race) in order to magnify a passion that is never so sublime and authentic as when it transcends the differences that separate them, but also to make their union a perfect fusion (two strong individuals "become one," are "all for each other") and their disunion a monstrosity ("Without her, without him, I cannot live").

The reasons for the disjunction change over time, which allows the romance novel to renew itself, while maintaining a canonical structure. While the characters are, in the most archaic forms, separated by natural elements (shipwrecks, storms), the causes for temporary disjunction become, over time, more social and psychological. In Quebec, in the nineteenth century, girls were prevented from marrying because of nationality or religion, while in the interwar period, more varied obstacles arose, linked to class differences. In the immediate postwar period, lovers tend to despair more over misunderstandings or incompatibilities of character. In any case, the main characters always reconcile at the end of the story. We have become accustomed to the happy ending, where the two lovers, in a passionate embrace, promise to marry. But an unhappy final conjunction, involving the death or disappearance of one or both characters, is also possible. We have only to think of the model popularized by *Romeo and Juliet*, a play in which the two lovers are reunited in death: as long as the narrative sanctions their final reunion, it is still a romantic work. As we shall see, this tragic motif was abundantly reproduced in the novels of nineteenth-century Quebec, under the influence of the Gothic movement and a certain form of Romanticism.

In sum, we can say with Constans that "the romance novel is [the novel] of the triumph of love."[20] This apparently tautological formula is fundamental. The essential message of the romance novel is that outside of love there is no salvation, and this is true as much for the heroine as for the hero. Love is the cardinal virtue that governs the actions of the characters and gives meaning to their lives, even against their will, for they are often its playthings. The resigned spinster and the hardened bachelor come to understand, at the end of many stories, how empty their lives were without love and how, in the arms of their partner, their existence is now perfect because it is "complete." Summing up the essential message of the romance novel, one of the characters of our corpus exclaims, at the end of his adventures, that life has given him "the most incredible gift ever: love, happiness, family... everything."[21]

Our corpus

Based on several years of research using reference works and historical sources,[22] our inventory includes more than a hundred romance novels, covering a wide variety of styles and collections. This long-term research has enabled us to draw up a list of emblematic works, from the origins to the present day. The simple constitution of this corpus is in itself an important contribution to knowledge, since it reconstructs for the first time the history of a paraliterary genre previously neglected by research in Quebec. By studying a multitude of novels, most of which are little known, if not completely forgotten (hence the need to summarize them), our synthesis demonstrates not only the persistence of a genre that has long been thought absent from literary history, but also the heuristic quality of texts whose value has been regularly denied by disregarding them as "dipped in rose water" ("*écrits à l'eau de rose*").

However, despite our best efforts, our catalogue is not exhaustive. For the period before the Second World War, many works of popular literature are difficult to trace because they were not preserved, and the identification of titles corresponding to the criteria of our research thus remains uncertain. Not surprisingly, we discarded many novels because, in the end, they deviated, despite their promising premises, from the romance genre. Likewise, a number of "true" romance novels undoubtedly escaped our scrutiny. New challenges in establishing our corpus arose in researching works from the 1940s onwards, only in reverse: at a time when popular literature was enjoying more widespread distribution, propelled by, among other factors, inexpensive formats such as the paperback and the dime novel, the number of romance titles skyrocketed. The extent of this mass production is evident in the rise of romance pulp fiction works published from the 1940s to the mid-1960s, which alone included more than 3,800 titles written by Quebec authors in eighty-one series produced by forty-nine different publishing houses. In this case, it was not the limited presence of sentimental works that posed a problem, but the difficulty in choosing representative titles from among the astronomical quantity available. Part of the selection process was made easier by looking at the sales figures of a few bestsellers, but our research admittedly often advanced in the dark, as we sorted through the titles ourselves, from one discovery to the next.

In addition to meeting the criteria proposed by Constans, we added two other strict requirements, so as not to get lost in the literary output. First, the novels had to be written in French by Quebec authors and, second, they had to circulate beyond the periodical press and be published in book format.[23] As for the decision to include only French-speaking Quebec authors in our corpus, we should note that this has not prevented us from occasionally referring to an exogenous production when it appears necessary to draw a quick portrait of texts that dominated the Quebec market and influenced, in the background, its development. We decided to limit analysis to romance novels published in book form[24] to avoid being overwhelmed by the vast quantity of possible material to cover, since periodicals abound in romantic stories which are often published in serial form.

While scrupulously respecting our set criteria, we have made room for certain nineteenth-century works that are somewhat beyond the scope of our study. Among these exceptions are the novels of Rosanna Eleanora Leprohon (née Mullins), an English-speaking Montrealer educated at the convent of the Sisters of the Congregation of Notre-Dame, whose plots drew on Canadian history and who has been described, admittedly with considerable exaggeration, as "[b]y taste and education, [...] a Frenchwoman who writes in English."[25] We also included some of the founding novels of Quebec literature, such as *L'influence d'un livre* (1837), *Les fiancés de 1812* (1844), and *Charles Guérin* (1853), in which many passages shed light on the emergence of a "romantic imagination," before the birth of the romance genre per se. In the same spirit, we also look at some short stories published in periodicals from 1830-1860 that have the unique feature of including more tragic denouements of the romantic plot, compared to the books of the time (very small in number, we might add). These different texts elucidate the gestation of the romantic imagination in Quebec and are essential to understanding what the romance novel would become, from the end of the nineteenth century until the Second World War.

Given that the romance novel has taken different forms throughout history, we are interested in its genesis and multiple mutations up to and including its current incarnations. We have been careful to trace this specific literary genre's developments, without, however, ignoring other types of production that overlap with it (for example, the photo novel and, more recently, "chick lit" and the new adult novel) and without completely overlooking works that are emblematic of its limits (for example, *Maria Chapdelaine* or *The Tin Flute*, which are not romance novels). In our opinion, the reinventions (in the plural) of the romance novel (in the singular) are what make its exploration fascinating. Despite the ever-changing cast of characters and circumstances of thwarted passion, the romance novel, at first glance, seems to repeat the same story over and over, that of "girl meets boy." And yet, from another perspective, it tells a story that is never quite the same, not only because each love story is unique from the viewpoint of subjects that love "with all their heart," but also because the authors try to weave the materials of their time into an original narrative framework, even if this comes at the cost of plausibility.

We include many footnotes that allow us to contextualize our interpretations, not only in relation to works on Quebec literature, but also, more broadly, on other national literatures, especially those of France, England, and the United States. In our view, American scholars have often worked in ignorance of French-language romance and their French-speaking colleagues have done the same with respect to English-language romance. We maintain that knowledge of both traditions can significantly deepen and refine our understanding of the historical development of the genre. The situation in Quebec, at the confluence of American and European currents, only makes this methodological principle even more essential.

Six major periods

Without denying that there are constant and numerous overlaps in time and borrowing between sub-genres, we have schematically divided the history of the romance novel in Quebec into six periods, which correspond to our six chapters. These six periods can themselves be grouped into two broad blocks. The first block (1830-1940) is defined by the fact that love is channelled towards something other than the couple (heritage, religion, homeland, social milieu). This fact explains why the analysis of this first block focuses on singular works that translate the love code into a socially acceptable language, as well as on publishing houses whose function was to formulate an edifying discourse. The second block (1940-2020) is defined by a love that is now turned towards the couple. Whereas the first block emphasizes the reasoning and sense of duty of the engaged couple, who had to think of something other than themselves when they got married, the second block celebrates the passion of the couple and personal happiness. This revolution (more than just an evolution) propelled the romance publishing market to an enviable position among other popular sub-genres such as crime and spy novels.

In the first chapter (1830-1860), we observe a period of incubation, that of "repressed" love, while the romance novel seeks to establish its foundations. The works included in this inaugural chapter are chosen from among adventure novels, Gothic novels, and novels of manners that harbour a romantic discourse that had not yet been fully established. With the emergence of the first real local romance novels, love is "sublimated" (second chapter: 1860-1920), while being strongly torn between duty (patriotic and religious) and passion. Some of the works that stand out from this still very limited local production can be interpreted individually. Not surprisingly, when love is "domesticated" (third chapter: 1920-1940), it is also the most disciplined love in the entire history of the romance novel. During this period, love is all but a "child of bohemia": the heroine's and hero's ability to express their desires had never been so constrained, so much so that, in our corpus, the romance novel, as a genre centred on the triumph of the love, comes close to being self-effacing. Tenderness and respect replace the passionate outpourings which do not seem, over this period, to be an indispensable ingredient of marital happiness.

With the upheavals brought about by the Second World War, and during the period of prosperity that followed, love is "celebrated" (fourth chapter: 1940-1965). The possibility of flirtation appears, the fiancés no longer being necessarily chosen from the extended circle of relatives and neighbors. Fuelled by the heroine's obsession with finding a husband and leaving the family nest, the romance novel experienced a dazzling vogue in the form of "dime novels." After the Quiet Revolution, love becomes "serial" (fifth chapter: 1965-2000), in the triple sense of "serialized," "reborn after every heartbreak," and "trivialized." Following a brief period of waning interest which saw few romance novels being published, we observe a revitalization of the genre at the turn of the 1980s. The surge of Harlequin novels (which entered the Quebec market in 1978) set the tone for this period, which celebrated free love, albeit by restricting this sexual freedom to a very conventional framework, under the pretense that sex is most fulfilling when partners are in love. Incorporating a more feminist perspective, romance novels for teenagers also express the search for a passion that no longer ignores sexuality. Finally, in the most recent period (sixth chapter: since 2000), love continues to flourish in chick lit, new adult novels, and homoromance. Sexuality seems more uninhibited than ever, and the fragility of love is now a fact recognized by everyone, without the dream of true love having disappeared "despite everything."

CHAPTER 1

Repressed Love (1830-1860)

The diary of George Stephen Jones, written between October 1845 and April 1846, offers a rare glimpse into the presence of romantic love in the nineteenth century, a time often imagined to be governed by the necessities of everyday life. The son of an English-Anglican priest and French-Canadian Catholic mother from Quebec City's Saint-Jean neighbourhood, George makes the acquaintance of Honorine Tanswell, also from a mixed marriage. The story of their courtship reads like a veritable novel, from the discovery of their mutual attraction to their eventual exchange of vows. At first not understanding what has come over him, George finally realizes he is in love. Over several months devoted to courting his lady, he experiences feelings that are quickly transformed into a devouring passion. He writes in his journal: "Honorine, Lovely Honorine, O how I love you, my lovely wife, my better half."[1] From then on, George's happiness hangs on this affection, and when it is compromised by the opposition of Honorine's father, he declares that no other man could have ever experienced so much pain. The journal ends rather abruptly, but we learn from the archives that George and Honorine enjoy a very Christian union shortly thereafter.

Clearly, love did indeed exist in French-Canadian society in the first half of the nineteenth century.[2] But, unfortunately, historical sources have left us little record of French Canadians' state of mind during this period. In any case, even if they had, we would probably be disappointed: the dominant ideology inhibited the impulses of passion, privileging moderation in interpersonal relations.[3] This restraint is evident in the attitude cultivated by the period's elites with respect to novels, and reading as a pastime was seen as suspect. "Bovarysm," the dreamers' escape from reality, was of great concern to censors, who condemned activities that would entice readers to surrender to their romantic tendencies.[4] Countless letters, sermons, editorials, and tracts warned the population against the sirens of the imagination and attempted to redirect people's attention to more urgent and respectable occupations. As we read in the *Cours abrégé de belles lettres* of the Collège de Montréal, "The reader's enjoyment, which seems to be the skilled novelist's intended goal, is but a secondary end to the primary one, which should be the instruction of the mind and the correction of morals."[5] Consequently, a model for proscriptive censorship condemning and prohibiting "bad" literature was gradually implemented alongside a model for prescriptive censorship based on the widespread dissemination and promotion of "good" literature.[6]

The elites' mistrust toward fictional works held back novelistic production in Quebec. Over the course of the nineteenth century, less than one hundred novels were published, and they were very often accompanied by prefaces that made heavy use of rhetoric to justify the publication.[7] The romance novel, which thrived on human passions deemed "base" or "shady," was particularly subject to this suspicion, and its emergence was subsequently hampered. Lovers abound in these stories, as we shall see, but the obstacles they face indicate that, most of the time, their primary concern is not the quest for happiness in love. Published in 1837, *Les révélations du crime ou Cambray et ses complices* confirms this: love "is the most violent and the most ardent of all the passions."[8] One could therefore never be too careful.

In order to understand the romance genre's gestation over a period that saw few published novels and none that meet our criteria, this introductory chapter will consider examples that fall somewhat outside our definition, by invoking works belonging to other genres: Gothic and adventure novels, novels of manners, and short stories. This detour is justified insofar as it contributes to enriching our overall analysis by introducing, in parallel, the framing of the romantic imaginary in the first half of the nineteenth century. Up until 1860, three main discursive strategies stand out and inform our understanding of the romantic imaginary in literature; we will examine these, in order, in the opening sections of this chapter. In the first case, Gothic and adventure novels transformed romantic passions by using the pretext of more-or-less fantastic adventures, all the while relating them back, *in fine*, to moral preoccupations. Attributing a certain authority to passion, these works favour excess, immoderation, and unrestrained urges (eroticism, crime, vice), without ever sanctioning the deviance; this entails stretching accepted norms beyond tolerable limits, all the better to then rein them back in. However, we will also see how, in the second case, these same texts uphold love as the ultimate goal and promote an individualistic moral that revolves around two people meeting, declaring their love, and "completing one another." Not surprisingly, a third narrative strategy intervenes which consists in stifling wild and unwieldy passions in favour of more sensible relations. In the section titled "The heart has its reasons that reason knows," we will see that the novel of manners restricts love to a pleasant and ingenuous discourse, the respectability of the romantic sentiment hanging in the balance between sincere inclination and social decorum. In a fourth section, we will examine a corpus that is less well known but essential to the genesis of a romantic imaginary in the nineteenth century.

Through happenstance, we unearthed a plethora of short stories, published in the press, featuring the often ill-fated love of young characters separated by death. Shaped by a Romanticism reminiscent of Chateaubriand, these texts achieve a synthesis of Eros and Thanatos, one that would leave enduring traces in the romance novel in Quebec, particularly in the recurring figure of the heroine tempted by suicide. Paradoxically, the fatal outcomes in this fourth section evoke both the avoidance and celebration of love: love born dead is contrasted with love born in death, the stories making use of this artifice to express the profusion of love, all the while condemning it.

Of love and adventure

Whether featured in papers or, more rarely, in volumes, texts before 1860 that do not overlook the vagaries of love are torn between order and adventure, to cite the title of Jacques Blais' study.[9] Moderation, as repeated time and again, was the virtue of good people, and worthy suitors were to be judged by the control they exercised over themselves; conversely, the impulses of passion were considered dangerous, because they were susceptible to opening the great gates of Eros. Nonetheless, in the period's stories, the conquest of the heroine frequently constitutes a narrative thread, and several works leave an opening, however discreet, for the stirrings of love. This can be explained by the fact that distinctions between literary genres in nineteenth-century Quebec were not clearly established; on the contrary, novels proposed "tendencies," and combined a plurality of themes and styles within a single text. This is how the Gothic novel "incorporated [the romance novel] into its plot to not confuse the reader."[10] The same held true for the adventure novel, which, as Nathalie Ducharme has demonstrated, devoted more space to romantic intrigues than its European counterpart.[11]

To explore the treatment of love in the pages of Gothic and adventure novels, two works will serve as our guides: the first French-Canadian novel *L'influence d'un livre*[12] (1837) by Philippe Aubert de Gaspé Jr. and *Les fiancés de 1812*[13] (1844) by Joseph Doutre. Both of these authors, inspired by French Romanticism, incorporate a discourse on love that seemed already settled in the eyes of the French-Canadian intellectual elite of the time. It is interesting to note that *L'influence d'un livre* almost became a love story.[14] Philippe Aubert de Gaspé Jr. thought of writing a novel in which, "after forcing [his] hero through countless tribulations of thwarted love, [he] ended by granting him happiness for the rest of his days."[15] He abandoned his project once he realized that it would have only rehashed a number of clichés. Yet the author's clear renunciation in no way prevents *L'influence d'un livre* from being representative of works that, though seeming to give little space to romantic intrigues, still provide captivating representations of them. Against the backdrop of a few tried-and-true elements of the Gothic novel—diabolical apparitions, phantoms, murders—Philippe Aubert de Gaspé Jr. gives free rein to the emotions of Saint-Céran and Amélie, the daughter of Amand. Abbé Casgrain did not miss this, and, twenty-three years after the death of Aubert de Gaspé Jr., he republished the novel under the title of *Chercheur de trésors*, taking care to modify or delete elements from the original text that could inflame unrestrained desires.

In the Gothic novel, the heroine—a lover who is prevented from loving—is often the victim of a villain: the hero has to confront the scoundrel and overcome a series of obstacles, set against a back drop of ruins, castles, and forests, in order to be reunited with his beloved. While love is certainly present in this literature, it does not respect the invariants of the romance novel as defined by Constans. In *L'influence d'un livre* for example, the hero and heroine do not experience the disjunction that normally keeps readers in suspense until the final reconciliation.

Philippe Aubert de Gaspé Jr. himself, perhaps still preoccupied by his initial idea to write a romantic story, makes light of the fantastic plot twist that brings about the happy ending of his story: "A young girl turning the final pages of this book might observe, 'They are going to marry so soon, without even the smallest quarrel? How strange. Ducray Dumesnil [*sic*] is far more adept at devising stories.'"[16] This ironic remark, addressed to a female reader, contains a wealth of information. It suggests, for one, that romantic intrigues were already clearly associated with a female readership, enough to single out the female reader. It also confirms that the referential corpus for the romantic imaginary was French serial fiction.[17] Indeed, the narrator of *L'influence d'un livre* compares himself to François-Guillaume Ducray Duminil (1761-1819), an author often considered the father of the popular French novel[18] and still in fashion at the time. Kenneth Landry has estimated that of the seventy-seven Québécois novels published as volumes in the nineteenth century, close to 80 percent were also published in serial form, which most likely influenced the content of the stories.[19]

In *L'influence d'un livre,* the author uses the intensity of the love at first sight between the main protagonists as a narrative pretext. Saint-Céran, a young man from a good family and upbringing is out taking a country stroll when he encounters Amélie, a young girl of fifteen who, like him, is inclined towards melancholy. "Love was born in that first glance. In the words of a modern author, 'we were made for each other [...].'"[20] If a heart can be set alight in an instant, in a single glance, it is because romantic feelings escape reason, upset the rules of decorum, sometimes to the point of being indifferent to the norms governing legitimate unions. Love at first sight embodies the ideal of love because it reveals that love is complete in itself and can only be explained by the mystery of passion.[21] In particular, distinctions based on social standing, class or money seem meaningless, unbearable, even, to those who are truly in love.

The hero of Gaspé Jr. goes on a long tirade against parents who try to convince their daughters to ignore their hearts and trade their feelings for the prospect of a wealthy husband.[22] He swears he will devise a plan to free Amélie "from her foolish father" so she can share his own "life and fate."[23] In short, Gaspé Jr. presents love as something that is impulsive, invaluable, and unmotivated, asking nothing in exchange but love itself. To the maxim of a modern society that says emotions have no place in business, he responds with the adage that love has no price.

The explosive force of love stems from a violent impulse that seems to respect neither god nor master. However, at the same time that Gaspé Jr. affirms that one can love in "seeing one another" and that love is the "most powerful passion of the human heart," he also suggests that this type of intoxication is the source of many errors and should not be left unchecked. The first novel of Québécois literature set the parameters within which attraction between two individuals could be expressed and defined the behaviours expected of a good hero and heroine. The woman should be pretty and fragile, but not too enticing or servile. The man should be strong and faultless, but not too seductive or poor. Thus, Saint-Céran's marriage to Amélie, thwarted by the opposition of the young woman's father (who, among other things, finds the suitor not rich enough), only takes place once Saint-Céran becomes a doctor. For her part, Amélie avoids the coquettish behavior that Saint-Céran so abhors, a stance without which the book could not "have concluded with a marriage."[24] We can surmise from these passages that matters of the heart, as disinterested as they might appear to be, are still held captive to economic and moral considerations. Individuals who are destined to love each other are influenced as much by their social conditions as by their subjective dispositions.

Like *L'influence d'un livre*, *Les fiancés de 1812* by Joseph Doutre is not a romance novel but also devotes some space to a romantic intrigue.[25] The author was inspired by *The Mysteries of Paris* (*Les Mystères de Paris*) by Eugène Sue, a series that became the great success of the nineteenth-century popular French novel.[26] In its pale Canadian imitation, the main character, Gonzalve, experiences "the strong passions that the charms of an enchanting lady arouses"[27] and confesses to loving Louise de Saint-Felmar "with all the force of his soul." "I love her," he writes, "as the son loves his mother, as the mother loves her daughter. I love her still more than all that. Her memory grips and breaks my heart. I devour this memory, I do not abandon it for an instant. My heart is empty without it... and she deserves all the adoration on earth!"[28] Louise de Saint-Felmar, who is as captivated as Gonzalve after their first exchanged glance, returns his vows of eternal love. They are immediately united by unbreakable bonds.

Physiognomy forming an integral part of the laws of romantic literature, a person's outward appearance is systematically related to his or her character. According to a universally redundant convention that is the basis of the popular genre's accessibility, the clothes make the man (or woman): fine gloves, an elegant hat, and shiny shoes are the marks of a distinguished personality. Moreover, one's soul is reflected in one's face. In the description of individuals, the beauty of a person's facial features is a mirror of his or her good character. With respect to Alphonse of P., the friend of Gonzalve of R., the author writes that "with the conformance [*sic*] of an admirable body and charming face, he had established between his body and soul an exact correspondence."[29] As for Louise, who is described as "divine," she is presented as "a flower of beauty, feeling and virtue."[30] Gonzalve praises the physical charms of his enchantress, such as her "slim and languid figure," pink lips, "lovely bosom," and "alabaster neck." This list of the ideal woman's attractive features makes use of typical clichés and remains chaste while hinting at something more suggestive.[31] When Louise whispers the "enchanting words" in his ear: "I'm yours for life," Gonzalve cannot help noticing the "gentle sway of her beautiful bosom."[32] In *Les fiancés de 1812*, the emotion aroused by the physical beauty of the heroine is inseparable from the attraction she elicits from men. Nonetheless, this sexual appetite does not stray from but rather leads to virtue. Cloaked in a religious language (a woman is an "angel" and a "sacred object"), love is presented as an act of devotion.

It is clear that the two young people in *Les fiancés de 1812* are made for one another, but they encounter a stumbling block on their path to happiness: more noble than Louise's father, Gonzalve is also more poor, and this defect seems unpardonable in the eyes of the miserly father-in-law. Though wanting to lead a life respecting the rules of law and good taste, Gonzalve has no choice but to forsake the connections that tie him to his community in order to follow the "divine law" of love. He insists, like so many before him, that he no longer follows any rule but the one dictated by the passions of his heart. Judging others from his own position, he is convinced that no one can escape the emotions that torment him. "From the moment I came of age in society," he declares, "I have known no other master but love. In all the circumstances that life has since led me to, it has been the driving force of all my actions. And if I had to judge the majority of men from my own experience, I would not hesitate to say that man is created to love."[33] Given to uncontrollable impulses, Gonzalve denies anyone the right to select his future spouse. He vows to overcome obstacles and "devote himself fully and forever to the service of the passion that subjugates him," and he "sees the possession of his lover to be the single goal he must attain to achieve the state of happiness that marks the end of tribulations for any man and guides the actions of his life."[34]

Following his example, his ladylove transgresses the "sacred ties" that bind a daughter to her parents, cleverly evoking the

Holy Scriptures: "A woman shall leave her father and mother and shall cleave unto her husband." She declares to her parents: "Yes, despite the sacred ties that nature has imposed on me, despite my attachment for you and even for my father, I cannot deny that it is still with a kind of joy that I take my distance from you! Should I not follow in the footsteps of the husband that heaven and my heart have chosen for me?"[35] The association between heaven and the heart, as motives for love, is not anodyne: Louise "recognizes" her other half, her "heart" instantly loves him, and her individual will is left powerless before the outpouring of love. Her decision is made. "I beseech you," she writes to her parents, "to spare yourselves the trouble of looking for me. Should you find me, a greater force would defend my retreat. My fate is now forever linked to Gonzalve's. I must follow his lead everywhere that destiny takes him. My life will be too short to prove the steadfastness of my love to him; I will stay with him to my grave."[36] Rejecting the union with the "monster" that her father tries to impose on her, she ends up marrying Gonzalve thanks to a stratagem organized at Saint-Felmar's expense.

Like *L'influence d'un livre, Les fiancés de 1812* affirms the absolute liberty of love without assuming all the consequences: the novel ends with the reconciliation of Louise's father and his son-in-law. The two spouses and the old man hug and "merge into one soul [...] three hearts, one of which seemed destined to eternal separation."[37] But one senses that this finale is but an artifice to distract from the premise of the rest of the novel, which presents love as divine and encourages young people to "sacrifice everything on its altar." Despite the misfortunes that have befallen him, Gonzalve cannot resist blessing "the day [he] saw, for the first time, the most loveable of women!"[38] "It was," he writes, "the most beautiful of my life! Oh yes! I cherish that blessed day when Louise, appearing like a shining star, inscribed the seal of eternal love on my soul! I cherish the luck that led me to her, that set my gaze upon her!!"[39] Critics of the period who read *Les fiancés de 1812* were not mistaken in seeing love as "the dominant passion the author sought to develop" by "lending it, in some parts, a truly lyrical language."[40]

With *L'influence d'un livre* and *Les fiancés de 1812,* Québécois literature made the novel into a great echo chamber for romantic excitement. The lesson contained in these works—that love is so powerful it can overcome any resistance—is presented as an inspiration for their readers. While fleeing to reunite with her love, Louise meets a father and mother and convinces them to let their son marry a girl of the people. "You told us," they sighed to Louise, "that you left your parents to follow your lover. This touched us and also made us understand that it was wrong to restrain a son's affections. [...] happiness resides less in one's standing than in the feelings of the heart."[41] Herein lies the scandal of love for a society accustomed to an entirely different hierarchy of values.

The language of love

The novels of Gaspé Jr. and Doutre subtly develop a romantic code at the intersection of Gothic, adventure, and romance stories. This new conception of feelings affirms the self-referentiality of love. As with art for art's sake, science for science's sake, or faith for faith's sake, love justifies itself, so much so that the couple is presented, in common discourse, as a self-suffient dyade. This is true as much with respect to the immanence of the moment of near absolute completeness it embodies ("to live on love and fresh water") as to the transcendence that it projects (love is "divine").[42] There is no reason to be in love, apart from the pleasure one finds in it alone. Anyone is worthy of love if they possess a pure and noble heart that is entirely focused on the affection that ties them to their "beloved." The sincerity of the commitments ensures that a union between a woman and a man, the only attraction tolerated at the time, is not entered into for self-serving reasons. This is why the heroines and heroes often come from the best families and are distinguished by their bravery, integrity, and upbringing, all of which assures the readers that they are motivated by lofty sentiments.

To better understand this, let us return to Doutre's novel, *Les fiancés de 1812*, which represents in some way, as we have seen, a school of feelings. We learn that love is something "sacred." Women who are loved resemble "angels" whom we must raise "altars" to in order to pay "homage" to them, much as one worships idols. Just like in a religion, nothing should interfere with the worship devoted to Cupid. The man who is in love must devote his life to the love of his heart's choosing.[43] As for women, their submission is clearly just as total. Louise composes a song for Gonzalve in which she declares wanting to "die or live under his law."[44]

In *Les fiancés de 1812*, love is an ecstasy, a blessing. Gonzalve vows to "devote himself fully and forever to serve the passion that subjugates him."[45] Louise's resolution is no less exuberant: she declares to her parents that she will follow her beloved "to the grave."[46] From this premise it would mean that separation from the loved one inevitably constitutes a calamity. According to Doutre, there is no "worse state than to be separated from the one we love."[47] Such a separation appears "cruel," filled with "the most horrible suffering."[48] Far from cooling the passion of hearts in love, with true love, distance makes the heart grow fonder. Locked in a dark room by her father and prevented from seeing her beloved, Louise clings even more desperately to her desire, the persecution ultimately serving to "fuel her passion."[49] Pushed to her limit, she is driven to flee her father and reunite with her lover in what she calls a "pilgrimage of love." The journey becomes the source of multiple misadventures that put her life and honour in danger. In *Les fiancés de 1812*, just as force is powerless to "sow love in hearts," it is also unable to extinguish love's flames once set ablaze.[50] But, there is something even worse than being separated from the person one hopes to spend their life with: marrying someone one feels no affection for. Confronted with her father's decision to marry her to a stranger, Louise is reduced to tears, driven to despair, ponders death, and likens her engagement to a "funeral ceremony."[51] Gonzalve, on the other hand, always has the option of going to fight in the war and dying on the battlefield.

During this period, love relates to nothing other than itself, only to the joy of loving and being loved. It thus contains a great deal of mystery. Those who have never encountered love cannot really know what it's about: "no one, unless having known love, has any real idea what it is."[52] Doutre depicts love as an irrepressible drive, a violent inner turmoil. A person smitten by love cannot dream of anything else, cannot devote themselves to or even live for anything else. The object of one's affection at one's side is all that matters. When this object is withdrawn, the mind cannot stop thinking about it. "The absence of a cherished object is so cruel that not a moment passes that one's mind is not consumed by it; and the minute a word evokes its memory, the heart becomes so full, so pleasantly distracted, that it spontaneously exudes love, as though paying tribute to itself and the object of one's every thought."[53] Gustave's Greek wife Alpina represents the counter-example to this rule in Doutre's novel. She proves to be unworthy due to her cheating and lies. She is described as "vile" and "contemptible," despite her declarations to repent. Gustave, on the contrary, lives up to love's demands; even after all that Alpina has put him through, her image still enters his thoughts, and he cries in spite of himself "over the loss of the most adored of women."[54]

The love portrayed in *Les fiancés de 1812* conveys an individualist moral, insofar as the loved one is always unique in the eyes of the person in love. When trying to describe Louise's beauty and charm to his friend, Gonzalve struggles for words, resorting to a string of superlatives: "How can I give you an idea of who she is? The sun that illumines the world, the light breeze that sighs in the forest, the siren who pierces the ocean's waves—none are equal to her charms."[55] And if Gonzalve is unable to do justice to Louise's beauty, it is not only because she is supremely magnificent, but also because she is beyond comparison, and one has to see her and speak to her to understand how irresistible she is. "In her most simple state, devoid of any ornaments or jewels, my Louise would seem unique to you on this earth, if you were lucky enough to receive one of her glances."[56] The person who is loved is not interchangeable, and love is thus also most true when it is the most subjective.

The idea of love being self-sufficient shattered some of the older norms governing marriage. *Les fiancés de 1812* celebrates the weddings of three unusual couples: the penniless noble Gonzalve and the daughter of millionaire Saint-Felmar, the Canadian Eugénie (Alphonse's sister and Gonzalve's good friend) and the Irish-American Brandsome, and Alphonse and the Indigenous Ithona (member of the Saulteaux Nation and also presented as an "Indian," a "savage," and "girl of the woods"). The story of Alphonse's and Ithona's relationship prompted Brandsome to make this striking remark: "Truth be told, I have never read such a beautiful novel as the one you've made with our friend the savage. I don't recognize myself. I'm afraid if I return to New York I could fall in love with some black woman."[57] This racist comment reveals fear as much as it does fascination: with love, the passage suggests, one can break even the most powerful taboos.

When love is not an end in itself, when it is driven by calculated and self-serving motives, it flounders. Louise's suitor, chosen by her miserly father for venal reasons, is detestable: inspired by greed, he wants to marry Louise "with the goal of sordid exploitation."[58] In this respect, Doutre's novel seems to have been written, at least in part, to denounce the vices of parents who, throughout the ages, privileged money over love.

Recalling Horace's maxim *Virtus post nummos* ("virtue after riches"), the author decries, in particular, "the sometimes very cruel constraints" of parents who "interfere with their daughters' affections."[59] Doutre recognizes that "the human heart is given to weakness" and that "a heart too gentle and open can often be drawn into unworthy affection."[60] But in recent times, he argues, parents' "obstinacy" in selecting their daughters- and sons-in-laws "is based on vile monetary speculation or, to some degree, more-or-less, family standing. [...] Which has made this song's refrain in our time so true: *Montre tes écus / Pour plaire à Vénus* (Show your crowns / To please Venus)."[61] Doutre launches into a long diatribe, not uncommon in nineteenth-century European romance,[62] against marriage for money as the true antithesis of marriage for love. He sees this type of arrangement based on "calculating the wealth of Hymen's contenders"[63] having bitter consequences for the newlyweds. He warns that, married against their will to greedy men, women face a life of despair and early death, while their husbands, forsaken by indifferent and negligent wives, turn to alcohol, gambling or adultery to seek the solace they cannot find in their marriage:

> What is the usual outcome of these speculative marriages. The wife has been sacrificed to [economic] interest. She is condemned to spending her sad days in the perpetual company of a man her heart detests. The husband, in his wife, does not see the degree of affection he believed he had earned; he seeks distractions for his ennui elsewhere; he becomes spendthrift, cruel, then miserly when the money is running thin. The result is domestic conflict, poorly educated children. Finally, all of the family's problems are compounded, in direct proportion to the rapid onset of animosities and misunderstandings.[64]

Doutre anticipates the objections of those who think money is necessary to the couple's well-being. A woman, he does not hesitate to write, who "chooses a friend with a character and heart suited to her own, be he a simple heir of Job," is guaranteed happiness for the rest of her life. "If he does not enjoy fortune, the generosity of his nature, nourished by a constant love, will overcome all of life's difficulties. The piece of bread he offers his wife will be worth more to her than the shiny bracelet adorning the wrist of the millionaire's lofty companion."[65] Since love is self-sufficient, it makes up for everything.

It is this language of love as mystery and individualism that Doutre's novel reaffirms. With *Les fiancés de 1812*, French-Canadian literature channels and develops the romantic revolution that sees in conjugal relations the mutual discovery and confirmation of individual subjectivities. In this view, the lover exists only in the eye of the beholder, to the point where lack of recognition from the loved one can lead a person to madness, suicide, or death from emotional anemia. As Doutre writes, all lovers give their souls to the one they love. In so doing, they no longer live except through their loved one, can no longer exist without them. The romance novel, drawing on this conception, was soon to be born. But it first had to overcome stubborn resistance from a certain elite who were very aware of the potential dangers of a passion that risked inverting the hierarchy of values of that time. Narrative strategies were thus developed to recognize love, all the while assigning it a place that did not overly disrupt the traditional organization of French-Canadian society.

The heart has its reasons that reason knows

The idea that love cannot be imposed from without, that it somehow operates on a higher level than social mores, conformed to the codes of canon law. The latter insisted on full liberty in conjugal matters—no one could be married against their will. However, it is important to understand the extent to which this consensual theory of Christian theology contained revolutionary implications. Each new union could result in the deprivation of the rich or the promotion of the poor and, more generally, the subversion of social distinctions.[66] Since families no longer had the means to defend their heritage against unwanted sons-in-law, individuals could impose matrimonial choices that ran counter to the wishes of their guardians. Indeed, studies have observed the evolution of free choice based on personal affinities in rural France from the 16th to the 18th centuries, a phenomenon that no doubt also affected New France and Lower Canada.[67]

The more couples focused on their love, the more distance they took from their communities, the more they escaped prescriptive norms and undermined the pillars of the social order with their indifference. Understandably, impulsive love was feared to have negative effects on more lasting relationships, august traditions, and respectable alliances. To prevent this deviancy, an important disciplinary regime was gradually established over the course of the 19th century. "Too many material and cultural interests were at stake to leave the choice of a partner to the whims of youth,"[68] historian Serge Gagnon rightly observed. It was a question of channelling the seemingly antisocial power of romantic emotions into more acceptable behaviours. In other words, once the passion was identified as such, efforts were quickly made to contain it by putting it to use in the reproduction of the social order. French Canadians were thus encouraged to marry people within their milieu, to seek partners belonging to the same group, of the same status and from the same village. "As a whole," concludes Gagnon, "the matrimonial institution was bound by a body of written and unwritten rules that sought to ensure the triumph of social, religious and cultural homogamy."[69] This is a key observation that helps explain why the criticisms of marriages of interest were so strong at the time. Far from celebrating the freedom to love whomever one wanted, the criticisms of these marriages more often than not concealed a defence of marriage based on class.

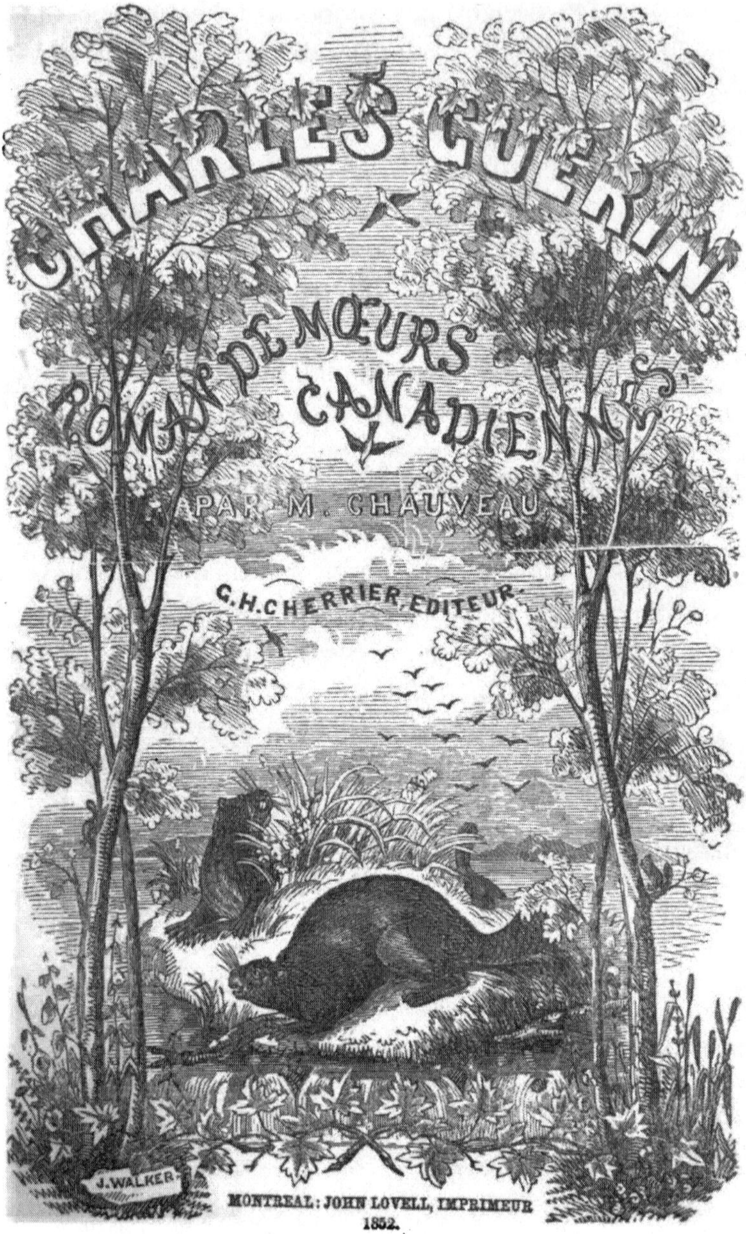

Pierre J. O. Chauveau, *Charles Guérin. Roman de mœurs*, Montréal, John Lovell, 1852. Illustration de John Walker.

This is how, along with Gothic and adventure novels, romance novels before 1860 shaped a discourse that generally aimed to curtail and regulate the expression of love. The list of examples is long of works that sought to convince readers that to be happy meant respecting convention and entering into marriage with those sharing one's condition. An example that stands out, due to its central place in Québécois literary history, is the novel by Pierre-Joseph-Olivier Chauveau, a young author who was also the sitting member for Quebec County and later the first premier of Quebec. *Charles Guérin* first appeared in the pages of the *Album littéraire et musical de la Revue canadienne* (1846-1847) before being published as a book in 1852 by Georges-Hippolyte Cherrier. Taking on the role of editor for the first time in Quebec's literary history, Cherrier wrote a preface in which he tries to disassociate *Charles Guérin* from the French novels then in fashion, notably those of Eugène Sue. Of Chauveau's novel, he insisted, there is "barely a love story in the work: indeed, the substance of the novel seems to many to be a pretext for depictions of mores and a few political and philosophical dissertations."[70] The book can thus be read, assures Cherrier, without fear of offending any sensitive minds.

Charles Guérin implicitly presents a thesis on the subject of good and bad reading material, an occasionally recurring theme in the discourse on the romance novel in Quebec. We foresee the hero's future difficulties upon learning at the story's outset that he grew up in a house full of bad books. When his father dies, the priest has no choice but to resort to an auto-da-fé and burn "nearly the entire library of Mr. Guérin."[71] But the seed had been planted. As a student in Quebec, Charles devours the "most fashionable" Parisian novels, which stir his imagination and undermine his intellectual faculties. He succumbs for a brief time to the charms of a woman immersed in the *Lettres à Sophie*, a collection published in 1792 that contains the correspondence between Mirabeau and Sophie de Monnier, his mistress. The narrator implies that this literary licence clearly spells the young woman's misfortune. Her opposite, the heroine Marie, is as "devout as an angel."[72] She doesn't have to fight off succumbing to such vices, since she spends her spare time immersed in wholesome and pious reading that adds a "philosophical"—that is to say, composed and sensible—tone to her thought.

Rather than "the influence of a book," as in the novel by Philippe Aubert de Gaspé Jr., here it is a question of the influence of books. Interestingly, the idea that the romance novel was suspect more than any other genre because it distracted readers from reality, immersing them in a world of dreams incompatible with everyday needs, is a recurring theme in the romance novels themselves, more than in other literary genres. These works frequently contain passages denouncing the unrealistic worldview of characters who imagine being able to experience the passions they read about in books, and and just as many excerpts recounting how the characters portrayed are living a real-life romance novel. This tension—the romance novel conceived as both an impossible dream and an ideal—resurfaces in Chauveau's *Charles Guérin*. By setting his heroine apart from some of the licentious female characters portrayed in French novels, Chauveau sought to lend credibility to a romantic story that, nonetheless, still only existed on paper.

Charles Guérin is interesting for our purposes because, despite the editor's warning, it is not only the choice of profession that awaits the eponymous hero after finishing his studies at the Petit Séminaire de Québec. He also has to decide between the allure of the lovely Clorinde Wagnaër, the daughter of a wealthy merchant from Jersey who has her sights set on the Guérin family assets, and the charms of Marie Lebrun, a farmer's daughter from his same national background. From the outset, the narration draws attention to all of Clorinde's flaws. We learn that this "foreigner's" daughter is a socialite who loves dancing and that we should be very concerned "for her salvation."[73] If this weren't enough to entirely discredit her, even her physique is couched in darkness: "She has very dark hair, but she has such a beautiful figure and such beautiful black eyes!" exclaimed Marie Lebrun. "She jokingly told me she looked like a black woman next to me; but that doesn't stop me from wishing I had her figure."[74] Charles' image of Clorinde is also marked by alterity. The first times he sees her she seems "like one of those Andalusian beauties whose poetic portrayals one has read about in the popular novels."[75] This exoticism should have been a warning to the protagonist from the start, but since his imagination has been long corrupted by frivolous reading, he is unable to contain his desire and fulfill his duty to do the right thing.

Incapable of competing with Clorinde's enticing looks and wealth, Marie Lebrun seems condemned to gravitate in a world that is "well below" that of Charles. Next to him, hailing from the city and fresh out of college, the farm girl appears undignified in her status and dress, despite her solid convent education. On the other hand, she seems superior to Charles in her simplicity, modesty, hard work, respect for ancestral traditions and language, which is "more correct, more elegant, more poetic than that of most women," not to mention her "melancholic and soft eyes, her beautiful hair so smartly styled, a smile that is so gentle and intelligent, a complexion that is so fresh and so pure."[76] Marichette, as the villagers affectionately call her, the seemingly "rather vulgar," "poor little farm girl," is soon transformed in Charles' eyes into "a young person full of seductions."[77] This transformation confirms the need to respect class, religious, racial, and ethnic endogamy, which is decisive in shaping romantic relations, especially since it tellingly coincides here with a condemnation of Clorinde, whose higher status is not suitable for Charles: "Among the novels that his friend Voisin suggested he read, he did not find a single one where the man was indebted to the woman for his existence [...] Consequently, Mademoiselle Wagnaër, with her slender waist and black hair and in spite of or, rather, because of her dowry made but a very short appearance in Charles Guérin's dreams. He was not in love with her for more than fifteen days."[78] By inserting such considerations into his love story, Chauveau makes love, unlike a romantic representation, an *amor fati*, that is to say, a "love of social destiny."[79]

In misunderstanding one another's feelings, the two main protagonists of *Charles Guérin* remain distant until chance leads them to recognize their real shared affection. A sleigh accident luckily brings them together, with the important nuance that (deviating from the typical romance novel) the real saviour of the young damsel in distress is her father and not her suitor. The novel maintains the theme of rescue dear to romance but only ironically: Marie's exaggerated gratitude and Charles' quixotic imagination end up persuading the latter that he really did save the young woman from danger, "and, like all saviours and protectors, he became tenderly attached to the protected one."[80] There comes a time when Charles, "after so many muffled sighs, so many imploring looks, so many unfinished sentences, and a thousand other hesitations made for our readers, dares to say quietly, slowly and mysteriously, as it is always said: 'Marie, I love you!'"[81]

A realistic and grounded country girl, Marie is not gullible and clearly perceives her admirer's fickleness. "Since there is a lot of poetry and fiction in your love, based on what you tell me, and that these things may come and go, I run the great risk of going back to being Marichette at any moment, at least in your imagination."[82] Marie is right. Charles will be once again seduced by the allure of Clorinde and, to purge once and for all his "exalted brain" from all the bad books that clutter it, he must visit Marie's library to discover works that should have always been among his own, such as *L'imitation de Jésus-Christ*,

Fénelon's *L'éducation des filles,* François de Sales' *L'introduction à la vie dévote,* Madame de Sévigné's *Lettres,* and Madame de Genlis' *Adèle et Théodore.* Randomly opening *L'imitation de Jésus-Christ,* Charles lands on the following passage, which will serve as a prescription to follow: "Love is circumspect, humble and fair. It is neither loose, nor light and never dwells on things of vanity. It is temperate, chaste, firm and tranquil, and it makes for a good guard in every sense."[83] In following these rules of the sentimental life, Charles can hope to have a good marriage. While the bad novels presented unreasonable passions as legitimate, the respectable books taught him the proper way to be in love: soberly, chastely, humbly, and reasonably.

Chauveau reiterates in this novel the idea that true happiness is stamped by the seal of moderation. Outbursts are restrained and effusions are restricted. Contrary to romantic love that shows its worth in outpourings and excesses, the love portrayed by Chauveau is all the more strong and true because it is sensible, calm and moderate. In one of the last scenes of *Charles Guérin,* the hero declares his feelings to his sweetheart, who is dressed "simply and elegantly" and waits for him in a lovely sitting room decorated with care. "In theatre, it would have been the moment for our hero to fall to his knees and break down crying. In real life, between people who are somewhat civilized, one takes a chair and sits down to continue the explanation more comfortably. This is what Charles does, at the sign of Miss Lebrun."[84] A marriage is quickly decided, which, unexpectedly, also makes it possible to resolve the problems raised by the will of Charles' boss (having died, leaving him his fortune) and thus "prevent his goods from leaving the family and render the *three thirds* of the succession more *undivided* than ever."[85] In *Charles Guérin,* as such passages suggest, the heart has its reasons that reason knows. The novel recounts a story that hardly resembles a fairy tale: Cinderella does not exist and Charles Guérin is not a prince. Both from good backgrounds and well educated,

Charles and Marie are set to marry, and once the union has been celebrated, Charles will return to live in a rural parish and establish himself as a prosperous farmer.

As André Sénécal rightly observes, the romance novel that Chauveau could have written is ruined by the ideological thesis that subordinates love to the imperatives of its milieu. "In the final analysis, the motives for the sentimental intrigue do not obey the laws of passion. There is a lot of romance in Marichette's awakening of love, in the romantic idyll between Clorinde and Charles, but, in the end, this romance gives way to a moral determinism that ultimately depends on ideological demonstration."[86] If Charles ends up marrying Marie rather than Clorinde, one senses it is because the preservation of the nation and social class to which he belongs demands it, especially since he himself does not seem as enamoured as he tries to convey. As for the novel's two heroines, love for both is a sacrifice that is made more acceptable by painting an ideal image of women to better subjugate them. Marie renounces her happiness while waiting for Charles to return, having given her heart without demanding his in return, and Clorinde at the end of the story takes the veil under the name of Sister Saint Charles. *Charles Guérin* thus effects, in relation to *L'influence d'un livre* and *Les fiancés de 1812* the same rupture that separates Gothic and adventure novels from the romance novel in France: the hero's romantic quest is replaced by political and social ambition.[87]

The study of *Charles Guérin* is very instructive in the history of fictional representations of love. Like other novels of manners of the period, Chauveau's text, seen from a certain perspective, is a romantic breviary. It provides the codes for understanding one's place in society and the consequences of refusing to adhere to them. Fearing the anarchy that could result from ill-considered unions, the whole art of nineteenth-century French-Canadian novels consists in trying to channel the romantic intrigue into acceptable goals, without denying the characters their free will. Chauveau compares the situation in the United States, where young people marry when and how they please without advice from their parents, to that of French Canada, where "the absolutism of the parents, especially in rich families,[88] still strongly reflects the Ancien Régime. We would not presume to say that paternal authority is stern and unyielding, but it surely has the greatest influence on the most important acts of life: the choice of a state, and that of a spouse. The best parents, through their entreaties and tears, sometimes impose their will on decisions that should be free, for the very reason that they are irrevocable."[89] The American regime seems too lax, and that of French Canada no doubt too strict. Chauveau seems to plead for a happy medium where romantic sentiments are honoured without placing the social order in danger, midway between the unacceptable follies of a marriage of inclination and the trivial proprieties of a marriage of reason.

"God is watching us": short texts with a romantic flavour

To understand the genesis of the romantic imaginary in the nineteenth-century Québécois novel, we have to integrate analysis of short stories centred on romantic intrigues published in periodicals. These texts do not disavow the triumph of love, but this victory most often ends in death, which is an original feature, nearly an obsession, that distinguishes this type of story from the longer versions.[90] While allowing the great reaper to come for the young couples, who would have been normally destined to form their union on earth, these texts make death not so much the end of love as its ultimate achievement. Unlike the rest of our corpus, these works culminate in associations between Eros and Thanatos that are as sudden as they are unexplained. Thus the text "Fatalité," written by a certain D. F*** and published in *La Ruche littéraire* in November 1853, begins on a joyous note:

two fiancés are madly in love and getting married the next day; their last evening together, filled with sighs and anticipation, provides a glimpse of their bright future. However, on returning home, the man is fatally struck by a falling block of ice in the Quebec suburb, and his fiancée, devasted, takes the veil.[91]

Generally, three scenarios emerge from the corpus of short romantic texts. In the first, love serves to punish those who love without respecting the norms of their community. In this case the outcome is often accompanied by diverse stigmas, including painful deaths, distressing problems and financial losses. In the second type of scenario, death serves to remind readers of ideas that are more elevated and grandiose, more noble than human passions. The ideal of sacrifice finds full expression here, romantic duty drawing on religious duty and striking the same sensitive chords. In the third type, death is used to magnify the love between the protagonists of the story. It adds an element of eternity to human stories that, thanks to this literary ruse, have no end and can be frozen forever in the moment of their greatest purity and most sublime expression.

The first scenario is the most banal. Death punishes deviant or delinquent behavior. In particular, it is a question of recalling that wavering virtue inevitably leads to confusion, misfortune, exile, to the convent, to death. Female characters who play the socialite or coquette are a particular target for this dreadful outcome. This trope can be found among others in the widely known legend of "Diable à la danse" (Devil at the dance),[92] a fantastical story reappearing a number of times over the course of the nineteenth century in newspapers and magazines, such as *L'avenir* (Charles Laberge, 1848) and *Au coin du feu* (Joseph-Ferdinand Morissette, 1883). We discuss here the oldest written interpretation, added by Aubert de Gaspé Jr. to the chapter "L'étranger" in *L'influence d'un livre*. Even though the version of Gaspé Jr. was not initially published in a newspaper, it stood out enough from his novel to quickly become a separate pub-

Philippe Cusson, *Légendes laurentiennes,* Montréal, Éditions de l'Agence Duvernay, 1943. Illustration de Louis-Joseph Dubois.

lished piece in *Le Répertoire national ou recueil de littérature canadienne* compiled by James Huston in 1848.

"L'étranger" (The stranger) recounts the story of Rose Latulipe, a pretty girl whose ways are sometimes "indelicate" if not to say "scandalous."[93] During a Mardi-Gras party, and though engaged to Gabriel Lepard, Rose falls under the spell of the devil, whose horns and claws are cleverly camouflaged under his magnificent clothes. At the antipodes of the model of whiteness and purity imposed on the female subject, the devil figure, whose erotic charge is well known, embodies "the primacy of the body and its instincts, always lurking deep within beings and against which the battle is sometimes lost."[94] Seeing the devil dancing with Rose, the "poor" (in both senses of the term: broke and pitiful) Lepard "bit his lips with such force that they bled."[95] Very handsome, rich and seductive, the devil is the archetype of the stranger. Having accepted being his "forever,"

Rose gives him her hand, but then pulls it back "letting out a small cry," having been pricked, that is to say, metaphorically deflowered. The priest arrives just in time to chase off the evil one and save the heroine from eternal damnation. The carefree Rose, realizing the gravity of her error, hides herself away in a convent. Three years later, she "joins her heavenly maker."[96] Gabriel Lepard, the rejected fiancé, miserable as sin, forms part of the crowd attending the funeral.

One of the functions of popular stories is likely the temporary lifting of restrictions, and this is precisely what happens in "L'étranger," which evokes the fantasy of a union between "a poor country girl" and a rich bourgeois, between an uneducated peasant and an elegant city-dweller, between a French-Canadian woman and a "stranger." It is no coincidence that the ending—Rose's entry into the convent, then her death—represents only a few lines in a story primarily concerned with recounting Rose's escape from a life of duty into a world of pleasure. The conclusion of "L'étranger" nonetheless emphasizes the unfortunate fate that awaits those who break the laws of their community. The father is particularly guilty: "crazy" about his daughter, he gives in to her whims, which can only lead to an inversion of hierarchies, to the overturning of tradition and disruption of the natural order.[97] Conversely, in wanting to escape her position in the name of her passion, by refusing to listen to the advice of an old aunt and, especially, by not consulting her father before agreeing to dance with her partner, the heroine condemns herself. Death puts an end to a love that should have never been born.

By invoking death, the short story seeks to preserve the social order by putting an end to love stories that risk making the characters deviate from their expected trajectories. Death seals the fate of impossible love, that is to say, prohibited love. Shifting the perspective, the story "De Québec à la chute Montmorency" (From Quebec City to Montmorency Falls), by

Malvina D., is another eloquent example of how norms governed matters of the heart in the first half of the nineteenth century. In this text, the lovers are separated by Marie's father, a government employee who wants his daughter to marry an Englishmen, "to be well seen by the powerful people he serves."[98] Despairing at the news of this decision, Alfred, the hero, does not hesitate to ask Marie to escape with him by jumping into the Montmorency Falls. Astonishingly, in an era when suicide constituted the surest way of ending up in hell, Marie seems at first enchanted with the idea. "To die!," she replies, "to die with you would be happiness!"[99] However, when the time comes to commit the irreparable, the young woman notices a quiet young girl from the neighbourhood kneeling down and praying, nearby. Exclaiming: "God is watching us!" Marie backs away and returns to her father's. Eight days later she is married with the foreigner. From the night of her wedding, she becomes "crazy... crazy... yes crazy!"[100] Incapable of disowning her father and her homeland (and probably her religion, though this is not stated), Marie's character faces either real or symbolic death, which indicates the fate reserved for anyone betraying the injunctions of French-Canadian society.

Little needs to be said of the death sentence imposed on guilty unions in these short texts. More interesting for our purposes are the moments where death reminds the living that the pleasures of the here-and-now are few and far between for Christians. Death is used by the authors to sublimate love in a greater, more noble ideal. We thus see passion being frequently not denied but transcended and transubstantiated in and through death. This comes as no surprise in a society based on a Catholic ideological foundation. Death, more than love, is the great event for Christians and, at that supreme moment, it is not surprising to see human loves reunited, or else dissolved before the love of God. The influence of Romanticism only reinforced this fascination with sacrificial love.[101]

Louise Chawinikisique, a story by Georges Boucher de Boucherville first published in 1835 in the pages of *L'ami du peuple, de l'ordre et des lois*, recounts the sad story of a young Indigenous woman saved from drowning by Saguima, a brave warrior who, like her, is from the Algonquin nation.[102] They fall in love. Saguima comes to the rescue again to free her after she is abducted by Canatagayon, a young Mohawk chief. When Louise catches smallpox, Saguima, saving her a third time, stays by her side as she loses consciousness. "Leaning over her, he supports her drooping head on his arm."[103] He has the idea of breathing in the illness that is consuming the woman who means more to him than his own life. Assuming the traditional fairy tale role of prince charming, he saves his love, who is literally on the edge of dying, with a kiss. "His mouth pressed against her mouth, he seemed to breathe in her soul; and he received on his lips the poison that instantly infused the blood in his veins. He felt that he had drawn death from the bosom of his lover, and he was happy to die for her if he could save her."[104] This suggestive scene is followed by a hellish night, when Louise, suffering from fever, has nightmares filled with terrible images. "A dreadful sleep, the sleep of death, that you often only escape by entering into the sleep of eternity!"[105] The next day, Louise comes to her senses and recovers almost instantly. Her chest still burns with a "devouring fire" but it is now the "fire of love," a "love as pure as her soul," and "grateful for all that her liberator has done for her."[106]

Though the two lovers face a series of setbacks caused by war or the forces of nature, the greatest obstacle, the main impediment to their union is Saguima's refusal to convert to Catholicism: "[Louise] wanted to devote her life to him; to love him with all the power of her soul, because her soul was also burning with love. But her religion prohibited her from loving an idolater [...]."[107] She is ready to sacrifice everything on the altar of her love, except for her religion, because love cannot escape the supreme blessing of God, consecrated in Christian marriage. The alterity of the Indigenous figure, constantly marked by excess or deficiency in the literature of the period,[108] provides the opportunity to exalt the "grandeur of the purity of the soul" of Louise, who personifies Christian duty in the face of savage lust, or at least the violence of the pagan impulse. "Saguima, who sees so much passion and virtue in this young virgin, admires the power that created it."[109] But even though amazed by Louise's inflexible attitude and sensing "something supernatural"[110] in her refusal to unite outside the "sacred bonds" of marriage, he cannot understand how one can both "love truly" and prevent oneself from loving in the name of one's religion. "Your God," resumes Saguima, "he would punish you for loving me! And you want me to love your God; the one who prevents you from loving me, who is the cause of my despair. Oh! No, no, never! He is a monster!..."[111]

Declaring himself "ready to shed his blood to the last drop to defend the one he loves more than himself,"[112] Saguima has, as might be expected, contracted smallpox in saving Louise. He decides to secretly leave her so as not to contaminate her but collapses before getting far away from their campsite. Louise finds him, accompanied by a missionary encountered on the way. Transfigured, she becomes a veritable catalyst for the divine message in order to convert the dying Algonquin. When she announces to Saguima that he will be Christian, she "appears to be detached from the earth," "radiating the glory of the elected" and "Saguima, in looking at her, believes he is seeing the angel of the deserts who has come to speak to him in the name of God."[113] The missionary baptizes Saguima, then joins his hand with Louise's. The young man dies as soon as the missionary has pronounced his last words: the warrior who brought death upon his enemies has given himself to death in saving the one he loves, and she in turn gives him eternal life before, the text implies, walling herself up in a hopeless grief.[114] When Louise dies, at an unknown age, she is buried by his side, having known no destiny besides that of virgin and martyr. The love between the two Indigenous characters both kills them and saves them.

In the third type of recurring scenario that we may find in short texts from the first half of the nineteenth century, tragic events at the end of the story assure the lovers that their love will last forever. In other words, their death guarantees the permanence and serenity of their affection. An excellent example of this fantasy can be found in a brief narrative by Ulric-Joseph Tessier titled "Emma ou l'amour malheureux. Épisode du choléra à Québec en 1832" (Emma or the unfortunate love. The cholera outbreak in Quebec in 1832) (1837). A mix between romantic intrigue and Gothic decor is the pretext for recounting the story of Emma Dornière, a young girl from a good family destined for a happy marriage with her suitor, Eugène. The beautiful heiress, filled with delight in knowing she is cherished, has a bright future ahead of her. But cholera has engulfed Quebec. After spending a day with her aunt in the country, Emma, who had a bad premonition, returns home devastated: she finds her mother seriously ill. The mother dies, then Emma catches the disease. Her thoughts go to her fiancé, with whom she imagined spending peaceful days. "Alas! I expected to enjoy life and I had devoted it to you! Next to you I was to find the crown of happiness, but heaven wanted otherwise. Taken by a fatal end, I mourn our cruel separation [...]."[115] Feeling her strength wane, she surrenders to the will of God. "Emma said her goodbyes to her father and, turning her eyes to heaven, she addressed her final prayer to the Eternal. In this moment, her face was glowing, a pale glow reflected in her features... she expired!"[116] With Emma gone, Eugène has no more reason to live. In a barely disguised variation on the final scene of *Romeo and Juliet*, he goes to the grave of his fiancée and literally dies there of sorrow, after realizing that Emma, who took opium to alleviate her pain, had been in reality buried alive due to a misunderstanding. Readers can nonetheless be consoled for this dismal ending in knowing that the betrothed will be "reunited in the celestial region," in the "destination of angels."[117] Confirming that the conjunction has indeed taken place, their parents arrange new funerals and bury them together in the same grave.

What stands out in the three scenarios found in short romantic stories published in the French-Canadian press in the first half of the nineteenth century is a tension. On the one hand, burning passion is not disavowed. Love embodies an intense and uncontrollable feeling that consumes lovers but cannot be denied without renouncing an essential aspiration of human existence. On the other hand, we sense an effort to redirect this aspiration toward a more suitable ending, in the absence of which the emotional irruption is defused by having the characters die. When passion does not culminate in the fulfillment of divine or social duties (faith, work, family, social class, homeland), it is promptly removed from the story through the artifice of a dramatic conclusion. Passion can thus be fully expressed in French-Canadian short stories, as long as it is suppressed in the moment it surfaces. Loving each other until death means loving each other in death. The protagonists are born in love and die in the world. For them, the cradle of love is their tomb.

This literary sensibility clearly borrowed from the Romantic movement and more specifically Chateaubriand, whose influence is reflected in the themes of impossible love and the reunion of the lovers in a shared tragedy. But more fundamentally, if sensual emotions were quickly banished from the world in short stories, it was probably because they were deemed unacceptable by a society that saw a powerful source of chaos in them.[118] Literature opened a window onto the abyss of passions, was gripped by vertigo, and promptly closed it. It is thus not surprising to find the budding romance novel in French Canada characterized by a rather restricted gestation and apprenticeship. It was important to warn those freely succumbing to their attraction to the other sex and breaking the rules of morality that they would be severely punished or only find love in death.

A respectable love

Postulating that love is both dangerous and essential to human existence, the French-Canadian literary discourse of the first half of the nineteenth century attempted to reconcile social expectations and liberty in love. In the stories, the most common solution to this aporia was to contain the expression of romantic passion within the institution of marriage and, in doing so, make it conform to the rules of the community to which the characters belong. In other words, while affirming that love is wild and untameable, the authors proclaim that this sentiment cannot exist outside of the Catholic sacraments and different social control mechanisms associated with them. Only a socially acceptable love was possible in their eyes, any other affection being blindness, lust, depravity, or caprice.

A good example of this can be found in *Le pirate du Saint-Laurent*, written by Henri-Émile Chevalier, a French immigrant to Montreal. Published in serial form in 1859, this adventure novel includes a long digression in which the author wonders what love is, without really knowing how to answer the question. For him, this sentiment seems to be an insolvable enigma that no poet, artist or philosopher has managed to penetrate. Proof of the spontaneous and pure character of love can be found in the "most disparate couplings, most shocking contrasts, and most revolting anomalies" that it provokes between beings that everything should have kept apart.[119] At the same time, Chevalier is careful to situate the hero's attraction in his own story, *Le pirate du Saint-Laurent*, within the strict normative frameworks of his epoch. Thus, in *Le pirate du Saint-Laurent*, it is only when the veil has been lifted on the heroine's origins, once her status of "bastard" has been refuted and her heritage (most likely) restored, that she can confess her love for the rich Alphonse. And from this moment, the only possible outcome for them—an outcome so natural that it is not even discussed and goes *without saying*—is a Catholic marriage. Chevalier may very well admit that love provokes "the most disparate couplings," but he is quick to implicitly proclaim at the end of his novel that his characters cannot be fulfilled in love other than by uniting as a couple before the altar and honouring a national and class homogamy.

During this period, it was out of the question to let personal impressions, mysterious and unpredictable by nature, interfere with the reproduction of the social order. Maintaining control of impassioned emotions required the sanction of marriage and the community. Since the Church had to consecrate the union, the religious institution retained full control over the declaration of vows. And since the parents, the entire community even, took an interest in the marriage, they were in a position to remind liberated young couples of their duties. While a man reaching the age of majority had a right, in theory, to marry whomever he wanted, the novels and short stories maintain that it is better to "abandon a young girl one loves [...] and who can make him happy" than to marry against the wishes of his father and risk being disowned and disinherited.[120] Marriage blessed by the spiritual father (the priest) and the biological or adoptive father is presented in the novels, with remarkable force, as the normal, expected, inevitable, irrefutable conclusion of romantic feelings. It is only in respecting this prescription that the heroines and heroes can hope for a happy life together. Any other outcome condemns them to an atrocious (physical or social) death.

By presenting loves stories as part of a Catholic marriage recognized by the community, the novels and short texts published prior to the 1860s upheld the preservation of the social order.[121] Rather than fully embracing the logic of the romance novel, in which love always represents "the supreme Value to which others are correlated or subordinated,"[122] they channel the expression of human passion through the more prosaic values of the Church and French-Canadian community, to the extent that love itself tends to be denied in the act of marriage. Rural literature (*du terroir*) pushed this negation of romance to its limit. The role of love in the first rural novel published in Quebec, *La terre paternelle* (The paternal land) (1846), by Patrice Lacombe, is completely neglected. The word love rarely appears in the pages of this novel and, when it does, it is to refer to love of self, love of one's neighbour, or love of God.

However, as our analysis of works in this chapter has demonstrated, we can indeed observe a slow though laborious evolution of the expression of romantic love in the literature. The necessity of love is already present in the first novel of French-Canadian literature, *L'influence d'un livre,* and Doutre's novel *Les fiancés de 1812* portrays characters who say they want "to die or live under the law" of love. Even the novels and short stories that assign an ancillary role to love, compared to religious and social duties, convey in their conservative lessons that romantic passions, however concerning they may be, are common. Attempts to defuse the subversive power of love already attest to its growing importance in the minds—and hearts!—of French-Canadian men and women. These discursive strategies become even more apparent in the following period.

CHAPTER 2

Sublimated Love (1860-1920)

Starting in the 1860s, the development of the French-Canadian literary field was bolstered by the commitment to recounting the deeds of the national group. In founding *Les soirées canadiennes* in 1861, the writers surrounding Abbé Henri-Raymond Casgrain set the tone for the period, reflected in the incipit borrowed from Charles Nodier: "Let us hasten to recount the delightful stories of the people before they have forgotten them."[1] While the reputation of the fictional genre had not improved much, it seemed like a lesser evil if it served to recall History with a capital H. Gothic and adventure novels thus gave way to a surge in historical novels, when they weren't cleverly camouflaged within them. The same was true of the romance novel, which was beginning to discreetly take shape in the writings of some local authors.

It would not be an exaggeration to say that an author wanting to be widely read at the time in French Canada had to write entirely or partly for women. This was already the case in the previous period, which explains, according to Nathalie Ducharme, the less figurative role given to female protagonists in French-Canadian adventure novels, as compared to their European counterparts.[2] At the same time, literature was assigned the task of recalling the nation's accomplishments. These two injunctions (writing for women and for the homeland) were not easily reconcilable, because gender differences were then based on structural oppositions: public and private, reason and emotion, authority and submission. This is undoubtedly why novels published in French Canada between 1860 and 1920, seen through the sentimental lens, reveal a tendency to disguise historical novels as romance novels, probably in order to seduce a larger pool of female readers. By including the romantic dialectic in their titles, these books appear to promise various adventures involving two protagonists who are unjustly separated but will be happily reunited in the end. And this is more or less what happens in these works, except for the fact that love does not play a determining role but serves, instead, as a pretext for reconstituting the saga of the French-Canadian people. This stands out in *Charles et Éva* (1866), by Joseph Marmette: the didactic purpose of the text continually diverts the reader from the romance advertised in the title. The narrator himself, who seems to be uncomfortable with such a hastily concluded love story, exclaims in an amusing *mise en abyme*: "You move on swiftly when it comes to matters of the heart, Mister novelist!"[3] And in fact, one could say that, as a general rule, the French-Canadian novel of the second half of the nineteenth century also "moves on swiftly when it comes to matters of the heart."

Nevertheless, around ten novels form an initial corpus of romance novels corresponding to the invariants of the genre. This is due in part to women's entry in the literary field, but also to a greater distinction between the popular novel and the serial publication, the latter privileging a mixing of genres. Published over an extended period, the serial novel had to be continually renewed by developing the storyline, adding new twists, and integrating a variety of themes, which explains why the Gothic, adventure, and historical stories published in the newspapers of the period incorporate numerous secondary plots recounting disappearances, kidnappings, duels... and thwarted loves. Conversely, the more a literary text was conceived in book format, the more it tended to specialize in precise genres. With the growth of book publishing, this laid the foundation for an initial corpus centred on the quest for love.

In the first section of this chapter, we look at an English-Canadian female author who was strongly influenced by British-American literature, Rosanna Leprohon. As Montreal's "Jane Austen, she opened up perspectives on mixed marriages that the majority of French-Canadian authors were quick to close down, convinced that only people who resembled each other could form a union. In the second section, we examine the novel *Les Ribaud*, which focuses even more on the sacredness of passion. In the third section, we analyze one of the greatest forms of resistance to the romance novel at the end of the nineteenth century, the idea that human love must be abandoned or discouraged in favour of the more venerable love of God. In the fourth section, we discuss a novel that flirts with the rural genre, without really being a *roman du terroir*: in *Marie-Anna, la Canadienne*, the heroine is a Maria Chapdelaine figure who has not completely renounced her love. The fifth section ends with a veritable American-style success story that stands out from the rest of the corpus: *Amour vainqueur* (Victorious love) (1915), whose title speaks for itself.

Virginie Dussault, *Amour vainqueur*, Montréal, J. R. Constantineau, 1915.

A Montreal Jane Austen

Born in Montreal in 1829, Rosanna Eleonora Mullins studied at the convent of the Congrégation de Notre-Dame in Montreal and married Doctor Jean-Lucien Leprohon in 1851.[4] We decided to include two of her works in our corpus because of their exemplary value for analysis of romantic discourse in the Québécois novel, and also because they seem to have been more appreciated, in the period that interests us here (1860-1920), in their French translations than in their original English versions.[5] Her publications in English-language newspapers (her work includes sixteen texts of fiction and around a hundred poems)[6] slightly preceded her entry into the French literary world, when Joseph-Edouard Lefebvre de Bellefeuille (the nephew of Doctor Leprohon) translated her novel *The Manor House of De Villerai*. Under the title *Le manoir de Villerai, roman historique canadien sous la domination française*, the book was published by l'imprimerie Plinguet et Cie in 1861. This was followed by the John Lovell publication of *Antoinette de Mirecourt or Secret Marrying and Secret Sorrowing*, which soon became a success among French-speaking readers thanks to a translation by Joseph-Auguste Genand published as a series in *L'Ordre* under the title *Antoinette de Mirecourt ou mariage secret et chagrins cachés*. In 1865, the novel was published by C.O. Beauchemin & Valois and saw a wide distribution, eventually being republished in 1881 (by J.-B. Rolland & Fils)[7] and reprinted in 1886-1887 in the periodical *Les Nouvelles soirées canadiennes*.[8]

Leprohon's popularity is not surprising, given that her work essentially inaugurated the romance novel in the French-language publishing world in Quebec.[9] In Europe, as in the United States, freely choosing a spouse and the valorization of conjugal love came earlier to English-Protestant culture than it did to French-Catholic culture.[10] Thanks to her education, Leprohon could easily borrow motifs from British literature, whose most celebrated female authors of the time included Ann Radcliffe, Jane Austen, and Charlotte Brontë. Austen's masterpiece *Pride and Prejudice* (1813) seems to have made a particular impression on her. In her novels, as in Austen's, a woman must decide on her matrimonial future by weighing the options herself, without her parents having much of a say. To do so, she must carefully read the character traits of her potential suitors by relying less on their titles, positions, and possessions than on their manners. This exercise is more difficult than it appears, because different points of view affect the opinions one may have of the same person. As such, the fact that Leprohon's characters are one-dimensional and embody a number of archetypes (interest, gentleness, bravery, devotion) does not deter from people having multiple contradictory interpretations about them, which makes the romantic quest all the more complex and captivating.[11]

The action in *Le manoir de Villerai* (1861) takes place in 1756, on the eve of the British Conquest. Imagining a sort of monarchist France transplanted into America, Leprohon evokes a world populated with aristocrats and knights, and animated by august customs. However, we should not be misled by the fact that the story is situated in a distant past and appears, on first view, to be a historical novel. The work is definitely a romance novel, in the full sense of the term.[12] To add a cloak of legitimacy to a generally devalued production, novels of the second half of the nineteenth century frequently borrowed from the historical novel. Apparently ceding to the demand for a patriotic glorification of the past, these stories only use the latter for their decor. And this decor is rather flimsy—the mansions where the sumptuous balls are held often seem straight out of a fairy tale, rather than a Canadian reality. The aristocratic style of the characters serves more to impart a "castles and shepherdesses" aspect to the love story that is about to unfold. As for the historical events that serve to frame the works, they are primarily used to justify the obstacles to the romantic quest, which of course constitutes the hero's and heroine's real motivation. Entering the romance novel by the back door, but entering nonetheless, these pseudo-historical novels primarily elicit the reader's interest in the romantic impulses of two protagonists seeking a common path to happiness.

In Leprohon's works, we are witness to a "struggle between duty and inclination."[13] The plot is constructed around three characters who cannot get married, either because of differences of class or lack of affection. Blanche De Villerai is the seigneuress of the fief of De Villerai whose since-deceased parents promised her in marriage to the French military officer Gustave De Montarville. Though only a child at the time, she was forced to make a promise that cannot be easily broken. As her aunt explains to her: "If you do not like him [de Montarville], you have no alternative but to learn to like him. [...] [A young lady's] parents select. That is their duty—hers obedience."[14] De Montarville moves to France for six years. The evening of his return, the sky is stormy, the landscape is desolate and cold and, most importantly, he is late, which never bodes well in romance novels. The two characters seem to have everything needed to be in love—beauty, intelligence, bravery, rectitude—but there is no spark between them. Blanche argues that she does not know Gustave well enough to feel anything other than friendship for him. She mocks the tradition of parents choosing the spouse for their daughter, who has no say in the decision. As for Gustave, no sooner has he returned when he notices Rose Lauzon, a young girl who, despite her humble background, "appears quite a superior person altogether."[15] Raised by the governess of Miss De Villerai and sent to the same convent to complete her education, Rose has left Gustave smitten. Against all expectations, he declares his love for her and promises to make her his wife before God and men.

Rose, who refuses to betray Blanche, rejects Gustave. However, she has not seen the end of her troubles. The novel emphasizes on several occasions that Rose's flawless beauty is a source of cruel suffering for her. This angelic beauty leads to her rupture with Blanche, her benefactress, who suspects Rose of plotting against her by stealing her fiancé, an act that, were she to go through with it, would lead to Blanche's dishonour. Indeed, what would people think of a rich heiress being outdone by a humble peasant girl?

Rose finds refuge with an old patroness from Montreal, who takes her under her wing and treats her not as a servant, but as her companion. By chance, Gustave sees her walking down the street. He confesses that he has not been able to forget her. After an hour-long discussion, he gets an admission of love from Rose and gives her "a shower of kisses on her hands."[16] However, a marriage between them still seems impossible. The outcome of the story is based on a twist of fate: while paying a charity visit to the poor, Blanche contracts smallpox. The illness disfigures her, without entirely ruining her looks. Rose immediately offers to be her nurse and take care of her. Thanks to Rose's company during her convalescence, Blanche is reunited with her "sister." Confiding to De Montarville that he will never be but a brother to her, she understands that Rose and Gustave are destined for each other.

> Gustave, I have read more deeply than you think into your own generous heart—I have understood its struggles, its sufferings, its noble devotedness. I have fathomed, too, the secrets of another heart, than which a nobler never beat in woman's breast; one who loves you as no woman ever yet has done—better, a thousand times better than I have ever loved, or ever could learn to love you; and who, despite her inferiority to yourself in point of wealth and station, can alone, I feel convinced, render you happy. She is the wife, Gustave, I would give you. Need I say, I speak of Rose Lauzon?[17]

Having freely chosen celibacy, Blanche is no longer opposed to the marriage of Gustave and Rose. The two lovers leave

Canada for France after the defeat of the French armies. Their life together is not free of suffering, the novel tells us, but "whatever were the trials that subsequently swept over their household, they found in the deep fond love uniting their hearts, solace and balm for all."[18]

In the conflict between love and duty that Leprohon's novel depicts, neither can prevail. The two heroines, Rose and Blanche, have a greater sense of principles than the other characters, but, at the same time, they are also the ones who show that the impulses of the heart cannot be betrayed with impunity. While one refuses to enter into a marriage of convenience, even against the promise made to her parents, the other renounces a marriage of love in the name of social norms. One senses that Rosanna Leprohon has borrowed the ideas expressed in *Strictures on the Modern System of Female Education* (1799) by Hannah More, an author who instructed women to not abandon the self-control, modesty, and delicacy of their sex, nor the "dignity of their rank."[19] It is for transgressing this cardinal rule that Pauline de Nevers, an acquaintance of Blanche De Villerai, will be punished. Pauline is fickle, playing with love and etiquette, thinking only of pleasure, new dresses and jewellery, crazy for balls and soirées. She enjoys making new sentimental conquests and breaking hearts. The moment she feels loved, she rejects the object of her affection. A simple marriage proposal is enough for her to feel contempt for a suitor. She finally marries a major who is revealed to be a tyrant: he engages in debauchery and squanders her fortune. After the latter's premature death, the "desolate and now penitent woman"[20] accepts going to live with her pious aunt and devotes herself to works of charity with her. The message is clear: one doesn't trifle with love, any more than with the principles of polite society.

Set against a backdrop similar to that of *Le manoir de Villerai*, *Antoinette de Mirecourt* recounts the story of a love hindered by differences of nationality.[21] The eponymous heroine of the novel, a young girl from a good family, is invited by her cousin, Madame d'Aulnay, for a stay in the city. This is the only example of a heroine from the corpus of this period being authorized to leave, even temporarily, the paternal home.[22] This is also where the problems arise. Deprived of her father's protection at only seventeen years old, Antoinette is everyone's plaything. Her cousin manipulates her by involving her in schemes that are not suitable for her age. She attends social gatherings and meets two British military officers there: Major Audley Sternfield and Colonel Cecil Evelyn.

Not interested in the partner her father has chosen for her (the meek Louis Beauchesne) and poorly advised by her cousin, Antoinette is driven into the arms of the major. Though the affair between the two characters makes up a large part of the text, the reader soon discovers that this love story is not the right one. From the beginning, Sternfield's unpredictable character is betrayed by his nickname, the "irresistible," and his wheedling voice. Antoinette soon develops doubts about her relationship, regrets that are confirmed by the behavior of Audley, who is becoming unbearable towards her. In emphasizing the "charming naivety" and "timid vivacity" of the colonel (whose rank in the military hierarchy is above the major's), the narration makes it clear from the start that Antoinette would be much better matched with the simple and discreet Evelyn. The scene of his meeting with Antoinette provides a host of clues that point to this. At the ball thrown by Madame d'Aulnay that Antoinette attends, Evelyn is among the first to arrive. He is described as "a tall, fine-looking man whose clear bright colour of dark blue eye betrayed his Anglo-Saxon descent."[23] He is a perfect gentleman. His reserve could almost be mistaken for coldness. His severe character is in direct contrast to Sternfield's, whose uncontrolled ardour becomes pernicious over the course of the story. To confirm Evelyn's uncontested superiority over Sternfield in the eyes of French-

Canadian readers, it suffices to note that the first is Catholic and the second is Protestant.

Many similarities can be drawn between *Pride and Prejudice*, published in 1813, and this novel by Leprohon—which is not surprising when one is familiar with the serialized processes used in popular literature. A number of scenes seem to be strongly influenced by Austen's famous work, like when Sternfield paints a very negative portrait of his colleague Evelyn during a ball at the beginning of the novel: he describes him to Antoinette as nothing less than an atheist and misogynist. More fundamentally, Antoinette's three suitors occupy functions in the story that are similar to those of Elizabeth Bennet's suitors. Evelyn/Darcy embodies the hero who is cold and distant but discreetly generous. While Evelyn proves to be heroic helping Antoinette's father during a snowstorm, Darcy preserves the honour of Elizabeth's sister. In both cases, the rescue is anonymous, without the hero's identity being known or his receiving any glory for it. Moreover, the coldness of the two characters is traced to the same cause: in the past, they both had a great love stolen from them, Evelyn by his own brother and Darcy by Wickham. The similarities between Sternfield and Wickham, both fortune hunters and deceitful characters in trouble with the law, are just as obvious. Even Antoinette's third suitor, Louis Beauchesne, who her father has chosen for her marriage, can be likened to William Collins, though the former is less caricatured, good French Canadian that he is.

In chapter eight, the Colonel and Antoinette are obliged to take a horse ride together, following a scheme concocted by Madame d'Aulnay. At first "indignant beyond measure at being thus arbitrarily forced on the society of so unwilling a companion,"[24] Antoinette quickly changes her mind. A gun shot startles the horses and Evelyn protects Antoinette: "In that moment of deadly peril [...], quick as thought, Evelyn catches his companion, and murmuring, 'Forgive me,' threw her out on the snow-covered ground."[25] Taking refuge in a farmer's house, the two protagonists warm up. Antoinette is impressed by Evelyn's bravery. The latter admires her composure and, for the first time, revels in her beauty, when he sees her in a maternal role caring for the farmer's children. After the false start of the episode at the ball, the promise of the union jeopardized in the inaugural meeting is now sealed. Before parting, "Colonel Evelyn kindly holds Antoinette's hands [...]."[26]

Audley Sternfield tries to convince Antoinette that she loves him, and he makes persistent advances that, due to her extreme shyness, she does not know how to reject. Knowing that her father would never consent to her union with a British Protestant and that he could disinherit his only, still-juvenile daughter, the major commits the ultimate sacrilege by plotting to make Antoinette accept a secret marriage. As soon as this union is blessed by a Protestant minister, Sternfield becomes possessive, jealous, and tyrannical, as his new spouse refuses to make the marriage public and consummate their union. His intrusions become increasingly excessive, to the point where Madame d'Aulnay's chambermaid exclaims: "One would think he was the master of the house."[27] This invasion of the heroine's physical space is a common theme of romance literature that, in describing one person's entry into the life of another, inevitably raises questions regarding the distance between the protagonists. From covert glances and stolen kisses, to violent intrusions into the private space, there is a wide range of symbolic and physical gestures that reveal or mask the conjunction (for heroes) or disjunction (for rivals) between the characters.[28] The woman must know how to mitigate these encroachments in order to avoid having her "secret garden" violated, and metaphors of penetration and chastity abound in the descriptions of this complex dance.

In *Antoinette de Mirecourt*, it is obvious that something is wrong with the way the major behaves towards his wife.

Intrusions into the heroine's space are followed by undesired physical advances. Antoinette, concentrated on some sewing work, "heard not the servant's announcement of a visitor, and it was only when enfolded in Sternfield's arms that she was aware of his presence."[29] Further into the story, a menacing Sternfield justifies his advances towards her: "let me [...] press for once a husband's kiss on that proud brow, which has, heretofore, so scornfully refused it. Do not say me nay! I again repeat, 'tis wrong to push a desperate man too far!"[30] Antoinette refrains from replying to Sternfield's words, for fear of provoking him: "interpreting her silence in his favor, [he] threw his arm around her, and kissed again and again her brow, her silken shining hair."[31] Finally, despite being formally forbidden to come to her father's place, where she has taken refuge to recover her faltering health, Sternfield disguises himself to track her down. His ardour is now so extreme that it makes him violent, both psychologically and physically. Madame d'Aulnay even compares him to Bluebeard, who "was not half as bad as [him],"[32] a comparison full of innuendos for those who remember the tale.

Terrified by her husband's outbursts, Antoinette stood "motionless with changing cheek and beating heart."[33] She cannot count on the help of her entourage, who are unaware of her situation, and she doesn't know how to react other than with silence. Incapable of expressing herself in words, she lets her body speak in her place. In the traditional romance novel, the gallant man should know how to be firm and master his ardour, whereas the woman can be more expressive in her attitudes, but only because she does not know how to avoid physically expressing how she feels: she bites her lip, blushes or turns pale, feels like fainting, and so on. In *Antoinette de Mirecourt,* this somatic expression becomes so pronounced that Madame d'Aulnay orders the heroine to control her non-verbal language: "but, mercy on us! Child, how dreadfully ill you look. [...] This will not do. You should never allow anxiety or grief to go farther than imparting a delicate pallor or pensive look to your features."[34] But the more Antoinette is consumed by anxiety, the more her beauty fades. Her value on the matrimonial market is at stake, and this is exactly what her father reminds her of with a remark that is "half dry, half-laughing," specifying that "it was fortunate she had her husband Louis ready chosen and secured, otherwise her fading beauty might render it somewhat difficult to procure an eligible one."[35] It is a cruel verdict for Antoinette, whose only fault in that moment, in her father's eyes, is that of being sick!

Things become complicated for Antoinette when she realizes that she is in fact in love with Colonel Cecil Evelyn. Torn between indifference, even aversion to a man she can no longer leave, and attraction to another who she cannot be with, she sinks into despair and suffering, even after a stay in the countryside. She then makes the only choice that can save her from the tyranny of her undesirable husband: her "supreme hope" lies precisely in her declining health. It is "with a strange quickening of her pulses she remembered that death might yet free her from a union, to whose consummation she now looked forward with inexpressible aversion."[36] In divulging her secret, the declaration she makes to Doctor Manby leaves no room for doubt: she is indeed planning a suicide. "Talk to me no more of drugs or palliatives, Doctor, unless you can give me one that will set this weary heart at rest for ever."[37] This recalls the trope introduced in the short stories analyzed in the preceding chapter, which established that it is through suffering, even agony, that heroines take their place in history and become masters of their destiny. Illness or death paradoxically represent for them a way of acting in the world.

The last pages of Leprohon's novel provide a providential solution to the young woman's dilemma. Louis Beauchesne, furious about Sternfield's domination over his former love, fatally injures him in a duel and flees to the United States. After visiting her dying husband and forgiving his wrongdoings, Antoinette is struck with "brain-fever" and slips into delirium. As expected, the illness is temporary, because clearer skies are on the horizon for her. Though the novel states that it is the doctor's "watchful care" and great "medical skill" that cures her illness, readers surmise that she recovers because her two other suitors are no longer in the picture. Audley Sternfield, chosen by a cousin (Madame d'Aulnay) corrupted by vulgar books, has been killed in a duel, and Louis Beauchesne, chosen by a father attached to tradition, has been exiled. Antoinette can thus give herself to Colonel Evelyn and enjoy a bright, loving marriage.

Leprohon's novel encapsulates the new romantic moral of the modern family, which proclaimed with growing intensity that conjugal love was the "very essence of marriage" and the only sentiment that could "ensure happiness on earth."[38] Nonetheless, Leprohon's writing remains conservative and therefore acceptable. In the two novels summarized here, passion exists, but we note that it can also be a poor guide. The heroines and heroes might experience something like love at first sight (even if slightly delayed in *Antoinette de Mirecourt*, in the horse accident scene), but they must scrupulously search their hearts and, especially, weigh the social consequences of their inclinations before succumbing to their passions. Leprohon also remains "honest," like other novelists of her time, by confining romantic attraction to the marital institution. Licentiousness is absolutely forbidden. A man should not show interest in a woman he does not want to marry (even the ghastly Sternfield conforms to this rule), and a woman should not accept being courted by a man without considering making him her husband. Coquettish girls and conceited boys prepare for a dark future. Once the declarations of love are made, the couple can fully express their feelings, but only without ever transgressing the boundaries of decorum. Kissing hands or eyes, holding hands, and languorous looks are permitted.

Leprohon does however stand out in French-Canadian literature by letting her heroine reject her father's choice without being stigmatized.[39] In both *Le manoir de Villerai* and *Antoinette de Mirecourt*, the father's first choice of fiancé is not respected. This determination to override the father's wishes should be read against the backdrop of the heroine's broader refusal to be limited to her community of origin. In *Le manoir de Villerai*, the novelist allows Rose to have an exogenous marriage with a man who, on top of being French, is of a higher class, and who she even follows to his native country, abandoning her homeland. In *Antoinette de Mirecourt*, the heroine further breaks group ties and marries an Englishman. When Louis reminds her that they have lived "in the same circle," belong "to the same race," profess "the same religion" and had grown "accustomed to one another since their earliest childhood," Antoinette replies that the familiar circumstances of their growing up together has taught them to regard each other as brother and sister. For someone who dreams of love with a capital L, Louis's affection towards her seems too tepid, too sober.

It is likely that Leprohon's personal trajectory, as the daughter of an Irish father and Swiss mother, and having herself married a man from an old French-Canadian family, made her more open to this mixing, which was quite unusual in romance novels of the period.[40] The romantic imperatives one finds in her work greatly contribute to distinguishing *Le manoir de Villerai* and *Antoinette de Mirecourt* from other publications in French of the time. The triumph of love in a French-Canadian society trying to preserve its faith, race, language, and traditions does not come without conditions, and, in the writings of French-language authors, love is anything but exile from one's class and nation: it is a return to the fold. Rather than an uprooting, it is an entrenchment of roots. The few rare escapes from the milieu of origin only reinforce the rule of closure on the same. Leprohon's audacity did not go unnoticed, and, though praising the morality of her work, critics did not hesitate to denounce the liberties she took with the traditional community's rules of endogamy. Joseph-Édouard Lefebvre de Bellefeuille, who praised *Le manoir de Villerai* upon its release and was its translator, reproached the writer for having married the heroine of *Antoinette de Mirecourt* to two English men. He understood why the union with Sternfield was "portrayed as excessively sad; it is the deserved punishment for a secret marriage made against the parents' wishes and the laws of the Church."[41] However, he was disappointed that the second was not also cursed but marked, on the contrary, "by all sorts of happiness and bliss."[42] "It is true that Col. Evelyn, Antoinette's second husband, was Catholic; this is something, but it is not all that I wish to see in the spouse of one of my young compatriots: he is not [French] Canadian."[43] A much more satisfying conclusion, in Bellefeuille's eyes, would have been Leprohon "painting an expressive portrait of the misfortune, hardship and disgrace forever attached to both unions in *Antoinette de Mirecourt*..."[44]

Loving her love

In Leprohon's novels, love triumphs while also respecting the conventions of the period. Tradition is preserved, despite transgressing the taboo of socially or ethnically mixed marriages. A generation later, Ernest Choquette (1862-1941), a doctor and man of letters, goes one step further in distancing his work from the traditional constraints around love. In his first novel, *Les Ribaud: une idylle de 37* (1898), he marries his French-Canadian heroine to an "Englishman." The title, which pairs the promise of a historical novel (the Rebellion of 1837) with that of a love story (a romance), arouses intrigue and no doubt explains a part of its success with the French-Canadian public. The work was popular enough to have been published in a second edition in 1926 and adapted for the theatre under the title *Madeleine (épisode de 1837)*, in 1927.

Les Ribaud begins with the death of Doctor Ribaud's son, killed during a duel with an arrogant Englishman. To avoid adding to her torment, his sister Madeleine is told that her brother died during a hunting accident. Four years later, in 1836, Madeleine meets one of the witnesses of the duel, Captain Percival Smith, who she had already briefly seen marching at a military parade. It is mutual love at first sight. The young eighteen-year-old girl falls under the spell of the young soldier, and the latter cannot resist the beauty's allure. The father is mortified when he learns of his daughter's liaison with a "hereditary enemy" of his "race." Having himself been in love at twenty years old and knowing the "heartcrushing" feeling of being separated from one's flame "in the full bloom of love," he thinks of poisoning Percival with drugs from his medicine chest. It is clear that the action will take place at the crossroads of love and duty and that the battle between these two theoretically absolute values will decide the characters' fate.

From the outset, Madeleine feels like the heroine of a novel. She confides her joy at loving and being loved in her diary. But the confrontations between the Patriots and the English make her gradually aware of the drama she is embroiled in: she loves an enemy of her people. She is torn between respect for her father, an ardent patriot, and her attraction to Percival. "My father on the one side… Percival on the other; what I adore on the one side and, on the other, what I love…"[45] The feelings she is experiencing become a source of torture. She does not want to bring shame upon her father or her nation, but, at the same time, she knows that her love is stronger than her will, that this love has taken full possession of her, and that the call of duty is not powerful enough to prevent her from fleeing with her handsome English captain. Everything should have steered her away from him, and yet she can't stop thinking about him. She is gripped by "this irresistible need to love" that never comes twice in life. Not knowing what to do, she prays to God: "God has to make a miracle: he must wrest from my heart the love he allowed to enter and take root there, just as he must wrest from Percival's heart the love he has for me. Otherwise, if I have to still love him, if he's going to still love me too, I feel that I would never have the strength to refuse following him, even as an enemy, even as a murderer of my own people, and that, with only the sign of his hand, I would run to him, into his arms [...]."[46]

Caught between dishonour and the loss of love, Madeleine chooses love. Choquette maintains the traditional division between a more feminine private sphere and a more masculine public one. Madeleine is overcome by her feelings because politics is not her domain. Her primary concern is being beautiful, seeking the tender company of a husband and starting a family.[47] Percival embodies, by comparison, masculine resolve. If Percival could not remain bravely on the battlefield or loyal to his flag, if he proved to be a coward by abandoning his people in the name of love, he would make himself unworthy of being loved. This is why Madeleine can ask God to extinguish Percival's love for her but conserve her love for him. "Like all women, Madeleine, in her big heart, [is] prepared to sacrifice herself... To being no longer loved... she accepts it, since all the pain would have been hers alone."[48] Just as Percival would dishonour Madeleine in not fulfilling his patriotic duty, at risk of losing her, she would betray him by not loving him, at risk of disappointing him. The gendered division between the private and the public sheds light on another invariant of the nineteenth-century romance novel: while the woman must leave the private sphere to find love, raising the issue of marriage with strangers, the man must return home to find love, which most often renders love affairs with exotic women suspect.[49]

Tormented, tortured, Madeleine runs to the church in Chambly to pray. She meets there the Abbot Michaudin, a good friend of her father. The priest tells her that, contrary to what she has been led to believe, her brother died in a duel with an Englishman and that Smith was one of the witnesses. Hearing this news, Madeleine feels "that something breaks in her heart."[50] "I am horrified with myself," she exclaims; "I am ashamed; I imagine the general feeling of contempt others must have around me [...] and I feel defeated, crushed..."[51] At this point in the novel we sense that nothing can save Madeleine's love for Percival. Marrying him would almost be like uniting with her brother's murderer. However, in a spectacular turn of events, the village priest, who we learn had himself one day loved, encourages Madeleine to pursue her passion. He assures her that there is no point in fighting it, because a love like hers "cannot be broken."[52] Moreover, he vouches for the honour, goodness, and generosity of Percival (with no mention of his being Protestant or Catholic), since the young man was only honouring his duty to his country.

With her priest's blessing, Madeleine pays a visit to Percival at his military quarters. She reiterates her love for him, vowing that it is impossible to love anyone but him now that she has given him her heart. She begs him to not shed the blood of her compatriots. She says she would rather die "than have her love attached to the shame of betraying her blood and race."[53] Percival hears Madeleine's plea and promises to find a way to be a brave and honest soldier, loyal to his national group, without compromising their union. He kisses her tear-filled eyes as the Angelus bell chimes.

The next day, the Patriot Rebellion breaks out and Doctor Ribaud takes the opportunity to plan an ambush. He seizes the chance to avenge his son and targets the regiment officer, who he believes is Percival, killing him after a few shots. Learning that her beloved has fallen in combat, Madeleine is convinced that he let himself be killed because of his love for her, preferring to die rather than betray his promise. She falls ill, delirious, remains laid out in her bed, lifeless. Like the heroines of romance novels before her, she is consoled in telling herself that death could unite her with her chosen love. Her father, devastated by the state of his daughter's health, feels responsible for her suffering. But, in yet another twist, we learn that Percival is not dead! To remain faithful to his love and his duty, he decided to enter battle as a flag bearer, allowing him to not desert but also not shed the blood of French Canadians (his good friend having worn the captain's clothes and been killed in his place, which seems to have no effect on anyone in the novel). Percival appears before Madeleine, who quickly recovers. They can get married with the blessing of Doctor Ribaud, who has been convinced to accept Percival as his son-in-law, because, otherwise, he would become like his own daughter's executioner.

Written by an author who severely judged the Patriots' actions, *Les Ribaud: une idylle de 37* does not raise questions regarding the language or religion of the couple formed by Madeleine and Percival. Or, rather, he does so, but only to provide a very provocative response: the novel aims to show that love is constituted in a way that "is resistant to all other feelings,"[54] and, in particular, to patriotic considerations.[55] Madeleine confesses that the Patriot uprising, the assassination of her brother by an Englishman in a duel, and her father's opposition would not have been enough to change her choice of fiancé, that her passion for the man "of her life" is too resolute and that a single gesture on the part of Percival would have sufficed for her to renounce family and country. As Ernest Choquette accurately writes, she desires, above all, "to love her love."[56] In this sense, one could almost see this novel as a rebuttal, twenty-five years early, to *The Call of the Race* (*L'appel de la race*, 1922). In Lionel Groulx's didactic novel, a priest gives his blessing to a divorce in the name of loyalty to his nationality, while in Choquette's work, the priest forgives renouncing one's nationality to remain faithful to one's love. The moral of *Les Ribaud: une idylle de 37* is audacious, if not downright scandalous, for the period.[57]

Several years later, in a long review of the theatre adaptation of *Ribaud* Louis Dantin (the pseudonym of Eugène Seers) is offended by the "logic of the situations" and the "veracity of the characters,"[58] in Choquette's story. He notes the succession of entirely unexpected and implausible developments: a young woman meets a soldier of the enemy camp to plead with him to renege on his duty; the soldier agrees to partially desert his position because of his love for her; his best friend takes his place without anyone in the army noticing; the battle smoke barely lifted, the officer appears at the house of the man who thought he had killed him but killed his best friend instead, to ask for his daughter's hand in marriage; the patriot father suddenly forgets his hatred of the other "race"—just a few of many situations, observes Dantin, that break "the logical threads and plunge us into a complete chimera."[59] But what especially shocks the literary critic then exiled in the United States, is that the love story itself lacks coherence. He accepts the idea that a great love is an invincible force that takes precedence over both family and patriotic duty, and that this theme of absolute love, "true or false, can, as well as any other, be the basis for a beautiful drama, since it is the same as that of *Romeo and Juliet.*"[60] Nevertheless, according to Dantin, in taking this literary approach, one has to consider all of the consequences and depict the heroes as "being moved by a driving, consuming, blinding passion," that turns the characters into "playthings of an invincible fate."[61] The contradiction between individual passion and collective duty is thus resolved by "misfortune, catastrophe," which, in Dantin's view, seems to be the only solution consistent "with both life and aesthetics."[62] It was in refusing to follow this basic principle that Choquette compromised his work. He wanted to have an outcome that was both logical and happy for a drama that could only be logical if it ended in misfortune.

In his review, Dantin took the liberty of rewriting Choquette's romantic story in order to make it conform to the literary canons as he understood them. He believed that the work would have had "more unity, more strength," if the author "had pursued his premises according to their inevitable evolution."[63] He could have then shown "Madeleine captivated, conquered, persisting in her crazy love, and the father Ribaud in his hatred; the priest terrified, powerless between them, but rejecting the role of Cupid's messenger; [Percival] brave and beautiful in his despair, going to battle as though to a suicide; transported fatally wounded, perhaps, to the home of the Ribauds."[64] The novel would end with a "great scene of crying: love revealing itself, shouting its pain to the heavens, and finally forgiven, sublimated by its defeat."[65] In short, Dantin wanted nothing less than to abolish Choquette's discourse and replace it with a tragedy in which patriotic duty bloodily triumphs over love.

Choquette's subsequent more regionalist novels seem to have anticipated Dantin's future critiques by avoiding happy endings. A work like *Claude Paysan* (1899), published only one year after *Les Ribaud*, has Fernande and Claude die, the first from a series of illnesses, the second from a suicide barely disguised as a drowning. In portraying the incompatibility of their love, *Claude Paysan* belongs to the category of "quasi" romance novels at the limit of our corpus, which deviate from the romantic quest as they unfold. In this second novel by Choquette, Claude's mother remembers being "deeply moved by the always charming appeal of love" at twenty years old, but how the "castles she erected under its deceptive mirage [...] then collapsed,"[66] foreshadowing with her words the tragic fate of her son. In the novel *La terre* (1916), the third and last of Choquette's, this moral is repeated even more insistently. Jacqueline, the daughter of Doctor Duvert, believes the fairy tales she has read in books recounting how two beautiful and virtuous angels come together in "the purest love" and achieve "the perfect happiness."[67] Her father responds firmly: "Chimeras and delusions, all of it; tales that fairies sometimes dream up for children but which the writer should not be telling older girls like you, because he knows that life's brutality is later going to contradict every page of his book, one by one. [...] You see, plans like yours, my little Jacqueline, can only come true in a dream, with your eyes closed."[68] Jacqueline will marry Yves, her lifelong suitor, but their marriage will take place on the condition that they become farmers, which, as the book's title indicates, is the main subject of the story. In the novels published after *Les Ribaud*, Choquette was no longer interested in using his work to exalt the "deceptive mirage" of pure love.

Martyrs of the heart and brides of God

In French Canada, the second half of the nineteenth century was marked by the emergence of a religion that was simultaneously more political and more intimate, arising from both a tight-knit network of social institutions and sentimental devotions. At the same time that the Catholic Church was trying to take charge of or influence French-Canadian national organizations (including schools), it was also trying to more subtly shape emotions and attitudes.[69] The dominant discourse was primarily based on mortification, patience, and humility. Suffering became the test par excellence for Christians seeking salvation. By calling on men and especially women[70] to sacrifice their desires on the altar of duty, to efface themselves, it was inevitable that carnal love be curtailed. It was not, however, the heart's impulses that were repressed in stories in the second half of the nineteenth century. Emotions are frequently accommodated in this corpus, which is notably confirmed in the abundance of tears that are shed. What prevents the French-Canadian novel from spawning a real romance corpus is the constant diversion of romantic impulses toward endings other than a man's attachment to a woman, or vice versa. The virtue of self-sacrifice, already present in several works of the previous period and still evident in the "feminine fidelity" literary trend of the 1930s,[71] constitutes a formidable obstacle to the expression of an all-too-human love.

This was perhaps never more clear than in the writings of Félicité Angers (1845-1924), alias Laure Conan, the first female writer to "pursue a career" in the French-language world of letters in Quebec. Though not part of the romance genre per se, her work must be considered precisely for the perspective it offers on how personal affections are redirected to avoid dealing with romantic passion. The few examples of her work that use romance novel motifs recast them in a mystical or patriotic light. *Un amour vrai* (1879), *Angéline de Montbrun* (1882), *À l'œuvre et à l'épreuve* (1891), *L'oublié* (1900) and *L'obscure souffrance* (1919) can be considered works of an edifying literature that aim to show how the inconstancy and fallibility of love cannot guarantee real happiness to those who surrender to it.

First published as a series in the pages of *La Revue de Montréal* starting in September 1878, Laure Conan's first novel *Un amour vrai* (A true love) was sold in book form the following year by Leprohon & Leprohon, and republished in 1899 under the title *Larmes d'amour* (Tears of love) without the author's permission. One could characterize this text as a quasi-romance novel, given that love does not triumph in the end. Vacationing in Malbaie, Thérèse Raynol falls in love with a handsome Scotsman, Francis Douglas. He also enjoys her company, and, in no time at all, they are confessing their love. But alas, there is a disjunction, and the cause is easy to surmise given the hero's nationality: he is Protestant. They still plan to marry, but, despite Thérèse's pleading, Francis categorically refuses to convert to Catholicism. Their happiness, initially so full of promise, now seems hopelessly compromised.

The only possible solution, in Thérèse's mind, is to sacrifice her life for Francis' conversion. "Oh my God," she exclaims,

LARMES D'AMOUR

PAR

LAURE CONAN.

LEPROHON & LEPROHON
LIBRAIRES-EDITEURS
1829, RUE NOTRE-DAME
MONTRÉAL, CAN.

"you will have mercy on him. You will illuminate this soul, one of the most generous that you have created. I ask you in the name of Jesus Christ, make me suffer as much as you please, but give him the faith, *without which it is impossible to please you.*"[72] A woman was then expected to take full responsibility for Catholic family morality.[73] She was the one who had to make the ultimate sacrifice in the name of her Christian duty. Laure Conan redirects this conviction by committing her heroine to an educational and redemptive mission. As soon as her marriage contract is signed, she makes a vow to the Virgin: she is ready to give her life in exchange for her fiancé's conversion.

Thérèse's wish is granted. She falls ill and dies in her wedding gown. The day after this catastrophe, Francis realizes his error and becomes Catholic. The morning of the funeral, "when the time comes to lay her in her coffin, Francis approaches and takes Thérèse's left hand, puts on her wedding ring, and then kisses her on the lips."[74] Finally united, the couple can celebrate in Heaven the bliss they were unable to find on earth. However, the plot is not structured around the three essential motifs of the romantic novel, there is meeting and disjunction but no real conjunction. We know that the death of fiancés or spouses poses no problem for a final reunion; they can reunite in the afterlife. In this case, Thérèse clearly promises to remain faithful to Francis, once dead: "Dear friend," she sighs before dying, "I will love you more in heaven than on earth."[75] But this declaration only works in one direction. Once converted to Catholicism, Francis indeed experiences sadness and grief (intermingled with the joy his new faith brings him). Nevertheless, from then on, his romantic quest is replaced by a religious one. Rather than being content to convert to Catholicism so he can eventually join Thérèse in paradise and consummate the conjunction of two pure hearts, he finds in the religious life a love that is greater than earthly love.

During his last visit to Thérèse's mother, Francis decides to add some pages of his own to the end of the deceased woman's diary, another way for the male hero to invade the heroine's space. This takes the form of a contradictory dialogue, a battle, in sum, between human love and the love of Christ. "Thérèse," he writes, "all the days of my life, I would have wanted to cry on this earth that covers you. It is by your side that I want to sleep my final sleep and awaken at the hour of the resurrection. But one must obey God. [...] My God, be my dream, my love."[76] In the last lines of this peroration, Douglas has made his choice. Thérèse's mother receives a letter in which he announces his entry into the Grande Chartreuse monastery. He thus must rid himself of the last objects that still remind him of Thérèse: a strand of her hair, her portrait, and, especially, her crucifix. The closer he comes to God, the further he is from Thérèse, reproaching himself for the moments he cedes to his grief for lost love as so many "failures." As his spiritual advisor reminds him, he must learn that "God suffices for the soul" and that "sacrificing everything to God is the greatest grace." Francis' last dying words are: "What should I fear? I am going to fall into the arms of He who I loved the most."[77] By this time, there is no trace of Thérèse in his mind, while she herself had sworn fidelity to him beyond death.

Interrupting the romantic plot halfway through, at the moment when Angéline's father dies, Laure Conan's second novel *Angéline de Montbrun* seems to deviate even more from the typical romance novel scenario. We will not undertake a detailed analysis of this work, already discussed elsewhere at length,[78] *a fortiori* because it is not in keeping with the invariants of the romance novel. It suffices to recall that Maurice and the young eighteen-year-old Angéline, a motherless orphan, have declared their mutual love and are engaged to be married. "Nothing, absolutely nothing was lacking to the young, charming, deeply enamoured couple. The future appeared to them enchanted. Both had that elated confidence, that illusion of security which people have who share a keen, irreproachable love, who will soon be united by a divine bond."[79] But Angéline's father dies in a hunting accident, and, devastated by the news, she is engulfed in her pain and becomes dangerously weak, to the point that her life is at risk. One day when she goes out, she faints and suffers a fall that disfigures her (in the first version of the novel, a tumour was the reason for her disfigurement). Despite the protests of Maurice, who vows to always love her and remain celibate if he cannot be with her, Angéline refuses to impose the torment of a mutilated spouse on him. Avoiding the inevitable infidelity of her suitor, convinced that his feelings would only wither at the sight of a face that has lost its beauty, she breaks the engagement.

Much like the heroine of *Un amour vrai,* Angéline revels in her heart being "reduced to ashes."[80] Taking a perverse delight in suffering, she seems to willingly substitute a joyful love for a sacrificial one, even though, the text suggests, she could have Maurice back and be happy with a single word.[81] She even seems to relish how the euphoria she briefly enjoyed increases her despair. "How many are there who love as they want to love, who are loved as they want to be loved? Infinitely few. As for me, I have had that happiness so rare, so great; I have lived an ideal, intense life. And I pay for this divine joy through dreadful sorrows, unutterable pains."[82] Angéline admits finding it difficult to "resist the temptation to sink into [her] melancholy, to allow [herself] to be engulfed by it."[83] She is constantly seeking "pain, that virile friend," the "cruel rending and the illumination of sacrifice," the "revelation of pain," claiming to be "like a wounded person who would have a bitter pleasure in aggravating his wounds, in seeing blood flow from them."[84] The mirror that once reflected her beauty has been exchanged for a diary in which she describes her darkest thoughts. In these pages, Angéline recounts her apprenticeship in the "most difficult knowledge: knowing how to suffer."[85]

Numerous commentators have attempted to read Angéline's sorrow through a biographical, psychological, or psychoanalytic lens.[86] In several passages, Angéline's love for Maurice clearly pales in comparison to her love for her deceased father. The latter was and remained after his death "all [her] happiness."[87] In the story, Maurice's and Monsieur de Montbrun's characters become intertwined, the ghostly "he" used to speak of her father and her fiancé "finally fusing them into a single object of love, the Father."[88] Other studies have focused instead on the fictionalization of Conan's supposed real love for a local politician.[89] However, these types of interpretations overlook the fact that Angéline's love is revealed in the very dynamic of loss. What is important is not Angéline's love for this or that person, but the fact that these individuals allow her to live impossible loves that nothing, "neither separation, nor time, nor religion, nor death," can take away from her. Angéline says of both her father and Maurice "Woe is me! However much I tell myself that I no longer exist for him, I love him, as only the unfortunate ones can love."[90] Though Angéline describes herself as "a woman who needs to be loved,"[91] she places herself in a situation in which she will never be loved again.

Mary Jean Green is quite right to compare *La Princesse de Clèves* and *Angéline de Montbrun*. In both cases, the heroine renounces the "love of a handsome young man with whom [she] is passionately in love, and who is eager to marry her," though there is "no real legal or moral barrier to the marriage," but she "chooses to retreat to a secluded life of virtue."[92] The explanation for this surprising decision is consistent in both novels: Angéline is convinced, just like the Princess of Cleves, that her suitor's attraction to her will fade over time and this appears to her "so dreadful a misfortune"[93] that she prefers to renounce marriage. This tragic ending has long bewildered literary critics in France (for *La Princesse de Clèves*) and Quebec (for *Angéline de Montbrun*), who did not understand how someone can so easily forgo one's desire. As the two novels' texts themselves reveal, the explanation is nevertheless simple: in the ideal version of human love, only women, Conan recalls, are capable of fidelity, because their desire for the other sex is not based on physical attraction alone. Aside from "a few rare exceptions,"[94] men, unlike women, end up becoming indifferent and cold when their fiancée loses the "enchanting charm of her beauty,"[95] even when, in the excitement of the first encounters, their love "seems as deep as the ocean." To Maurice who called her in a letter his "immortal beloved," Angéline responds that this "beautiful phrase," this "heavenly phrase," however "delightful" it may be to her ears, is deceptive. In reality, she says, "there is no eternal love" and "the dream of endless love, always sought, has been sought in vain on earth."[96] To enjoy immortal love, a woman must have immortal beauty and thus immortal youth.

Contrary to the heroines, who persist in their feelings despite difficulties, men are susceptible to losing interest in the object of their affection, and it is thus no coincidence that male infidelity became a central theme just as female authors were first making their entry into the literary field, in both Quebec and France. For the character of Angéline depicted by Laure Conan, the situation seems hopeless, but the woman's reconciliation with love becomes possible thanks to the intervention of a priest, who convinces her to turn to the consolations of Heaven (much like Madame de Clèves, who spends the rest of her days devoted to holy works). Following his advice, Angéline consummates a union with her "heavenly father" and "sacred nuptials" with the "divine crucified one," both of whom, Father and Son, promise to love her forever. Maurice, rejected, seems to really be suffering in the last letter he writes to Angéline, when he begs her to give him another chance to prove his fidelity. The young woman turns out to be inflexible. With her angelic name, promised to the Virgin by her father, she seems to fulfill her destiny by being "devoted to God" and "obliged to love Our Lord with the love of a virgin and a wife."[97] She recognizes, in particular, that Jesus Christ is the "Loving Saviour" and that she must renounce human love in order to be His, because His love alone is truly "eternal, incomprehensible love."[98] At the habit ceremony of her friend Mina Darville, who has entered the Ursuline convent after not being able to marry the man she loves,[99] Angéline takes the mockers of perpetual vows to task. For her there is no love but eternal love, and any love that ceases to be reveals its intrinsic falseness. "Shame to the heart which, once it loved, can anticipate that it will cease to love."[100] In secluding herself and giving herself to God, she shields herself from the betrayals of human love.

In the very last line of the story, Angéline all but orders Maurice to respect her decision, exclaiming "Spare me this ultimate pain; may I never blush to have loved you!"[101] In so doing, she does not proclaim the value of human love but, rather, consigns it forever to a bygone past. It is important to note, however, that, beyond being a novel that speaks of love without being a romance novel, *Angéline de Montbrun* also downplays the emotive charge typical of romance novels (generosity, grace, tenderness and immortality) to focus more on religious aspirations. The mystical alternative to romance that Conan's novel proposes goes far beyond the paradoxical call for abstinence that infuses nineteenth-century romance novels, which often entails the heroine sacrificing her life in a state of bliss. In *Angéline de Montbrun*, the martyr Angéline does not end the love story but instead sublimates and redirects it toward the only true love, completely changing the meaning of the initial story. While the literature is filled with heroines who give their lives for their loved ones, hoping to reunite with them in heaven, Angéline de Montbrun refuses to end up like Thérèse Raynol, who sacrifices herself in vain (dying in her wedding gown and betrayed by Francis Douglas, who loves God more than he ever loved her). Faced with Maurice's apparent tepidness, Angéline rejects him before he changes his mind. Condemned by choice to become a *vieille fille* (a term whose pejorative connotation in the French-Canadian imaginary is well known[102] and distinct from that of its English counterpart "spinster"[103]), Angéline vows to forget about Maurice and gives herself to "Jesus Christ, who alone loves us as we need to be loved."[104]

While in both novels cited by Conan the final message is the superiority of divine over earthly love, in *Angéline de Montbrun*, the turn to divine love is done in the name of true human love.

It is the betrayal of human love, its broken promise to be forever absolute and unfading, that leads the heroine to choose divine love. In this sense, we must reconsider the initial hypothesis and conclude that in this work by Conan, divine love is only truer because it is a substitute for a human love that is always too weak and fallible. It is in failing to find a human love faithful to what it should be, that is to say an eternally passionate and pure commitment, that Angéline turns by default to another love in which she can be infinitely loved, cherished, admired. One could even say that, despite its conclusion, *Angéline de Montbrun* is more of a romance novel than *Un amour vrai* since it is not so much a question of Angéline substituting divine love for human love as it is her seeking in divine love the bliss of a human love always destined to disappoint women.

Understandably, it is the message of *Un amour vrai* and not that of *Angéline de Montbrun* that recurs in several works of the period, which could have taken the typical form of the romance novel if not for their final conclusions. The theme of self-sacrifice is also not exclusive to women, though it does primarily concern them. In *Entre l'amour et le devoir* (Between love and duty) (1912) by Louis Gérenval, another narrative that begins as a love story before sabotaging its initial premise, it is the hero who chooses the religious calling. René Pelletier has a bright professional future ahead of him. Having become involved with a pretty young girl from a good background, he cannot dispel the feeling of a great emptiness in his life. He abandons the idea of marriage and writes to his fiancée that he has decided to become a Jesuit. "In kissing the feet of Christ that were placed in my cell, I experienced the indescribable pleasure of obeying love and duty after putting myself between them."[105] As in so many other novels of the period, passion is redirected toward a higher aspiration, that of God. In this imaginary, love cannot take the absolute place demanded by the strict codes of the romance novel. It serves, rather, as the premise for a drama that leads the characters to discover a love that is "truer" than simple human affection.

Endogamy in the romance novel

In *Angéline de Montbrun*, Charles de Montbrun consents to giving his only daughter on the condition of keeping her close to him. The offer he makes to his future son-in-law is not without originality: "I have left my daughter completely free to accept you. She did not refuse, but she asserts that she will never agree to leave me. Think about it, my dear, and see if you have any objection to marrying *me*."[106] This comment nonetheless reflects a reality. In a traditional society, any divergence from one's group and its tastes is perceived as an obstacle to the couple's harmony, because their union serves to renew the previous social order through the fusion of two families. The husband simply replaces the father next to his daughter, just as the daughter replaces the mother for her husband. The interchangeability of roles confirms the continued existence of the social order, which the engagement should seek to prolong rather than disrupt. This attitude is present in French-Canadian novels from 1860 to 1920, and the readers thus witness the recomposition of a family through marriage, rather than observing its dissolution due to the departure of its members. The novel sets out to show that, contrary to what we might think, marriage serves to renew family ties rather than undo them.

To defuse the subversive power of love, always susceptible to confusing social relations through "impetuous" and "rash" unions, nineteenth-century novels adopt two strategies: they either make the lovers orphans or depict them as belonging to the same family. In other words, the solution consists in not having a family or remaining within one family.[107]

On the one hand, many children are raised by a single parent or are orphans, which is a common characteristic of popular novels across all periods and corpora. Usually, the sons are raised by their mother, and the daughters by their father, when not by their parents-in-law. The obstacle, for them, is not only being "nobody's children" and excluded from respectability, even normality, and thus easily subjected by popular authors to the twists and turns of the plot. As orphans, boys are also expected to be virile and independent figures by becoming adults at a younger age. Likewise, having no parents leads girls to seek an early marriage to find a family through union. With no hereditary ties, no constraints arising from existing family networks, no need to deal with the transmission of a heritage, and no concerns about their marriage upsetting former family relations, orphans can live their love story more freely.

The strategy of making the lovers family-less can be found in *Les fiancés de Saint-Eustache* (1910) by Adèle Bibaud, which takes place during the Rebellion of 1837. Lucienne Aubry has been an orphan from the age of five and raised by her aunt and uncle. Pierre Dugal, fatherless, is hired by the family as a tutor, when Lucienne is twelve years old. Over time, they fall in love. The story revisits the myth of Pygmalion, with Lucienne being compared to Galatea. The young girl is said to have "been alone to deal with life's hardships, without real protection, [...] without even a family's affection so needed in childhood" and that the "devoted tenderness" of Pierre helped her to finally be happy.[108] Better still, Pierre's mother has "this mother's tenderness that [Lucienne] was missing [her] whole life" and would be proud to call her a daughter.[109] Taking refuge in Saint-Eustache, the novel's two protagonists are preparing to get married when the Patriot Rebellion breaks out. Pierre dies heroically at the side of Chénier, while "the death knell of martyrs falling one by one tolls, drenching the soil of the homeland with the purest of their blood."[110] Lucienne also receives a fatal blow in trying to protect the doctor from enemy fire, but the scene unfolds with an improbable joyfulness that results in the lovers' final conjunction in the afterlife: "'Dear protector, do not cry for me, I am happy to die, I'm going to be reunited with Pierre.' And with her fiancé's name on her lips, she dies smiling."[111] There will be a union of the two orphans, but beyond the grave.

The other strategy adopted by the romance novel to prevent love from disturbing the social order consists in finding a way to contain it in the family. We are thus confronted with the paradox of love being presented in numerous works as both absolutely essential and entirely superfluous: no one can marry without love, but marriage does not serve to cultivate love. Having always been made for each other, the protagonists' first encounter is a reunion, and their acquaintance is a recognition. Still defined by its absolute liberty, love strikes two people destined to love each other. The novels thus repeat that love is born of resemblance and one should seek a partner from a similar background. In other words, the characters must fall in love with their alter ego. More precisely, choosing a partner comes "naturally" between individuals who already regard each other as "brothers" and "sisters." This gave rise to a strong emphasis on endogamy in novels from the period 1860-1920.

The endogamy in romance novels reflects not only the reserve expected of young people, girls in particular, whose discovery of love is limited to someone already approved within a restricted social sphere. But even more so, it stems from the need to prevent foreign elements from breaking up the family and to thus encourage the most perfect love of resemblance. It is not surprising to observe the heroine's and hero's closeness from their first encounter in the corpus, and it is tempting to see in this proximity the theme of "sibling lovers," a characteristic trope of the romantic trend. "Obsessed with incest,"[112] romantic authors explore several combinations (father and daughter, mother and son, etc.), while making incest between the brother and sister the most common theme.[113] This is how, from the point of view of a traditional society, love becomes socially most desirable when it is morally most unacceptable.[114] The Church of course had to firmly condemn incestuous unions and sought to quite strictly regulate the degrees of affinity and family ties acceptable for marriage.

The romance novel of the second half of the nineteenth century clearly understood the dilemma faced by the traditional society, torn between wanting to identically reproduce the social order and rejecting an endogamy that was too extreme. The corpus reveals a society confronted with a Cornelian choice: to accept people marrying whomever they want would be chaos, but to accept sisters marrying their brothers would be horrific. From the moment they are evoked, generally through a form of euphemism, incestuous relations are subject to opprobrium. The only destiny in store for heroines and heroes who dare break the incest taboo is misfortune: their abominable love can only end badly. Consequently, among writers who fuse "sibling attachment" with "sexual desire to constitute an idealized erotic love," death "disrupts or closely follows upon the consummation of that love."[115] Nevertheless, the temptation of incest haunts the romance novel. Striking a fine balance, it is still always aspiring to maximum intimacy without leading to the complete closure of families upon themselves.[116]

The most common trick for suppressing the revolutionary power of romantic passion is to create family ties between children who are from different families but are *like* brothers and sisters to each other. For example, the plot of *Le secret de la marquise* (The Secret of the Marquise) (1906) by Adèle Bibaud (whose fantastic plot twists are typical of the paraliterature) is entirely centred on this rhetorical strategy, while also respecting the three invariants of the romance novel. Hector and Louise, cousins who grew up together at the Château de Montreuil, are in love. The motif of incest is more than obvious: "Madame de Montreuil had raised these two children under the same roof, they grew up together, sharing their joys and sorrows, loving each other like a real brother and sister, up until the day they both suddenly realized there was a more affectionate feeling."[117] The Marquise de Montreuil, the mother of Hector, condemns the growing bond between them. She tells her son that Louise is in reality his sister, conceived with Monsieur de Montreuil before they were married. Hector is devastated. Alone in his room, he collapses and accidently bumps his hunting rifle, which goes off and seriously injures him. Meanwhile, Louise's nanny Marie, who has been sick for some time, is on the verge of dying. In a dramatic turn of events, she confesses that in fact Louise is not the daughter of the Marquise. The two women had given birth the same day, and the two little girls were entrusted to Marie. One of the two girls succumbed to illness at a young age, and everyone thought it was Marie's natural daughter. But the nanny had previously exchanged the two babies' identities in order to provide a better life for her natural daughter, Louise. The marriage between Hector and Louise can be celebrated.

In other works, the representation of incest is sometimes more subtle, without deviating much from this model. Pushed to its limit, the ideal scenario involves children who have lived under the same roof, as in Édouard Duquet's *Pierre et Amélie* (1866), in this case, two cousins by blood, raised together and often found "sleeping under the shadow of trees surrounding the cottage, in each other's arms, face against face and blending their sweet breath."[118] The two protagonists love each other from a very young age: "And how could it be otherwise? They had sucked the same milk and slept in the same cradle."[119] Pierre is very partial to Amélie, who he calls his "sister," and she does not act differently toward her "brother." In a similar way, in *L'épreuve* (1900) (The ordeal), by Paul-Émile Prévost, the lovers are not biologically related, but have known each other from a very early age, since Paul often visited the home of the Monteil family: "This is how they grew up, with their feelings and tastes in perfect harmony."[120] In adolescence, their love for each other is declared in the most natural way, when exchanging a chaste kiss makes them shy away and blush for the first time. "They looked at each other overcome with emotion and trembling, they were in love and hadn't understood it."[121]

Thanks to this trick, the emergence of romantic feelings for the protagonists is situated in a previous time in such a way that it unfolds as expected, as though it were self-evident. While in numerous romance novels, the lovers recognize each other as soulmates without ever having seen one another, here, the story foregrounds instead the inverse relationship: the lovers recognize their love after having lived together. Without being siblings, they are already part of the family. Their union changes nothing in the present situation and only sanctions an existing reality. They don't have to establish a new home, when all is needed is to take their place in the inherited property that has always been theirs. There could be no better way of ensuring the identical reproduction of the social order.

Conversely, the obsession with bastardy makes sense in light of the fear of social disorder. Characters who play the role of villains bear the infamy of shady, dubious, obscure and impure origins. Of the thirty-two adventure novels studied by Nathalie Ducharme, at least twelve include a minor female or male character who is not sure of their roots and is suspected of being born out of wedlock. According to her, the emphasis on these individuals' violations of the rules is important "not so much for the religious and moral transgression they imply as for the effects they have on the legitimacy of the family and value of children."[122] The celebration of endogamy and its opposite, the condemnation of bastardy, can thus be read as a metaphor for the importance of fidelity to one's origins. In the most stereotypical novels, the heroes' rivals are born in another country, have dark skin, have not received a Catholic education, and have been raised by negligent parents. They do not really belong to the community they seek to become members of through marriage. Also, far from encouraging unions with mysterious princes or young women of no pedigree, French-Canadian romance novels are generally inclined to protect their readers, male and female, from involvements with "foreigners," a characteristic that will be further accentuated in the rural *roman du terroir.*

An "Iphigenia resignation"

In the second half of the nineteenth century, love is often pushed aside in the name of homeland, religion or heritage. The rise of the *roman du terroir* at the end of the nineteenth century did nothing to reverse the trend, the woman having no place beyond being a good match, a docile wife and mother of many children. In rural novels, love's fire is extinguished, for fear of rural folk being caught up in their emotions and losing sight of what Louis Hémon referred to as the "essential hierarchy of things that count."[123] In *Maria Chapdelaine,* the quest for love is, as we know, soon disavowed.[124] Having eliminated Maria's only true love, François Paradis, the author confronts Maria with a moral alternative: she has to choose between the American dream embodied by Lorenzo Surprenant and the fidelity to tradition represented by Eutrope Gagnon. Inspired by voices that show her the path to follow, Maria chooses the latter. Forgetting her own inclinations, she accepts the hand of the farmer "the spring after this, when the men come back from the bush for the seeding."[125] *Maria Chapdelaine* confirms the impossibility of love for women and the superfluity of love for men.[126]

These observations illuminate the reading of a novel by another French author, Fernand Baboulène, who lived in Canada from 1906 to 1914, around the same time as Louis Hémon, and pursued a career as a church painter and decorator. *Marie-Anna la Canadienne* (1913) proposes a somewhat more romantic

Floris Bluther [Fernand Baboulène], *Marie-Anna, la Canadienne,* Québec, s. n., 1913.

version of *Maria Chapdelaine,* without ceding to the sirens of passion. In a review on the "La vie au foyer" page in *La Presse,* Colette (the pseudonym of Édouardine Lesage) congratulates the author "for having taken an unbeaten literary path and bringing, in a plot that is so interesting, very noble attention to excluding anything, however small, that could be harmful to Christian morals and sentiments. This is clearly as it should be in a purely Canadian novel."[127] Specifically addressing female readers, she assures them that they will enjoy every page of this "fresh and charming work."

The heroine who gives the work its title, Marie-Anna Carlier, keeps company with the bourgeoisie of Grandes-Piles, in Mauricie. Described as having "the most beautiful eyes in Canada,"[128] she has a natural complexion that has "more transparency in its warm pallor than many faces decorated with clever artifice." Like the other heroines, her "divine beauty" is inscribed in her purity. Her "eyes like two hearths of vivid tenderness" are the "mirrors of a serene, limpid, virginal soul whose whiteness evokes angels."[129] Many admirers languish at her feet, but she claims indifference to their advances. She ignores, in particular, the attentions of Henri Chesnaye, her childhood friend, who is struggling to complete medical school in Quebec. This endogamy is presented as an obstacle, along with the fact that Henri is awkward and shy, which discredits him as a suitor. To the warnings of her friend Jeannette, who says if she doesn't accept Henri's hand in marriage, she "will have to renounce marriage altogether" and "prepare to grow old all alone," Marie-Anna wearily responds: "This all would be for the best."[130]

Marie-Anna's disposition changes when, thanks to a storm, she meets Jacques de Villodin, a Frenchman visiting Canada. Born into a family of old Norman nobility, he lives, when in France, in the Château de Rézenlieu-Villodin, which exudes an air of luxury and distinction. Though born abroad, the traveller, who is described as "strong-willed, stubborn, submissive to prayer and rebel to orders,"[131] is not as foreign as one would think. Marie-Anna realizes this during a stroll with Jacques, who begins singing the praises of Canadian landscapes. "In no other country," exclaims Jacques, "have I been so stirred in the depth of my soul by such an abundance of beauty![132] His admiration for the "wonder of Canadian nature" confirms not only that he is a free, dreamy, and romantic person, but it also indigenizes him; in other words, it "Canadianizes" him. The "young man's sincere enthusiasm" flatters Marie-Anna "in her sentiment of being a good Canadian."[133]

Marie-Anna finds herself becoming susceptible to Jacques' charms. The two characters eventually confess their mutual attraction. Jacques feels possessed by an unknown passion and vows to sacrifice everything for his new love. "Do not turn away from this adoration that reaches God in touching your soul," he murmurs to Marie-Anna. "Let me love you as you deserve to be loved. You have been my whole ambition, you will be my whole pride, your homeland will be my homeland, your dreams will be my dreams... you will be my wife! . . ."[134] Despite the words "your homeland will be my homeland," it is understood that he wants to leave Quebec and live with her in France.

Letting herself be seduced by the handsome foreigner, Marie-Anna feels a growing desire to abandon everything to follow him in order to "spread the wealth of tenderness within her."[135] She vaguely suspects, however, that her weakness for a Frenchman and an aristocrat is not acceptable and that she may be doomed to suffering by giving in to such an attraction. While Jacques is about to enter a misalliance of class by marrying a "little Canadian woman," Marie-Anna is preparing to enter a mismatch of "race" by going to live in exile. Jacques may well protest that the young woman he loves "has more nobility in her little finger than the powdered marquises of Paris have in their entire person"[136] and that one should not stoop to considerations of fortune when it comes to matters of the heart, but his parents are categorical: they will never accept what they consider to be folly.[137] In the other direction, Marie-Anna may try to defend Jacques' Christian and Norman qualities, but her mother will not consent to a marriage "that would take her only child away from her, like death, ten years earlier, had taken her husband."[138]

Baboulène could have allowed his characters to love each other in exile (for Marie-Anna) or in poverty (for Jacques), leaving them to live happily together somewhere in the old country or Canada. But, faithful to the morals of French-Canadian literature of the period, he chose instead to describe the inner turmoil that plagues the two protagonists. Jacques' torment comes in outbursts and is compared in one passage to the chaos of the Shawinigan Cataractes. He becomes more violent, rebellious and irritable than ever. For Marie-Anna too, "the romance becomes agonizing."[139] She feels she is going "mad, her heart roiling with emotion, calling her mother and God, whispering Jacques' name, listening by turns to her implacable conscience and her resuscitated love. The demon of temptation has taken her by the neck and shaken her like a poor little thing determined to die rather than give in."[140] This cannot go on, and a door must be opened or closed.

It is Marie-Anna who first comes to her senses. She turns away from Jacques under the influence of her mother, who reminds her of her filial duties. Right after praying in church, "the holy thought of sacrifice [penetrates] her soul."[141] Awareness of her responsibilities has tamed the passion, stifled the affection. Resigning herself to marrying Henri, she makes the "cold-blooded" choice of a man she doesn't love. She knows that in doing so she is preparing herself for a difficult and dreary life, but she accepts her fate with resignation, in the name of a higher ideal. "Oh, the sacrifice! Before this holy idea becomes salutary, oh but the suffering one must endure!"[142] Like Maria Chapdelaine, Marie-Anna, experiencing the oxymoron of "a kind of painful joy," listens to the voices of reason and tradition instead of following her heart. Giving up the life of the château and her prince charming, she refuses to follow a path of love that would also be one of exile. Jacques, for his part, recalls that he "belongs to one of these old families of France, [...] heir to a pious, chivalrous tradition, living from century to century in the honour of an impeccable name."[143] Reproaching himself for behaving "like a valet," he gallantly cedes his place to his rival, Henri Chesnaye, who had never given up his assiduous pursuit of Marie-Anna.

In the novel's final pages, Jacques makes Marie-Anna vow to remember him, and one senses that she will keep her promise and never be able to forget him, since he remains the first and thus great love of her life. In marrying Henri, Marie-Anna fulfills her mother's wishes, but absolutely nothing in the story suggests that she will erase Jacques from her memory. On the contrary, the intimacy of the final scene constitutes an excellent example of a "conjunction of hearts," which is why, despite the semi-victory of love, we can include the novel in the category of romance novels. Even separated, the lovers still remain forever united with each other, notably because Jacques saved the heroine's life and left in her heart "the immortality of his memory." "You will long live happily when I am not here, because my soul will stay close to you like a swarm of kisses, a song of caresses that hums every night around your great affectionate heart."[144] Love as a value is thus not repudiated. At the end of the novel, Marie-Anna does not stop loving her first and only love. If, as the last page of the novel claims, "first loves never last,"[145] it is not because they disappear but because they cannot be fulfilled.

François Paradis' death in the forest corresponds to Jacques de Villodin's return to France. But while Maria Chapdelaine was lost to love and could never even feel regret, Marie-Anna Carlier continues to be inhabited by the memory of Jacques, while also trying to live an ersatz love with Henri. Though the novel's conclusion is somewhat brighter, fans of romance novels seeking a happy ending were likely left somewhat confused. In a review of Baboulène's novel published in *Le Devoir*, one author could not refrain from expressing his disappointment, considering Marie-Anna's attitude unworthy of a true romance novel. "This Iphigenia's resignation [referring to the Greek heroine who accepted death for the salvation of her group], however commendable, seems to diminish the interest we feel for this young girl, whose heart so deeply belonged to Jacques de Villodin and who through virtue willingly accepts the hand of another. The reader wants a heroine to not give her hand without her heart and not confine herself to a painful resignation."[146] During this period, with few exceptions, half-victories of love were often the only choice readers had when buying works published in Quebec, and they had to learn to settle for that.

Victorious love

Among all the romance novels of the 1860-1920 period, the most revolutionary work from a sentimental education point of view was completely overlooked by critics of the time. Its spectacular originality is however undeniable. As is already evident in its title, *Amour vainqueur* (1915), Virginie Dussault's work resolutely distinguishes itself from novels like *Martyr de l'amour* (Martyr of love) by Français Pierre Zaccone, which portend sadder and more tormented stories.[147] In fact, the discourse Dussault's novel engages in is so far from what conservative minds were ready to hear that one wonders how such a work could have been published in 1915. It is no doubt because when Dussault self-published her one and only work, printed by J. R. Constantineau in Montreal, she was isolated in Bonnyville (Alberta) and removed from the literary networks governing literary production in Quebec.[148]

The heroine of *Amour vainqueur* meets the hero in their home town of Guigues, in Témiscamingue.[149] Ninie and Rogers soon declare their love and promise fidelity to each other. "Ninie had received her first kiss of love from Rogers who had never received nor given any! Ninie had received this first kiss, on the waters of Témiscamingue, wearing her first formal gown, in her native country, and from a young man from her country! [...] First kiss of love, first formal gown and native country!"[150] By emphasizing the importance of the "young man from her country," while signalling the transition to her "formal gown," this passage introduces the main aspects of the heroine's quest. She will be faced with the challenge of reconciling a love affair with a native son and a material success that cannot realistically be attained in a village outpost of Abitibi.

Ninie leaves her village to study in a convent in Chatham, Ontario, in order to learn English and the rules of decorum of "high society." Rogers, for his part, has begun studies to become a lawyer or a doctor. They try to correspond in secret, but the convent nuns intercept their letters and they both think the other has abandoned them. Still without news from his beloved, Rogers, in frustration, decides to become a priest. Ninie returns to Montreal to work and "succeeds beyond all expectations," though her precise job is not mentioned (she seems to perform the duties of a secretary for some important company, in which she is climbing the ranks). When by chance she sees Rogers at the Grand Séminaire, she realizes that their relationship is hopelessly compromised. She takes a trip to the United States to join one of her aunts and ends up meeting a rich businessman, the New Yorker Harry Mitchell, who instantly falls in love with her and promises her heaven and earth. Ninie does not like him, finding him to be quick-tempered and dominating, besides the fact that the memory of Rogers never really leaves her. She breaks up with Harry and returns to Canada. Furious, Harry tries to kill her on Mount Royal, but she is saved *in extremis* by Rogers who—as luck would have it—happens to be passing by. After having to leave the Grand Séminaire due to an illness, Rogers had become a lawyer. The two lovers are finally reunited and engaged.

The story could have ended there but, in a final twist, the infamous Harry plots vengeance and catches Rogers in a trap. Rogers is wrongly accused of fraud and sent to prison. Without news from Rogers, Ninie once again thinks he has abandoned her. While staying in Témiscamingue, she begins seeing another wealthy businessman, Walter Burrage, without being enamoured of him. Returning to Montreal after receiving a mysterious telegram, she is astonished to learn that Rogers is in jail. She takes steps to have his case appealed and manages to get him acquitted. A "true, idealistic love, that is the very foundation of all noble aspirations,"[151] can at last seal their final reconciliation. At the end of the story, we find the two lovers married and living an authentic success story. "We are very happy," confides Ninie; "we live lavishly; we live in New York; my husband Rogers has succeeded in all of his ventures, since what will soon be three years that we have resided in this city; he is very rich now."[152] The novel ends with the two lovebirds leaving on a lavish trip to Europe.

What is immediately striking in Dussault's story is of course the heroine's desire for professional success. When she was only seven years old, the young Ninie had announced to her mother that she wanted to receive a good education and "go far, far, very far."[153] In wanting to "create her own future for herself,"[154] Ninie clashes with the marmoreal heroines encountered up until now in our corpus. In moments of weakness and doubt, she engages in a veritable self-flagellation to convince herself that she has enough strength and resources to make it on her own. When Ninie learns, for example, that Rogers is going to become a priest, she considers returning to live with her parents but then changes her mind. "Recalling her firm decision to make a life for herself that was out of the ordinary, and all of the sacrifices she had made to achieve this up until then, she repeats again: I will prevail, I will leave in my path, with the thorns trampled underfoot, my heart in shreds if I must, and I will prevail!"[155] In fact, over the course of an evolution that resembles that of self-made woman, Ninie relies exclusively on herself to achieve her goals,[156] to the point where even marriage briefly seems to her like an obstacle to her social advancement now that she has "made so many sacrifices, to get educated" and taken "so many steps to find an enviable position."[157]

What drives Ninie's irrepressible desire for social mobility is her wanting "to earn a lot of money," so convinced she is that "the world is only based on money."[158] As a young girl, she confides to her mother: "I have courage, mummy! And I think I would not be afraid to go far so I can come back like papa with big silver coins […]."[159] After leaving for the convent in Chatham to learn English, the language of business, Ninie reflects on her future following her studies. "She had accomplished the first of her dreams: to acquire knowledge, to get an education; all that was left was to accomplish the second: to become rich and show gratitude for her parents."[160] Fidelity to parents, at least in thought, recurs several times in the text, but Ninie's hope in "making her parents proud of her" serves above all to camouflage ambitions that would otherwise be judged as selfish. She reiterates her wish to acquire wealth in Montreal while taking a stroll on Sherbrooke Street where she sees "expensive carriages transporting people with happy faces and exuding only joy and happiness." She then thinks to herself, "me too, I will have money!"[161]

As much as the novel tells the story of a "victorious love," it also depicts the heroine's material success. In Montreal, the young girl who had grown up in a small rural village in Abitibi-Témiscamingue is first lodged in a "modest and simple roomette; with only a small white bed and table making up her ornaments and furniture."[162] It is only when visiting one of her aunts who lives in New Bedford, Massachusetts that she discovers with delight the magnificent American cities "where everyone heads straight to their goal, attending only to their own business, without the least care for others, for what others are doing around them!"[163] This initiatory voyage is a veritable revelation. After visiting the cities of Boston, Hartford, and Meriden, the narrator states: "What impressions must have stirred her soul encountering these Americans, so grand in their manners, so accustomed to living with all of the comfort that money can buy."[164] Far from feeling out of place, Ninie, perfectly bilingual, enjoys the vast American cities and does not experience the least nostalgia for her hometown. "She likes the United States, the temperate climate suits her!"[165] Published at a time when the French-Canadian population was still traumatized by the exodus to the United States,[166] *Amour vainqueur* has no interest in the "little Canadas" or factory workers of Lowell and Woonsocket. On the contrary, when Ninie returns to visit Témiscamingue, the child prodigy prefigures a sort of female *Survenant*, and the villagers are fascinated by the stories of her travels: "every night, friends and neighbours came to the family house to hear her talk about Montreal and New York, and to ask the young girl all sorts of questions regarding business."[167]

How then does one explain the fact that Ninie does not marry Walter Burrage or Harry Mitchell, two incredibly wealthy and highly coveted men? Burrage is not very handsome and his conversation is boring: he does not have a "taste for the joy of building castles, of planning a shared future that would be beautiful and grand!"[168] As for Ninie's lack of interest in Harry, it derives from the latter's having two major shortcomings. He does not respect her professional aspirations, as she explains in a letter to her mother: "He is proud and does not suffer contradictions; I should have the right to my ideas; sometimes when I dream of the future, he laughs at me [...]."[169] Moreover, Harry lacks determination. She describes him as "having a proud, pretentious character, as a commercial type, without any dream for the future, any ideal."[170] Harry is not able to "satisfy all of the ambition in Ninie's soul; she wants more dreams from him, more adventures than his monotonous, ordered life has to offer."[171] This statement is quite surprising given that Ninie accompanies Harry to all kinds of distinguished *soirées*—including a famous New York garden roof party—and travels the American cities with him in shiny cars. More generally, one wonders how someone doing "big business" in New York could lack ambition...

Ninie's disinterest in Harry is more likely due to *Amour vainqueur* upholding the principle of endogamy dear to the traditional French-Canadian novel. Rogers comes from the same village as her, is Catholic, speaks French and, though now rich, started out like Ninie with nothing and entirely "made himself" (twice even, since since he lost his entire fortune due to Harry's scheming but was able to rebuild it, as if by magic). Rogers and Ninie are of the same "race," both in the literal and figurative sense of the term. This is also suggested by the inclusion of an epigraph in the chapter describing Rogers' return, which is the only quotation from the work of a Canadian author, in this case, Octave Crémazie. In discovering the urban life, Ninie had, at the beginning of the novel, stopped believing in the "declamations of speakers who, on the campaign trail, proclaimed to be the champions of patriotism."[172] However, seeing her parents and friends again in Guigues, as well as the "picturesque sites" of Témiscamingue, she cannot suppress a feeling of visceral attachment to her country. "She had never felt so moved reading patriotic poetry."[173] In a strange patriotic outburst, Rogers, happy to be reunited with Ninie, exclaims: "Long live those who love and have been loved! [...] Love is the motive for all great actions. Through love, one defends his family, his parents! Through love, one defends his Alma Mater! Through love, one defends his Homeland!"[174] Carnal love has become a vehicle for attachment to the nation.

As the authors of *La vie littéraire au Québec* observe, "*Amour vainqueur* is undoubtedly a title that anticipates a lot about the future, but it addresses more bluntly than any other the issue at stake—the place of the female subject and emotion in the "national" French-Canadian text."[175] Contrary to most of the heroines in our corpus, Ninie, though choosing to marry a French Canadian from her village, refuses to sacrifice her destiny for the benefit of her nationality. She wants freedom, wealth, and great love, and if she abandons Harry Mitchell and Walter Burrage for Rogers (with an English name), it is to speak better English, live in Westmount or New York and travel in the company of the love of her life. Contrary to Maria Chapdelaine, who has to settle for Eutrope Gagnon, Ninie marries a Lorenzo

Surprenant who has the looks and charm of a François Paradis. This audacious attitude anticipates, several decades in advance, the serialized novels published between the 1940s and 1960s.

Derisory loves

For the elites at the turn of the twentieth century, love was simultaneously unsurpassable, indispensable, and universal. Women, in particular, could not resist the call of Cupid. They over-invested in love, which became more than ever their domain, while the men were conversely called upon to over-emphasize work, each gender being assigned a more-or-less restricted social and physical space corresponding to the private and public spheres. The *Guide des amants* of 1889 described women as being "constantly occupied with their emotions," and having "no other goal on earth but to love, no other happiness than being loved. Love, as we have said elsewhere, which is but an episode in a man's life, is [a woman's] whole existence."[176] But this specific female trait did not prevent men from also being invited to the lovers' ball. They could not completely ignore love, insofar as this sentiment had come to be regarded as an essential dimension of the couple and of social life more broadly.[177] One would therefore expect the 1860s-1920s to celebrate the "victory of love." But, while recognizing an absolute love that theoretically rejected any objection or compromise, the elites understood all too well that French-Canadian society as a whole risked being influenced by passions that respected "neither god, nor master," answering only to the "beautiful eyes" of lovers. The control of love had to be as strict as its celebration was strong. The romantic sentiment was heavily monitored from the 1860s to the 1920s, even more so than in the Gothic and adventure novels of the previous period. Despite the rhetoric promoting marriages of love, the romance novel was bound by a tight net of conventions.

As we have seen in the previous chapter, the difficult birth of the romance genre was a result of romance novels unlocking an imaginary that no longer venerated old social structures, true love being measured precisely by its disregard for anything or anyone, by its madness, disorder, and fiery, volcanic eruptions, an impulse as unpredictable as it was absolute. In novels from the 1860s-1920s, some heroines and heroes express vague desires to contest social obligations. A sign of the power of their love, it is in the stories that do not respect homogamy that the attraction between a man and a woman has a greater chance of flourishing in all its purity. Rose Lauzon breaks free from her social class by marrying the aristocrat Gustave De Montarville, Antoinette De Mirecourt and Madeleine Ribaud are able to pursue a marriage of love with an Englishman, Marie-Anna pines for a Frenchman from France. While the protagonists of *Amour vainqueur* are born into a similar milieu, they enjoy throughout the story's unfolding a rising social status that leads them to implicitly reject their rural origins.

Generally, however, in order to avoid transgressing the dominant society's boundaries, to avoid, that is, the loss of institutional control over personal emotions, writers placed clear limits on the romantic imagination. With few exceptions, between 1860 and 1920, the conclusion barely changes from one book to the next and is confined to repeating that young women and men are rewarded when they respect the social norms and punished when they do not. In this literature of proprieties and principles, emotional expression is given less space, the works seeking above all to instruct readers on the rigid rules that should govern their relationships. While pretending to speak of love, the works illustrate how romantic sensations are not self-sufficient, how they are derisory compared to other human aspirations. In other words, they seek to defuse the explosive potential of an untethered love by warning against the illusions and dangers of a passion that is too fiery, too undisciplined, too "free." The exceptions of *Les Ribaud*, which puts love before everything, and *Amour vainqueur*, which makes the American dream the condition for romantic happiness, only confirm the rule.

Highly regulated, the French-Canadian novel from the 1860s-1920s generally portrayed human love in a less-romantic way or sublimated it in divine or patriotic love. The following period, coinciding with the most constrained romantic discourse in the entire history of the romance novel in Quebec, would become even more strict in its manner of dictating the morally and socially acceptable boundaries of love. The sublimation of love as passion is replaced by enclosure in the domestic sphere. Instead of flight, it will privilege the cage, one that is as golden as possible.

CHAPTER 3

Domesticated Love (1920-1940)

In France, from 1830 to 1880, the portion of romance novels in the overall production declined, in favour of novels of manners and historical novels.[1] The genre would see a notable revival there in the first decades of the twentieth century, when it became a product of mass consumption. The expression *roman d'amour* began to spread, driven among other reasons by the phenomenal success of the 1910 publication *Esclave... ou reine?* (Slave or queen?) by Delly (the pseudonym of brother and sister Frédéric and Jeanne-Marie Petitjean de La Rosière). Another extremely popular female French writer, Alphonsine Zéphirine Vavasseur, writing under the pen name of Max du Veuzit, published, from the turn of the century, novels that invariably described a man and woman meeting, being separated, declaring their love and ending up united. In addition to Delly and Max du Veuzit, there was Magali (the pseudonym of Jeanne Philbert), who also published an impressive number of novels with increasingly catchy titles, including, *Ève enchaînée* (Eve in chains), *Martine au cœur secret* (Martine with the secret heart), *Dans la geôle enchantée* (In the enchanted jail), *La reine prisonnière* (The prisoner queen), *Idylle en montagne* (Romance in the mountains), and *Un mari tombé du ciel* (A husband out of the blue). In England, a similar literature was emerging at the same time, notably with the publication of *Jigsaw* (1923), the first of some 700 novels by Barbara Cartland, known as the "queen of romance novels."[2]

Presented as "very moral" works that could be left in the hands of young girls without fear, the titles by Delly, Magali, and Max du Veuzit were associated with the "Catholic" side of the romance novel and were thus extraordinarily popular in French-speaking Quebec. Women's magazines hastened to reproduce the texts of these "pink novelists" to meet the demand of their subscribers, especially their female subscribers. Founded in 1919, *La Revue moderne* (which became *Châtelaine* in 1960) represented an important vehicle for this literature in the place it accorded to stories "that passionately interested female readers who like fine books about love that end in marriage."[3] In 1927, for example, the magazine announced the release of the novel *Le Prince charmant*, by French writer Alphonse Croizière: this "short and delightful love story," they write, "ends like all our young lady readers want their romance novel to end. All those who dream of prince charming will adore this lovely story of two hearts seeking and finding each other…"[4] Again in 1927, *La Revue moderne* offered with each new subscription the gift of "a nice romance novel." Even a conservative daily like *Le Devoir* could not resist publishing serialized romance novels, including in its pages no less than seven titles by Delly during the interwar period, beginning with *Esclave… ou reine?* in 1913. The daily indeed boasted that the novel was a huge success among the faithful readers of Henri Bourassa's paper.[5]

Over time, French novelists became household names among French Canadians. Some twenty or thirty years after the publication of their first best sellers, it was said that these authors found a vast public in Quebec "because of their intrigue, charm and morality."[6] In 1949, a survey conducted by the Bibliothèques de la ville de Québec under the auspices of the Société d'éducation pour adultes, revealed that both male and female readers greatly appreciated romantic works. In the capital's libraries, 73 percent of works borrowed were novels and, among those, the writings most in demand were those of Delly, followed by Max du Veuzit.[7] In the 1950s, among the seventy-five authors represented in the "Petit-format" collection, the most popular paperback collection in Quebec at the time, Magali topped the list (thirty-seven publications), followed by Delly (twenty-three), and Max du Veuzit (sixteen).[8] These authors were so fashionable in Quebec that parents chose to name their children after the characters of their favourite novels![9]

The craze for so-called BCBG literature[10] (*bon chic, bon genre*, roughly "good style, good attitude") reveals an important reconfiguration of romantic codes in French Canada. From this point on, heroines were destined to become good wives and mothers, all else being conditional on the attainment of these two supreme goals. Of course, unlike the previous period, human love now wins out over divine love in these novels, but we will see that in French Canada, love in the so-called Roaring Twenties and Dirty Thirties remained sensible and unemotional. Novels from the first period often take place in an idealized rural setting and serve to promote the triad of work, family, and fatherland. Those of the second period, from 1930 to 1940, depict main protagonists who are doctors and lawyers from fine families in an urban context and make love a pretext for maintaining social status. However, the change in the characters' locations and occupations should not obscure the essential theme, which is that the victory of love now comes at the price of domestication. The authors were indeed too preoccupied with patriotic lessons, Catholic morals and practical concerns to bother too much with sentimentality, and there was no question of them sanctioning an image of marriage that would make it a voluptuous, romantic dream, like in the movies.[11] The "passionate and flimsy stories,"[12] denounced by the encyclical *Casti Connubii* on Christian marriage (1930), were thus systematically viewed with suspicion. When the question of love was raised, it was almost always to exalt love of the French language, love of the land, love of ancestors, love of the Church, love of God, love of traditions or love of the homeland, when human love was not reduced to a sober, bourgeois pleasure.

This more conservative discourse can be understood in part by looking at the editorial structures that accommodated it. While in the previous period, the romance genre was mostly confined to publishing at the authors' expense with the aid of printers or newspaper editors; starting in the 1920s, established publishers took over with the goal of disseminating an apologetic and nationalist message.[13] At a time when the literary field was slowly becoming more autonomous under the triple effect of demographic growth, the democratization of the book market, and mass education, the elites were not content to censor and repress a romantic discourse that was too liberated, but were also trying to "shape the sayable."[14] This development is not without repercussions on the definition of our corpus. Though we have tended up until now to analyze each work individually, the present chapter and the ones that follow, without entirely abandoning a case-by-case approach, privilege where possible a global study of a growing and diversifying production. This is why instead of undertaking detailed analysis of individual works, we have chosen to highlight certain elements that are most representative of and pertinent to our discussion across a range of novels.

After identifying the consequences of the transfer of divine love to the consecration of the Christian marriage as the true purpose of the couple, we will discuss the pronounced rejection of the figure of the foreigner by showing how the alterity of the male protagonists in the stories is discarded in favour of a unifying "we" ("nous"). We will then trace the chronological thread of the interwar period to identify the romantic ideal in regionalist and bourgeois romance novels. We will see how moderation becomes an essential dimension of an emotion previously defined, in contrast, by its excesses and transgressions. Two new elements emerge at the end of the period that set the stage for themes taken up after the war: the introduction of a rhetoric emphasizing the importance of maternal love in the couple, and the pervasiveness of the fragility of romantic love as a cause for disjunction, particularly for men, who are at greater risk of being unfaithful.

Slave much more than queen

Based on a reading of the summaries alone, one has the impression that the novels of French authors like Delly refer alternately to a penal or princely world. The ambiguity of the heroine's fate infuses the works more than ever, oscillating between submission and majesty in relation to the man she takes as a husband. *Esclave... ou reine ?* captures in three words the essential question facing all married women. The young girl caught in the claws of a harsh and tyrannical husband can only hope to make him tender and loving to ensure her happiness in a household from which she cannot escape, once the vows are taken. Thanks to her unwavering Catholic faith, she can believe, like Lise in Delly's novel, that her jailor will repent one day for making her suffer and attempt to repair, through constant attention, the wrongs committed against her. She must hope that her husband will tell her, like Prince Ormanoff: "From now on, it is you who will reign, and I will be the first of your servants."[15] Indeed, the novel *Esclave... ou reine ?* ends on a remarkable reversal, to say the least, for the young tormented wife: "The sceptre had changed hands: it was now in the entirely beneficent hands of the young woman who Prince Serge surrounded with passionate adoration, seeing and promptly satisfying her every desire, only complaining, half-smiling and half-serious, that she was never capricious."[16] This *deus ex machina* fosters the dream of an absolutely happy marriage, wherein the husband only uses his strength to better serve his wife, and the wife only uses her influence to better devote herself to her husband. Even in the more subtle versions of Delly's writings, the moral contract between the main characters remains unequivocal. In *Cœurs ennemis* (Enemy hearts) (1924), Lord Walter Falsdone declares to Orietta: "Nobody knows me well. I'm taken for a pleasure-seeker, an arrogant man, a skeptic, incapable of attachment. Yes, for a while, I was that. But I can be something else. You can make me into something else, Orietta, if you love me as I wish—like no one before you was able to love me."[17]

Without analyzing this French literature in depth, we note that it belongs to what Ellen Constans calls the "Catholic romance novel," a genre that had the advantage of being "suitable for everyone," despite the virulence of some critics from the most conservative circles. "Engagements and marriages sanction what Delly calls 'permitted love': earthly love authorized and blessed by the Church. It is contrasted in the stories with the kind of passion that brings moral and social disorder."[18] This type of romance novel, which glorified the heroine's role as mother and wife and made women the guardians of Christian values, was perfectly aligned with the program of "prescriptive censorship"[19] that dominated at the time in Quebec. It celebrated passion, but within marriage itself, because it was in the unhappy union that conjugal bliss became possible for a wife who thought herself condemned to a life of boredom and abuse. In the vale of tears of her marriage, she had to bear her cross before seeing the doors of an absolute comfort open before her, where she would be queen.... of the home. It is easy to understand why this line of thought had such an immense impact in French Canada during the interwar period. Belittled in life and law, women found themselves at the mercy of their husbands once the marriage was celebrated. Not only was there no escape route for them, but as soon as the vows were pronounced they became legally, socially, and economically subordinate to their husbands. The relationship between the spouses was clear: the husband's duty was to protect his wife, and the wife's duty was to obey her husband. In such a context, day-to-day routine soon shattered any illusions about married life.[20] The indissolubility of the Christian sacrament combined with a legal framework that infantilized women typically transformed marriage into a "tomb of love."[21]

Many French-Canadian romance novels of the period, while recognizing the value of love, sanctioned the married woman's submission, for the reasons mentioned above. In *La mystérieuse inconnue* (The unknown mystery woman) (1929), the encounter between André and Annette provokes in the latter a sudden and equally inexplicable "need to devote herself, to sacrifice herself for the being she loves": "Just by seeing him, by hearing him, she had become his slave. He was indeed the man she had sometimes fantasized of, the man who would one day become the master of her life. He was the male made of strength and beauty without the conceit of power."[22] In another novel, *La petite maîtresse d'école* (The little school teacher) (1929), Madame Vermette consoles the heroine: "You see my dear, we women are made for harmony and obedience. We must constantly appease and submit our will to the will of the stronger."[23] In the home, the husband orders, the wife obeys. Not only is the man described as enterprising and the woman as fainthearted; the woman also takes on a subsidiary, ancillary role in the couple. The heroine can sometimes appear slightly superior to the hero due to her education, which remains a prized value in a part of the corpus. But even these differences in education do not change the hierarchy within the couple. A passage from *Fleur lointaine* (Distant flower) (1926) is quick to re-establish the limits of the heroine's "power" over the hero: while the woman "reserves the right to educate [her husband] and give him advice," she must submit to her man, "it is understood."[24]

Love in this context plays an essential role. Thrust into a home where a man she barely knows acquires full authority over her overnight, the French-Canadian woman had no choice but to embrace the conviction that love continues to grow once the union is consummated.[25] She had to believe that love was a product of marriage as much as its promise. The "path of love" metaphor, which already existed in the nineteenth century,[26] made the romantic relationship a learning experience, a project. The woman especially needed to believe in this dream, because only love made it possible to find domestic bliss in activities that would, in other circumstances, be perceived as so many chores (cooking, dishes, washing the floors). A marriage needs love, declares a female character in a novel by Blanche Lamontagne-Beauregard, because "otherwise, it is hell..."[27] And conversely, the romance novels reiterate that with love, it is "paradise": when done with love, the most thankless feminine tasks become easy, light, even enjoyable, so long as one takes pleasure in pleasing. Thus the "rosy" novel promises a rosy life for women, without changing their fate one iota.

In *Celle qui revient* (The girl who returns) (1930), the only daughter of Antoine Lajoie, a wealthy farmer, loves dresses, jewellery, and chiffons. One easily recognizes the model of the "frivolous" heroine, recalling Rose Latulipe. Spoiled by her mother (in such cases, the parents are almost always the first to blame), Louise has become vain and does whatever she pleases. She forces her parents to accept a marriage with a poor labourer from the parish. After three years, he realizes that he will never be able to make his spouse into a good housewife. Arguments erupt over frivolous spending and Louise returns with their child to live with her parents. Regretting her impulsive act, she misses snuggling in her husband's arms and offering him affection. She realizes that a woman must acquiesce to her partner and that it is up to her to make amends by learning to be more considerate and docile in the future. Answering the call of duty, the tamed shrew returns to live with her husband and they both emerge stronger from the ordeal. Philosophical, her father exclaims: "In books, the novels always end after the marriage… but in life it's a bit different. My daughter had to learn some hard lessons to convince her that on earth, things do not always work by following our desires, however compelling they may be."[28]

Celle qui revient quite accurately represents the new moral of romance novels, which incorporate the view that marriage is not the crowning of love, but only one step towards it. What these texts recount, consistent with the prevailing social discourse, is that this tender affection can develop within the union if both partners enter into it in good faith, learn to fulfill their respective functions, and know their place, which is not far from the moral of arranged marriages. Reflecting this change, fewer novels use the artifice of lovers knowing each other from the cradle or belonging to families with long-standing ties, as was prevalent in the second half of the nineteenth century. Spouses have to patiently weave the fabric of their love, and the story of their meeting can thus be a kind of agreement on their chances of attaining domestic bliss, in a near or distant future. Far from being an impetuous passion, love appears as something that is calm and pure, stable and peaceful, discreet and gentle, rather like a friendship. The message tends to emphasize the harmony between the spouses, in a world where "simple hearts know nothing of romance and [where] a solid affection can replace the first tender feelings and create happiness all the same."[29]

Stranger to love

The English expression "love knows no bounds" can have a double meaning: love is inexhaustible and it has no boundaries.

Such a conception of love clearly has no place in the interwar period in Quebec. Seeking to prevent a disruption of meaning that could undermine ethnic and social homogeneity, romance novels, whether regionalist or bourgeois, continued to encourage the reproduction of the social order. The preservation of the nation remained an essential condition governing the flourishing of love in the Christian marriage. Though mixed marriages had hardly been encouraged in the past (with the exception of a few happy outcomes), "foreigners," defined here in ethnic terms, were never more absent from the romance and broader literary landscape than during this period, which took an even more marked racist and xenophobic turn with the consolidation of the regionalist novel.[30]

The plethora of works denouncing mixed unions testifies to this dread of the foreigner: only three of the "chosen" in the corpus of romance novels from the period are not French-Canadian. Roger in *L'Amour et l'épreuve* (Love and ordeal) (1940) is French, and two heroes are of Indigenous origins in *Un de Jasper* (One from Jasper) (1933) and in *Mon sauvage* (My savage) (1938). These two novels are interesting insofar as they justify mixed marriage precisely through the two heroes' belonging to a familiar milieu. The alterity is surpassed, even erased, by conformity to the social and cultural stereotypes of the period. When Danielle, in *Un de Jasper*,[31] discovers that the handsome doctor working in a rich holiday resort in Jasper is in reality a "Red Skin," her ideal seems crushed. However, Danielle learns to tame Pascal, which comes quite easily given the highly euphemized "savage" nature of his character. He is above all a man of science, educated and "civilized." There is very little about him that recalls the "woodsman." In Laure Berthiaume-Denault's novel, the alterity introduced by Michel Côté is addressed more directly. As Daniel Chartier has observed,[32] Côté's identity inspires both fear and fascination in Liliane, in a novel that sometimes recreates, sometimes tries to efface cultural stereotypes. Following Danielle, Liliane judges the Indigenous identity to be acceptable, even desirable, provided it is contained within the parameters of "civilization." Of all the novels in the corpus, *Mon sauvage* comes the closest to distancing the couple from the French-Canadian milieu, but Michel, who has become a government official responsible for defending his people's interests in Ottawa, still exercises his profession "among the Whites."

The suspicion cast on love expels the figure of the stranger from romance literature, even an "outlander" like the character of Germaine Guèvremont's novel. Conversely, the absence of the foreigner in French-Canadian novels renders the expression of a sudden, absolute love more difficult. The characters in the nineteenth century who were raised as brothers and sisters have been replaced in the interwar period by heroines and heroes belonging to the same village (in the regionalist novels) or the same social class (in the bourgeois novels). This no doubt explains why scenes of jealousy are rare in our corpus. Normally, love sees in its object of affection an incomparable, singular, irreducible subject, an ineffable reality. Since the object of love is unique, and the individual cannot live without it, the possibility of its loss is a source of unbearable anxiety. Jealousy becomes proof of affection, though the lack of confidence it signals usually implies one loves too much or poorly, since love requires a delicate balance between dependence and independence, desire for possession and indifference, display of emotion and reserve. But while jealously makes "a huge appearance" in the European literature of the end of the nineteenth century, to the point that one could be justified in considering it "a literature of jealous passion,"[33] we observe nothing of the sort for this period in French Canada. The interchangeability and immutability of the novels' characters make the expression of any possessive feelings somewhat superfluous.

In the "sentimental anti-novel" *Trente arpents* (1938) (*Thirty Acres*, 1940), Ringuet describes how Moisan, considered a good catch himself amongst the villagers, had seen in Alphonsine a "good fit": "his conception of her was not in the least romantic. On the contrary, he had a very good idea of what he might expect from her. She was strong and sturdy and not afraid of work; she would be able to run the house and help in the fields at harvest-time."[34] Moisan begins frequenting the home of Alphonsine's parents, and this suffices for all the locals to understand that she will be his wife. Given it was not a romance novel, *Trente arpents* did not likely contribute to the development of a "romantic" or "sentimental" rhetoric. But what indeed emerges in reading the romance novels of the interwar period is their lack of interest in passion. This explains why, among all the works published over this period, volumes corresponding, even remotely, to our model of the romance novel, are rare.[35] Many French-Canadian novels of the period include a romantic quest that does not result in conjunction. The works of Jovette Bernier, Éva Senécal, Michelle Le Normand, Harry Bernard, and Rex Desmarchais foreground love, without however allowing it to really bloom, as Adrien Rannaud has shown.[36]

In sum, in the interwar romance novel, one loves according to one's position, class, and "race," and in loving this way, not much love is needed. Insofar as people marry individuals from their milieu,[37] it is not important to know them intimately. It suffices to recognize them socially and thus settle for more impersonal qualities when choosing a partner.[38] This is also what the regionalist novel reaffirms when it adopts the trappings of the romance novel.

The regionalist romance novel

In a context of sublimated, diverted, suppressed and denied love, studying the collection "Le Roman canadien" published by Éditions Édouard Garand, never ceases to be interesting. Described by Jacques Michon as a "unique phenomenon" in the literary history of the early twentieth century, Garand "appears to be both one of the first to break through to a wider public and a pioneer of the French-Canadian popular novel."[39] The materiality of novels in the collection "Le Roman canadien" (the publisher's main collection), published in brochure format, already says a lot about the targeted public. The colour-illustrated covers, catchy titles, ads, and crowded text printed in two columns and rarely exceeding sixty pages, all testify to the product being intended for mass consumption. Added to this were strong distribution strategies: Garand's novels were not only sold in batches to the government but also distributed in news-stands, bookstores and by mail through a subscription system. The novels appealed to a broad public: the first print run of 3000 copies in 1923 rose to 10,000 copies by 1926. Primarily published between 1923 and 1932, Garand's complete production included more than 185 titles.[40]

The collection "Le Roman canadien" proposed, as its name suggests, to establish a "Canadian publication of Canadian novels, written for Canadians by Canadians and printed in Canada by Canadians."[41] The overarching message was linked, to different degrees, to the nationalist project of the period: good patriotic sentiments flowed in abundance amidst an avalanche of incidents specific to adventure novels and novels of manners.[42] But while the production was oriented toward adventure stories and melodrama, the joys and torments of passion were not forgotten. Though respecting the codes of traditional Christian morals (the protagonists exchange at best—or at worst!—only chaste kisses[43]), and making the family, the nation and the Church the ultimate horizons of collective life, a number of scattered stories in the Éditions Édouard Garand catalogue make room for love.

Among the published books of the period, we have thus identified around twenty works that satisfy the parameters of the romance novel, as we have defined them. One of these is

Le triomphe de l'amour (The triumph of love) (1929) by "Mme Graveline." The novel depicts the life of a tall and graceful young girl, Dolorès, the only daughter of the rich Comtois family. She is loved by Robert Neuillie, who is however injured in a duel with a Frenchman who had offended the honour of his bride-to-be. He is declared dead and laid to rest. His fiancée then joins a convent to become a missionary nun in Africa, which seems to confirm that there was no vocation, other than religious, for a single woman of the time: she had to take the veil, whether that of a bride or of a nun. But in an unexpected twist, we learn that Robert is alive, and he reappears the day the young woman is to take her perpetual vows. The mother superior refuses to tell Dolorès the news of her loved one's "resurrection." "Sister Comtois entered here voluntarily. She wanted to devote herself to God and I am not going to trouble her with your story... She believes you are dead... so much the better... Dolorès Comtois is dead also... for you... forget her."[44] The hero is not satisfied with this declaration. "Forget her... one can see, Madame, that you have never loved... 'Who knows,' she says, her eyes briefly filled with tears."[45] The fable cannot help recalling Rapunzel, prisoner in her tower. Seeing the doors of the convent close on him, Robert concocts a scheme and manages to communicate with Dolorès who, far from having banished him from her mind, had been crying over her lost love every night since entering the community. The lovers are reunited *in extremis* and the fantastic story ends with their marriage, which is joyously celebrated. The moral concludes that the most beautiful wish one can offer newlyweds is that they love each other forever.

Dolorès' choice to leave the convent reveals an evolution toward a more frank recognition of love.[46] Nevertheless, the acknowledged power of love is not accompanied by an openness to desire, and, under the eye of the Catholic authorities, carnal love remains suspect. In most of the Éditions Édouard Garand stories, the female characters are beautiful, but the value of their beauty is downplayed. As for the male hero's physique, it is sometimes completely overlooked, and he may even be presented as not very attractive. In *Le cœur est le maître* (The heart is the master) (1930), the entire narrative is structured around the ugliness of the hero, who has been disfigured in the war.[47] At the beginning of the story, the male character, Gérard Sautet, is persuaded "that no girl will want him anymore." However, the moment he experiences a romantic feeling, his looks improve. "His very ugliness had glimmers of virile grace."[48] His mother confirms his new beauty: "Just as you are here, before me, joy in your eyes, love shining in your face, you are handsome, charming—and I would fall in love with you—if I wasn't already!"[49] In the eyes of the person who truly loves him, the toad is transformed into prince charming. "This injury," exclaims the heroine, "is the proof of his valour and nobility. It is another beauty... more dignified than the other kind, more noble, more profound."[50] Clearly, these representations aim to convince female readers that it is better to spend one's life with a nice boy whose physique is not very appealing than with a bad partner, however seductive he may be.

In the same vein, the exceptional charm of the female characters so dear to the conventional romance novel is downplayed here in the description of the bride, reduced to mentioning her "cute manners" and "impish little faces." While the typical romance novel tends to associate the power of seduction with women of ill-repute, these novels go even further in denying any too obvious sensual appeal among their heroines. In a discourse that meets Catholic and nationalist expectations, feminine modesty coincides with an effort to make the ideal woman docile and self-effacing, submissive and fragile, pure and virginal. In *L'enjôleuse* (The charmer) (1928), the author denounces Héliane's clothing, her too-short skirt and bare arms violating the clergy's dress codes and making the "socialite" an obvious object of desire.[51] Meanwhile, at a time when the consumer society promoted in women's magazines was beginning to impose its own rules, Éditions Édouard Garand felt obliged to at least partly accept the increasingly influential fashion trends. The heroines in these stories sometimes express their frustration in being dressed like "country girls" (*habitantes*) and their desire to resemble "the ladies from the city."[52] The solution was to adapt the canons of female modesty to the demands of fashion by finding a compromise between the woman being *artificially* stunning and desirable and being *naturally* beautiful and loved. Since the balance between an "erased beauty" and a "dazzling modesty" was not easy to achieve, authors had to come up with all sorts of contortions. Deeply embedded in the texts of Éditions Édouard Garand, as in many other publications,[53] this paradox between physical beauty and spiritual beauty reveals one of the important tensions of the romance novel.

In the BCBG novels, two people love each other not because of their looks or physical attraction to each other, but because they make, in the opinion of others and especially the parents, a good match. The man typically has a "situation," that is to say a job that will bring him enviable status and a decent salary. Most importantly, he is a hard worker—idleness being a man's worst fault, which can only lead to debauchery, gambling, and drunkenness. In *La dame de Chambly* (The lady from Chambly) (1925), by Andrée Jarret (the pseudonym of Cécile Beauregard), the sight of a drunken passenger on the tramway, leads Madame Beauchemin, witnessing the spectacle, to have apprehensive thoughts: "— Oh! My child, if you knew how I thought of you, in front of this disgusting spectacle… Yes, of you. I said to myself if ever my little Yolande had to make her life with such a being, I would rather lose her immediately and never hear another thing about her."[54]

Conversely, the woman is pretty, but not too seductive, because this would mean she is vain and extravagant. The rest of Andrée Jarret's novel illustrates this without subtlety. A veritable Montreal-born Cinderella, Bernadette does not have the looks of her sister Aurore, and the family makes a point of reminding her of it often. Bernadette's mother is consoled in repeating to herself that her daughter is perhaps less attractive, but that she will nonetheless make "a good little wife, especially for the country…"[55] In the meantime, the best thing her daughter can do is make herself useful by cleaning the house from top to bottom. In line with the classic fairy tale scenario, Bernadette undergoes a transformation thanks to an intervention from "Dame de Chambly," an old woman, a sort of fairy godmother, who takes her in as a cleaning woman and educates her. Bernadette corrects her language errors and, now prettier because more cultivated, marries the lawyer Jules Larose, who appreciates her precisely for her manual skills. The precious Aurore is doubly rejected: she who had her sights set on Jules has to settle for marrying the farmer Donat, whose parents had destined him for the brave Bernadette. And even Donat himself is hesitant: "if I believed Aurore would remain coquettish after marriage, I would give her up immediately, because, once married I want to be able to sleep with both eyes shut."[56]

The romance novels of the 1920s thus emphasize the domestic qualities of women who are later destined to become "good wives." In *Fleur lointaine* (1925), the heroine is compared to Nausicaa from *The Odyssey*, washing her clothes, like the Bible's Rebecca, a water carrier, as well as to the chatelaines of French legend, spinning wool with "their white hands."[57] The novel is also interesting from another point of view: even though it takes place in a bourgeois milieu and the heroine's family is rich enough to have servants, this practice is clearly regarded as wasteful when the girls and women are able to do the work. "The Desautels had up until then escaped the tyranny of the lackeys, both the maids and the chauffeurs; the cohabitation of two households united had relieved them of this hassle: the girls were there to ensure the service."[58] One of the story's characters, a Frenchman, is delighted by this. "This is something that is not unpleasing to me," the new guest thought to himself, "these ladies do not believe they are lowering themselves by seeing to the care of the household. The bourgeois prejudices from my country have not yet taken root here."[59]

By thus undermining the presuppositions of the romance novel, the regionalist novel develops prosaic plots in which passion is continually defused. One could say of this trend, echoing *Charles Guérin*, that here too, the heart has its reasons that reason knows. In the stories of the period, marriage is reduced to a simple contract; the spouses must be sincere friends and demonstrate loyalty, confidence, and devotion. Affection, in this case, is limited to fulfilling their respective conjugal duties. Each must accept his or her role in the couple: the husband will be the provider, and the wife will be the mother and housewife who knows how to cook, decorate tastefully, receive guests, keep the home in order, attend to needlework, and balance the budget.[60] This element constitutes one of the central changes to the heroine's status with respect to the previous period. Raised in a privileged milieu, the nineteenth-century heroine had few domestic concerns and could devote herself entirely to affairs of the heart, however complicated they might be. In this interwar period, to be a good wife, one had to know how to "keep house." When in *Un cœur fidèle* (A faithful heart) Marie's mother is called to the bedside of her grandmother, Marie, still young, must take over the household chores at a moment's notice. "She quickly acquired the practice she was lacking and Gros-Jean [her father] did not seem to notice much that his wife was not there."[61] Setting aside the interchangeability of the two female subjects, we note here instead the satisfaction Marie experiences in fulfilling her role as "woman of the house"; once married, she will be able to "quickly carry out her mission as a housewife."[62] Even in the novels that present a less clear-cut point of view, this message is hammered home. Household tasks are for women and it is on the basis of being able to perform this practical work that their conjugal appeal is to be measured. To be in love for a woman is to have a husband who puts food on the table, and for a man, it is to have a wife who correctly attends to keeping the house in order. It would be difficult to cultivate an attachment more mundane than this.

The measure of feelings

In the regionalist romance novel, which was promoted by Éditions Édouard Garand, love is a medium through which characters, presented as sensible and honest, can learn the "ways of goodness." The heroine especially evokes the charms of a "moral seduction."[63] Her heart is simultaneously devoted to the man she loves, her family, her country and God. Nonetheless, if the novels of the period are chaste and puritan, it is not only because they seek to ensure the triumph of Christian marital norms; more fundamentally, it is because the moral they adopt is based on an ethic of moderation and rationality that denies the romance novel's transports of emotion from the start. Loving wisely is deemed so important that the feelings described by the protagonists are more like a quiet esteem than a fiery passion. Bodies no longer yearn for love. Characters no longer faint or torment themselves to the point of losing their minds (being "drunk with love," "crazy in love") or bursting into tears—no less dying from love! Such excesses, so frequent in the preceding periods, no longer have their place in the works of the interwar period.

On this subject, *Un cœur fidèle*, published by the Bibliothèque de l'Action française, makes the issue of measured feelings so central that some would say it is not a romance novel at all. It recounts the story of Marie Dumont and Jean Beaulieu, two neighbours who have loved each from early childhood and who took their first communion together. Jean is "a handsome young man, stocky, with a somewhat heavy build," but his "conception of things suggests an exceptionally beautiful and noble soul, as one encounters sometimes among country folk."[64] Marie, for her part, is ravishing "with her complexion of lilies and roses, her bright and intelligent eyes, her lips with a delicate smile, framing two rows of teeth as white as ivory pearls."[65] As Jean begins making plans for marriage, Eusèbe Landry, the wealthiest farmer in the parish, widowed for eight years and childless, proposes to Marie. She sees in this offer a means of ensuring her future, but, in any case, the decision is not hers. "Since her parents say that this man will give her happiness, she would be imprudent to not listen to her parents' advice. In the convent, one often spoke to her of obedience to the parents. It would bring misfortune to contradict them."[66] Since Marie was educated at the residential school of the Sœurs de la charité de Cacouna and obtained her teaching certificate, her parents have great hopes for her union, and Jean does not fulfill, in their eyes, the basic criteria. "Now that she is educated, Marie should only love a man who is educated. The young Beaulieu, who abandoned school very young, is not an acceptable suitor."[67]

The "affair" is quickly concluded and, one month later, Marie is wed to Eusèbe. Marie has suffered from her parents' poverty, and she appreciates the material advantages of an alliance with a rich widower: "it is not unpleasant for her to have the perspective of a comfortable life so soon."[68] "Tempted by so many new things shining in the distance" and dazzled by the "riches" hidden in Eusèbe's country home, which "almost has the air of a manor house,"[69] she already sees herself "as Madame Landry, the wife of an esteemed man, living in a beautiful house where there are a lot of dishes and furniture."[70] The novel's discourse continually confirms her resolution, notably through the voices of neighbours attending the wedding. To one who states: "She will not be happy [...] It is her mother who forced her," another retorts: "She will be happy as long as she likes. A woman is always happy with a good fellow of means. Church warden, school commissioner, not bad looking either, with a nice piece of developed land and a stable full of animals, you think that little Marie made a bad choice?"[71] Then a neighbour drives the point home: "You see that smoke coming and going? Love is like that. Gone with the wind. Beauty doesn't put food on the table. And love is always there when there are qualities. I'm telling you the little Marie will be happy."[72]

While Jean, cruelly wounded by his thwarted love, chooses to migrate to the United States, Marie is enjoying a quiet life with her husband. But tragedy strikes. After barely a year of marriage, Eusèbe catches a cold and dies. Courageously, the widow takes over managing the farm work "without deviating from the traditions of her race."[73] Five years later, Jean returns. Marie sees that he had always kept his heart for her. They marry "after the harvest."[74]

As long as we accept the idea that love is possible without excessive passion, the parameters of the romance novel are respected in *Un cœur fidèle*. The two protagonists know each other at the beginning of the story and we find them again at the end. The union between Marie and Eusèbe is just one episode of the disjunction, prolonged by Jean's departure to the United States; if not for this absence, they could have gotten married sooner. Also, they never stopped loving each other: the proof is in the scene when, during her first wedding, Marie is overcome with sadness thinking of Jean with his "sweet face, his child-like voice."[75] The sight of Jean leaving "more sad than the other nights, with deep sorrow in his heart, perhaps crying silently [...] scares her."[76] Marie gets a hold of herself. "She banishes these thoughts that appear sacrilegious to her. It is wrong of course, bad to go back to the past like this. Now that she loves Eusèbe Landry, that she has become his wife, she should not think of old times."[77] But even happy in marriage, Marie has a troubling dream. "One night she dreamt that hordes of sheep were grazing on their land, facing the sunset, which gave their white fleece a pinkish hue, while further up the field a mysterious shepherd was smiling at her: he had the features of Jean Beaulieu. She awoke feeling very confused, overwhelmed by a sensation that only faded little by little."[78]

What *Un cœur fidèle* tells us is that the invariants of the romance novel can be respected as long as the couple in love is united in a way that conforms to the dominant group's expectations. Eusèbe personifies the means by which Marie, though not in a calculated way, is able to be with her true love in the end while also ensuring her wealth. In the beginning, Jean has certain shortfalls. He is not educated and is just starting out on uncleared land, while Eusèbe distinctly specifies to Marie when asking her to marry him that "his new wife, after his death, would have all that he possessed, including money he had loaned."[79] Finally, Jean does not appear without flaws: he attracts the attention of American girls while visiting the country and also chooses to live in exile for five years in Massachusetts. It is only upon his return, having suffered a lot and aged from much crying, that he becomes worthy of his childhood love. He is only lacking wealth, which Marie can now happily provide.

In his comments on *Un cœur fidèle* in the *Dictionnaire des œuvres littéraires du Québec*, Maurice Lemire questions Marie's ability to love. "This novel of imprecise meaning could be a simple and naive country idyll, but Marie seems incapable of really loving, because interests one would find more or less respectable in other settings always interfere with her feelings."[80] Perhaps the question is better explored through the lens of the place accorded to Marie's real desire in the French-Canadian romance novel of the period. The conservative ideology demands that she respect the choice of her parents, follow the diktats of religion, spend her time on earth living a moderate life and founding a family (which Jean will no doubt make possible: Eusèbe indeed dies before having impregnated

Blanche Lamontagne beauregard, *Un cœur fidèle. Roman canadien*, Montréal, Bibliothèque de l'Action française, 1924.

Marie, and one can see the sheep in her dream as symbolizing children to come). Marie's first desire is clearly announced when Eusèbe asks for her hand in marriage: "It is Jean Beaulieu who she loves the most,"[81] she confesses to herself. But this desire is quickly relegated to the dreamworld, and then postponed for later in the name of duty. It is only fulfilled at the very end of the story when Marie chooses to marry Jean Beaulieu over any other suitor. *Un cœur fidèle* is indeed a romance novel, one that rewards the heroine for her submission and offers her a more solid, more mature love. A sign of the wisdom that comes with contrition, the two characters, like Maria Chapdelaine and Eutrope Gagnon, will get married, but only "after the harvest."

The main scenario of *Un cœur fidèle* contrasts with another story that author Lamontagne-Beauregard could have developed in the novel. At the beginning of the story, a cousin from the United States, Rose-Alma, arrives at Jean's parents. She is used to going to the movies and the beach, as well as "strolling in the parks."[82] She lives a carefree life "while waiting for the rich man who will fall in love at first sight and become her husband."[83] Earning a lot of money in the factories, she goes out "every night [...] dressing or undressing according to the latest fashions," using her "artificial charms to attract perfumed and curly-haired young lads looking for romantic adventures..."[84] For Rose-Alma, "being pretty, attracting attention, seducing men, sowing and reaping smiles—this is all there is to life in her eyes. She leaves a trail of perfume in her path, and the folds of her silk dresses make a captivating swishing sound. A real enchanting doll!"[85] When she meets Jean, she is charmed and openly flirts with him. The author compares this attempted seduction to a "new novel," but Jean, to the great regret of the American, remains unresponsive to her advances. "Rose-Alma, with her sparkling eyes and fiery lips, finds that the novel is not moving quickly enough: she nonetheless already sees a budding romance on the horizon. She anticipates the moment when her cousin, conquered like so many others, will kneel at her feet. But she waits in vain."[86] She waits in vain, just like the readers who would have enjoyed this kind of love story! Lamontagne-Beauregard did not allow herself to write such a novel. For her, on the contrary, it was important to reiterate that "simple hearts know nothing of sentimental excitement."[87]

Bourgeois love

Beyond the efforts of publisher Édouard Garand, the absence of editorial collections specifically devoted to popular novels led to an important disparity in this type of content. The romance

Andrée Jarret, *L'expiatrice*, Montréal, Édouard Garand, 1925.

genre was left to its own devices and blossomed where it could. But the Québécois novels that adhered to the invariants of the romance novel had one thing in common: they privileged the bourgeois class. It thus becomes tempting to associate them with the category of the "urban bourgeois novel," as defined by David Décarie, a category that gained momentum precisely in the 1930s.[88]

The bourgeois novel affirmed with renewed force the centrality of the conjugal relationship in the romantic project. Just about everything in the novels of the preceding period focused the lovers' attention on something other than themselves, whether it be the extended family, the religious community, or the nation. The rare examples that depart from this model, like *Amour vainqueur*, conclude with a happy ending worthy of fairy tales, and the lovers are presumed to be happy without posing questions about the challenges of married life. Protagonists in the novels of the 1930s, for the first time with such clarity, seek happiness in a world of their own. While in the regionalist novel, family happiness was extended to the entire community (village, relatives), the bourgeois romance novel focuses on two individuals joined by their affection. Love consecrates the meeting of two unique beings making a home together and not content to only continue a lineage, if they seek to preserve a heritage at all.[89] It is the first time one could really say that *les amoureux sont seuls au monde* ("lovers act as if they are alone in the world").

This does not mean that the bourgeois romance novels of the 1930s impose no social constraints on marriage, quite the contrary. Love is still and always the pretext for maintaining social status. To be in love, one must be happy, and to be happy, one must enjoy a minimum of comfort. The difference between these novels and the ones of the preceding period, is that when the action took place in an aristocratic milieu, the hero inherited colossal fortunes and, when it took place amongst peasants, the hero remained faithful to a land "that never let anyone down." Questions of money were thus not posed directly, especially since the characters' value was not defined by their wealth. The prince could marry a poor girl on the condition that she had an aristocratic grace (acquired or innate) or blue blood, and the farmer could marry the daughter of an upstanding family on the condition that she was not an urbanite in her tastes and values. The situation is different in the bourgeois romance novel, since capital constitutes the very basis of bourgeois identity. It is thus hardly surprising that fear of deprivation by possibly losing one's fortune is present to different degrees in many works of the period. In *Nicolette*

Auclair (1930), Armand, who Nicolette has set her sights on, is discredited by Major Le Roy, who also wants to marry her.[90] The novel's conclusion exonerates Armand: he has become a prosperous broker and can now form a union with Nicolette.

The idea that love is an alliance between people of the same status and that it sanctions a class-based endogamy infuses the entire corpus of bourgeois novels to such an extent that usually it is so self-evident there is no need to mention it. *Les voies de l'amour* (The paths of love) (1931) is an exception to this rule. The main character's equivocations between Lucille, a working-class girl, and Andrée, the daughter of a rich merchant, are presented without any qualms. "Lucille [is] beautiful, elegant, kind beyond doubt," reflects the hero, "but, in the end, her social condition is not very enviable, whereas Andrée, equally beautiful, it seems to me, just as elegant and kind in a perhaps more reserved way, is the daughter of a rich, honoured and high-ranking man."[91] Unsurprisingly, it is Andrée who wins the contest. Though emphasis is placed on Andrée's "long-standing wealth," which suggests a lingering traditional or aristocratic vision, what emerges from *Les voies de l'amour* is the extent to which love is a matter of class belonging, whether this membership be old or new. If the hero no longer finds "in their evenings the same grace, the same elegance" in Lucille "despite all the money he has spent on her gowns,"[92] it is because Andrée, with her education and class origins, has a bearing that is naturally more distinguished and a gift for conversation that is more "sensible," "knowledgeable," "intelligent," and "consistent."[93] Especially, more "accustomed to splendour," Andrée reveals, compared to her rival, "tastes that are more simple but however more refined."[94] Her simple way of dressing "denotes this innate taste for beauty in its simplicity, for elegance in its modesty."[95] She is not one of these upstarts who, like Lucille, "spends for the pleasure of wearing something as compensation for previous deprivations and the little she always had."[96] The comparison turning entirely to the advantage of Andrée, the hero of *Les voies de l'amour* questions the attraction he felt for Lucille in the past: "How could I have preferred Lucille to Andrée ? I don't understand it today [...] What is love if not a sentiment whose origins are unknown, that comes from where? that leads where? A word, a gesture, a glance is the spark that lights the devouring fire. But where is the reflection?"[97] Lucille's "beautiful eyes," "like those of a serpent," her "enchanting voice," her "marble complexion," her "elegant figure" had hypnotized the hero and made him forget about Andrée's education and intelligence, not to mention her fortune. He blames his youth and inexperience.

In its promotion of a Victorian ethic (defending private property, personal initiative and puritan mores), the bourgeois romance novel is not so distant from its regionalist counterpart as one might think. The virtues emphasized are still those of work, family, good morals and moderation. As before, the choice of a spouse should still be based on discernment, careful consideration, and attentiveness to the qualities of sobriety and endurance. For the man, respectability is conditional on a marriage with a woman who is educated, well dressed, of good taste, who knows how to keep house, and comes from a good family. For the woman, maintaining status in the social class is ensured by marriage with a man who has an honourable and lucrative profession, which explains how the age gap inevitably increases to the benefit of men, in proportion to the importance accorded to the husband's social position. In the corpus of this period, it is not surprising that over half of the heroes are doctors (or medical students) and lawyers, and the others are not lacking in wealth: high-ranking officials, reputed surveyors, architects, prosperous brokers, and rich heirs.[98] When the relation of wealth is exceptionally inverted between the man and the woman, strong rhetoric is employed to excuse this breach of the genre's rules. For example, in *Ce que peut l'amour* (What love can do) (1943), by J.-Wilfrid Pion, a priest has to intervene to convince a man who resembles a "prince" and a "knight" to marry a rich heiress who is madly in love with him.[99] At the end of the novel, we learn that the fiancée's father has offered to take his future son-in-law on as a company associate.

We should not be misled by the fact that some female characters are represented in bourgeois novels as salaried workers. Women have a job, either because they want to escape a suffocating family home or because they are orphans or from a poor family background. Moreover, they do not take this decision lightly; the desire to "make it," to become rich like Ninie in *Amour vainqueur*, is not what drives their professional choices, and their work environment is rarely fulfilling for them, except when used as a part of the plot to introduce a romantic encounter. Marriage typically puts an end to the heroine's job so she can concentrate on her conjugal "career": conceiving and raising children, cooking, and housecleaning.

A striking exception to this rule is *Anne Mérival* (1927), by Madeleine (the pen name of Anne-Marie Gleason Huguenin), published in serial form in the pages of *La Revue moderne* (and never released as a book prior to its contemporary electronic version). Though this novel introduces themes found in the bourgeois novel and could be considered a precursor to this trend,[100] Madeleine's story is original in that it depicts a career woman who does not renounce her professional aspirations. Anne, a young journalist, falls under the charms of Paul Rambert, a married politician. However, she is also engaged to Jean Deschâtels, a medical student. Torn, like so many heroines, between emotion and reason, she doesn't know how to resolve the dilemma. The more she thinks about it, the less she can resign herself to returning to her "little hole of a village" and accept becoming, as *Madame Docteur* Deschâtels, her husband's "submissive slave." At the same time, there is no question of her pursuing an adulterous relationship. But everything works out for the best: while Jean, in a gesture that seems out of spite, decides to leave for the European front, where he dies, Paul becomes a widower, which authorizes Anne to give in to her "forbidden love." This love is a true love, even if for Anne it comes after her engagement with another and, for Paul, after another marriage. Anne knows now that she never loved Jean, having felt only a vague tenderness for him. As for Paul's first wife, the novel explains that she was ill-suited for him. A friend of Anne's tries to reassure her: "Paul Rambert may have married a woman before you, Anne, but you will be his wife, do you understand me, and he, he is truly the one who was put on earth to provide for your happiness. Your marriage will thus be one which is said to be "written in the stars."[101] Hearing these words, "which promised her paradise on earth," Anne "rejoices."

This novel stands out in the interwar corpus. On the one hand, it affirms the heroine's right to continue working once married and to make her voice heard in the public arena. On the other, it seems to defend passionate love. For Anne it is clear that love is something other than a calm river; it is a torrent, a volcano, a devouring emotion. "I understand what love is now," she exclaims. "A great feeling that takes us away, that ravages, massacres us, perhaps, but it is unique and unlike any other..."[102] Under this innovative guise, Madeleine's story nonetheless sets out a strict framework for the expression of feelings. Anne can only admit to herself she has feelings for Paul once he has become a widower. A strong-willed woman, she still believes that her personal accomplishment naturally leads her to the altar, because it involves the discovery of a great love. Also, while affirming Anne's choice to not return to live in her village, the novel presents the two characters as belonging to the exact same social class. Anne's father had been a doctor, a respected speaker and a close acquaintance of Wilfrid Laurier. He would have been destined for a great intellectual and political career if he hadn't chosen, through excessive modesty, to bury himself alive in a little village and die there prematurely. Anne is of the same calibre as her father. "Also," notes Paul, "you resemble him a lot, your father, and the more I look at you, the more I see him... The same eyes, the same smile, the same posture... Do you know that yesterday I couldn't stop thinking of you?..."[103] Since Anne is the double of her father, who is himself the double of her future husband, her choice of Paul over her milieu of origin is less of a betrayal. Together they will share "the incomparable joy of well-matched souls." She will act as secretary for him, in a role that evokes the nurse-doctor relationship found in the American "nurse romances" of the 1930s.[104]

Maternal love

During the interwar period in French Canada, the notion of love was more than ever linked to family responsibilities, understood in the broadest sense.[105] To love is to love through children that the spouses have together. In the context of the "revenge of the cradle" and the confinement of the woman to the domestic sphere, couples, it was said repeatedly, cannot love each other without wanting children. The old adage of French-language tales ("they married and had many children," which already contrasts with the English version "they lived happily ever after") can almost be inversed and reformulated as "they had a lot of children and loved each other." In sum, in the romance novels of the interwar period, a couple who loves each other is a couple with children, something that the corpus of the preceding period had not yet introduced. From *Les fiancés de 1812* and *Amour vainqueur* to *Antoinette de Mirecourt*, the children of the couple are non-existent.

The recentring of romantic relations on maternity in the stories comes with two consequences, one bad, the other good, from the point of view of the expression of passion. Let us start with the bad. Conjugal love being channeled through the duty of raising children, the spouses are allotted distinct and complementary tasks. The man is the provider, and the woman is the child bearer and manager of domestic tasks. Defined primarily by their roles vis-à-vis their progeny, and not by their feelings for one another, the spouses risk staying together for reasons that have only a weak relation to passion. Moreover, since the division of tasks in the household leaves childcare to the woman, she is the one expected to surround them with needed affection. However, a mother's love for her children is unique in that it can be accomplished selflessly, requiring no reciprocity. A mother can and should love despite ingratitude, pain, and sorrow. Rejected by her children, she might experience profound sadness, but she can never stop fawning over them, without altering her nature. Since the object of her love is displaced from the husband, with whom relationships should ideally be egalitarian, to the children, with whom relationships can be unidirectional, it is irrelevant whether the woman is loved or neglected: for her, what she could never endure as a spouse is acceptable to her as mother.

Seen from this perspective, marriage as portrayed in the romance novels of the interwar period includes neither great effusions nor great affection. It is not only that the idea of a "weak sex" and a "strong sex" informs the discourse that confines the woman to her kitchen. It is also that in marriage, the great love is not so much between spouses as it is based on the mother's love for her children. This maternal love is nothing like the gentle affection of the period following the Second World War. The expectation is that, through love, the mother demonstrates mortification, renunciation. Her love must be a form of self-surrender. Hundreds and hundreds of stories repeat this lesson, which is even woven into the love stories. For example, two chapters of *Le château des illusions*, despite being a romance novel, are titled: "A mother's heart without love is a well without water" and "The heart of a mother is a treasure of devotion."[106]

This description of maternal love would be rather depressing in a history of the romance novel if the sombre portrait it painted was not tempered by another element. In terms of the expression of passion, the recentring of romantic relations on maternity had one positive consequence. The definition of the nuclear family as the unit of production within which each partner fulfilled a precise function also implied a perfect psychological harmony between the spouses. Partners who were too different risked living in conflict. The happiness of conjugal life depended not only, as we have seen, on maintaining the national community and social classes, but also on the complementarity of temperaments. An older man would thus hesitate to marry a much younger girl, just as a girl of humble origins would abstain from marrying someone too rich, a French Canadian from choosing someone of another nationality, and, especially, a Catholic from considering union with a Protestant. More fundamentally, one sought to marry someone who shared the same tastes and ideas, and this desire for social homogeneity encouraged the democratization of conjugal relations.

Romantic stories thus began to focus less on a shepherdess meeting a prince charming who will save her and more on a virtuous young girl meeting a protagonist who closely shares her condition, with the two being briefly separated due to unfortunate events. The romance novel, which naturalized the inequality between the sexes, thus also challenged the hierarchization of these relationships. The couple would unite two different but equal individuals. While the complementarity of roles encouraged men to desire women who were educated, work-oriented, modest and virtuous, and women to seek men who were hard-working, courageous, frugal and prosperous, equality between spouses encouraged them to seek life partners. It is thus not surprising to see the characters in novels striking a delicate balance between "the heart's choice" and the "good match." This meant falling in love with someone who did what one could not do, while somehow being totally like-minded—not an impossible but rather complex mission.

Insofar as it implies respect, love elicits a reciprocity between the man and the woman in the couple. The equality of love (partners must love each other equally, because not loving enough is to not truly love; love is sincere and total, because only total love is sincere) is echoed in the equality within love (one loves another self, an alter ego, a better half, a life companion). In contrast to contractual equality (legal or commercial), the equality of love is unique in being expressed through a double submission, a double deference. The person loved is admired, venerated, adulated. In the strict sense, one can love neither one's master nor one's slave, and yet, in love, one accepts becoming the "slave of love."[107] Indeed, the classic image of the marriage proposal is the young man kneeling in a position of submission and admiration, vowing to forever be the knight in service to the queen of his heart. Promises abound in the moment the engagement ring is offered: "I promise you eternal adoration"; "I will live only for you"; "your wish will be my command." The wife who risked being reduced to a servant bound to household chores and caring for children in marriage is transformed into a queen thanks to love. What woman of the interwar period would not have been overwhelmed by the promise of this metamorphosis?

French-Canadian women were not deceived by the dream being offered to them. When they saw through the declarations of love a masquerade leading straight to domesticity and submission, some sought consolation for this depressing future in the "literature of resignation," which taught them how to bear their cross on earth. "That's life," declares the main character of *Yolande la fiancée* (1935), "true happiness is bought with suffering and worry."[108] But for those who preferred to dream of a better life, romance novels offered an escape, a vision of profound joy and a brighter future. In *La Revue moderne*, a reader rather astutely confides that she reads Delly because "it makes [her] dream of things that are perhaps impossible, but it is still better to fantasize than further immerse oneself in the sad reality."[109] In this fantasy, the romance novels make the readers believe that it is possible to be both submissive and loved: loved because submissive, and submissive because loved.

The declaration of love

When love is declared, two questions present themselves: first, do I truly love the person I am attracted to? Second, does the person I love truly love me? Novels from the 1830s to the 1930s were very quick to answer these questions. It was unimaginable to present a legitimate union between two people who were not profoundly in love or, at least, destined to love one another, and romantic feelings were always reciprocal and equally sincere. In the 1940s these certitudes began to be cast in doubt. It was understood from then on that human nature was more complex and that love stories were more uncertain than fairy tales allowed for. Too many suitors had broken their engagements after promising eternal love, and too many marriages ended in disaster. This is what the novels of Adrienne Maillet (born in 1887) and Albertine Laperle-Bernier (born in 1900) observe.

Nicknamed by the critics the Magali or Delly of Canada, when not compared to Colette Yver,[110] Adrienne Maillet does not generally adhere to the Dellyian framework,[111] and her work cannot be included in the category of the romance novel as we have defined it.[112] This is because most of her plots are based instead on a melodrama and revolve around Cornelian dilemmas arising from maternity outside of marriage[113] or marriage without maternity.[114] They are in fact closer to "victim novels" that often describe how women, separated from their children due to a fault (light and excusable) or misunderstanding, have to face a series of challenges before being pardoned or redeemed.[115]

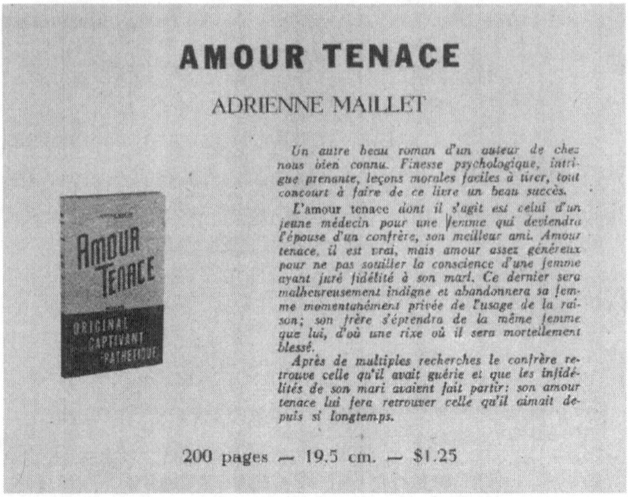

Revue dominicaine, vol. LVI, Tome 1, janvier 1950, p. xiii.

Seen from this perspective, attempts to demonstrate the presence of a feminist revolt in this production fall short due to a lack of knowledge about the genre.[116]

Two of these works, both of which recount the misadventures of a woman who has chosen to marry the wrong man, nonetheless stand out from the rest of her work and more closely resemble the canonical scenario of the romance novel. In *L'oncle des jumeaux Pomponnelle* (The uncle of the Pomponnelle twins) (1939), Denise marries an adulterous and alcoholic husband.[117] Though the latter ends up losing his mind and being interned, Denise cannot get remarried with her friend and childhood love, Jean Pomponnelle. Fifteen years later, her husband dies and the widow can reunite with Jean, who has never stopped thinking of her. The other single novel by Maillet belonging to the romance genre is titled *Amour tenace* (Tenacious love)[118] (1945) and revisits a similar scenario. It depicts two young men, one who is elegant and handsome (Jacques Dulac), and his friend who is timid and loyal (Roger Vaillon). From the first pages, the novel describes the first as selfish, dishonest and mean-spirited, and the second as generous to the point of being selfless. However, the tender and beautiful Lise marries the first and her love for Roger, awakened when she learns of her deceitful husband's betrayal,[119] remains suppressed until Jacques' death, without ever "tarnishing her conscience." After a long search, Roger finally sees her again and the two can enjoy their "tenacious love."

More interesting for our analysis are the works by Albertine Laperle-Bernier. Her novels take place in the most bourgeois of settings: the characters travel by air, own fabulous cars, pass their summers at their cottages, enjoy yacht excursions, dine in chic cabaret restaurants, attend the Saint-Viateur church in Outremont, and live in opulent houses on Desmarchais Street, in Verdun. These texts are not, however, bourgeois novels. The men are architects, important lawyers, businessmen or men of independent means, but the girls can be of modest backgrounds, and the story really revolves around a love that is indestructible and pure. By authorizing the social migration of the heroine who finds her prince charming, while replacing the carriage with the Chevrolet, these texts already prefigure the production of the postwar period, proclaiming that love cannot live on fresh water alone. They also reflect an expansion of the matrimonial market that makes the quest for love more difficult.

Built on conflicts between the duties of friendship and the call of passion, *Dans la nuit sombre* (In the dark night) (1942), in particular, includes all the invariants of the romance novel. Claire, an orphan, is boating on a lake when a furious storm breaks out. Just as her death seems imminent, she is saved by Philippe Richard, who saw the drama unfolding from the window of his cottage. Overcome with emotion, she falls into the arms of her "prince charming" and, her head resting on his shoulder, whispers to him that she loves him. "The stranger has no response to these so natural, so spontaneous words, but his arms become more comforting, more protecting for this poor little warbling bird."[120] Claire is immediately conquered: "'Love is a song from heaven,' said a famous poet. Even if you do not invite it, it invades you without your knowing. I mean to say open and expressed invitation because, in the heart of every living being, there are always open arms that call for, that claim love."[121] Philippe is not indifferent to the young girl's allure, but his best friend, Charles Langevin, has also succumbed to her charms and, to avoid causing Charles grief, he decides to bury his feelings. When Charles declares his love, Claire rejects him, seeing him only as a good friend. In a new and interesting twist, it is the silence that now becomes the obstacle to love. The declarations of love are so convoluted, the characters become mired in a dialogue of the deaf. Each is trying to guess the other's thoughts without ever formulating precise questions. Philippe does not know what his best friend Charles thinks of Claire, and Charles does not know what Claire thinks of him, who herself does not know Philippe's feelings, who, finally, does not know that Claire loves him! Charles first learns that Claire does not love him, then he guesses later that Philippe loves Claire, before unexpectedly discovering, at the end of the novel, that Claire loves Philippe. Charles decides to work on bringing them together, and the novel ends with a marriage.

By the same author, *La voix de l'âme* (The voice of the soul) (1944) begins with the character Solange, an orphan raised by nuns, finding a position as a maid for the Forget family. She becomes acquainted with the rich and physically attractive heiress Edmée. "Tall, agile, admirable hair, blue-green eyes of incomparable beauty, dazzling teeth, a proud bearing, she was created to be adored on one's knees."[122] Solange, by comparison, resembles when she sleeps, "the living incarnation of the virgin at rest. Her jet-black hair darkly frames her divinely pure face."[123] Edmée's fiancé, Gérard Dagenais, leaves for Halifax to plead an important case. Edmée asks Solange to answer his letters because this type of correspondence bores her. Gérard discovers in the letters an entirely different woman than the one he left behind and was thinking of breaking up with, finding her to be too capricious and whimsical. "My dear," he writes, "oh how I love you! I am ashamed to admit it, but I think I love you more than before our separation. With this letter from you I have known a little more of your soul, which the beauty of your face always made me neglect."[124] Solange plays along and falls in love with Gérard. She begins dreaming of him and imagining that his letters are destined for her. For his part, Gérard admits to being more filled with love with each new letter, because "a love letter, is the voice of the soul who writes it and whose faithful echo intoxicates the one who receives it."[125] Meanwhile, Edmée has fallen for Bob Foster, a single twenty-eight-year-old, whose parents live in the United States and who is always cruising all the pretty girls.

Having won his case, Gérard returns to Montreal, where he dances one night with Solange. She then has the confirmation that Gérard is the man of her life. "No man had this power like him to make her quiver all over, trembling with indescribable emotion. No man could make her tremble like him at the very sound of his voice, like a reed bending under the caress of a powerful wind."[126] She would rather be dead, because she knows her love cannot be fulfilled. She refuses the advances of a good match, a chemist who works in an important laboratory, because she feels nothing for him beyond a close friendship. At the announcement of Edmée Forget's and Gérard Dagenais' engagement, Solange decides to leave the Forget home, but when Gérard asks her to take care of his aging mother and to live with her, she cannot say no. Gérard, who Edmée has left to marry Bob, begins visiting his mother more and more often. By accident, he discovers that Solange wrote the letters he received while he was in Halifax. He becomes cold towards her. Solange loses the will to live and takes refuge with a cousin in the Laurentians. Gérard realizes his mistake and runs to join Solange to confess his feelings for her: "you made me see so many things, I am happy, happy! As I had never hoped to be. Don't you see we must have been born with the promise of meeting one day and loving one another?"[127] The novel ends with a finale worthy of a Hollywood film: "With tender words, he asks for her promise to become his beloved wife. Her only response is to offer him her lips. Intoxicated with happiness, they exchange a first kiss of love. And appearing on the horizon like a dream, they see the marvelous vision of their future."[128]

An overview of the works of Laperle-Bernier would be incomplete without saying a word on *Le château des illusions* (Castle of illusions) (1949), composed, as one critic correctly observed, "in the style of Magali."[129] The novel describes Geoffroy Vigeant's childhood with an unloving mother who married his father for his money. His parents end up separating (his mother eventually dies from a heart attack after losing an important sum of money gambling and his father enters the Jesuit mission). One day when he is asked to attend a ball with a young girl named Gisèle, Geoffroy is surprised to find himself attracted to her, but he learns from a devious source that she had arranged to be escorted by him. This confirms his view that marriage is a trap and that all women are despicable. He vows to take revenge. One day while taking a boat ride with Gisèle on a lake, he convinces the young girl to jump into the icy water on the pretext of a bet with a friend, simply for the satisfaction of humiliating her. He quickly regrets his gesture, but the harm is done. At the end of the novel, he has the courage to confess his misdeeds in a letter: "To think of being forever separated from you, my tender love, I feel my heart beating to the point of breaking. Gisèle, I love you! I love you more than anything in the whole world. For me, you are happiness, life!."[130] The novel's final pages take the form of a fairy tale or "castle of illusions," which is the name of a magnificent cottage that Geoffroy's uncle has bequeathed to him. The two lovers finally resolve the *quiproquo* that separated them:

> For a long moment, he held her in his arms against his chest, feeling her heart beat. His head resting on her beautiful silky hair, which infused his lips with a sweet perfume of fresh lilacs, he whispered:
>
> — I knew you would come. I was waiting for you.
>
> — Why have you waited so long to write this letter? she said, in a sulky tone while gently forcing him to ease his embrace.
>
> — Why! But I believed that you would hate me! I believed I had lost you forever. Oh! Gisèle, you do not know how happy I am to see you here next to me. It is the most beautiful day of my life. Come...sit down here, he said, leading her toward a rustic bench, tenderly taking her in his arms.
>
> A smile sparkled in her eyes.
>
> — Me! hating you... she whispered.
>
> — You forgive me?
>
> — I do not have to forgive. You acted believing you were paying me back for something I did not do, it is true...but you were sincere.
>
> — What! So you knew that?...
>
> — I met your friend André, by pure chance, over tea at Madame Orner Marignan's, he told me everything.
>
> — What!...
>
> — Shh! she said, posing a finger on his lips. I promised to keep it a secret. He knew you were unhappy because of me. He's a brave soul.
>
> — I love you Gisèle!
>
> — I love you too, she said, offering him her lips for a first kiss.
>
> He felt an inexpressible happiness rise within him, based on his infinite love for the woman tenderly nestled against his heart.[131]

Since Geoffroy's and Gisèle's affection is authentic and unselfish, they will not end up like Geoffroy's parents, doomed to despair for having accepted a marriage without love. Their happiness will be eternal because their love is "infinite."

The titles of Laperle-Bernier's three novels could have been variations on Shakespeare's *Much Ado About Nothing,* read in reverse: in these stories there is *a lot of silence for nothing.* Having written the entry on Laperle-Bernier's work for the *Dictionnaire des œuvres littéraires du Québec,* Léonce Cantin clearly understood the underlying plot of the novelist's three works: "In each of the novels, the young protagonists are lonely romantics, dreamers, victims of their silence before their loved ones."[132] The barrier to their love is a lack of communication, an inability to express their feelings, a retreat into soliloquy. "The novelist continues the "cult of unhappy love" and arrives at a rather simple ideology: the obstacle to happiness is to be found in the characters, who are both weak and idealistic, inclined to fatalistic suppositions and silence; despite these defects, she makes them believe in happiness, which always triumphs in the end."[133] The dark clouds dissipate above the protagonists' heads and give way to a sunny sky through the magic of a love that can finally express itself.

Our love

The period between 1930 and 1940 is marked by three cardinal changes to the grammar of romantic narratives. First, the love between the couple is partly transferred to the woman's love for children. At a time when the life expectancy barely surpassed fifty years old,[134] a good wife was primarily a good mother, the French-Canadian woman spending most of her life looking after the home, with little time to devote to the couple. While this lack of love may have taken on a morbid aspect in the collective unconscious (while America was fixated on the story of a young ten-year-old girl named Dorothy who realizes "there's no place like home," French Canada was obsessed with the fate of a child of the same age, Aurore, horrifically abused by her parents and killed as a result of their torture), the romance novel held up an idealized image of the domestic universe. It sought to demonstrate the grandeur, nobility and joy of the woman who sacrifices her whole life for her children. In this literature, the romantic discourse was not primarily directed toward the husband but rather toward the family, and it did not require perfect reciprocity, because a mother's love was invariably defined by sacrifice. Domesticated, the result of an agreement between partners having distinct functions within the home, love could not be easily expressed with all its force. The few novelists who countered this image in their writing positioned themselves on the margins.[135]

Second, love maintained its endogamous structure but also began to adopt more bourgeois values, even in the regionalist genre. Love united young people belonging to the same social class and sharing the identical values of restraint, sobriety and good taste. Love thus flourished between people who were socially destined to love each other. The romance novel was often abandoned altogether as a genre, with the search for a good match replacing the "savage" pursuit of unbridled passion. Relatively well educated, assured by the consoling words and benevolent advice of their parents,[136] the heroines are rarely placed in desperate situations and their action consists in pining for someone who is their equal, as much by class belonging as by the complementarity of their functions in the household. Only in this way could one hope to enjoy, once married, "the incomparable joy of well-matched souls," as Anne-Marie Gleason Huguenin describes it in *Anne Mérival*.

Third, and in relation to the above comments, while the novels of the preceding period depicted individuals who were "destined to love each other," this period sees the heroines and heroes beset with doubts, regrets and questions, and the romantic narrative is constructed around their questioning and hesitation. The objective obstacles (war, religious or ethnic incompatibility, etc.) that in the past created disjunction are gradually replaced by individual, psychological causes. This reversal stems from the growing focus in novels on the couple, now placed at the centre of the story. Two relatively free individuals (the woman often lives with an old aunt in the city and has a little job) seek union in a singular relationship; they are presented as responsible for their happiness and misfortune. In the novels of Laperle-Bernier, this theme is pushed to its limit within the romance genre, since the heroine and hero have no obstacles to overcome, apart from the silences and *quiproquos*. The characters of the previous period who could not be together despite their love are replaced in her stories by individuals who are separated by nothing major, apart from their inability to declare their love.

This shift in the romance novel toward the celebration of the model nuclear couple coincides with an empirical change in social relations. Real French-Canadian marriages began to increasingly sanction the institution of the couple. Without being isolated, newlyweds became more autonomous with respect to traditional community ties, especially if they lived in the city. This evolution can be observed in the change in meaning of the newlywed trip: while at the turn of the twentieth century it was an occasion to visit the extended family, it later focused on the intimacy of the honeymoon.[137] The expression "our love" illustrates this transition to a more self-referential romantic relationship. The "us" of love, as sociologist Roch Hurtubise rightly observed, could no longer be reduced "to the sum of 'I' and 'you.'" It became "an autonomous entity, a new construction resulting from the love between the 'I' and 'the other.'"[138] The individualist aspect of love, present from the original institution of marriage, was magnified over this period, even if the regionalist and bourgeois novels did everything to contain its corrosive implications. These social upheavals are what the romance novels of the 1920s-1940s convey above all, despite their great diversity. These changes paved the way for the increased emphasis on the couple, young and surprisingly free, that infused the serialized novels of the 1940s and 1950s.

CHAPTER 4

Celebrated Love (1940-1965)

For our purposes, the period extending from 1940 to the mid-1960s is undoubtedly one of the most fascinating. The war, followed by economic growth and consumerism, propelled Québécois society into a new romantic register that even the Catholic elites could not escape,[1] even if their message, however revamped, remained traditional. The elites still maintained, as before, that passionate love should be avoided, the selection of a fiancée or fiancé being above all a matter of reason. "When making their choice," warned Father Marcel-Marie Desmarais, "the [marriage] candidates should judge more with their head than with their heart and their eyes."[2] Physical attraction was severely condemned, insofar as it could lead to excess, misconduct, and impulsive, thoughtless decisions. Above all, they preached that love was only acceptable if it entailed some transcendence, because self-sufficient love was intolerable. While the centring of love within the couple was accepted, the idea that conjugal happiness could flourish without anyone or anything, not even children, was strongly denounced.[3]

The romance novel that emerged over this period is fuelled by these conflicts, and, without departing from the original model and premises, was somewhat reinvented, proposing other ways of living a love story that differed from those of the preceding period. We note in particular a greater acceptance of sexual desire, a tolerance that was strongly condemned by conservative elites, who criticized the postwar romance novels for their "excessive exaltation of carnal beauty" and "scenes of seduction" likely to awaken "bestial tendencies" in young readers' minds.[4] Despite their vehemence, such denunciations were powerless to stem the popularity of this renewed romance novel, which had become, for many Québécois, "a true passion."[5] According to a study conducted by the Jeunesse ouvrière catholique in 1955, a quarter (25.4%) of the young workers (male and female) who were members of this organization, though devoted to moral purification, read an average of four romance novels per week.[6] These novels were purchased either at newsstands or grocery stores or through subscriptions to magazines that reproduced them in series.

The Québécois romance novel thus enjoyed a golden age at the height of the Duplessis era. On the one hand, and we will not return to this topic, authors like Delly, Magali, and Max du Veuzit were still popular with the public. Collections like "Petit Format," launched by Léo Cadieux in 1947, and book clubs like the Cercle du Livre romanesque, created by Pierre Tisseyre in 1952, continued to widely distribute BCBG romance novels. Without denying the importance of this production, we focus here on serialized romance novels for two reasons: 1) they were all written by Québécois authors, and 2) they have received little scholarly attention, though their influence was exceptional. For the period from 1940 to 1965, François Hébert catalogued no less than 11,000 popular dime novels, including 238 series covering several genres (cowboy, detective, spy, romance), published by 66 editors.[7] Among these, collections titled "Mon roman d'amour" (My romance novel), "Roman d'amour mensuel" (Monthly romance novel), "Roman d'amour spécial" (Special romance novel), "Les plus belles histoires d'amour" (The most beautiful love stories), etc., provided the public with an impressive variety of love stories. "All of the series editors

[had] their romance collection, from the biggest (Police-Journal, Bigalle, Bavard, Irène) to the smallest [...]."[8] The phenomenon was remarkable, to say the least, and it had the sales figures to match. According to Jacques Michon, in the mid-1940s, the Éditions Fleur de Lys launched one romance novel per week, with a typical print run of 5000 copies, which rose to 10,000 copies five years later.[9] Each novel sold for 10 cents, the total gross income of Éditions Fleur de Lys for this collection alone representing the sum of $50,000 per year, at a time when the Québécois worker's average annual salary was $2000.

The proliferation of this romance literature stemmed from several factors. From an economic point of view, technological and industrial advances enabled the low-cost production of small volumes, which, barely fifty years earlier, constituted luxury goods that only the wealthiest could afford. Simultaneously, an era of personal aspirations fuelled by postwar prosperity replaced the period of contrition brought on by the Great Depression, when almost the entire family income was devoted to essential expenses.[10] From a demographic point of view, the changes were also considerable. The postwar period in Quebec saw both the triumph of marriage and a decline in births. Young women were rushing into marriage, to the point that girls barely twenty years old without a boyfriend despaired of possibly never finding a husband. On the personal level, differences between the rural and urban milieus decreased, as did the distinction between more- or less-educated individuals. It was the advent, at least imagined, of a gigantic middle class composed of interchangeable nuclear families.

The bliss of conjugal life has undoubtedly never received so much praise. The investment in public discourse was astronomical, with ads about domestic comfort growing exponentially.[11] In this fantasy world of cars, bungalows, televisions, and refrigerators, the ideal of maternity continued to dominate, though somewhat differently than before, when women were invited to "leave for the family" (i.e. marry and have kids). Henceforth, they would have two or maybe three children,[12] which allowed them to live a fulfilling life without denying their femininity. Surrounded by their husbands' affection, showered with constant expressions of gratitude, they seemed to enjoy a quiet happiness made up of little daily pleasures, a happiness that contrasted with the life of chores and humiliations experienced by their mothers. This discourse revisits and overlaps with that of the romance novel. In the 1945 annual issue of the magazine of the Ligue ouvrière catholique, *Le Mouvement ouvrier*, a journalist recounts attending a meeting of engaged young women a few weeks before their marriage. "Their comments," he writes, "are those of young women from every background. They are living the intoxicating joys of a beautiful dream. The engagement period should never end for them. Their fiancé is the ideal husband; he has a few little flaws, not many—, and he will correct them later; they even compare their life to the novels of the *Revue Populaire*."[13]

After explaining why the dream of love (almost invariably coupled with a desire for social advancement) suddenly seems to occupy such an important place in the popular culture's imagination, we will discuss how the postwar romance production centred the romantic ideal even more on the couple, whose members begin flirting and seeking out urban pleasures. The heroine's desire for emancipation from the family home had never been so explicitly expressed. In previous periods, the heroine was often just a simple object of exchange between her father and her fiancé. Now she takes full charge of the "hunt for a husband," in a quest sprinkled with (moral and physical) obligations and pitfalls. In thirty-two pages, dime novels recount this moment of vertigo when the woman, having to choose a near-stranger for a husband, fully commits to a decision. If she is lucky and wise, she will be rewarded with a life of material comfort that her mother and grandmothers would never have dreamed of.

A husband who loves me

In her study of popular songs from the 1940s, Chantal Savoie notes the extent to which romantic relations occupied a central place in the form of a "fantasy life."[14] She sees in this the affirmation of an individualism that, more oriented toward the private sphere, disrupted the old values "oriented towards the interests of the collective, the maintenance of the established order and social utility."[15] This interpretation is correct, but one should add that if so many women wanted to believe in the fairy tales of popular songs, it was because the alternative was too discouraging for them. On the one hand, Québécois women who rejected the religious vocation could only establish themselves in society by getting married. From this arose the obligation to find a husband who would make it possible to ensure their development as individuals after leaving the paternal home (it was only in 1964 that women obtained full legal rights in Quebec). In *La fille sans nom* (The girl without a name), the fiancé is nicknamed "my solution,"[16] which says it all. On the other hand, free union being strictly prohibited and divorce being anathema (the first law legalizing divorce in Quebec dates to 1968), marriage was seen as both a source of fulfillment (if it was filled with respect and tenderness) and space of confinement (if it was not). The ideal of love is heightened in this inescapable situation, as we have seen in the previous chapter.

In the present section, we propose the hypothesis that the passionate love depicted in novels of the 1940s and 1950s serves to mask the heroine's real quest. By becoming the wife of a respectable man, she goes from being a young girl (fragile and vulnerable) to a (socially recognized) woman. Never before had love and marriage been such a requirement; never before was the woman in such desperate need of a husband to exist; and never before, in the history of the romance novel, were the characters as unequal in their premarital relations than in the

Jeanne Zéphire, *La Jalouse*, Montréal, Éditions Police-Journal, 1952.
Illustration d'André L'Archevêque.

postwar period. Even completely dispossessed and diminished in the previous works, the heroine (orphan, poor, rejected) conserved a certain status in relation to the hero, who she could only marry due to the degree of endogamy that linked her to him. After untold suffering punctuated with dramatic fainting spells, illnesses and suicidal thoughts, the heroine ends up finding a family, a heritage or refuge with a sympathetic older woman. Returned to the bosom of good society, she regains her outward dignity (the reflection of a perfect inner dignity) that she had temporarily lost. Later, in the years following the legalization of divorce and mass entry of women into the workforce, the heroine could carve out a place in society without needing a husband (summed up by Gloria Steinem in the popular slogan "a woman needs a man like a fish needs a bicycle"). Between these two poles, between the necessity for endogamy and the recognition of women's autonomy, the heroine of romance novels endures a period of great anguish: she cannot go without a husband, and the ideal husband is the one who distinguishes himself most through his wealth, intelligence, and strength. This is why the heroine nurtures a romanticism that is unequalled in the history of romance literature. The tale of Cinderella never seemed so necessary in the eyes of the young women readers, who were not quite as naive about these fictions as one might believe.

We see here the two central motifs of the serial romance novel, already apparent in the interwar production, but pushed to their extreme: to be someone, a woman needs a husband; but to be more than a housewife to the latter, she also needs love. The stories thus recount how a woman manages to find a home through the only avenue available to her at the time, through engagement, and how this quest leads to her meeting a man who is respectful, kind, generous and loving. Caroline Barrett noted in the only previous study on the romance dime novels of the 1940s to 1960s: "one thing is certain, however things turn out for the heroines of romance novels, whether ending in happiness or misery, they only live for and through men. The exterior world, the social reality does not exist, there is only Man and Love."[17] It would be more accurate, however, to write that for them, there is only the "Husband and Love," insofar as marriage and love form an indivisible whole. The symbiosis of love and marriage is so self-evident in the novels that the declaration of love and marriage proposal happen at the same time, when they are not implied. "Mathilde, I love you, I adore you and if you want to cure me, you will be my wife,"[18] or again: "He offered her this diamond ring, which meant he loved her."[19]

To reinforce this outcome, sexuality is, as in the past, entirely contained within the framework of marriage. Besides virginity before marriage and the exclusive heterosexual relation after marriage, nothing can exist.

This makes it easier to understand the incredible popularity of the romance novel of 1940s and 1950s, especially among women.[20] The romantic story was not much concerned with men, because they could actually, culturally and symbolically enjoy their bachelor's life for longer: in 1951, when the age of legal majority was fixed at twenty-one years old, the average age of marriage was twenty-three for women and twenty-seven for men.[21] This almost suggests an inversion of expectations according to sex: men sought a situation so they could get married, while women sought a husband so they could have a situation,[22] as expressed in the fact that, once "established," they were often referred to with the first and last names of their husbands. Without a husband, young women were either minors or old maids in the making, which was hardly better. In a context where nuptiality and conjugal union formed the horizon of a fully lived life (90 percent of women got married, a record in Quebec's history), women who missed the chance to transition from their status as the father's daughter to the husband's wife, were condemned to being the wives of no one, which meant being worthless.[23]

This rite of passage from the father's house[24] to the husband's was not easy. Young women of the postwar period not only had to elicit the "engagement kiss," while avoiding dishonourable kisses, but also choose a husband who would not make them scorned servants, confined to domesticity. Adèle Lauzon sums up in three short sentences the fears of women of her generation: "If she is not rich and remains in the home, [the married woman] often spends a life devoted, day after day, year after year, to tiresome, thankless and solitary tasks. If she is rich and idle, she will perhaps lead an easy life, but one deprived of the profound satisfaction of an active life. She will be but a flower in her husband's lapel."[25] We recognize here, a hundred years later, the musings of Flaubert's heroine, and we recognize them because they have been, until recently, the sometimes secret, repressed or shameful reflections of all married or about-to-be-married women since the advent of modern society. The only difference is that this questioning of marriage, once stifled by a discourse of duty and sacrifice, was heightened by an emerging ideology that celebrated personal happiness. In 1963, the American Betty Friedan provoked outcry by raising a disturbingly simple question: "Each suburban wife struggled with it alone. As she made the beds, shopped for groceries, matched slipcover material, ate peanut butter sandwiches with her children, chauffeured Cub Scouts and Brownies, lay beside her husband at night—she was afraid to ask even of herself the silent question—'Is this all?'"[26]

Increasingly educated, women could aspire to work that ensured them a small income and were relatively free compared to their parents' generation. They could dream of something other than cooking, sewing and ironing for a herd of children and husband who treated them like servants or housekeepers. They could oppose, in sum, the conjugal institution's transformation of the eternal happiness promised by the wedding night into a hell of solitude, platitudes, and servitude. Women needed to know that once the marriage ceremony was over everything would work out well for them. The romance literature was there precisely to allow women to dream, to promise that finding a husband did not mean having to grieve the loss of their happiness. It presented marriage as a perfect state of grace that, through the magic of love, entailed a double submission: of the woman to a man, and of the man to a woman. One could say in this respect that *Tes désirs sont des ordres, ma chérie* (Your wish is my command, my dear)[27] perfectly condenses in its title the hopes of young girls of the postwar period thinking of marriage. In this sense, the romance novels were not more critical of women's situation as they were alienating: they clearly delineated the frameworks of what women could aspire to.[28]

Love on a dime

If readers, especially female readers, could go through dozens of volumes recounting, in the end, always the same story, it was because the works gave ongoing expression to their desire for happiness, threatened by a disjunction that contained little real suspense, since it was understood that these stories generally ended well. However, the relief in knowing that Cinderella would meet her prince every time could not quell the insatiability of a desire infused with anxiety. The leitmotiv of the happy meeting of two beings never managed to bore the readers.[29] This seemed especially true with the serialization and mass commercialization of romance novels, when literary production acquired a momentum and adopted a format that resembled, in many ways, assembly-line production. Magazine stories, dime novels (literally "romans à dix sous" or "novels for 10 cents"), pulp fiction and paperback novels respected strict rules regarding the number of pages, the illustrations used, the frequency of output and even the content, with the narrative plot typically following a very stereotypical premise that authors could not easily deviate from.[30]

The elites perceived the growing popularity of these 16-to-32-page serial novels, printed on low-quality paper and illustrated with catchy covers, with suspicion if not fear.[31] They were scandalized by the growing success of inexpensive texts (10 cents instead of 1$ to 2$ for regular format books), quickly churned out by journalists or authors of Québécois radio soap operas. To counter the influence these stories were having on young Catholics, the clergy tried to produce romance novels that would be acceptable from a traditionally moral point of view. The dime novels from the collection "Amour et aventure" (Love and adventure) launched by Fides in 1947, were to replace what the editors regarded as "rubbish [...] that reduces love and marriage to the level of the most imbecile animality."[32] These "morally safe" novels, which did not comply with the genre's codes, did not fool the fans of the dominant romance literature, and the public snubbed stories depicting heroines who were not beautiful or enterprising, heroes who were not rich or powerful, and a conjugal bliss that wasn't glamourous or exciting. This failure testifies to the development of a market with already well-established rules and the existence in French-speaking Quebec of a readership perfectly capable of exercising its critical judgement with respect to the available options.[33]

The Québécois public's rejection of the titles proposed by Fides was made easier by the extensive local production of romance novels published in booklet form and widely distributed from Gaspésie to Abitibi, and from Lac-Saint-Jean to Montérégie.[34] Sales figures reveal the immense popularity of this literary genre (in 1945, Éditions Lanthier alone boasted of selling 130,000 copies per month.)[35] Éditions Police-Journal distinguished itself in the genre by publishing, alongside other series (such as "Les Aventures étranges de l'Agent IXE-13, l'as des espions canadiens" [The strange adventures of Agent IXE-13, the ace of Canadian spies]), an impressive number of romance novels, in a range of collections interchangeably titled "Roman d'amour," "Mon roman d'amour," "Roman d'amour mensuel," "Roman d'amour spécial," "Roman d'amour populaire," and "Les plus belles histoires d'amour." Very common during the war and postwar period, the practice of retitling and rejacketing (buying shipments of popular novels from Europe and substituting their original jackets for new jackets sporting the name of a Quebec publisher) might have us believe that dime novels were mostly imported, but the romance series published by Éditions Police-Journal were produced in Quebec and

Henry Chevalier, *Le baiser sous l'érable*, Montréal, Police Journal, c. 1944.

written by Québécois authors.[36] Given the size of this publisher's output of romance series, which included 878 titles published between 1944 and 1965, we have chosen to focus here on this corpus, with occasional reference to the production of other dime novel publishers.[37]

Since the Éditions Police-Journal texts were published under pseudonyms (a common practice for the popular romance novel of the period), it is difficult to determine whether these stories were written more by women or by men.[38] Knowing that many authors shared common pseudonyms over the years, it is likely that the use of recurring names for the "Amour" collection was intended to produce a serial effect to encourage sales (if you liked the last Jeanne Zéphire book, you would probably like the next), rather than being based on a real authorial style. It is interesting to note that while the first dime novels published in 1944 featured men's names (Firmin Bibeau, Julien Dorsac, Fernand Labranche, Roger Saint-Yves, Henri Chevalier), women authors became more prevalent over the years (Pauline Verchères, Roxane d'amour, Roxane d'Avril, Fleur Desneiges, Betty Forest, Mimi Estival), without eliminating the male names altogether.[39] This feminization of authors probably reflects the conventional idea that popular romance novels were written "by women, for women."

Dime novels from the "Amour" collection always tell the same story: a young woman discovers love and finds herself a home. Of course, over the years, romance novels increasingly incorporate the reality of women's work.[40] However, this does not, in our view, reflect a period in full transformation[41] but is simply one of tricks used to ensure the heroine's transition to the "career" of a wife. The tasks of nannies, school teachers, secretaries and nurses are described very generally, salaried work being indeed secondary to the heroine's actual objective, which was to escape her parents' supervision. Work is often a way for female characters to earn the money needed for little outings to the city, cafés, dance halls or movie theatres. Exceptions, like the secretary marrying her boss or the nurse marrying a doctor, only reinforce hierarchical relations that are transferred from the household to the workplace. The heroine knows that once married, she will normally renounce her profession, if she has one. This is evident in *Le roman d'une garde-malade* (The novel of a nurse), a "personal diary" that sets out to describe the splendours of the nursing trade but comes to an abrupt end with the heroine's marriage. The heroine feels that the world of work was for her in the end just a step toward discovering her true vocation: "I just reread my diary. It's strange… I hardly ever speak of my patients anymore. […] And these pages seem more those of a young girl 'in love' than a head nurse."[42]

Seen from this perspective, the heroine's level of education and practice of a trade are not indicative of a real desire for professional emancipation; these attributes aim to show rather that she is ready to leave the family nest and is mature enough to make life decisions, the most important of which is choosing a partner. She is already beginning to cut ties with her family insofar as her salaried work requires leaving the family home by day and allows her to access a larger matrimonial market in the evenings and on weekends. The fact that she sometimes gives part of her salary to her parents sends a double message: it inverses the normal relationship between children and parents by making the heroine the provider for her own parents, thus revealing her maturity; it also expresses the limitations of living under the family roof, of having parents who are preventing her from fully enjoying her youth. Likewise, the absence of the parents or, appearing as a novel theme, their incompetence, facilitates the heroine's transfer to a new home. She has no choice but to become an adult, since she cannot be the daughter of immature individuals. And becoming an adult for a French-Canadian woman in the 1950s of course always means getting married.

All of the aspects that we have evoked here can be found in *Souffle de passion* (Breath of passion) (1947), by Betty Forest.

In its description of the tribulations that lead the heroine from dissatisfaction to final bliss, this novel is particularly revealing of the imaginary of young Québécois women in the immediate postwar period. Ruth, the fifteen- or sixteen-year-old eldest of a family of six children, has to help her mother with household chores. The latter is a loving, though authoritarian, woman who is "a little backward"[43] (in other words, "old-fashioned"). Ruth longs for and aspires to more; she wants to partake in cheerful preoccupations like other young people her age. Aware of the "pointlessness" of impetuous revolts, she knows that a well-behaved young girl cannot throw off the parental yoke with impunity. While she can oppose her mother's decisions—at least by questioning them—she is still not free to govern herself. Though discreet, the crisis is real for the young girl who dreams of going out and having fun. To escape the chores imposed on her, she doubles down on her studies, hoping one day to find a job that will give her more freedom.

At the end of the school year, Ruth, the top student in her class, wants to interrupt her studies to work as a salesclerk in a store. Her mother recommends that she take a "specialized course" instead, which the heroine ends up reluctantly agreeing to after insisting on how senseless education for women was: "But mom! I could work right away, because for a girl it's not the same!"[44] After completing her studies, Ruth finally enters the workforce. As a stenographer, she earns "18 dollars in the first week, which is double what her friends earned six or seven years earlier."[45] However, she is soon disillusioned: not only does her mother keep nearly all of her salary, but she is still not free in her comings and goings. The heroine quickly realizes that she still lacks autonomy.

At seventeen years old, Ruth has her first taste of freedom. She obtains permission to attend a party thrown by her friend Jeanne. "Ruth was happy to spend the night at Jeanne's, laughing with other young people, enjoying the sound of music and twirling on the dance floor."[46] During the evening, she meets Marcel, a young man who Ruth first sees as a means of getting away from her family. On this subject, the text is unequivocal and clearly depicts Marcel as a lifeline, notably when he asks Ruth to go to the movies with him and she agrees "mainly because" she did not have enough money "to allow herself this luxury very often."[47] It does not take very long for the two characters to develop a complicity, though one without passion, because Ruth still sees Marcel as a means to an end. "If she broke off with him, she would be bored to death. And Ruth was tired of being bored."[48] But her dependence on Marcel makes her narrow circle of activity even more intolerable, at a time when her age and work should allow her to enjoy more independence. She "suddenly becomes aware of her subjection."[49]

When she succumbs to the charm of one of Marcel's friends, Claude Bernard, who is preparing to leave for war, Ruth feels a last impulse to rebel. The "daydream" motif, a recurrent theme of romance novels, makes her aware of her solitude and distress. She knows that she will not have love with a capital L with Marcel but nonetheless resolves to marry him, through a sense of gratitude. In fact, "she doesn't think she has the right to reject the man who never did her any wrong, who made her first outings possible, who was the source of her first amusements, who sort of freed her from the kitchen [...]."[50] The future that Marcel promises her is a life of monotonous regularity. "With him, she is sure to have some peace of mind. He loves her and can give her a decent life."[51] Once married, their passionless relationship is reflected in a suburban life that is routine and devoid of the excitement that, as the novel mentions, makes life worth living. Loved like a "sister of charity," and not a desirable woman, Ruth ends up reproducing, though more comfortably, the boring existence of her mother as mistress of the house and mother of two children.

During nights of insomnia, she is surprised to find herself thinking of Claude, who made her discover "the strange sensation of a love that nothing can hinder." Unable to turn back and become a child again, Ruth can also not undo the sacred bond of marriage to a man who inspires no profound feelings in her. Like many heroines in the romance novels that came before her, Ruth contemplates death as a possible solution to her malaise, and this perspective becomes the repressed heroine's veritable distress call: "When Marcel returns, exhausted after a day's work, she knows he is tired to death, so she wants to die too, lying in the flowerbed, her face buried in the grass, with both hands over her ears so as not to hear the beating of her tired, wretched heart."[52]

Happily for Ruth, "destiny" brings Claude back into her life five years later. Now a pilot, he travels from village to village offering plane tours. It is easy to guess what happens next: the reunion of Claude and Marcel is sealed by a flight that ends badly. Only Claude survives the crash. Ruth and Claude can finally confess their mutual attraction. At the end of the story, Ruth gives birth to Claude's child and fully savours the joys of maternity for the first time, because, as she confesses, during her first pregnancies, it was Claude's child that she wanted to have... All's well that ends well... though not without some convoluted detours. And, let's not forget what preceded the *deus ex machina* that brings about the happy ending: in Betty Forest's novel, Ruth longs for pleasure (cinema outings, city adventures, evening dances) and freedom, and she suffers under the parental institution's, then marriage's, attempts to force her into a precise role, that of a servant. The status of wife and mother only becomes acceptable at the very end, when they are associated with true passionate love. It is this passionate love, and it alone, that makes it possible for the family home to be something else for her, even living in a beautiful house in a comfortable neighbourhood, other than a place for accomplishing "servile [...] tasks."[53]

We could provide many other examples of this promise of a love capable alone of transforming the more-or-less gilded cage of conjugal life into a fulfilling experience. This discourse in romance dime novels supports the idea that mass-market production contains, alongside a myriad of alienating representations, "certain modes of transgression."[54] The heroine of this period dreams of getting rid of her apron to have an entirely different role than that of simple housewife, despite the dominant social discourse's attempt to impose that role on her. She only accepts becoming the ideal homemaker if this role is transfigured by the love of her partner. It is only in being revered, desired and recognized for who she is, for her unique character traits, that she consents to move from the residence of her childhood to the conjugal home. It is her beauty and intelligence that creates the condition for equality in the marriage, in her view, through the abolition of hierarchies in love (when it is not their reversal, the husband becoming the knight serving the queen of the home). This "love on a dime" both confirms and denounces the gap between dream and reality for women in the postwar period.

The (relative) triumph of flirtation

Up until the Second World War, strict boundaries were set for the game of love. The elites condemned outings and parties, considered sources of moral disorder, and encouraged parents to habituate their children, especially young girls, to spending their free time with the family.[55] Opportunities for encounters were kept to a strict minimum, as this type of distraction almost always led, they warned, to serious transgressions. Marrying someone from one's own background was thus inevitable, since there was never an occasion to propose to anyone else.[56] All of this changed with the social intermixing created by industrialization and the mass movement of people from the countryside to the city. Since social circles could no longer be restricted to family and neighbourhood networks, love stories between individuals who had known each other since birth became less and less credible. This created the need for young people to have more opportunities to meet strangers. Before, men visited the young girl at her home; now, the young girl was going out with boys: these simple words are indicative of a veritable revolution in romantic relations.[57] Courting, which had formerly been a public act that took place in private, became a private act that took place in public.

Since choosing a partner was considered a necessity and meeting someone from one's local circles was less likely as in the past, flirtation became the latest thing for young people of marrying age who were ready to "settle down." Flirting constituted the best way to test the strength of mutual affections. A province-wide study conducted by the Jeunesse ouvrière catholique (JOC) on 1500 young workers in 1961 (and the findings appear to be valid for the previous years also) revealed that among 14-to-17-year-olds, "the search for romantic experiences [was] the basis of their leisure lifestyles. [...] The purpose of leisure time among our adolescents (according to the numbers and facts) seems to be meeting a boy or a girl."[58] Considering that the survey was based on the responses of members of the JOC, as well as workers and residents of Jonquière, Trois-Rivières, Chicoutimi, and Montreal, it is safe to assume that the phenomenon of flirting had become an inescapable reality throughout the province.

Despite outcries from conservative elites, romantic experiences for boys and girls were "strongly provoked and directly promoted 'as a series of normal experiences' by a large part of the ideological content"[59] of novels. For example, in *Le plus beau cadeau* (The most beautiful gift), by Paul Verchères, the heroine asks her grandmother if she should be chaperoned by her father or mother when receiving an escort. "No," she answered. "I might be old-fashioned, but not that much. My reasoning is as follows: Parents should allow their children an amount of freedom that is fair and reasonable. Their continual and annoying supervision is a veritable insult to their child."[60] Living on ancestral land cleared "during the heroic times of Curé Labelle," the heroine of *Le plus beau cadeau* refuses to follow tradition and give her hand to the next door neighbour farmer's son, choosing instead to marry a brilliant lawyer from Montreal who she met by chance. The conclusion of this Éditions Police-Journal dime novel is all the more remarkable given the contradictory clues of the paratext: the cover page depicts a young blond-haired women gazing with admiration at a brave and smiling farmer, and the brief preface claims that the novel was written at the request of the publishers to revive "our good old customs, which form the strength and future of our race and are nearly eternal in their extension."[61]

Once rare in the stories, restaurant or cinema outings become increasingly common, as do strolls and evening dances featuring the popular foxtrot, and one-step. The protagonists play bridge and tennis, and even go shopping together, without being under the continual watch of their parents. Recognizing the need to date many partners before marriage, these novels advise young people against hasty declarations that may end in disappointment, echoing the countless warnings of advice columnists to think twice before making the final choice of a partner.[62] Since the family is no longer the reference for approval of the suitor, the young people themselves have to show discernment by not falling into the arms of the first to come along.

The dime novel *Le doux pays des amants* (The sweet land of lovers) (1954) offers advice to readers who might be tempted to skip the steps leading to marriage. An aunt reminds Marcelle that there are thousands of boys and that, if she ever lost the one she thinks she loves, she would find many others in his place. It should not be assumed after a first dance or date that one's escort will necessarily become her husband. "It was the panic of a young girl that you had… an optical illusion, as my husband would say, when you thought that Raymond would be your prince charming simply because he took you out dancing, one time... to be kind to the young girl who couldn't go home. One has to know how to distinguish between love and gallantry, simple politeness. It is not because a young man has shown courtesy to a young girl that he should court her the following week."[63] It is better to not be hurried in love, since the consequences can be devastating. The aunt emphasizes that the bonds of marriage, once celebrated, cannot be undone. "Be prudent, my dear... be prudent... you know, love, or what one believes to be love, is deceptive... an entire life can be ruined by love... and there is no going back afterwards..."[64] Made wary by her aunt, Marcelle realizes that it is a common error among young girls her age to want to throw themselves into the arms of the first handsome boy to come along. "You know, when leaving the Convent, [girls] want to get married within two months... thinking that, otherwise, they will remain old maids. But with time, we understand so many things. We want marriage, but we want to choose also, not to jump on the first one and say "yes" for fear of never having the chance to say it again."[65]

These fine words are suggestive of a very romantic, very sentimental discourse. But what becomes evident in reading the romance dime novels of the 1940s and 1950s, is the extent to which they depend, even more frankly than before, on external qualities to judge the validity of a romance. No work reveals this better perhaps than *Hasard ou destinée* (Chance or destiny) (n.d.), a novel by Pol Delval published by one of Éditions Police-Journal's main competitors, l'Imprimerie Bernard. The story begins by insisting on the fact that Viviane, an orphan with a meagre income, is an ugly woman who, because of her ugliness, knows she will never be loved. She laments not being able to have some of the happiness prettier women enjoy. Her only hope is to accept the hand of the village notary, Mr. Durand, but he too has an unprepossessing appearance and clumsy manners, which defeats the purpose. François, a foreigner staying in the village while recovering from a breakup with a Hollywood actress, advises her to work to increase her income, dye her hair, wear makeup and lipstick, and to make herself some new dresses inspired by the best fashion magazines. "Go spend a day in the city in a nice beauty salon, for once, make an extravagant purchase, learn from the experts and take their advice."[66] He also offers her this opinion: "You don't owe anyone anything, you are entirely free to do as you please."[67]

Knowing enough English to get by in the big city, Viviane decides to move to Montreal and offer her services in a flower shop. She continues to improve her appearance by going to a good hairdresser and exercising at the Palestre nationale sports centre. She has become "almost pretty." François, who is visiting, invites her to a nice restaurant. "The young girl [has] nicely styled hair topped by a little green hat, and her makeup is carefully applied; in short, François is happy to be walking alongside such a chic companion."[68] When Viviane returns to her home town, her uncle, far from criticizing her new look, commends her for it: "My how you have become more and more pretty... the city suits you..."[69] The notary, perhaps inspired by Viviane, who he always found to his liking, has gained around ten pounds (prosperity and plumpness being a common association) and has begun dressing with more taste. "He did like me, he took care of his appearance, and he is almost a handsome man..."[70] Their marriage is celebrated one month later. "The notary Durand, whose good business provides a large income, is very rich and refuses nothing to his wife."[71] As a sign of his incomparable success, he is elected to parliament. The birth of a son transforms Viviane's body even more: her breasts increase in size, her hips become rounder. "She is dressed by the best designers in Montreal, once a year the couple treats themselves to a trip to New York, and the young woman brings back gowns that make her even more elegant."[72]

In *Hasard ou destinée*, the regionalist ideology that emphasized the rural woman's hard work is replaced by a discourse that focuses on the delicate physique of the heroines, whose image borders on the caricatural model of the trophy wife. The oppositions between women and men in relation to body image become even more apparent than before the war. While women's beauty is described with reference to diminutive features (slim figure, small stature, dainty feet, fair skin, blue eyes, blond hair and tapered fingers, with the occasional exception of an ample bosom and hips), men's appeal is attributed to their imposing presence (broad shoulders, tall stature, muscular build, powerful voice).[73] While clothing and cosmetics are used to showcase the body of each woman as unique, for men, they serve to elevate his status and render him anonymous behind his function (thus the allure of men in uniform).

Hasard ou destinée shows the extent to which the discourses had changed since the 1920s. In an expanded and thus more competitive matrimonial market, great wealth, previously regarded with suspicion (as a sign of class divide within a national group imagined as homogeneous), is henceforth legitimized for men, and coquetry, a formerly unacceptable flaw, becomes an indispensable weapon for women seeking a partner. The heroines of dime novels, having perfectly integrated the postwar norms, know they no longer have a choice: they have to attract attention and arouse desire, the art of seduction being one of their strategies of romantic conquest. In *L'amoureux de Noranda* (Noranda's lover) (1951), Nicole is spoiled by her father, but her immense wealth is not enough to hide her obesity, lack of taste in clothing, and hideous hairstyle. "Laurent also cannot help noticing the young girl's lipstick, which is much too dark and does not go at all with her style and even less with her dress."[74] For the spark to be lit between the two main characters, the young twenty-one-year-old girl has to lose a "considerable" amount of weight, highlight her features with skillfully applied makeup, and wear shoes with "very high heels."[75]

The novels incessantly repeat the same theme: it is impossible to be attracted to an ugly woman. If the housewife has to be fresh and attractive to prevent her husband from "looking elsewhere" and "jumping the fence," the same holds true, *a fortiori*, for the fiancée, who could have her betrothed stolen by a more enterprising woman. While the regionalist ideology praised a woman capable of performing tasks for others (washing the floors, caring for children, etc.), the new ideology conveyed by *Hasard ou destinée* promotes a woman who is primarily devoted to working on herself (makeup, hair, jewellery, etc.) and doing for herself what others demand of her. In a huge reversal that has very little impact on the role of male domination itself, the discourse of self-effacement (reserve, self-sacrifice, contrition) is replaced by one of merit: the woman pays obsessive attention to the appearance of her body because she "deserves it." From now on, she must "make herself" beautiful to love herself and be loved, the mirrors reflecting her multiple "imperfections" and "flaws," which must be endlessly corrected: how tragic to see that first wrinkle, and how many lotions need to be applied night and day to hide any trace of it! While the man pursues a career to be worthy of love, the woman makes searching for love a career in itself, sparing no expense or effort.

The sensuality of dime novels

In the prewar novels, love represented the very negation of sexuality, going so far as to assert that young people should suppress their carnal desires in proportion to their level of attraction. The more ardent the love, the more sexuality had to be effaced in favour of wise and platonic declarations. Gallantry, devotion, and oaths of fidelity all contributed to repressing sexual impulses and replacing them with a romantic ideal capable of channelling desires into more acceptable goals. In the prewar novels, the girl was pure and a virgin, the fiancé was sweet and attentive, and both swore to having only chaste thoughts about one another prior to marriage.[76] Love thus served to enclose the protagonists within rigid sexual norms. Sexual relations, almost completely absent from the corpus even in the form of metaphor, were only alluded to with a few vague signs[77] and confined to the boundaries of the strictest decorum, which amounted to making the physical attraction between the two characters almost incidental, despite the insistence on their unparalleled beauty.

Without engaging in sensual excess, the postwar dime novels explore the question of flirtation and desire, though often through using the counter-model of the rival, who is prepared to abuse her charms to seduce the hero. The character Suzy Jasmins, whose legs "concealed nothing" and were "made for caresses," is one example among others.[78] But, far from remaining reserved and pure, the heroine must also now know how to be desirable so as not to leave the field open to her rivals on the matrimonial market, which leads to a certain eroticization of the "meeting ritual."[79] The more the period advances, the more the works employ suggestive titles, such as *Un baiser d'extase* (A kiss of ecstasy) (1961), *Le professeur de caresses* (The teacher of caresses) (1962), or *Une nuit scandaleuse* (A scandalous night) (1963), which evoke infinite lustful possibilities. While being careful to not veer into the realm of the tease, that is to say, to not be judged as "easy" or "light," because that would entail losing her honour, the heroine of dime novels knows she has to become an expert in the art of flirtation, master the laws of appearance, and make her availability known, but within limits. The transition from girl to wife is more perilous than the transition from boy to husband, for the good reason that the woman cannot succumb to her partner's desires at the risk of passing for a "slut."[80] While a man's "little infidelities" are peccadillos, the woman's slightest meanderings are judged with the full implacability of Christian morality. Women who lose their virginity before marriage or, worse, become pregnant outside of marriage,[81] must pay the social price. Readers are thus drawn into a journey full of pitfalls and traps, captivated by the sophisticated or naive attempts of the characters to give of themselves without losing themselves.

In our corpus, kisses, formerly very chaste, are now legion. In *Le survenant amoureux* (The romantic outlander) (1958), which has a particularly enticing cover, the heroine Gertrude allows herself to be kissed by the womanizer Philémon Boisvert, even though she knows he has also kissed her sister and her cousin. The voyeuristic scenes go quite far, because Gertrude is witness to these kisses, and perhaps even more. Hiding behind a combine, she is mortified by what she sees, but readers' desires are no less satisfied. Wearing an "outrageously lowcut dress," Colette is "leaning back against a large tree." Philémon "leans over her," takes "her head in his hands and plants a kiss on her crimson lips." "That's it," the breathless Gertrude says to herself. "She's going to give herself to him now!"[82] Despite his flirting ways, Philémon ends up being exonerated when he confesses to Gertrude that she is the one he truly loves and has been since their first encounter.

Scenes like the ones found in *Le survenant amoureux* lead to indictments of male behaviour, judged as being weak and fickle. The heroes' hesitations become the source of numerous plot twists that reveal their fear of commitment. They are presented as potentially lecherous characters whose passions can only be calmed by their true chosen love. Though already observed in the preceding chapters, the situation has become more common: it is the men who are mostly responsible for the disjunction, due to their frivolity and infidelity. In *Mon beau soldat* (My handsome soldier) (1952), the situation borders on the ridiculous. Since he cannot meet the woman he thinks he loves (Suzy Jasmins) on the night of his return from war, Gabriel decides to go out on the town with Colette Lalande—who is in reality the one he really loves without knowing it, because she was the one writing letters to him on the front, which she was signing with Suzy's name. Gabriel spends the entire weekend with Colette, very surprised by the complicity that develops between them. He does not hesitate to kiss her on two occasions. "You are allowing me to be happy before she [Suzy] arrives,"[83] he explains in the simplest way possible... Reading these words, it is not surprising to find one of Éditions Police-Journal's titles exclaiming *Au diable les hommes!* (To hell with men!) (1952) and taking as its premise: "All men are brutes. They give you hope, awaken your passions and then, bam... they run away or sneak off."[84]

The subject of eroticism in dime novels merits one further observation. All too often, the acknowledgment of sexuality in the novels is seen to follow a curve that goes from censorship to free expression. According to this interpretation, the languorous looks of 1900 give way to kisses on the cheek in the 1930s, kisses on the mouth and neck in the 1940s, and sensual caresses in the 1960s, before giving way to actual sex scenes following the Quiet Revolution (a period of profound social and cultural transformation that took place in the 1960s and 1970s). From the point of view of the romance novel, this approach is misleading, because it overlooks the question of the sexualization of love itself. Before 1960, and one could even say before 1975, Québécois novels that base love on sexual relations are very rare. They are limited to evoking the physical attraction between the story's two main characters, that is, to eroticizing their mutual affection, without directly portraying the physical impulses they feel for each other. Repulsion toward obscene literature certainly played a role in this silence, but, more fundamentally, the body does not appear to be central to the romantic relationship in this literature, which based its fantasies on a more poetic, more ethereal aesthetic, even in stories that claimed to be daring.

In other words, the fundamental difference between the nineteenth- and twentieth-century novels is not that there is less sexuality in the former and more in the latter. It is the role sexuality plays in the expression of love that changes. While it is clear that the French literary tradition has not been averse to erotic currents (from Marquis de Sade to Pauline Réage), historically, women's desire had been sublimated into a quasi-religious experience. The founding novel of French romance literature confirms this: while the Prince de Clèves is dead and nothing now prevents her marrying the Duke de Némour, the Princess de Clèves renounces her desire in the name of her love. Postwar Québécois dime novels continue this sentimental tradition that makes love the founding act of desire. Eroticism is implied in relationships, making men handsome and, especially, since it is their only real capital, women beautiful, but they stop at any sexualization of feelings for women, who must continually defend themselves against the words and actions of men who are too forward in their advances. The female body can somatize the confusion and joys of the heart, but the heart should not be privy to the appetites of the body. In the dime novels, inclinations expressed through sexual impulses are judged to be lewd, vulgar, and dirty, and this condemnation is definitive for woman, leaving them in a somewhat strange state, where sexual desire, although their very means for attracting men, does not exist for them.

Between taking and being taken

The prewar romance novel generally did not recognize women's true equality in judgement and action. Placed at the centre of the story, the heroines, like the princesses of children's fairy tales locked in their towers, were not the masters of their destiny. More often than not, they waited for events (in other words, Providence) to make their dreams to come true ("One day, my prince will come," as in Walt Disney's 1937 song). In this literature, while the hero's identity was based on what he did, the heroine's was based on what was done to her. In general, women are described as passive, weak, and ingenuous "prey," whereas men are described as active, muscular, and "hunters." This sheds light on an intriguing fact: while the heroine is the main character of the stories, since her search for a spouse is more necessary for her than for him, marriage itself being her "vocation" and "career," she is not the primary agent of what is happening, a role delegated to the hero. This imaginary reflects a normative framework that still expected men to make the "first moves,"[85] invite the woman to dance, take the lead, make the first kiss, propose marriage, and so on.

All of this can still be found in the Éditions Police-Journal novels. The roles given to the heroines are neither monolithic nor unique, and there is a proliferation of characters in the industrial production of romance dime novels that never ceases to amaze. That said, though the heroine of the Éditions Police-Journal novels enjoys more autonomy in her pursuit of a good match than in the past, though she does not only hide and suffer while awaiting an outcome beyond her control, in short, though the inequality of the sexes—presented as natural and universal—does not entirely inhibit her ability to take initiative, she is still very often torn by events and reduced to crying in silence. Her newly acquired freedom only confirms rather than denies her inability to face the world without a man by her side. Her vulnerability is just one of the obstacles on the path to her affirmation as a woman, among many others that vary according to the author's imagination.

Louise Duval, the heroine of the book by Mimi Estivale, *Au bord de la faute* (On the edge of failing) (1947), provides an interesting trajectory by evoking several recurring themes in our corpus. Like so many other characters of romance novels, she is a motherless orphan who has also partly lost her father, because he is a drunkard who cannot fulfill his parental obligations. The author exploits Louise's opportunity to live unhindered romantic adventures. She confides to Marc: "my father takes very little care of us all… I mean with respect to our comings and goings…"[86] Worse, before driving off to spend an evening with Marc, Louise's father practically pushes her into his arms, leaving her surprised and even upset by this breach of parental duty: "'Go on kids! Have a good time,' said Mr. Duval as he was going back to the house. 'Have fun and don't think of anything! You're only young once.' He let out a grotesque laugh that luckily muted the noise of the motor. Louise felt uncomfortable, sensing the implication of these words."[87]

This precocious and total freedom leads Louise "to the edge of failing." Tired of the family burden weighing on her (she has to take care of her young brothers and sisters and give her salary to her father, who spends it on alcohol), she comes very close to revolting by giving herself to Marc, the son of the boss of the company she works for. "I told you that no one cares about what I do! I even feel like not going back at all, if that can calm your fears!"[88] The story of a first car ride outside the city's limits conveys the sexual tension of a hot summer night, during which "no breeze" stirs the leaves, Louise complains "that it is hot" and, above the sound of the motor, Marc can clearly hear "the young girl's panting breath."[89] It is during the second car ride that Marc feels "Louise's body no longer resisting."[90] "Immersed in the intoxication that washes over her," somewhat like her father unable to ward off the demon of alcohol, Louise is "burning with desire." "'Marc,' she says after a few minutes, 'Marc… take me anywhere!'"[91] This is all it takes to encourage physical contact, initiated of course by Marc, who "presses his lips on Louise's without her fighting it" and "prolongs the slow caress of his arms, the gentle pressure of his fingers."[92] As in many romance novels, this fondling is characterized by a brutishness that embarrasses the heroine, who feels invaded and trapped in her space. When Louise composes herself and tries to break free of his embrace, Marc "pulls her back close to him" and kisses her "angrily."[93]

Brought to the edge of the abyss, the young girl realizes too late that in seeking to become a full woman through the consummation of the sexual act, she is failing to meet the condition *sine qua non* of her change in status—her transition to marriage—and risks ending up in the "monstruous" condition of an "unwed mother." Luckily, Marc has fallen in love with her. He intends to marry her, but not without first being assured of the strength of her virtue. Before making a decision, he turns to the advice of his father, mirroring, in reverse, the heroine's relation to her father. After hearing his son's doubts about marrying Louise, because "he would only have to lift a little finger, and you know what would happen, right?", Marc's father makes the following ambiguous statement:

> Listen Marc, I don't know what advice you want from me exactly, but if you love her it's simple... You see, there are good girls and bad girls... Between those two, there are no other... And often, it is the man who turns the woman into a bad girl, Marc. You know, when I met Stella, your mother, when I knew that she loved me, I could have taken advantage of this unreserved love... Today I regret nothing...[94]

Strange advice, in sum, that ends with "What exactly did you want to know from me, Marc?"[95] Against all odds, Marc has understood: "'I know everything I wanted to know,' said Marc, 'and I thank you, dad.'"[96] From then on, he devises a plan. He decides to convince Louise to spend the weekend with him, without a chaperone, at the family cottage. What he doesn't tell her is that he wants to introduce her to his parents. It is a trap, in sum, to test her moral qualities. We understand that if she accepts to stay with Marc without a chaperone, without batting an eye, he will leave her.

Initially, Louise is thrilled at the idea of a romantic weekend. But, little by little, she is consumed by remorse, especially since, prior to her departure, her father has sobered up, promising new calm in the family home. Once seated in Marc's car, she realizes the full danger of the situation. And the more the heroine's unease grows, the more Marc tends to act "as master..."[97] Sitting in a car that is taking her who knows where, Louise oscillates between "regaining control of herself before it's too late" and "giving herself in advance through silent acquiescence."[98] It is in the conditional that she asks her escort if he "would agree to" making a U-turn and taking her back home. She then formulates her request more clearly: "I am serious, Marc. Very serious even... I would like to go back, even knowing you will think of me what you want..."[99] She insists again feebly until, powerless, she simply puts her fate in Marc's hands: "I have no way to force you to go back, Marc; to really expect that of you after having accepted without hesitation..."; to which Marc responds: "I knew that you would come to your senses."[100]

The transfer of Louise's fate is fully accomplished: faced with a father who refuses to fulfill a guardianship role, Louise must in principle assume her own freedom. But she is incapable of doing so, neither by giving in to carnal temptation, nor by resisting and preserving her virginity when she finds herself, isolated in a car engulfed by the forest, at the mercy of the hero. Her will is limited to asking Marc to fulfill his role as fiancé, which is to protect his love by taking her only after a Christian union. It is the hero who decides in the end. Louise's pleas to turn back are helpless against the determination of a man at the wheel of his car who resembles an animal ready to jump on his prey. The rest of the trip continues in near silence, because Louise, feeling "anxious," recalls "books she read about retreats in the woods where the hero would bring the heroine, counting on the discretion of a quiet servant to prepare the love nest and facilitate illicit affairs."[101] Marc is not worried about Louise's frightened demeanor; he knows he has saved her virtue, because his objective was not to deflower her, but to introduce her to his parents, who were waiting for them at the cottage. He thus expects that "soon the young girl will be loving and sweet and submissive again... He even thought to himself: grateful."[102] Louise's rescue is accomplished, Marc having heard in the young girl's protests *in extremis* the pangs of her moral conscience.

One might think the story's emphasis on the experience acquired by Marc (who "is no longer a child" and is "now a grown man" *a fortiori* since his return from war) has no other purpose than to highlight, by contrast, the heroine's weakness and inability to seize the reins of her destiny. It would be more accurate, however, to say that the opposition implicitly reveals the necessity for both protagonists to establish themselves in life, one because he is ready to assume the responsibilities of an adult (he was a soldier, an indisputable sign of masculinity), and the other because she already plays the role of mother for her brothers and sisters and can no longer be confined to the status of a child with an irresponsible father. The same obligation of autonomy nonetheless plays out differently for Marc and Louise. Unquestionably cast in the role of victim, Louise suffers hardships for which she has no antidote, short of her own death. This story, like so many others, foregrounds the theme of female suicide, and Louise thinks of this every time she is seized with despair."[103] Luckily for her, the end of the novel resolves the question of suicide as a solution to daily misery once and for all, when Marc orders Louise: "Never speak again of suicide! Neither of river, nor of stream!"[104] For her, love replaces death.

Based on a relation of opposition, the two main protagonists of *Au bord de la faute* conform to the usual model of the romance novel and are quite representative of this literature.

In the Éditions Police-Journal dime novels, as in romance novels more generally, the heroine is never complete: the hero is there to correct her original imbalance between deficiency and excess. In *Au bord de la faute*, Marc is the boss, Louise is his secretary; he is rich, she is poor (she gives all her money to her alcoholic father); he is the son of bourgeois parents, while her father is a source of shame ("her father is not worth much,"[105] observes Marc). But Louise's problem also stems from a surfeit of emotion, an excess regularly associated with a "feminine essence" in this type of production. The hero's assessment of his fiancée's personality is unequivocal and sounds like a condemnation: "Nothing about you is mediocre, nothing is half done. It is always extreme, in reactions and sensations, and this is all very bad for the soul and the heart..."[106] While the thirty-two pages imposed by the dime novel format do not provide enough space to formulate a clear solution to Louise's flawed temperament, the readers know that the presence of the hero, rich and determined, will ensure that her financial problems and anxieties are resolved.

A man leads to a home

Perhaps the greatest surprise to emerge from Éditions Police-Journal's "Amour" collection is that love is not the main quest portrayed. One might object that romance novels speak of love, that it is precisely their essential function and plot. However, in the works of the "Amour" collection that correspond to the three invariants of the romance novel, love does not occupy the place we might normally ascribe to it. Like the postwar Hollywood films that end with a kiss as the young protagonists begin their life as a couple, the "Amour" volumes stop just where the love story, strictly speaking, should be starting. Instead of describing a love story, they recount the characters' tribulations, from their first meeting to their final reconciliation, with all of the suspense centred on the multiple disjunctions that lead to the reunion in the final scene. The fact remains that the romance novels published by Éditions Police-Journal are not really interested in the description of love itself, whether with respect to the stirrings of the heart or the poetry of passion, and they are most often limited, in the available space, to portraying an initial love-at-first-sight attraction. When the story depicts characters who do not like each other at first, it makes this *quiproquo* an obstacle to overcome, which allows for a variation on the same theme.

In this sense, one could say these dime novels narrate the journey to love. And this outcome is so important because the real issue of these postwar texts is the girl's transition to womanhood, which in this period is only possible through the mediation of a husband.[107] The search for a man represents the woman's means for leaving the family home, something she would not be able to accomplish otherwise, despite the new possibilities offered by the job market. This is why meeting a man has such a central place in these stories.[108] This meeting camouflages a much greater purpose: in finding a husband, the woman can indeed be a "queen," "homemaker," and mother, but also become a person endowed with agency and free will, with varying degrees of autonomy. In other words, by settling down and starting a family, she makes, so to speak, *a room of one's own*. This redistribution of roles provides the underlying suspense in stories whose only acceptable outcome is a happy ending, since the alternative is far too tragic.

In an ideal world, the husband builds a "love nest" for her, a place where she can be fulfilled and that contributes to her freedom and happiness. In this ideal love, there is an immense promise of escape, comfort, and pleasure. The heroine of the romance novel moves from her childhood home and breaks ties with family and friends in exchange for the promise of finding bliss in a better life centred entirely on the couple, thanks to love. The assurance of the spouses' happiness in the conclusion of the story is expected to continue naturally for the rest of their lives, since true love can never die. It is this happy ending that female readers (married or not) aspired to in devouring one romance novel after the other. Are the letters to advice columnists not signed with pseudonyms like "Someone Wanting to Be Loved," "Someone Who Loves with All Her Heart," "Someone Wanting to Know Love"? Readers nourished the hope of meeting a handsome and generous "Adonis" who resembled the heroes in the love stories they avidly consumed.[109]

The most important theme of these dime novels, beyond the love story, is the woman's destiny being fulfilled by taking up her role in a home. This explains the narrow focus of the stories on an intimate world most often centred on everyday life, that is to say, the home, in stark contrast to the open, exterior spaces depicted in the crime, spy, and western novels also published by Éditions Police-Journal, but destined for a more male readership. Female characters enter the public sphere only for the time needed to migrate to their new conjugal space. In *Le doux pays des amants*, Marcelle dreams of seeing Kythira, the small Greek island whose mythology is associated with the pleasures of love, but when she gets there and sees the inhabitants' poverty, she is disillusioned. Before leaving again for more enchanting destinations, she has to return to her hometown to attend a funeral. That is where Raymond declares his love for her, giving her "all that [she] hoped for, all that [she] asked out of life." "Finally, my darling," he whispered quietly in her ear, "we have arrived... in the sweet land of lovers..."[110]

For the heroine of the Éditions Police-Journal, there is no *room of one's own* without a man. Since the convent is no longer an option for her, the only place outside the family home is the conjugal nest. "You don't understand," exclaims the heroine of *Dernier baiser* (1956), "that my future, my life, is you!"[111] Since the criteria for choosing a husband are based on the reciprocal attraction of two subjects, the woman's fate depends on discovering love. Without love, without a man, and thus without a home, the woman is either doomed to the fate of old maids, failures and outcasts, or destined to face social or even actual death.[112] Love must therefore be part of the story, even if it is understood that, because of this very dynamic, it may incorporate many practical, calculating, motivated, and "careerist" considerations.

Roman d'une orpheline (The novel of an orphan) (1946) tells the story of Sonia, a young girl whose father died while fishing and who was abandoned by her mother and left to the care of the Durand family. At thirteen years old, Sonia is adopted by Germaine and Richard Badeau, who need a maid. When she is seventeen, she meets Julien Houle, the rich son of a lawyer whose goal is to become a doctor. They fall in love and get married in secret. Julien's father objects to the union and has the marriage annulled. This is when Richard, madly in love, declares his feelings for Sonia. His wife Germaine is in the way, so he takes a gun and kills her. Sonia is afraid for her own life, but Julien, after a year-long absence, reappears as her saviour: his father has just died and he is free to settle down with the woman he never stopped loving. Not only can their love flourish, "merited by their suffering, strengthened by the ordeal," but, more importantly, Sonia, who has lived with others her entire life, will "finally have a home" and will be able to live "in the house of her dreams."[113] The novel ends with the image of "two very young silhouettes, embracing in a long kiss, in the pretty little house that Sonia and Julien call home."[114]

Since it would be unthinkable for a woman to set up house on her own, the heroines either bide their time in the family home until they are of age or move into a substitute family home that prepares them for the big leap into marriage. In an original way, *Au diable les hommes!* (1952) bases the heroine's desire for independence on her struggle to keep the apartment she shares with her best friend. Made wary by a man who had given her false hope, Réjeanne Gilon promises herself to never fall into the trap of love again. However, her desire to live a single life takes a rather catastrophic turn, since, without a man at her side, she can only afford to pay for an ugly "shack" full of "defects."[115] When she is informed of an increase in her monthly rent, she is outraged and decides to wage a legal battle against her landlord (while raising public awareness through a very contemporary method: a "sit-in" in a park!). After epic confrontations, Réjeanne falls in love with the opposing party's lawyer, and they end up getting married. We learn that the rent will be reduced to its original price, but this fact is rather symbolic, because Réjeanne will no longer be living in her shabby apartment.

In *Dernier amour* (Last love) (1947), Rolande Garnier has just married a widower, Luc Dercourt, a rich and attractive insurance broker who lives in Outremont. The disjunction begins the moment the newlyweds set foot in the opulent home, where Eugénie, the old cleaning lady and staunch defender of Germaine's (the dead wife's) memory, is in charge. Thus begins a war between Eugénie and Rolande, which revolves around governance of the household and leaves Luc totally passive and powerless. It is important to emphasize the extent to which Rolande's goal is not so much to be loved by Luc as it is to literally conquer the Outremont home, by getting rid of the cleaning lady and the memory of Germaine. "How would Rolande take living in the house of… the other?"[116] After insisting on ordering sirloin steak from the maid for supper, Rolande tries from that first night to bend Eugénie to her will. From the outset, she proves to be a better bookkeeper than the old servant by teaching her a new classification system for the bills. This intervention instantly elicits Luc's admiration: "Luc was looking at Rolande. A new woman had just been revealed to him. A woman of authority that Eugénie would not easily sway. […]

He no longer recognized Rolande, and this new woman pleased him even more."[117]

From this moment in the story, Rolande is transformed into a cold and authoritarian character. She asks Luc's permission to redecorate the house, because she "finds the layout of the rooms terrible."[118] Luc himself "timid" and "stuttering" remains perplexed by Rolande's "sudden sour tone."[119] The next morning at breakfast, she brings it up again: "We'll take the large bedroom in front, leaving the one we occupy now for the guestroom."[120] However, this is the late Germaine's room, and Luc once again does "not dare" mention to Rolande that she would thus be sleeping in the room of her rival. Faced with his inertia, she takes him into this room only to discover that all of the objects that belonged to Germaine are still there and that the room is meticulously maintained by Eugénie, "who lets nothing accumulate that could sully this sanctuary..."[121] Rolande then becomes "furious" and "loses her temper": "The small bedroom will do for the new wife... Not the large bedroom, not the sun, the nice wall, the fresh evening air... oh, no!... The small bedroom... So you have never forgotten her, the dead woman?"[122] Even when she commands him to choose between her and Eugénie (or, symbolically speaking, between her and the memory of his dead wife), Luc remains indecisive, feebly defending his attitude on the pretext that speaking to Eugénie would "only exacerbate things."[123]

Meanwhile, Rolande has managed to effortlessly win over the friendship of Gisèle, the hero's little girl, without Luc's knowing it. He doesn't even have time to introduce them. They get to know each other while he is at the office and they soon become close. The cordial relationship that develops between them can be explained by the hero's original need at the beginning of the story, when he was looking for a woman to assist him with his daughter's education. It is only natural that Rolande take charge of Gisèle's education. The two women, aided by movers, reorganize the rooms of the Outremont house (which costs a tidy sum of $300, the narrator notes) and dismiss Eugénie, who is allowed to choose some of Germaine's clothes and promised a year's salary in compensation. Germaine's other effects are shipped to France "to clothe a poor cousin from that country..."[124] The couple can finally live completely happy in "their home," the story ending on the words of a remorseful Luc, who regrets not having known how to behave.

The underlying logic of the romance novel as the quest for a home is palpable in a work that, by contrast, reverses the usual tropes of this type of story. Though it does not respect the invariants of the romance novel, *Mère et fille rivales* (Mother and daughter rivals) (1953) clearly reveals the inseparability between husband and home, but in a finale that consummates the tragic failure of the quest. At twenty-four years old, Marcelle Lacroix no longer wants to be treated as a child. However, her mother watches her closely "like a leech." Marcelle meets a young man, Laurent, who is unkempt and unprincipled. One night when they have both had a bit too much wine, Laurent grabs her and pulls her onto the living-room sofa, where they make love. Since Laurent has just declared bankruptcy, marriage will have to wait. Marcelle's mother, a rich widow who resembles her daughter like a sister, has had her eye on her future son-in-law from the beginning, and she seizes the occasion to seduce him by promising to pay his debts. Marcelle discovers their secret when she catches them kissing and caressing each other. Unmoved by her daughter's outcry, Madame Lacroix declares that it is her home after all and that a daughter should not judge her mother. The unscrupulous Laurent ends up marrying the mother, hoping she will support him. Prisoner of a milieu that accepts neither abortions nor births out of wedlock, Marcelle leaves for Trois-Rivières to give birth in a private clinic, without telling anyone she is pregnant. Laurent begins to despise Madame Lacroix-Beaulieu who, sensing that her husband is cheating on her, has him followed and finds him in the arms of another woman. She renounces him and reunites with her daughter, who has delivered a stillborn child. Consumed by sorrow, she accompanies her daughter in her final moments. Meanwhile, Laurent dies in a car accident. Madame Lacroix-Beaulieu decides to sell her house and personal effects and enter the convent of the Soeurs du Précieux-Sang to wash away her sins.

In *Mère et fille rivales*, the heroine's obligation to move to a new home is first temporarily compromised by her lover's bankruptcy, then definitively by his assumption of the role of the father in the family home. Marcelle, who thought she had found in Laurent a path to a new identity as a responsible woman, is relegated to the status of daughter when she protests against the injustice done to her. Her mother is scathing: "Keep quiet, you insolent girl… After all, I am in my house."[125] No longer having a place of refuge, Marcelle could have accepted her infantilization, but since she is carrying a child, an irrefutable sign of her transition to adulthood, she finds herself cornered with no way out. All she has left is to give birth in secret and die. Laurent, for his part, married to a rich widow who "has the dough" and only loving her like a son-in-law, spends his days having fun and wasting his wife's money, in other words, acting like a child. He will have to die too, because a child cannot marry his mother. Madame Lacroix, having failed in her task as a parent by playing the seductress must also die by retiring from the world. "Deep down, she was not a bad person… She was coquette and had lost her senses somewhat… She was well paid… Everyone was unhappy… Happiness was no longer possible in this house."[126]

The texts of dime novels hammer home a seemingly simple point: the young girl must leave her milieu to know love, and she must know love to leave her milieu. The problem is that to think of marriage she can no longer be a child. The man must desire an adult woman, that is to say, someone who demonstrates relative independence and maturity, even in an embryonic state. However, the transition from girlhood to womanhood involves a double ambiguity. On the one hand, the husbands-to-be, who are ideally seeking equals, continually treat their fiancées as minors, which legally they are. Thus, in *Le courage de l'amour* (The courage of love) (1947), Marcel tells Jeanne, an orphan in her early 20s, that he will give her a spanking when he comes back to see her, which he does, laying her over his knees and referring to her as a "little girl." [127] '—To see and hear you, one would think you're only 15 years old. —It's a little too young for you, eh?' I said mockingly."[128] Marcel retorts by asking his "ambiguous lady" to kiss him other than "as a child of 15 years old." The Lolita fantasy (Vladimir Nabokov published his novel in 1955) is not far off.

On the other hand, since the sign of women's maturity is their sexual awakening, the novels' heroines are already partly women under the family roof. In *Dernier amour*, the author defends the idea that a thirteen-year-old can already be considered a big girl. This adolescent maturity is inevitably expressed through a sexual affirmation. Luc, the father of young Gisèle, is dismayed to learn that his daughter has twice kissed (oh! "very chastely") her "knight-servant," "a very nice 14-year-old schoolboy."[129] His new wife however sees no problem with it: "At her age, you would have never spoken of kissing so casually... But she is of her generation, and don't forget that at 13 years old, these little ladies know more than we think... and know the difference between a chaste and an unchaste kiss..."[130] This discovery of the woman's condition as a sexual being in a person still seen by her parents as a dependant is fraught with tension. Some young girls are at the mercy of paternal figures who try to coax them into their beds and have to fight off advances of unfit fathers or stepfathers.[131] In *L'enfant de la misère* (The child of misery) (c. 1945), a sixteen-year-old adolescent is impregnated by the husband of a couple who adopted her after her parents' death. "I'm like a good father to you, no?"[132] says her adoptive father after abusing her. Women are depicted as either remaining a child in a woman's body or experiencing womanhood from a child's point of view. It is thus not surprising to find an implicit paternalism and incest in many dime novels of the period.

In romance dime novels, the quest for love represents the search for a place where the ideal of the girl as object of maternal affection and the idea of the woman as object of sexual desire are reconciled. A place, in other words, where the heroine can be both belittled and desired. On the one hand, the heroine is a child, a little girl. She appears very fragile in the arms of her virile, strong, valiant and accomplished fiancé. On the other, more than ever, there is no love without sensuality, without eroticism. In *Nuit divine* (Divine night), for example, the story revolves around ridding the heroine of her girlish "sentimentality" so she can transition to the status of an adult woman. "The man in him beckoned the woman and not the child, the young girl still brooding in Denise. He had counted on his wife being a woman—not a weak, uncertain and doubting child. And Paul had been right."[133] After much turmoil, Denise becomes enough of a woman to give herself to her husband, and enough of a child (the men sometimes call their women "dolls") to let herself be led by him. She will be rewarded with a nice marriage that will reconcile her identities of girl and woman, ingenue and vamp.

Rich and virile men

It is worth considering what fantasies or dreams are included in the romance dime novel, beyond the heroine's immediate point of view. What does this type of production tell us about the latent "musings" of postwar Quebec at the outset of a period of unprecedented economic growth? To begin with, one could say that, well beyond the simple valorization of the city or technology, the fictional discourse gives ample space to financial questions and displays a clear admiration for material success. This is perhaps not surprising given that these novels were addressed to people who suffered, directly or indirectly, the hardships of the Depression and saw economic prosperity restored during the war. But if wealth is so important in these novels, it is primarily because money, success, and consumption signal that the characters are ready to stand on their own two feet, which is particularly crucial for the men, since the responsibility of supporting the family rests on their shoulders.

The worst flaw for a man is to be an idler or a drunk, which ultimately amount to the same thing. A man who refuses the Protestant work ethic can achieve nothing of value. Not having a job or a stable situation is akin to admitting incompetence as a provider and disqualifying himself from the outset as a suitor. Continuing from the previous literary period—particularly at the height the bourgeois novel's popularity—, the man must be a good catch, which means to be prosperous or at least destined for a comfortable life. Wealth is a mark of autonomy, and the model man earns a good living and can provide material security and comfort for his future wife. But many of the Éditions Police-Journal stories nonetheless caution their readers. Not only is the world of luxury restricted to those who know how to use it properly, but it must also by all means stay under the cloak of love. Without affection, wealth is a trap, just as sexual desire without love is reprehensible. Women cannot be interested in men only for their money, because this would encourage a sort of "legal prostitution." Those who measure the size of their partner's wallet before searching their hearts have unpleasant surprises in store for them.

This is what Marie learns the hard way in *Cendrillon et son beau prince* (Cinderella and her handsome prince). Marie is engaged to Louis Laporte, who the family has nicknamed "the Prince of Wales." While hospitalized following a minor surgery, she hears a visitor say to her bedside neighbour that Louis has been having a love affair with a married woman for the past twelve years, which he intends to continue after his marriage. Adieu calves, cows, pigs, meals at the Ritz, and honeymoon in Havana! Marie will instead marry Marcel, a broker from Toronto who loves her "with a love like everyone else's."[134] And now that love is really part of the equation, wealth is possible. Marie's mother, who had been poor her entire life following the premature death of her husband, marries a wealthy businessman who lives in Outremont and often works in Toronto.[135] Marie is not left out: she receives an immense inheritance from the mother of Pauline (whom Louis happily betrayed her with), since Pauline and Louis have drowned to death after an ugly dispute in a rowboat.

Cendrillon et son beau prince stipulates that the husband of Marie's mother, a certain Mr. Lambert, is originally an American and that his name should be pronounced with an English accent, even if he speaks "an excellent French."[136] This remark is not innocent. The characters in the "Amour" collection stories reference a dream world that has become almost exclusively American and is revealing of the aspirations of a readership looking to new models.[137] This admiration for Americanness[138] is evident in the representation of space, in a trend that had already begun with the bourgeois novel of the 1930s. Whether going on a honeymoon or simply taking a vacation, the characters often travel to the United States, with New York being a favourite destination. That this space belongs primarily to the world of fantasy is more than obvious: there is no need to provide lengthy descriptions of the American city when simply mentioning its name will suffice. Given how vague the geography is, one may think that the authors never set foot there.

As noted above, male characters in the Éditions Police-Journal romance dime novels had to be rich, but they also had to be virile. And what is more virile than a handsome soldier?

Rare are the works that do not include, in one way or another, a reference to a world conflict, even if only as a backdrop. They do not hesitate to make use of the narrative possibilities of war as a theatre of exceptional exploits.[139] Produced far from the whistling of bombs and battlefields, the romance literature series seem to have retained only the heroic side of war. More often than not, the male protagonist enjoys the double status of a war hero and an accomplished businessman, combining the ultimate attributes of the perfect husband: physical strength and wealth.

In *Nuit divine* (1949), the homage to materialism and virility is complete. Both rivals and friends, Paul and René are vying for the love of their childhood girlfriend Denise. Their trajectories as self-made men seem exemplary: both men started out delivering newspapers, then worked in golf clubs instead of partying like the rest of their peers, and now own nice cars. "René's radio business has been doing well for several years, and Paul owns two gas stations in the city."[140] They are, at least due to their material success, men worthy of being loved. In this respect, the emphasis on Paul and René each having their "own car" is important. The luxury, often "convertible," car has the advantage of being both an exterior and interior space, where intimacy fluctuates between the pleasure of being seen or being hidden. It also powerfully combines the otherwise contradictory sentiments of security and freedom, saving and ostentatious spending, work and leisure. As for the heroes' fortune, it obviously ensures material comfort in a cozy home but also leaves open the possibility of escape. While the husbands return from work to their warm and restful homes, the wife cannot escape her condition as a housewife, so she dreams of staying in chic hotels that represent, for her, a privileged outing beyond the private space.[141] The honeymoon becomes a symbol of the bliss awaiting her as a wife and the freedom she is left with, once confined to the domestic sphere. This is why it is invested with so much magic and glamour.

Denise in *Nuit divine* is continually falling ill and fainting, like "a flower broken from its stem that has closed its petals."[142] Her fragility calls for a man of exceptional courage and determination. To find out who will be her chosen one, the two men in her life, René and Paul, will have to accomplish a series of exploits on the front as soldiers. René is the first to get a promise of marriage from Denise, but by a twist of fate he dies from cold shock after falling in a river, before even having the chance to prove himself on the battlefield. In a revealing association between war and love, the narrator assesses his love in these terms: "The young man lost everything, the chance to serve his country, the chance to die for his love, for his wife."[143] Denise, the grieving fiancée, endures a loss that she has no way to leverage socially, as she explains to Paul: "It is not only that René is dead, that I lost him. If he could have given his life for his country, I would have been proud despite my pain. But now—oh Paul! I have no one to give to my homeland."[144]

Denise has no choice but to marry Paul. But their wedding night ends in an argument that signals the lovers' disjunction. Believing that all is over between them, Paul offers Denise an official separation, but she refuses: "No, I cannot. I will never separate from you, as long as you are in the navy!"[145] Paul is surprised by this wording, which seems to leave very little place for affection: "He let out a wry laugh. [...]—And that's the only reason you refuse to separate?"[146] Not long after, Paul leaves for the front where he distinguishes himself by his bravery. "This world-weary man, whom death does not want to take" becomes "the greatest hero of the Canadian Navy." He "receives the highest decoration from the Prime Minister" and "the newspapers publish his photo."[147] All's well that ends well. Returned home, Paul is rewarded for his perfect virility, glory, and fortune with the heroine's total gratitude. There is no longer any doubt that he will be able to support Denise in her career as a wife, which she is preparing to fully and unequivocally embrace.

A sweet happiness

Examining the letters addressed to advice columnists in newspapers from the 1950s, one senses the extent to which many women were unsatisfied in their relationships.[148] A few of them, living on farms, compare their fate to that of a beaten and mistreated horse. They dream of a marriage based on tenderness and understanding, but the columnists in charge of answering them espouse a very conservative discourse, for a long time even insisting that "a woman who is a truly woman needs to be dominated."[149] They do not hesitate to remind their readers that while the husband has a duty to protect his wife, she has a duty to obey him, which clearly sets the terms of their relationship. Love is linked to marriage, marriage to procreation, and procreation to maternal devotion, to the salvation of the "race" or to a divine sacrifice, with little consideration, in the end, for marital affection.

The romance dime novels convey an entirely different image of the couple. In line with the expectations of the young generation,[150] the woman to be married with a crown on her head (as seen in the photos of the period) is presented with the image of the marvellous and magical couple worthy of a fairy tale. Romance dime novels focus on a brief period in the heroine's life involving the conquest of a man, because this search for love must end in finding a home. Nothing if not utilitarian, the "hunt for a husband" is cleverly sugar-coated but cannot hide this ulterior motive. In identifying with the novels' heroines, the female reader of the 1940s and 1950s can imagine herself exploring the streets of New York, frequenting clubs (like the *El Morocco* in Montreal, "the most chic club in town"[151]), drinking cocktails, going to see American films, driving around with a virile, rich, and attractive man, in a sports car... all this, thanks to love! "Gold diggers" are excluded from the race, because only those with a pure heart—like Louise in *Au bord de la faute*, who is said to be "thirsting for love" and susceptible to "a sort of complete submission,"[152] will be seen on the arm of the boss's son or a prosperous lawyer. It is Cinderella, not her wicked stepsisters, who is rewarded with the perfect marriage to a prince charming. In this sense, one could say that it is in the *interest* of love to be *disinterested*, that is to say, "blind," "free," and "spontaneous," the heroine's selflessness being ultimately the best "strategy" to attain her goal.[153]

There is perhaps no better way to highlight the discursive logic of postwar dime novels than by attempting a comparison to *Bonheur d'occasion* (*The Tin Flute*, 1947). Gabrielle Roy's 1945 classic and the dime novel do not belong to the same register, and it would of course be absurd to place them on equal literary footing.[154] However, they undeniably draw on the same fantasies.[155] As is true of the Éditions Police-Journal heroines, the happiness that Florentine Lacasse aspires to is one that involves an escape from her world, a way to access something better, where she might enjoy security, comfort, and inner peace.[156] When the young nineteen-year-old woman thinks of what Jean inspires in her, "all that she most longed for, admired, envied, swam before her eyes," and she imagines herself in the city with "its well-dressed, well-fed, contented people on their rounds of pleasure."[157] If one accepts our central hypothesis—that the romance dime novel is not so much a love story as it is the tale of a girl in search of a home—one can clearly see how Florentine embodies this quest. She wants to keep working, because, she "would have that much more" to leave a milieu she is ashamed of. "Giddy with pride and envy," she dreams of renting a house on Boulevard La Salle that is "almost as nice as the Létourneau place." "Why not? she said to herself. We have the money now. We're not obliged to live in Saint-Henri any more."[158] This house would allow her to escape a life of poverty, but it would also give her the opportunity to live in a home of her own, as "queen of the castle," and avoid

Radio monde et télémonde, 29 mars 1958, p. 8.

the fate of her mother, Rose-Anna, neglected by her husband and confined within the four walls of her apartment, without affection or hope.

The main difference between Florentine and the heroines in the romance dime novels, but it is significant, is that Florentine experiences the disappointment of love: at the end of the novel, she no longer believes in love. The hardships and disappointments she has suffered have hardened her heart "like a rock." "Her love for Jean was dead. Her dreams were dead. Her youth was dead."[159] This "love sickness"[160] envelops all of the characters in *Bonheur d'occasion.* Not only does Florentine's unhappy love backfire, but the other marriages in the novel also end in failure. Next to all of these "bitter-sweet love stories" (to borrow the subtitle of *The Tin Flute*'s English edition), the Éditions Police-Journal dime novels seem to recount entirely "sweet" stories of happiness, with the drawback being, however, that they are offered at a discount, so to speak. These are dreams on a dime that, though somewhat glitzy and enticing, still remain pathetic due to their "cheapness." Printed on low-quality paper, written in a hurry, and delivered without conviction, these stories of "sweet" happiness are perhaps no less sad than the disillusioned fates depicted in *Bonheur d'occasion,* as there is so much *sorrow* in their *enchantment.*

CHAPTER 5

Serial Love (1965-2000)

Completely overlooking the huge output of romance dime novels, a number of critics in the 1950s began lamenting the lack of true love stories originating from the Québécois imaginary over the past century. Monique Bosco, Jean Le Moyne, and Claire Martin, among others, claimed in unison that Quebec's literature had never produced anything but aborted or stillborn loves stories.[1] While the hypothesis of the general failure of romantic love in Québécois literature had long been uncontested, this supposed "disenchanted love" should have perhaps been read as a concession to the criteria of symbolic legitimacy. Once mass production had taken over the romance novel, the sub-genre was downgraded in the hierarchy of aesthetic values. It became systematically associated with entertainment and was considered even more degraded and insignificant because it was addressed primarily to women. Before the division of the literary field into spheres of limited and large-scale production, one could become known as an important writer even while publishing romance novels. Henceforth, this was no longer really conceivable. There were either writers worthy of mention in the histories of literature, or popular authors whose works were all the more easily suppressed, despite their massive output of titles and print runs,[2] because none of them seemed to stand out for their personal style or eloquence.

Once popular novels are taken into consideration, it can be easily observed that stories of triumphant love are not lacking in the pre-Quiet Revolution Québécois imaginary. One of the important postwar achievements was indeed to have combined love and marriage more than ever. In fact, to turn the question on its head, one has to ask not why love is absent in the Québécois novel before 1960, but rather why it indeed disappears as of 1960. It cannot be denied that the presence of love waned in the mass-market production at this time. While the Québécois romance novel had gradually gained an important readership, to the point of having its own widely distributed collections in the 1940s and 1950s, one might have expected its popularity to soar during the secularization of Québécois society. Instead, we witness an astonishing phenomenon: while a host of observers were stating at the outset of the 1960s that French-language Québécois literature was ripe for its first "true" romance novel, the entire romance novel publishing industry was plunged into crisis. For example, the Prix du Roman d'amour canadien was dissolved as soon as it was created in 1960, for want of manuscripts meeting the criteria of a romance novel,[3] and the publishers of romance dime novels (including Éditions Police-Journal) began closing their doors one after the other.

Quebec was not the only place to witness a decline in the romance novel. In France too, the 1960s was marked by the dark years of the *roman rose*.[4] Here as there, this sombre period did not end until the second half of the 1970s, that is to say, rather surprisingly, after the beginning of the sexual revolution. How can this disinterest, which lasted more than fifteen years (1962-1978), be explained? How could a genre that had generated thousands and thousands of stories, from the war to the end of the 1960s, have fallen into such stagnation? We propose three main hypotheses to explain this phenomenon.[5]

First, the internationalization of businesses in the postwar period likely facilitated the penetration of large European publishers and intermediaries of large American publishers into the French-language Québécois market. Mass-market literature lends itself particularly well to economies of scale, since the design and production costs of a book are fixed, with slight variations in printing fees, which increase very little when the print runs are large. In the 1960s, the Québécois romance novel thus lost out to a massive invasion of foreign products marketed by companies that could support large-scale advertising campaigns, along with an impressive catalogue of titles appealing to the varied tastes of their male and female readers.

Second, other cultural media probably began to encroach on parts of the romance novel market by presenting similar fictional scenarios in a more enticing form. This competition, which was already evident in the dime novel paratexts of the 1950s (for example, one ad from 1959 states that "Éditions Police-Journal publishes a romance novel every week [...] to read between your favourite television shows"[6]), became even more intense in the 1960s, notably with the arrival of Télé-Métropole (1961), which changed the face of television by offering more entertainment programming and drama series featuring women in more contemporary roles, alongside access to films that were a lot less censored (previously, when romantic films were not prohibited, scenes deemed too risky were cut out). In 1966, a young woman shared her story in an interview with the daily *Le Soleil*. She was eighteen years old, dreamed of marrying early, living in a pretty little house, and enjoying a quiet happy life. She would have been the perfect candidate to consume romance novels, except that she preferred listening to the crooner Bobby Rydell's albums and going to see romantic films at the movie theatre.[7] She probably resembled a lot of girls her age who, at the same time, were leaving reading behind in favour of popular songs, television dramas, photo novels, and films on the big screen.

Third, the codes of love also undoubtedly changed, which would in turn have an impact on the consumption of romantic

Amour digeste, no 5, p. 36.

stories. We know that the "flapper" works by Berta Ruck, Ruby M. Ayres, Netta Muskett, and Denise Robins (featuring emancipated young women who smoke and frequent jazz clubs, among other activities) were rarely translated into French (eight works out of 130 in 1940[8]) and more or less unavailable to the Québécois public for a long time. But the inverse was also true: Delly's novels or photo novels were never absorbed into the English-language romance market.[9] This is because British and American romance novels focused on different outcomes than their French counterparts, a fact that obscures their belonging to a common core of romance literature and parallel reproduction of many of the same motifs and clichés (such as the man's virility and the woman's fragility). At the cost of being overly schematic, it appears that, at one extreme, the English-language romance is more haunted by the possibility of sexuality without love, whereas, at the other extreme, the French tradition seeks more to sublimate a love without sexuality. While numerous British-American works recount stories of women threatened with assault and rape until the day love is declared (see the English classic *Pamela: Or, Virtue Rewarded*),[10] many French novels are constructed around the scenario of a woman who loves a man but cannot give herself to him (see the French classic *La princesse de Clèves*). From this point of view, the more "raw" sexuality described in the works in English compared to the "poetry" of the French works, stems from a more sexualized depiction of love (to the point of tolerating rape and normalizing flirtation)—as opposed to a romanticized sexuality (to the point of being removed altogether or euphemized in a "respectable" eroticism).

This opposition within the same romantic genre between Anglo-American "romance" and French "romance" is essential to understanding the evolution of the romance novel in Quebec starting from the Quiet Revolution, and it is this central hypothesis that forms the basis for our analysis leading up to the final chapter. To begin, we will develop our first observation regarding the Québécois romance novel being marginalized by the emergence of new platforms and media. Our second angle of analysis shows how, in the 1970s, Quebec novelists appropriated the typical British-American narrative structure to produce "rape sagas." Following this chronological progression, we will examine the huge success of the Harlequin romance novel, which seems to occupy the entire space of romance fiction in the 1980s. Returning to our central theme, we end by observing a relative resurrection of the romance novel in Quebec just where we might least expect it: young adult novels. This last section allows us to set the stage for the last chapter, where we postulate that "chick lit," which ensures the survival of the Québécois romance novel in the 2000s with a renewed narrative structure, owes its popularity in part to the rise of youth literature twenty years earlier.

Competitors to the Quebec romance novel

The general disinterest for the made-in-Quebec romance novel in the post-Quiet Revolution period can be linked in part to the resumption of French and Belgian imports after the interlude of the war, which kept European French-language publications off the Québécois market. Jean Pastureau provides a staggering list of French romance novel collections produced between 1939 and 1973, whose influence, as we know, did not spare Quebec.[11] What particularly hurt Québécois publishers was the appearance of French paperback collections offering inexpensive books, like the very popular Marabout (1949), Hachette's "Le Livre de poche" (1953), and J'ai Lu (1958). A 1984 analysis of the book market in Quebec found that, as a result of these developments, popular literature (including romance novels), which represented half of the French-language book market, was almost entirely abandoned by Québécois publishers to the benefit of foreign publishers.[12] The Québécois romance novel simply couldn't survive in this saturated commercial environment, where exoticism more than regionalism held sway.

While the invasion of the Québécois book market by foreign businesses played a clear role in the decline of romance novel publishing in Quebec, it does not explain everything. One need only recall that, in the 1960s, the book sales of Delly, Magali, and company also fell in Quebec, even though these authors were still very popular.[13] It was thus not only the romance book market in Quebec that was in crisis, but the global romance market. This was partly due, as mentioned above, to the competition of other media. Romance novels were in effect facing more and more direct competition, especially from television and cinema. Radio stations had of course long been broadcasting soap operas with romantic content, but this genre, outmoded with the advent of television, also went downhill in the 1960s, as though the visual element brought something irreplaceable to romance that orality and writing could not provide in a satisfying way.[14]

The founding of Radio-Canada in 1952 had already transformed the cultural landscape of Quebec. The proliferation of television sets in homes, the installation of broadcasting antennas across the province, and the addition of more programming hours (in the beginning, state television only broadcast eighteen hours per week) drew a growing number of Quebecers to the small screen. The arrival of Télé-Métropole (1961) brought even more variety to the television menu by adding more entertainment shows on top of the informational programming, which made it possible to meet the public demand for romantic stories. Starting in the 1960s, televised series began more openly expressing the intrigues of love and presenting female characters playing the roles of sweethearts and lovers with less restraint. Movie theatres were also showing a host of romantic films that were no longer subject to the wrath of censors. It is thus hardly surprising that, as revealed in a 1965 survey, French-speaking people were increasingly consuming their love stories through these two mass media. Even among rural and farm families, "love stories" were the "preferred subjects"[15] of television shows, and when French-Canadian families went to the movies, the survey showed, it was primarily to see "romantic films."[16] All of this inevitably eroded the romance novel market.[17]

One medium that is hardly ever mentioned but that directly impinged on the romance novel market is the photo novel, which was enormously popular "because it talks about love."[18] Originating in Italy in 1947, the *fotoromanzo* quickly spread to Latin countries (including those in South America) and entered francophone countries through widely distributed magazines. These magazines quickly found masses of buyers in Quebec. A survey conducted by the Ligue ouvrière catholique in 1960 revealed that a very large number of Quebecers, deaf to the advice of the clergy, were reading, in addition to the "little novels for 10 cents," the French magazines *Intimité* and *Nous Deux*.[19] In the 1960s, close to half a million photo novels were sold in the province per month.[20] "If you're not yet a reader of the photo novel," one writes in 1965, "you better start. Because these image books are published more and more, and you can't be fashionable without knowing the latest literary innovation of the century."[21] Fifteen years later, when the genre was in decline, there was still a million readers of photo novels in Quebec.[22]

The photo novel owed part of its success to its hybrid character, midway between the novel and the film, very close to comic books. In one photo novel scenario, the link is even explicitly highlighted: "This romantic drama made them cry, excited them, and at the same time gave them a kind of perverse pleasure, like the romantic dramas they saw at the movie theatre."[23] Presenting a "story between several characters, generally a conventional, melodramatic fiction, recounted in a succession of evocative photographs, accompanied by brief dialogues and commentaries (bubbles and legends) and published in popular magazines,"[24] the photo novel directly borrows elements from the seventh art: casting, directing, filming, and editing. They are "filmed" on sets with actors and actresses but "published" as stories linked to the feuilleton tradition. Also, the photo novels' use of known music and film personalities likely contributed to the readers' fascination with this popular genre par excellence, the power of fantasies being now measured using the yardstick of fame.

While the Québécois market was almost totally dominated by French productions and adaptations, we found evidence of a number of series published in Quebec. Even though the life span of these initiatives was very short in each case, a sign of the heated competition from foreign publications flooding the province with their unsold copies, they generated a certain interest on the part of the general public. There were a few newspapers (*La Patrie*, *Grand Journal*), magazines (*Femmes d'aujourd'hui*), and individual entrepreneurs[25] who tried their luck in this new commercial field and produced publications that, forgoing other photo novel genres (science fiction, detective, erotic, heroic) all seem to belong to the romance register. At the beginning of the 1960s, Éditions de l'Équipe (the same publishers behind *Amour digeste*, a magazine consisting of two or three short romantic pieces in each issue), launched the *Le Photo-Romans* [*sic*] *Canadien*, with catchy titles like "Ève et l'amour," "Simple et candide," "L'inviolable Catharina," "Amour interdit," "Destin tragique," and "L'amour d'un raté."[26] Featuring personalities like the actress Nicole Lord, the actors Jean Coutu and Serge Laprade, and the singers Tony Massarelli, Michèle Richard, and Monique Jetté, the magazine sold for 50 cents per copy. Around the same time, Éditions Publi Ltée published at least one photo novel shot in Montreal titled "L'école et l'amour,"[27] an imposing volume including no less than 500 images.[28] Éditions Populaires imitated them by publishing the photo novel "Le lit vacant,"[29] with the participation of Rosita Salvador. Toward the end of the 1960s, another business, Phototek, published a few issues distributed on a monthly basis from the collections "Mystère," "Aventure," "Passion," and "Amour" and sold for 15 cents each.

The overall presentation is of rather poor quality in these Québécois fictions. The texts in the legends sum up stories repeated in a few simplistic exclamations in the speech bubbles (stretched out on a bearskin rug in her apartment, a young girl cries: "Victor doesn't love me anymore. Boohoo! Boohoo!"), all the while offering up scenarios full of dreams and desires. The tension between a demand for realism and a demand for fantasy sets the tone for a production that can be described, on the one hand, as an overly prosaic depiction of ordinary and personal situations, and, on the other, as a pitiful succession of dramatic twists and pathetic stereotypes. The scenarios oscillate between insignificance and improbability. This paradox stems from the fact that the story recounted in the photo novel is reduced to fate, just as in the tales of old, but without a castle, prince, or princess. Abandoning any stylistic or aesthetic considerations in favour of a basic transposition in images, the photo novel exacerbates, in its simplicity, the basic elements of the romance novel by structuring them along a string of binary oppositions: her and him, innocence and aggrievement, weakness and strength, softness and hardness, purity and interest, etc.[30] Prisoners of these dichotomies, the stories unfold without finesse or subtlety, very crudely exposing certain cultural norms regarding the couple in contemporary society.[31]

The stories in Québécois romance photo novels, just like their French counterparts, rehash the classic "girl meets boy" scenario and resemble in many ways the dime novels studied in the previous chapter: two characters, a man and a woman, consumed by loneliness, must overcome various obstacles, helped or hindered by secondary characters who play the roles of assistants or opponents, before finding happiness in a communion of bodies and souls. Having little space to develop their stories or portray situations, the stories begin *in medias res* and get straight to the essential, magnifying the characters' traits, exaggerating the expression of feelings, making outrageous comparisons, and multiplying Manichean situations. The typical story of this popular production features a young girl almost systematically lacking support and obliged to work as a servant, typist, or factory worker. She meets a young man who has suffered misfortunes. Seducers and schemers lurk around them. The heroine is subjected to insults that she combats with abstention, abstinence, and abnegation, the cardinal virtues of women who structurally resist the "penetrating" (and *ipso facto* always potentially aggressive and dangerous) action of men. She will be rewarded with an honest marriage to an upright and hard-working man, who is not necessarily very rich.

In *Le correspondant impossible* (The impossible pen pal), published around 1969, Mireille and Sylvain no longer get along. In secret, Mireille has begun a writing correspondence with Gérard, whose romantic words excite her. When she meets him, she is disgusted by his ugliness (he has a huge nose) and makes it clear that they should no longer write to each other. Gérard persists and threatens her. Mireille confesses everything to Sylvain, who then asks his friends to help him teach the harasser a lesson. Mireille recognizes she was wrong to want to fall for someone else, and she accepts Sylvain's marriage proposal, insisting on the fact that she pays more attention to moral qualities than physical ones. Her new passion for Sylvain is based on his being more attentive than before, having not hesitated to fight for her.[32]

In 1980, Paf loisirs, owned by Belgian immigrant Henri Desclez, published *Romance*. Produced with a bigger budget, it was one of the last publications to make a foray into the genre, at a time when the golden age of the photo novel had come to an end. Though some of the Paf loisirs issues were translations of Anglo-Canadian series, the periodical nonetheless reserved space for local works. In "À toi pour toujours" [For you, forever], (1980) Julie is a secretary at an advertising agency. Unlike her colleague who spends her weekends watching television and eating peanut butter sandwiches, Julie believes she has found perfect harmony with Yvan and easily resists the advances of Paul, a photographer said to be unfaithful. But suddenly Yvan announces by letter that he is leaving her to marry someone else. When she meets Paul in a park, Julie realizes that she is the one "at fault" and nothing but a "foul egoist." The two begin seeing each other. Julie discovers that Paul hides a deep wound, caused by a woman who betrayed him. He is not hard-hearted because he is incapable of loving, but because he once loved and was scarred by it. By sharing his pain and opening his heart, he confirms that he can once again feel something for a woman whose intentions are selfless and pure. The fairy tale is complete. Their kiss awakens the man's dormant heart and the woman's dormant body. She is desired thanks to her love (for him), and he is loved thanks to his desire (for her).

Julie leaves Yvan to live in an apartment. She sees Paul in a restaurant with another woman and they argue. She seriously injures herself falling down a staircase and learns that she will probably never walk again. She pretends she no longer loves Paul in order to spare him the burden of caring for a disabled person. Later, seeing Paul again in a park, she makes a superhuman effort to approach him and is able to walk again. Knowing that she cannot live without Paul, she tries to find him and shows up unannounced on the doorstep of the house he has just purchased. A pregnant lady responds. Certain she has lost Paul forever, Julie berates herself and flees. But Paul runs after her and finds her as she enters a subway station. He tells her that the woman she saw was the wife of his brother and that he had never stopped thinking of her. The story ends with a kiss and these words: "Yes, my love! Kiss me! Love me!... forever!"[33] All of these events and plot twists occur over fifteen pages. It seems an image really is worth a thousand words!

It is easy to see the photo novel's countless variations on the theme of two people separated by obstacles on a quest for love: a possessive mother, a reversal of fortune, a morbid jealousy, a hypocritical rival and *tutti quanti*. This production offers readers the same experience as the romance novel but with less investment of time and effort. The photo novel's popularity attests to the Québécois imaginary having never renounced the triumph of love when other genres besides the acclaimed literature are included in the analysis. Both male and female readers still had a thirst for love. What changed is that they no longer inevitably sought this out in the pages of dime novels or Québécois novels. Other media, like the photo novel (but also television dramas and Hollywood films), peddled the same dream in a new form that was appealing, accessible and, as of the 1960s, taking over a growing part of the Québécois romance novel market.

Rape sagas

The third explanation for the absence of an important output of Québécois romance novels from 1962 to 1978 was, as mentioned, a dramatic change in the grammar of love that directly affected the romantic story script. It would have been astonishing for the social and cultural transformations of the Quiet Revolution to have no impact on romance literature. One of the most notable changes was that married women no longer had the status of being "incapable," a status that legally subordinated them to their husbands, like children to their parents, and women now had legal autonomy. The adoption of the first law legalizing divorce upended the questioning of love after marriage and made spousal affection an essential condition for staying together as a couple, now continually threatened by a breakup that was not only possible but increasingly common. Previously focused on the bungalow and family, love, devoted to the union of two completely free beings, became even more than in the past the ultimate purpose of married life.

Another fundamental change is that sexuality came to represent one of the avenues to love. With "free love," pre-marital sex, and rising divorce rates, the woman had to not only erotically entice a suitor on the way to the altar[34] but also find a way to keep him after their sexual relations were legitimatized in marriage. Henceforth, she had no choice but to accept love being expressed through sexuality. For the first time, she could be liberated in her desire. This revolution is evident in the shift in meaning of the expression "faire l'amour" (making love), which had previously been synonymous with "faire la cour" (courting).[35] It acquired the new meaning in Quebec at the end of the 1950s, which it already had in France and the United States since the 1920s. While in the past one could "make love" without sex, it was now possible to make love without love, though, ideally, the couple expressed their love by making love and made love to each other to express their love.

These transformations are reflected in the romance novel. In traditional stories, the celebration of love was a way of denying sexuality. The hero's decency was a sign of respect and affection, and, conversely, the vamp trying to seduce with flashy dresses and garish makeup represented a carnal desire at odds with the true love inspired by the young heroine who was chaste and innocent. Now that love was related to nothing but itself, it could more obviously integrate the sexual dimension, and sexuality came to occupy a more important and central place in the love stories, which had a decisive impact on the codes of fictional writing. It would be wrong to interpret this recognition of the place of sexuality as a simple evolution toward "free love." More fundamentally, it reveals a transition in literature from a type of love more common in Latin countries (inclined to gallantries, less common in the American corpus) to a more British-American type of love (inclined to divorce, as in the screwball comedy tradition, less present in the French corpus).[36] There is an illusion of continuity between them, because the stereotypical characters and central themes of the stories are the same: a young and pure virgin girl seeks a virile and powerful husband. Nonetheless, beyond these similarities, the drama that plays out in these stories is not really of the same nature.

What changed between the French and British-American romance novel traditions, as Anne-Marie Lugan-Dardigna rightly observes, was not the story itself but the issues at stake. While French romantic fiction revolved around "the price the heroine must pay for order to be restored in a given situation,"[37] the new focus was on knowing "how the heroine will end up submitting to the man who desires her."[38] The difference between the French and English romance novel traditions can be summed up in an image: on the one hand, the woman loves before feeling desire, and on the other, she desires before feeling love. In the first case, she must suffer a lot to atone for a desire nonetheless purified by her love, confronting several obstacles up until the final redemptions. In the second case, she must first experience her desire outside of love, which is only permissible by sublimating her fantasies and unconsciously playing and replaying rape scenarios. While the woman who loves ends up in the arms of a husband reformed of his old unfaithful ways (Magali's heroines, temporarily abandoned by their spouses, immediately come to mind), the woman who desires ends up in the arms of a lover who has become her love (the fate of Lady Chatterley, in the 1928 novel of the same name, is a good example).

The influence of the British-American literary tradition is especially palpable in Québécois works towards the end of the 1970s, in the wake of a feminist and sexual revolution that made the woman a desiring subject, not only an object of desire. The emergence of women's carnal desire paved the way, as we shall see, for a veritable sexual violence that replaced the French tradition's "noble" virtues of mortification and abnegation. Québécois writers of the period did not hesitate to directly borrow from the universe of *The Flame and the Flower* (1972), translated as *Quand l'ouragan s'apaise*, by Kathleen E. Woodiwiss, or from *Sweet Savage Love* (1974), translated as *Amour tendre, amour sauvage*, by Rosemary Rogers. These two American authors launched the trend of "rape sagas"[39] and contributed to popularizing a romantic code that had discreetly infused the British-American novel to some extent since the publication of Samuel Richardson's classic.

Author Marie-Claude Bussières-Tremblay (born in Chicoutimi in 1945) was representative of this new wave. Between 1978 and 1981, she published eight romance novels in rapid succession, including *Tendre Rachel* (Sweet Rachel), the first volume of a very popular trilogy. While, according to the Presses Sélect ad published in the newspapers, *Les oiseaux se cachent pour mourir* (*The Thorn Birds*) by Colleen McCullough transported readers to Australia, and *Nostalgie d'amour* (*After the Dream*) by Charles Kaufman, to Spain, *Tendre Rachel* was said to possess "the strength of our roots and our land."[40] However, since it takes place in Fort Hills and portrays characters with English-sounding names, Bussières-Tremblay's historical novel draws more on the usual plot of the British-American romance novel, amalgamating the most archaic elements of the genre (for example, the confinement of a weak heroine by a violent hero), while spicing up her novels with a sexuality clearly borrowed from the rape sagas. What indeed stands out most in the first tome of the series is the representation of a sexuality based on a power dynamic that goes so far as to justify aggression.[41]

Presented by her publisher as "vacation reading," *Tendre Rachel* sketches out the characters' identity from the first

Marie-Claude Bussières-Tremblay, *Tendre Rachel*, Montréal, Presses Sélect, 1978.

pages. We discover how the intrepid Rachel Conway trespasses on forbidden land and ascends the perilous Tête d'Aigle rock on horseback. When a storm breaks out, she is forced to take refuge in a cabin with the brutish Randolf Brewer, who she will have to marry to restore her reputation, even though there is no physical contact between them during the two nights spent together (the novel takes place in a distant past when, it is said, women's virtue had to be absolutely protected). Rachel is immediately disgusted by her marriage to an unfaithful seducer who has no qualms about sleeping with a series of women neglected by their husbands. She detests this man who is however immensely wealthy, the owner of a grandiose estate and "extraordinary with his imposing stature, his surprisingly wide shoulders, his muscular chest and arms, his strong and powerful neck."[42] Far from succumbing to the charms of a "man whose beauty made him worthy of an Olympic god" and yet is also a "mountain man, half beast, dirty and repulsive," she tells him to his face that she hates him "with all her heart."

We are on familiar terrain here. The heroine of Bussières-Tremblay's novel must learn to submit to a master, and the hero must recognize and develop his capacity for romantic feelings after having mourned the loss of a first love. The friction between two people affirming their individuality in discovering their complementarity (and thus becoming the "other half" for one another), creates a powerful tension, with every gesture being potentially interpreted as an opportunity for an attack or betrayal. What changes is that the heroine's love blossoms into a sexuality that is no longer taboo, without the female character being granted the agency to actively explore physical pleasures. Instead of surrendering, Rachel fights her desire for Randolf. Accepting to be his confidant and nothing else, she intends to maintain platonic, if not to say "frigid" relations with him, given that she is disgusted by the idea of sexual relations with a man. The novel goes as far as denouncing Rachel's puritanism. When Randolf realizes that her sexual education has made her disdain the union of bodies, he must initiate her himself to carnal pleasure. "Stop resisting, Rachel," he orders her. "There's nothing you can do, no more than the others. You are made like this, you of the weak sex, [once] a big, strong, virile man attracts you and makes you vulnerable."[43] Randolf teaches her that normal women "seek adventure, especially with strapping men who yearn to make them tremble with passion," and they "tease men with their pretty dresses, proactive gestures and beguiling looks,"[44] sometimes playing the offended virgin all the better to arouse them and get them into their beds.[45] Men think of nothing else, and, when he sees a woman himself, he never thinks of anything but her "alluring" body and "intense sexual appetites." He asks Rachel to reflect so she can understand "that there is nothing ugly about the human body and nothing dirty in copulation."[46]

Randolf's remarks are rather shocking, especially when associated with "male instincts" presented as "normal." "I'm not a dangerous maniac escaped from an asylum," protests the hero of *Tendre Rachel*, "but a normal man with normal reactions in conditions that are out of the ordinary."[47] Bussières-Tremblay's story does not even try to veil its underlying violence, as we see in this discussion between Randolf and his wife: "'Next to you,' says Rachel, 'I am so frail and your words seem so bizarre to me! Am I in danger?' He ogles her for a moment then starts laughing loudly, more than amused by her uneasy demeanour. 'You are very funny. Do you think Bluebeard warned his wives before killing them?' he asks mockingly. 'Would Blackbeard do otherwise?'"[48] Later, he slaps Rachel and, in another scene, feels authorized to rape her. Rachel, "powerless" under "his heavy body," is unable to wrest herself from his embrace. "Her screams are stifled under Randolf's mouth. She hits him with her fists [...]. Rachel no longer understands anything, and twists about to express her protest, to prevent him from pulling back the covers, from tearing off her clothes... in vain. When he gets up after his crime, he hurls triumphantly before leaving: "And what will you do now? Is there a law against a man raping his own wife?"[49]

Rachel soon becomes pregnant. The story nonetheless has a happy ending. Rachel finally agrees to physically surrender to Randolf, and he realizes that he has always been in love with her. "Only you exist, Rachel," he says at the very end of the novel.

"Only you can quench my desire, my needs, my hunger for your body, your embrace. [...] Forget my brutalities; tell me again that you love me, every minute, every instant. Everything will become easy." He leans over her, "his heart beating, to gently kiss her mouth. Finally, her feminine arms embrace him."[50] At the end of the story, the impenetrable hero and the young virgin are in a certain way intertwined, one accepting the intrusion of love (refused in the name of a masculinity that is insensitive to feelings), the other, sexuality (condemned in the name of a disembodied femininity). The cold-hearted hero and the frigid-bodied woman warm each through their contact with one another: both his heart and her drives are awakened, making an emotional and carnal fusion possible.

It is clear that the sensual historicals that Bussières-Tremblay adapts in her works seek to combine fairy tales and American dark romance stories.[51] Another novel by Bussières-Tremblay, *Suis ton destin* (Follow your destiny), also published in 1980, constructs a new scenario around the same violent power dynamics between men and women. Set in 1969, the quintessential year of the sexual revolution, the novel describes a young woman's attraction to a journalist, Jean-Luc Sullivan, who works in the same building as her and is always at the wheel of fabulous cars. "Luc [is] my little girl crush, I admire him. With his sports car, his prestige, he is so handsome, magnificent, so solitary and mysterious..."[52] Patricia finds a way to approach him and, after having too much to drink, lets him take her like a "child" to a hotel of ill repute. Jean-Luc takes advantage of her drunkenness, has his way with her, and leaves the city soon after to cover an important story abroad. Having lost her virginity and with no memory of her night at the hotel, Patricia finds herself pregnant with a "bastard" child. Not surprisingly, the story puts the blame on her: "I behaved foolishly, like a lovestruck, blind college girl."[53] She decides to keep her son, who she names Stéphane, and raise him alone. She meets Ronald Semey, who convinces her to marry him one day, whenever she's ready. Ronald has pale skin, a thin torso, and nervous hands, quite unlike Jean-Luc. Though gentle and understanding, he does not have experience with women, and his only sexual encounter with Patricia is disappointing, like a bad dream.

Jean-Luc reappears in Patricia's life. She discovers that he has done jail time for theft and drug trafficking. Forced as a child to prostitute himself with men by his incestuous mother, he split her head open with a shovel! Later, he beat women to the point of sending them to the hospital, killed a man who was after him for sleeping with his wife and raped at least one minor! No matter! Patricia cannot resist being madly attracted to him. In any case, what can she do? Her own four-year-old son, Stéphane, wants his "real" father. To drive the point home, Jean-Luc saves his son's life, then hers. One night when they are together in a cottage in the Laurentians, Patricia understands how hard it is to resist a man with such a muscular and athletic body, with skin so tanned from the sun and wind, and hair so blond. "She [is] conquered by his gruff and energetic manners, seduced by his air of an untameable devil and skilled conqueror, enthralled by his animalistic audacity."[54] Stretched out on a bearskin rug, she sees him suddenly lean toward her. "She struggles a bit, for the form of it, seeing his male face approaching hers and, when Jean-Luc's hungry lips meet hers, quivering, intoxicating, she feels all resistance melt away. How thrilling is the taste of his kiss!"[55] Mad with desire, Jean-Luc throws himself on her like an animal.

After their session, Jean-Luc reveals to Patricia that on their night together at the hotel four years earlier she had declared her love to him. "Today," she had exclaimed, "is the most beautiful day of my life! I'm going to become a real woman with you in my arms!"[56] She had confessed that night, while they were making love, that she was the happiest woman in the world. He too had been transformed by this night spent in the company of a virgin, something he had never known in his womanizing days. He realizes that he needs her, that she represents his last chance to be happy. "Jean-Luc began to laugh, a huge weight was lifted, that of his past, of a whole life... He would be a man like any other, a man loved and loving in turn, a husband, a father. It was over, the torture of his shameful past. Patricia knows everything and accepts him as he is."[57] He agrees to recognize his son and become a good family man.

Marie-Claude Bussières-Tremblay was not the only author to offer British-American style stories to Québécois readers. *Une biche pour le tigre* (A doe for a tiger) (1980), by Micheline Perron (born in Saint-Félicien in 1949), combines so many saccharine clichés that one loses count.[58] Having agreed to take part in an expedition to the farthest reaches of the Amazon to find a lost city, Patricia Corelly becomes the assistant of Christopher Van Dork, an archeologist whose reputation as a tyrant has earned him the nickname of "Tiger." Her first impression of her boss is based on his "animal" qualities: a bronze chest "studded with dark hair," an imposing stature, very muscular, a square jawline, jet-black eyes. "She can't resist admiring the virile strength that emanates from his entire person. How could one not have confidence in this man whose whole being seems to emit an assurance and spirit of unshakeable decision. His arrogant jawline and insolent look only accentuate the impression of steadfastness that he gives off."[59] By contrast, Patricia is described as a frightened doe, a child or a little girl.

Reciprocally defined as hunter and prey, the characters are attracted to each other. He undresses her with his eyes, examining the curves of her breasts and "perfect" hips. She feels "attracted by his virile body" and feels the "crazy desire to caress his manly chest, to feel those muscular arms wrapped around her."[60] Christopher comes close many times to taking her, without her being able to resist his attacks, but he stops just when she feels she is wavering, thinking his assistant is nothing but a "slut." He plans to teach her a lesson. From the novel's first pages, Tiger's misogynist and heartless words reveal him to be "an arrogant, proud and cruel man." Patricia does not hide her contempt. "'I hate you,' she spits in his face [...]. 'You're nothing but an insipid and cruel monster. I detest you...'"[61] Disconcerted by his kisses, she hurls at him: "And especially never try to touch me again, you repulse me...!" She swears to never again cede to his advances, "even if he were the only man on earth!"[62]

Yet she loves him and is only waiting for the moment when she will have the courage to tell him. One evening, back from their expedition, they find themselves at a party. With a brusque move, he grabs and holds her until she tires of resisting him. The doe, caught in a trap and unable to escape, lets herself be conquered by the tiger, because she knows that Christopher is no longer trying to fight off love. In the name of this sentiment, the rape becomes legitimate.

The characters of Bussières-Tremblay's and Perron's novels oppose each other due to their misperceptions of the situation. The disjunction arises from a misunderstanding that sets the characters against each other, making them adversaries. Love is transformed into hate. "I hate and despise you! Get away! Leave me alone! You are vile! You disgust me!" cry the heroines to those deemed unworthy of their affections. The confrontation turns violent. In these works, the man becomes hard, intransigent, and the woman becomes enraged and rebels. He pushes and shoves her, squeezes her arms. Frightened and exhausted, she gives in. The final pages have all the magic needed to resolve the misunderstandings and reunite the characters that were once tore apart.

We will not dwell on the staggering accumulation of clichés found in this type of production. What is original, at least on this level, is that the female characters in the works by Bussières-Tremblay and Perron like or learn to like the sensual pleasure of the sexual act, to not be afraid of coitus or the orgasm (even though these two words are never mentioned). The stories are filled with sexual tension, the heroine's obligation of virginity being lifted in scenes of rape and violence. Only at the end, in a sort of *deus ex machina*, are we reminded that one has to be in love to make love. The moral is preserved. However, romance novels written in Quebec had never gone so far in their contrast between a heroine, albeit rebellious and proud, who is confined, abused, and raped and a hero who seems a lot more like a beast than a prince charming. This hint of sadomasochism contains the seeds of future successful works like *Fifty Shades of Grey*, which we will return to in the next chapter.

The Harlequin explosion

It is not surprising that Québécois authors wanted to benefit from the success of the British-American romance novel tradition. In 1982, more than half of the books sold in Quebec were popular romance novels, the equivalent of ten million books.[63] However, within this market, works by American and British writers, like the ineluctable Barbara Cartland,[64] became increasingly popular and eventually outperformed the novels of Delly and Magali, which had formerly enjoyed such an immense success in Quebec.[65] A sign of this upheaval in the publishing world, in 1978—the publication year of the first volume of the *Tendre Rachel* trilogy—the Harlequin publishing house made a comeback on the Québécois romance novel market, after its first aborted incursion from 1958 to 1962,[66] and seemed destined to overtake everything in its path.[67] Soon, half a dozen, then a dozen new French titles were distributed by Harlequin each month in Quebec, with average sales of around 20,000 copies per novel. Total sales, which had already reached more than three million copies per year in 1981, climbed to a spectacular five million in 1985.[68] Across North America, the company, which had never been so dominant, controlled 80 percent of the romance novel market.[69]

Sketch of a 'clinch cover,' Fonds André L'Archevêque, P859, S2, SS2, D1, BANQ.

Clearly, something was happening in the world of romance that went beyond the adoption of more effective marketing strategies. In sum, the period saw a shift in the centre of gravity from "sweet romance" to a new dialectic relation between love and lust. Of course, Mills & Boon, which became Harlequin after the British company's purchase, had linked love and sex from the very beginning.[70] But the heroine's obligatory virginity before marriage was hermetically sealed, preventing any intrusion of real physical passion. The sexual revolution disrupted this overly prudish scenario. Seeing the success of *The Flame and the Flower*

(1972) and *Sweet Savage Love* (1974), published by its competitor Avon, Harlequin began introducing more-or-less veiled elements of the "bodice ripper" sub-genre (carnal desires, savage passions) in texts intermingling pain and pleasure, cruelty and tenderness. Stories with evocative titles (*Une envoûtante surprise* [An enchanting surprise], *Un désir inavouable* [An unspeakable desire], *Passion aux Bermudes* [Passion in Bermuda]) are filled with women in their early twenties who, despite almost always being sweet, sensible, frail and innocent, are fatally attracted to discovering their sexuality in the arms of a virile, savage and rich man in his thirties. Known as the "clinch,"[71] and emblematic of the Harlequin series, the cover image depicts a woman and a man partly undressed, locked in a passionate embrace. Though Harlequin was an immense factory churning out the most hackneyed sentiments, reiterating the well-known boy-meets-girl formula for the enjoyment of its readers, we should not overlook the sensual revolution that it set in motion and led to an explosion of the romance paperback market in Quebec as elsewhere in the world.[72]

According to some sources, 95 percent of the Harlequin readership is composed of women, and the company's directors primarily target them. In their discourse, they make use of the "eternal feminine" myth without batting an eyelid. In their words, "the woman is a woman everywhere in the world."[73] The truth, however, is that they have continually modified their French translations to meet the needs of their Québécois readership. The company, having learned from its past mistakes, adopted a marketing strategy that was both sophisticated and aggressive. This entailed a partial rewriting of the manuscripts in order to adapt the originals (written by British writers up until 1976, before bringing in American talent with Janet Dailey) to a new public. The head editors were not simply choosing from a stream of stories most likely to interest the readership of each region. The cultural references were also tailored to the expectations of a public primarily seeking relaxation and escape, but without leaving their comfort zone. The locations thus had to be just exotic enough to offer readers a change of scenery, but just familiar enough to not be too disorienting, which meant including the usual fantasies and clichés.[74]

The pioneering works of Julia Bettinotti and her team show that while the Harlequin novel's basic framework is quite fixed, it allows for a multitude of variations adapted to the different expectations of its readership, depending on their age, education, and socialization, as well as, more generally, their tastes, norms, and values.[75] Consistent with our hypotheses, what stands out in the translations for the Québécois public is that the raw descriptions of the characters' sexuality present in the original English version are erased and replaced, in the French translation, by more elliptical and sensual scenes. Contrary to the English text, which moves from carnal passion to tenderness, the French translation works in the opposite direction, with the exploration of the intimate giving way to a poetic, ritualized and almost mystical sensuality. A translator working for Harlequin confirms this: "The sensual scenes have to be 'toned down,' because the North American point of view differs from the French point of view. North Americans are culturally more pragmatic, and the sensual scenes are described in a rather precise, detailed, even cold way. In French, we work a lot more with suggestion, imagination, the unsaid, the feeling."[76] Instead of describing the sexual act, the French version focuses, for example, on the heroine's thoughts in the arms of her partner. The same holds true for marriage and the family, which recede more into the background in favour of a more dreamy, romantic, and poetic love. In English, consistent with the British-American literary tradition, the Harlequin novel represents a path to follow, a concrete objective (sex should lead to love, which then should lead to marriage), whereas, in French, it suggests more of a dream, a utopia (love should lead to sex), which is what justifies the censorship, in the French versions, of scenes in which sex is initiated by the woman.[77]

The Harlequin romance is often seen as an easily mastered formula that mechanically repeats simplistic, heavily formatted scenarios, being to literature what paint-by-numbers is to art. To make fun of the genre, Louise Leblanc published a parody in 1983 that won the Prix Robert-Cliché: *37 1/2 AA*.[78] This pastiche suggests that anyone who comes along could write a Harlequin romance novel. However, attempts to introduce romance collections in Quebec capable of competing with the international company were all unsuccessful. The marketing strength of Harlequin, which at the time already had an archive of 8000 titles, seemed unsurpassable. While encouraging subscriptions (which stabilized costs, reduced intermediaries, and eliminated returns), in 1981, the company counted 6700 points of sale in Quebec located outside of bookstores. More than half of the production was sold in grocery stores, and the rest in pharmacies, depanneurs, and metro stations.[79] Moreover, drawing on the knowledge of many sales and marketing experts, Harlequin made sure to gauge its target audience by increasing its surveys, focus groups, and readers' parties.[80] By privileging the romance category as opposed to single-title romance books, the romance novel giant's collections could meet the varied and precise tastes of its readers. Especially popular in Quebec were the collections Azur, promising "La force d'une rencontre, la magie de l'amour" (The power of an encounter, the magic of love) and Horizon, advertised under the theme of "Une famille à inventer, un bonheur à construire" (A family to invent, a happiness to build). These effective strategies explain Harlequin's ability to crush any competition. Two failed attempts by Québécois publishers to enter the romance novel market shed light on this situation: that of Cyrano (in 1991) and VLB éditeur (in 1998).

Having had their manuscript returned to them by Harlequin because it was written in French, Catherine Brisson and Gina

Élaine Sinclair, *L'espace d'un été,* [Laval : Cyrano, [1991].

Élaine Sinclair, *Patrouille de nuit,* [Laval], Éditions Cyrano, [1992]

Rosito founded their own publishing house in Montreal in December 1991, which they called Cyrano (the French film *Cyrano de Bergerac*, directed by Jean-Paul Rappeneau, had been released the previous year). The two women aimed to print one new romance novel per month "conceived and produced by Québécois authors"[81] and anchored in contemporary reality. With an annual subscription, customers received twelve titles at a cost of $3 each plus $2.10 for delivery, handling and tax. Brisson and Rosito thought they could capture 10 percent of the romance novel market in one year, but their hopes were dashed, and their adventure came to an end after the publication of only two titles from their collection "Évasion," *Patrouille de nuit* (Night patrol) and *L'espace d'un été* (It happened one summer).[82] Imitating the Harlequin works and limited to being ersatz versions of these, the two titles indigenized the Canadian giant's scenarios while embellishing the stories with a few local references (for example place names), but without changing the usual narrative thread.

Patrouille de nuit describes the torment of Vicki Wyllcox, a twenty-four-year-old police woman with brown hair, luscious lips, emerald green eyes, and slender legs. No man has ever resisted her. Born into a good family, she claims her independence and does not want to depend on anyone. The captain of her police station assigns her a new coworker, the twenty-eight-year-old Massimo Fiori, who is disarmingly charming. He personifies virility for her, with his black hair, steel blue eyes, arrogant nose, sensual mouth, feline gait and athletic body. The son of a wealthy entrepreneur, very cultivated, and a great conversationalist with a good sense of humour, he lives in Terrebonne in a pretty house bordering the Mille-îles River. Vicki falls under his spell. With him, she frequents the best restaurants, has getaways to Quebec City, is invited to a showing of the theatre piece *Broue*! One day, she gives herself to him:

> Massimo deftly undressed Vicki, while covering her in kisses. She gave in like a doll, because faced with Massimo's sensuality and virility, she knew all too well that she would be incapable of resisting and every ounce of her body desired this man. Then, he undressed himself in turn. She could not take her eyes off this magnificent muscular body. She surrendered completely to him. She had never imagined feeling so much pleasure with a man. Massimo made her his own and Vicki realized she would never be able to love another man like this, her love was so great.[83]

They encounter an obstacle on their path: Vicki cannot let go of the memory of Steeve Adornetto, a man she was in love with and who was killed two years earlier in a police raid. She feels guilty for betraying his memory, especially since he died trying to protect her. Towards the end of the novel, we learn that Massimo is in fact Steeve's brother and that he entered the police force to investigate his young brother's suspicious death himself. He did not reveal his identity before being sure that Vicki truly appreciated him for himself, thus explaining the troubling silences that led to the frequent quarrels between the two characters. Since he saved Vicki's life on two occasions (during a car accident and a hostage-taking), we sense that she must be twice as grateful to Massimo than to Steeve. Not to mention that she has become pregnant by him. Their reconciliation becomes natural and the novel can end on these words:

> She was ecstatic with pleasure. Massimo had made love to her like never before. Massimo gazed for a long time at Vicki, who laid by his side. "She's like an angel," he thought. He delicately replaced a strand of hair that had fallen on Vicki's forehead.
>
> — What's happening? she asked sleepily.
>
> — Go back to sleep, my darling, he said softly. Then he whispered: don't worry my love, because happiness can now be ours.[84]

L'espace d'un été is based on a similar framework as *Patrouille de nuit,* using the same motifs and sometimes even the same types of scenes. A recent orphan, the twenty-two-year-old Olga is a very attractive woman who is proud of her independence. One day when she is wearing jeans and a Guy Lafleur hockey jersey, people are amazed at how naturally beautiful and feminine she is. Studying to become a daycare school teacher, she accepts a temporary contract to look after the seven-year-old son of Tony Ramirez, a famous American architect who has moved to Montreal for business. Tony is a filthy rich widower of thirty-two years old, six feet tall, athletic, and oozing virility. Olga immediately falls in love with him, though promises herself she will resist this man who considers himself "superior." There is no lack of opportunities to detest him: she thinks he wants to take advantage of her, that he only wants her body, that he is in a serious relationship with a sassy American named Diana (although tall and with a model's figure, she has auburn hair, wears too much makeup and is over thirty), that he is seeking a mother for his son, that he wants to make her his slave. She keeps telling him he disgusts her and that she doesn't want to see him anymore. "Olga does not want Tony to know how much she could love him. — Leave me alone! I detest you! Then she slaps Tony and he pushes her violently after saying to her: — Go to hell!"[85]

But, whatever happens, Olga always ends up in her boss's arms. When he holds her, kisses her, and makes love to her (with a condom, it is duly noted), she feels transported "to seventh heaven." One sentence after another confirms it: "Never had Olga experienced such a sensation"; "Never had Olga felt so happy"; "Never had Olga felt so good"; "Never had Olga felt nor imagined that such pleasure existed." Having mourned his first wife and overcome the fear of suffering again, Tony sets out to conquer Olga. To curb his advances, she invents an affair with Steeve, a boy her age for whom she feels nothing but friendship. Enmeshed in both her own and Diana's lies (the latter having convinced her she was engaged to Tony), Olga is overcome by sadness, incapable of discerning what is true or false. Finally, realizing that their "relationship had been based on nothing but basic misunderstandings," Olga and Tony can confess their love. On the last page, Tony's son surprises them naked in bed and they tell him they are going to get married. All's well that ends well... over the course of one summer!

Patrouille de nuit and *L'espace d'un été* never managed to find their public. However, Éditions Cyrano's setbacks were no deterrent for the publishing house VLB, who in turn launched their own romance novel collection in 1998. Based on the back cover description, the "Tournant" collection promised dreams and emotions: "The birth of a great love is not an easy thing. Finding true love remains one of the most difficult quests. The lives of women and men who fall prey to this feeling are transformed by it, forcing them to make heart-wrenching decisions. The 'Tournant' is a collection of great love stories whose protagonists reach a turning point in their lives that might be their path to happiness."[86] The idea was to sell "intelligent" and "entertaining" little books of 200 to 300 pages signed by talented writers of popular appeal that were "well written" and "unpretentious,"[87] all of which was quite a gamble. In asking reputable authors to engage in "hack writing" and "commission" work under a pseudonym, Jean-Yves Soucy the director of the "Tournant" collection, took pride in allowing them to produce "light writing" without betraying themselves.[88] "Québécois writers wanted to explore new facets of their personality in writing this type of novel and maybe even embarking on a second career."[89] Moreover, by recruiting Québécois writers, he was aiming to add local colour to romantic pieces in a period of strong nationalist affirmation. "Of course," he admits, "we are talking about entertaining works that are accessible to a general public. But why not give readers stories that are written with a sensibility of our own?"[90]

The director of the "Tournant" collection planned on publishing four novels per year.[91] The inaugural novel, *Le cœur prisonnier* (Captive heart) (1998), by Béatrice Côté, the pseudonym, we are told, of a well-known writer, recounts a rather convoluted story. Julie Hénault, a thirty-four-year-old married bookseller, falls in love with Tom Stevens, an American movie actor engaged to a model. But she stays with Bernard, her friend from youth, who she is not able to betray, having believed he was the love of her life when she slow danced with him at a party. She remains at his side when he is struck by a rampant deadly disease. It is only once Bernard is dead that she regains her trust in life again and becomes involved with Tom. "Learning hundreds of lines by heart," confides Tom, "trembling at the first, sacrificing one's entire youth to ambition, is so much easier than saying 'I love you'... I'm loving for the first time, my darling." And Julie responds: "There's no second time, Tom. In love, every time is a first time."[92]

Just as with Cyrano's "Évasion" collection, *Le cœur prisonnier* is followed by only one other title, *Le rêve de Justine* (Justine's dream) by Michèle Brabant. In this novel, quite like the first, Justine and Mathieu (the latter married with children) are friends. Unsatisfied in their lives, they make a pact to attain their career goals, her as a writer and him as an engineer, but at the expense of the attraction they feel for each other. "I wanted him to pursue his dreams to the end," she moaned, "to not give up along the way, and I deeply hurt him. You know? I thought his dream should come before me, and I destroyed the only love that counted in my life. The only one!"[93] Twelve years later, their paths cross again by chance. Justine must now be nearly thirty-five years old, and Mathieu's children are teenagers or adults. Remembering their past love, they can no longer lie to each other and end up in each other's arms. "They remained for a long moment on each side of the door, uneasy, awkward, timid. The restraint that had weighed on them for so long made the least gesture troubling, the least desire agonizing, the least hope unbearable. [...] Then she held out her hand and put it in

Mathieu's. And this is how slowly, very slowly, they embraced each other and never wanted to let go."[94]

The two novels published in the "Tournant" collection did not meet the projected sales. The texts advertised as being "intelligent" and "cleverly written" failed on both counts: neither captivating nor well written, they were not accessible either. With their rather bland covers, hiked up prices, lack of physical descriptions of characters, absence of erotic passages, and neglect of the genre's stereotypes (the heroine's ravishing beauty, the hero's virility, the celebration of wealth and eroticism), the collection was dead in the water, just like that of Éditions Cyrano, six years earlier.

One of the main obstacles to appreciating the Québécois stories of the "Tournant" and Cyrano collections was likely their lack of exoticism. In its instructions to potential collaborators, Harlequin recommended that submitted manuscripts foreground travel, whether through space or, in the case of historical novels, through time. Integrating trips to foreign places was one of the strategies used to provide a change of scenery and enhance the element of escape, to the point that several passages in the Harlequin novels seem to have been taken, with little adaptation, from travel guides. The advertising promised characters involved in "romantic settings that will transport you to a new world, beyond the dullness of everyday routine."[95] The readers of Harlequin novels thus expected to discover, however superficially, places that were both concrete and dreamlike, where everything seemed possible. This is how enchanting titles like *La maison de coquillages* (The house of shells), *L'île aux mille parfums* (The island of a thousand scents), *La rose des Médicis* (The rose of the Medicis), *La jungle s'embrasa* (The jungle inflamed), and *Malakaï pour la vie* (Malakaï for life) held the promise of fascinating and exciting adventures, much more captivating than the ones offered by their pale Québécois copies. In *Patrouille de nuit*, holidays at "a big beautiful Canadian house" restored as an inn on l'île d'Orléans and supper at the "Le Québec d'antan" restaurant, serving pea soup and tourtière, have a hard time competing with the sumptuous villas, manor houses, ranches, and castles hidden in far-off regions where the enchantment of the place and magic of love intermingle. Set in a local décor and hopelessly banal, the Québécois substitutes for Harlequin novels were in some way condemned to fail from the start.

This publishing failure was not unique to Quebec. Attempts to compete directly with Harlequin were also unsuccessful in other national markets. For example, in France, the popularity of works by Delly, Magali, and Max du Veuzit abruptly declined with the introduction of the first titles from the Harlequin catalogue in French,[96] and the launch of local rival collections, like "Aventures et passions" and "Amour et destin" by the publisher J'ai Lu, would also see disappointing sales figures, with Harlequin monopolizing nearly 90 percent of the romance market in France in the 1990s. Publishing initiatives attempting to compete with Harlequin in Holland, Sweden, and Germany met a similar fate during this period.[97] One can only conclude that if Harlequin could be absorbed into the local culture, the local culture was not easily exportable to Harlequin. The inability in Quebec as elsewhere to create collections that could go head-to-head with the Canadian publisher not only reflects the company's impact but also its particular writing codes and paratextual elements, which only appear simple to those who have never attempted to master them.

The young adult novel

A number of Québécois authors published romance novels in the 1980s and 1990s. André Mathieu distinguished himself with a phenomenal production. Between 1978, the publication year of his first novel, *Demain, tu verras* (Tomorrow, you will see), and 2009, the year of his death, he published sixty-five books, including some romance novels.[98] A few other less prolific authors experimented with the genre, but, overall, romance novels for adults written by Québécois authors were rare. American, Canadian (Harlequin), British, and French publications captured nearly the entire market.

Though struggling to make forays into adult literature, there is one domain in which Québécois romance novels flourished: youth fiction. It should be noted that youth novels, all genres combined, were then enjoying unprecedented popularity across North America. In Quebec alone, the number of works addressed to readers under fifteen published between 1970 and 1990 went from six to 200, representing alone around a third of the total literary production.[99] Print runs regularly reached 10,000 copies per title. This popularity can be explained by the fact that young people preferred stories taking place in Quebec that they could more directly identify with rather than works focused on action situated in foreign countries.[100] Wanting to make the most of this boon, publishing groups began specializing in youth publishing. La Courte Échelle (1978), an offshoot of Éditions Le Tamanoir (1974), marked the generation that grew up in the 1980s. With their "Jeunesse/Roman" collection, launched in 1982, the publisher Québec/Amérique also carved out a place in this niche. As part of the social realist trend, the books of Québécois youth publishers sought to convey, as closely as possible, the real-life experiences of young readers.[101]

The problems evoked in young adult novels are concrete, sometimes painful, and the reflections found in them address subjects like life, death, mental illness, and drugs, but they also do not hesitate to provide their own original form of love stories.[102] Raymond Plante's *Le dernier des raisins* (1986) (*The Big Loser*, 1989), respects the three invariants of the typical romance novel, while managing to considerably renew the norms of the genre. Recipient of the Canada Council for the

Raymond Plante, *Le dernier des raisins,* Montréal, Les Éditions du Boréal, 1991. Cover illustration by Anne Villeneuve.

Arts Award and winner of the *Je suis livromaniaque* contest (to reward the most popular book among adolescents), *Le dernier des raisins* had such an important influence that some attribute a decisive role to it in the transformation of the youth novel in Quebec.[103] The story is simple, bordering on banal. François Gougeon considers his parents to be old-fashioned, especially his mother, who nurtures an outdated morality and clings to religious precepts. He lives in a "big and stupid" town in the Laurentians, Bon-Pasteur, where nothing important ever happens. The parish priest, Gilles Fortin, who is close to his family, still believes that relations between boys and girls are a source of corruption and sin. François makes fun of his sermons and almost sees religion as belonging to folklore.

On the first day back to school, François notices Anik Vincent for the first time in the high school hall: she is no longer wearing braces, and she wears makeup and dyes her hair. It's love at first sight. "There she was! Right in the middle of that big room where everybody's shouting greetings and talking all at the same time."[104] He is "girl-sick," with a "sickness you never quite get over."[105] Unfortunately for him, several obstacles stand in his way. He is awkward and shy, not particularly attractive, wears glasses, and has no talent for sports. Anik, on the other hand, is a real athlete and a formidable tennis player. "I was a loser. I was sure of it. I was a big loser."[106] To make matters worse, Anik has a boyfriend, Patrick Ferland, the son of a car dealer and one year older than her. Devastated, François devours, among other things, the complete poems of Émile Nelligan to drown his sorrows.

He desperately tries to find a way to get Anik to notice him. He can't sleep, his grades are falling, and he masturbates over issues of *Hustler, Penthouse*, and *Playboy* (the passages in question are nonetheless very discreet), all the while thinking of his crush. "Sex, sex, nothing but sex! I'm a bit obsessed with it, I'll admit."[107] While the high school is becoming a "hotbed of French kissing," François agonizes over not being able to seduce the beautiful Anik. He takes the school bus to run into her, sends her an anonymous Valentine's Day letter, plays a tennis match with her, which ends in disaster, asks her to work on a class project (on ads for the "Coup de coeur" underwear brand, whose slogan is "I pinched everything [from him], even his trunks," without arousing the least emotion from her. Everything begins to change when he makes a very successful class presentation, speaking of himself in unflattering terms but making the students laugh. He is invited to join the high school's improv league and helps his team win a match in overtime. Patrick tires of Anik and seems to be infatuated with a girl in his grade. During an altercation in a parking lot, Patrick violently hits François in the face. He collapses, his face swollen. Anik leans over and kisses him. All seems to turn out for the best: without even trying, he ends up having the best grades in his class, and his ease at winning improv league matches makes him a star at school. He caresses Anik "under her sweater." He feels all mushy. When she discovers his pink "Coup de cœur" underwear, she breaks out laughing: "Wow! Pink trunks with elephants! Super!" The tomboy girl has fallen in love with the sensitive guy (*homme rose*).

A similar plot is featured in *Une chanson pour Gabriella* (A song for Gabriella) (1990), by Bertrand Gauthier. Soon to be sixteen years old, Sébastien Letendre is overcome with heartache, because the girl he met in the previous novel left him for the captain of the school's sports team. "It's over, the beautiful dream of loving Chloé Beaupré for life! A first-class burial! And quite brutal! Passing by a locker, I see my dear Chloé. There she is, snuggling up with this other guy, kissing him. No mistaking it, it was really Chloé Beaupré in the caressing arms of Simon Lefort, the basketball team champion."[108] The pain is immediate, powerful. "But how do you protect yourself from the curse of heartbreak? How do you get over the devastation of lost love? It's a mystery. Nobody talks about it. Ever. When it happens to you, you're on your own. All alone."[109] He has to get the image of Chloé out of his mind, but he can't seem to do it. "Despite the great fear lodged deep in my heart, all day long, I yearn for a great love. Despite my bruised heart, I'm crying out for it, I want to taste love again in my life."[110] He feels too cowardly to fight Simon Lefort, this weakness being for him the sign that he is not yet a man, but on the contrary, "the most insignificant person on earth."[111] "It's obvious, I will never make a man of myself. And, deep down I have to admit it: I would have rather been a girl. At school, the teachers are always nicer to the girls."[112]

While the girls get noticed for their brilliant questions, the boys goof around. "I'm ashamed to be a boy."[113]

Less than a month after his breakup with Chloé, he crosses paths with a girl his age in the Espoir metro station. Judging by her strange behaviour, he thinks she is planning to kill herself. He thinks it would be atrocious to not help "such a beautiful girl" and abruptly grabs her to prevent her from committing the irreversible act. The young girl bites his hand deeply and runs away, thinking he is some kind of maniac. This bite mark seems to act on him like a love potion, sending a shock to his heart. He returns to the station several days in a row hoping to see her again. Finally, he finds her, approaches her, and realizes his mistake: she had only leaned over the tracks to feel the breeze of the metro tunnel on her skin. Sébastien gives her his telephone number and ardently awaits her call. The young woman eventually calls and invites him to meet her at the theatre to see a play. He dares ask her name. "Gabriella, Gabriella Sanchez, nearly 16, a heart filled with passion, a mind overflowing with ideas, a throat full of words, hands as warm as a June sun. Would you also like to know my Chinese astrological sign? I am a tiger. In the feminine, that makes me a tigress."[114]

What Gabriella didn't say, is that she is performing in the play and that she is even the one who wrote it. On stage, the young actress recounts her own story in a monologue, but without revealing the names. She explains how her family lived in Chile before Pinochet came to power and how, after the coup d'état, her father was arrested and tortured as a dissident, before disappearing. She speaks of her own suffering and her mother's sorrow and their thirst for justice. The audience applauds wildly. Sébastien is captivated by Gabriella's performance. "I think I have fallen in love with her. Without a single doubt. Madly, madly in love with Gabriella Sanchez."[115] Chloé (who has broken up with Simon) invites him to rent a film and spend the evening with her, but Sébastien's passion for the mysterious South American is not the least dampened. He begins taking intensive Spanish lessons and reading books on the history and geography of Chile. He has erotic dreams about Gabriella:

> Touching Gabriella fills me with desire. We caress each other. For a long time, gently, tenderly. And an immense pleasure sets in, infuses every pore of my skin. The great delight in feeling Gabriella's skin brush against mine all over.
>
> True paradise.
>
> Not only terrestrial, but cosmic.
>
> [...] I awaken suddenly.
>
> I feel all numb.
>
> I realize that, while I was sleeping, I must have ejaculated. The sheet is still warm and damp.
>
> Nocturnal pollution: the involuntary emission of sperm during sleep. Involuntary but rather enjoyable. Frankly, a better expression could have been found to define this so pure, so beautiful and so involuntary pleasure! No, I am not a polluter, I refuse to be. I'll leave that to factories, oil tankers, automobiles, smokers. Nocturnal, that can work. But polluter, never!
>
> In my dream, Gabriella and me, we were naked and beautiful, pressed against each other, cradled by our affection and immersed in immense pleasure.
>
> Is that pollution?
>
> In the minds of others, maybe.
>
> Certainly not in mine.
>
> What a delicious dream! If I could only replay it over and over![116]

But Sébastien is scared. He doesn't feel good about himself. "Suddenly I see myself in front of the mirror. I grew fast. I'm not handsome, not graceful [...] Who could love me? I'm not worth the trouble, not even a glance!"[117] And he has no talent. "What could a girl of Gabriella's calibre see in a guy like you? She does theatre, she is a musician, she is surely surrounded by handsome guys."[118] Next to this "talented, beautiful, fiery, lively, desirable and intelligent" girl, he seems way too ordinary, his life being only "filled with huge platitudes."[119] To impress her, he participates in a fundraiser for the poor at the Espoir metro station. She arrives just as he is about to sing a song he wrote for her and in which he professes his love. Gabriella takes him in her arms and responds "100 times yes" to his proposal to be "day and night, united in love, in the blissful joy of our bodies," while also asking him to cool his sexual appetite. For once, he feels perfectly fine in his body. "I will long remember this Saturday fundraiser at the Espoir metro station. The most beautiful day of my life. *Muchas gracias, Gabriella*. My love."[120] The "lamb" had managed to seduce the "tigress."

Other young adult novels feature heroines, instead of heroes, on a quest for love. In *Les vacances de Rosalie* (Rosalie's vacation) (1990), the twelve-year-old heroine is dating the red-haired Pierre-Yves Hamel. On vacation with Pierre-Yves in Florida, she is nonetheless courted by an American, Terry Wayne, who is a top surfer. One evening, Pierre-Yves catches them in each other's arms. Rosalie cries, not from sadness but from shame. "I realized that my great Viking hero was in trouble. That he was in danger. After all, dying of heartache can even happen to boys!"[121] Pierre-Yves decides instead to take a scuba diving course with the beautiful Anne, Terry's sister. To stop the attraction that seems to be growing between her friend and the American girl, Rosalie jumps in the water and pretends to be drowning so that she can be saved. The trick works and they are immediately reconciled. "Ashamed, I whispered in his ear: 'You forgive me, *Honey*!' Pierre-Yves Hamel made a surprised ugly face. He found the 'honey' so ridiculous that I had to promise I would never ever use it again."[122] On the last day of vacation, the reconciled lovers enjoy a walk on the beach. "Then the sun set. I took my big hero's hand and headed toward the dunes. I think we have never both been so happy."[123]

The lessons of *Le dernier des raisins, Une chanson pour Gabriella*, and *Les vacances de Rosalie* are revealing of a new way of writing the romance genre. Seven original characteristics emerge from these works and end up playing a decisive role in the subsequent history of the romance novel. In the first place, consistent with the broader evolution of the genre, sensuality and sexuality are no longer taboo, and the characters, though relatively young, evoke their fantasies, desires, and needs. "The love imagined by the heroines in the corpus as a whole," writes Marie Fradette in her analysis of Québécois novels for adolescents from 1940 to 2000, "must end in a solid relationship: for the French-Canadian heroines, love necessarily led to marriage, whereas for the contemporary heroines, it leads to a sexual relationship."[124] In the second place, anchored in a very franco-Québécois milieu, the works address concrete problems related to the transition to adulthood (menstruation, the first masturbation, contraception, etc.), which gives them a realistic tone that contrasts with the sentimentality of Harlequin stories. We see a blending of the romance novel and the coming-of-age novel, a combination that makes the initiation into sexuality a way of mastering the art of love, rather than the mastery of love being a preparation for sexual experiences.

In the third place, the fear of ending up alone, which in the past had almost solely haunted the girls, also now affects the boys, who are confronted with the possibility of never knowing love or sex, at an age when the teenage boy's confirmed masculinity depends on the seduction of girls. While most novels in the previous periods were written from the heroine's point of view (Harlequin made this one of its golden rules), a greater number of stories adopt the male character's point of view. In the fourth place, deconstructing the image of the tearful heroine and the chivalrous hero, the genre's stereotypes are blurred, even inverted. It is no longer a question of being confronted with a frail and weak girl and a determined and protective boy. We often see an inverse scenario unfold (the English translation of *Le dernier des raisins* is *The Big Loser*). In the fifth place, the adolescents affirm more than ever their independence from their parents. The latter are no longer there to chaperone or guide them, and school and neighbourhood friends occupy a larger place. In the sixth place, the stories are infused with humour. While they certainly tackle important issues, the characters never take themselves too seriously, defusing tense subjects with irony and self-mockery.

Finally, in the seventh place, *Le dernier des raisins, Une chanson pour Gabriella,* and *Les vacances de Rosalie* recount that it is possible to get over a heartbreak and to love more than once, which seems to be self-evident in the case of adolescent love. It is accepted that love can be temporary, that monogamy does not prevent different romantic situations from unfolding over time, which the mention of the characters' divorced parents serves to highlight. "My parents are separated," confides Sébastien to Gabriella. "I wonder why they get married, all these people, if it's only going to end in divorce. It totally boggles my mind, not you?"[125] One must learn to live with a mortal love. Knowing that love is fleeting, the characters engage in serial monogamy, having several partners they love over the course of their lives, while remaining faithful at the time of their relationship. A reflection of this transformation, satisfying endings come to gradually replace happy endings, shared lives and marriage proposals (whereas in the 1980s, half of the Harlequin novels end on a formal promise of marriage).[126] The characters no longer seek the total fusion of hearts of nineteenth-century romanticism, the complementary functions of the bourgeois novel, or the home-sweet-home of dime novels. The goal is more prosaic: it's just about being together, for a period of time at least. These elements provide some of the ingredients of the "chick lit" to come, and it seems likely that some of Courte Échelle's readers were the same ones reading novels by successful authors like Rafaële Germain a few years later.

Rafaële Germain, *Gin tonic et concombre*, Montréal,
Les Éditions internationales Alain Stanké, 2008.

Sexlove

After a period of uncertainty that followed the Quiet Revolution, the 1980s saw radical transformations in the romance genre. One change in particular merits mention: sexuality (and not sensuality or a mysterious passion of the senses), which was previously acknowledged only after the revelation of a total, absolute, and theoretically self-sufficient love, now comes before the declaration of love. Sexual attraction increasingly precedes and becomes the basis for feelings. The intensity of the orgasm is thought to be linked to the strength of the feelings that bring sexual partners together. "In the end, the real discovery," writes a hippie in the 1970s after living in a commune, "is that the quality of the sex more or less depends on the degree of love. You have to be in love to orgasm, it seems."[127] This observation is essential, because it once again makes it possible to attach love to something else: love is not only sought in the name of the homeland, the sacrosanct bonds of marriage, the children, or a complicity that runs deeper than friendship, but also and sometimes primarily in the name of a sexuality that is more rich, intense, pure, and pleasurable. One seeks love to have better sex. Sociologist Jean-Claude Kaufmann quite accurately used the term "sexamour" to describe relationships intermingling feelings and physical pleasure, the dream and pleasure of senses, the exploration of the heart and discovery of the body.[128]

In the 1950s dime novels, gestures of affection sometimes turned violent and embraced a fantasy in which physical torture was presented as a kind of "marvellous suffering." "He kissed me violently, brutally," says the heroine of one of these novels, "such that my head was thrown back and my lips were bruised."[129] However, this aggression remained veiled. First, sexuality was severely frowned upon, as the titles of postwar dime novels indicate: *L'abîme des passions* (The abyss of passions), *Baisers troublants* (Troubling kisses), *Un sale séducteur* (A rotten seducer), *L'enfant du péché* (Child of sin), *Le baiser qui l'a perdue* (The kiss that ruined her), *Femmes aux lèvres dangereuses* (Women with dangerous lips), *Il voulait son corps* (He wanted her body). Second, carnal relations between freely consenting characters, reduced to modest caresses and chaste kisses, were prohibited until the end of the story, which concluded rather abruptly on the promise of a forthcoming marriage. Finally, the sexual instinct was placed entirely in the hands of the man, with the woman being defined as the object of desire. He was sex; she was tenderness. A man who truly loved a woman respected her moral and physical integrity and only wanted to have sweet and platonic relations with her, only taking her virginity as an obligation of his conjugal duty and to "not prevent the family." The woman dreamed only of snuggling in the arms of her beloved or resting her head on his shoulder.

Bussières-Tremblay's novels go one step further, insinuating sexuality into the heart of the romantic story. Sexual relations take place before the end of the story. We note especially that women also experience desire. They are no longer satisfied with a love that starts out cold. There is no longer love without physical pleasure, neither for her, nor for him. In the Québécois rape sagas, the heroine is made to pay for her confession of carnal pleasure with great violence. Never before had scenes of rape and confinement—previously uncommon and discreet—been such a determining factor, such an integral part of the romantic relation itself. While heroines may have once been confronted with aggressors only to be saved from their clutches by the hero, now it is the aggressors themselves that some heroines fall in love with. Far from waning over time, this power dynamic becomes even more prevalent in the 2000s, as we will see in the next chapter.

The Harlequin novels are generally toned down. To avoid shocking the French-language public, the French versions present a sexuality that is more muted, euphemized, and romanticized than in the original English versions. But both the originals and translations are always based on a presumed demisexuality, that is to say, on a scenario in which characters feel a stronger sexual attraction for individuals they are emotionally attached to.[130] In the Harlequin novels, despite the erotic charge, we know and feel that the sexual relations can only be truly enjoyable, satisfying, and fulfilling when the partners are in love. Also, at least on the surface, these works recount how a woman can fuse her so-called natural need for love with her sexual impulses, which she thought she had to repress, and how a man can anchor his sexual impulses, which he is unable to control, in his emotions, which his innate virility or a previous wound had long stifled.

However, at a time when these unequal representations continued to persist, young adult novels, drawing on a realist current, offered an entirely different vision of sexual relations in the couple. Fragile boys who are unsure of themselves can seduce strong girls, as part of a sexuality that poses no threat at all but contributes, on the contrary, to reinforcing the characters' identity at a key moment of their personal development. Young women can no longer love without desire, just as young men can no longer desire without love, but this moral does not sanction physical aggression. On the one hand, *La princesse de Clèves* seems out of touch and, on the other, *Pamela: or, Virtue Rewarded* appears absurd. One might think that the perfect balance between sexuality and love has been achieved, except for the fact that it is rare to find the perfect combination of ecstatic love and fabulous sex. Disappointed with mediocre sex or half-hearted love, heroes and heroines are quickly relegated to the status of friends or fuck buddies, further complicating the quest for the ideal person and anticipating, fifteen years in advance, the advent of chick lit.

Since the cultural revolution, the union of bodies is considered a pre-condition for the union of souls. A man who doesn't desire a woman and a woman who doesn't succumb to pleasure in a man's arms have no chance of being happy together as a couple. The sexuality evoked in romance novels remains nonetheless intimately linked to love. The end of the cult of the heroine's virginity and the proliferation of erotic scenes should not, in this sense, obscure the framework within which love stories have evolved. Without sharing a heritage, without marriage and without the obligation to "consolidate love" by having children, the contemporary romantic novel still contributes to the construction of the modern couple through a continually renewed call for impassioned demisexuality.

CHAPTER 6

Love Despite Everything (since 2000)

Since the nineteenth century, the history of romance literature in the West is one of a gradual differentiation, and Quebec is no exception to this rule. Solitary writers of the first period, often self-published, were replaced by authors who wrote for established publishing houses, with the latter gradually introducing specialized collections that spawned increasingly specialized sub-genres. To get a sense of this, one has only to consult Harlequin's website, which provides a long list of collections tailored to different segments of its French-language readership: Allegria (tenderness and optimism), Azur (luxury and glamour), Audace (audacity and sensuality), Black Rose (suspense), Blanche (hospital drama), Darkiss (mystery), Dynasties (scandals and legacies), Gentlemen (male point of view), Horizon (family), Ispahan (Eastern countries), Jade (large format), Luna (fantasy), Magnetic (modern), Mira (detective), Nocturne (vampires and werewolves), Prelud' (psychology and comedy), Red Dress Ink (chick lit), Saga (series), Sexy (erotic), Spicy (sensual), Victoria (historical).[1]

As observed elsewhere, the Québécois romance novel market has seen increasing segmentation since the turn of the twenty-first century, the proliferation of titles being an indication in itself of a genre branching out to reach different publics. Éditeurs réunis alone offers around forty titles of novels "for her" that are more or less linked to romance, as well as titles in the category "Romance/Romantica."[2] Over the past twenty years, works with romantic content have explored a vast range of possible scenarios. The imagination of authors seems to have no limits at a time when self-publishing and digital desktop publishing make it possible to publish increasingly niche-oriented works. The nature of this production can be seen in a sample of novellas published in 2014 by the short-lived Éditions Laska, founded in Montreal to promote romantic literature in French, under the title *Romances d'aujourd'hui: une anthologie de romance contemporaine.*[3]

Focusing on key points, the last chapter of our overview of the romance novel in Quebec is brief. Rather than providing an exhaustive inventory of the field, which would in any case be impossible considering the proliferation of titles published under the most varied labels, we have decided to focus on four tendencies that revisit and prolong trends that emerged in the 1980s. In the first section we will see how, since Harlequin entered the French-language market in 1978, the Cinderella complex has remained very present in the literary landscape and continues to fuel the imagination of Québécois romance writers. We will then attempt to show how LGBTQ+ romance novels also recycle, within a once-marginalized, even taboo literature, a fairy tale imaginary. The beauty and prince charming, embodied here by a homosexual couple, become heralds of a romanticism that doesn't want to die. In the third place, we will see how elements of romance novels for adolescents are revamped in chick lit. Just like the young adult novels, chick lit novels are not all based on romance, but a good number of them borrow the romance novel framework. Torn between friendship and sex, they reiterate the importance of small-L love and its place in everyday life. Finally, we look at the so-called new adult trend, which, revisiting the rape sagas, took the Québécois market by storm, fueled by the worldwide success of *Fifty Shades of*

Grey (*Cinquante nuances de Grey*). The sadomasochistic love it portrays, particularly for the heroine, who has never been so reduced to the level of a slave, raises important questions regarding the current fad of violent sexual relations.

Finding one's destiny

Faced with the plethora of contemporary romance novels written "à l'eau de rose," as is said pejoratively, we have decided to restrict our analysis to two novels that won the "Prix Romance Milady: Le choix des lectrices québécoises." Since 2017, this prize is given to loves stories that are "full of spice" with happy outcomes and featuring heroines with a "determined, sparkling character," and with the aim of "giving romance a boost"[4] in French. The two winning novels of 2017 and 2018 were not written by just anybody. Suzanne Roy, the winner in 2017, published twenty-five novels over a ten-year period, many of which are romance novels. Chloé Duval, the 2018 winner, is of French origin, living in Montreal. She describes herself on her blog as a woman who, as a young girl "filled pages of notebooks with stories of knights slaying terrifying dragons with the sole aim of saving the damsel in distress" and who, today, "still tries to find in her stories the sweetness and enchantment of the fairy tales of her childhood."[5] Beyond their obvious differences in styles and themes, one could say that the two authors are fairly representative of the more naively sentimental current of Québécois romance novels in the place they attribute to love as destiny.

In her award-winning book *Un cadeau du ciel* (A gift from heaven), Suzanne Roy rehashes many of the clichés of the contemporary romance novel: an inflexible man who is disconnected from his feelings learns to love again with a young naive woman who, for her part, discovers sexuality. The novel's fantastic premise (the female character is actually an angel who inhabits the body of a beautiful young girl waking up in the hospital where the hero works), replicates the universe of a Guillaume Musso or Marc Lévy, in which love very often transcends the laws of human nature. The originality of this Québécois work lies primarily in the dual narration, with the chapters alternating between the female and male characters' descriptions of events and states of mind (Roy also makes use of this narrative strategy in most of her novels). But the heroine's relative lack of autonomy, given that she is driven exclusively by a sensual quest for love, places the hero in the position of a father or a Pygmalion who could easily seem outdated in the twenty-first century. The heroine's relegation to the status of a child serves to intensify a quest for self-fulfillment that cannot be attained, for the female character even more than for the male character, beyond its romantic purpose.

Un cadeau du ciel immerses us in the life of Elina, an angel whose task is to transport the dying to the afterlife. She is solely devoted to fulfilling this function, being totally indifferent to the fate of those she guides to a luminous door, not even knowing herself what lies behind it. She seems to be accomplishing her task well until the day when the emergency doctor, Éric Séguin, saves the lives of three people she was supposed to accompany on their journey to the beyond. Expelled from Heaven and sent down to earth, she is welcomed by Éric, who had recently felt her ghostly presence and wanted to communicate with her. Éric, completely devoted to his work and leaving no time for recreation in his life, quickly falls in love with this beautiful angel. With Éric, Elina discovers simple pleasures like enjoying delicious food and wearing nice clothes. Unfamiliar with human life, she is like a little girl inhabiting a woman's body, as the author adamantly emphasizes. She often wonders what God expects from her and whether he was entrusting her with a special mission by sending her to live among humans. In her despair, she seeks the advice of a priest and goes to a

Montreal church to pray. Her wings then become visible to the priest and the hero, who are both stunned by this unexpected spectacle. Elina's exceptional character is now evident, but her supernatural status only makes her more vulnerable in the eyes of Éric, who will do anything to protect her.

Elina has to wait all day for Éric's return. To distract herself, she watches cooking shows and discovers her culinary talents. Bingeing on American television films, she also becomes curious about all things related to love and seeks to learn more about this emotion that seems to be some people's ultimate purpose in life. Though Éric doesn't want to take advantage of a naive girl and a virgin, which would make him something of a pedophile (but the word is never pronounced), he cannot resist this woman who is "so beautiful and so pure, behind her kitchen counter," who makes him "truly happy."[6] Elina trembles all over when Éric tucks her into bed before going to sleep. "'In his arms,' she says, 'I feel not only human, but also like a woman. I never would have thought there was such a difference between the two.'"[7] She feels an intense shivering over her whole body, like a strange fever, and when she surrenders to her saviour, her body crying out for his caresses, she lets out a "savage, liberating" moan. "'Sex is marvellous,' she says after a long silence. 'Not sex,' replies Éric. 'Love.'"[8] Their increasingly risqué lovemaking only convinces Elina even more that she belongs to Éric rather than to God.

Un cadeau du ciel is clearly based on an implausible premise. But the scenario makes it possible to depict the heroine as a perfect virgin in an adult's body. Éric's best friend envies him when he learns that his girlfriend is a virgin: "Quite the lucky bastard you are! Something like that would never happen to me!"[9] At the same time, he tells Éric to be "a nice boy" and "be very careful with his little angel."[10] Éric himself cannot believe how lucky he is to have met someone so innocent and pure, literally a gift from heaven. Being "like a child,"[11] and knowing nothing of the world, Elina is particularly fascinated by chocolate and sexuality, which humans often miss when they die, and she savours them both before concluding that orgasms are "a thousand times better than chocolate."[12] Her destiny seems limited to tasting and being tasted, which the passages focusing on her culinary talents emphasize.

Elina swears to love Éric more than anything in the world. Éric, in return, is madly in love with her. With God threatening to reclaim the fallen angel as His, they decide to get married at the church and have a child as quickly as possible. They believe this will suffice to thwart the divine plans. Pregnant, Elina however learns that her stay on earth is coming to an end, but she doesn't dare speak to Éric about it, for fear of causing him too much pain. Immediately after giving birth, she falls into a deep coma and returns to Heaven. She learns that her indifference to the humans depending on her to open the door to the afterlife was the reason for her disgrace. Realizing how precious life is and how it is made up of a myriad of subtle and fleeting pleasures, she thanks God for this invaluable lesson. Meanwhile, the birth of his son cannot console Éric for the loss of his beloved wife. Now that he has known a kind of divine love in the arms of an angel, he is unable to renounce his love and thinks of committing suicide.

The hoped-for miracle happens: Elina comes back to life. She promises to never leave Éric again. He thanks God for giving him "the most incredible gift there is: love, happiness, family… everything."[13] He appreciates what life is worth more and values every fleeting minute. In the last chapter titled "What does happiness look like?", the author describes the young couple moving into an entirely renovated little house near what seems to be a pretty town overlooking the St. Lawrence River. Éric has decided to leave the city and accept a physician's job in the country, which leaves him more time to devote to family life. "He helps people improve their lives rather than helping them survive. It's nice."[14] As for Elina, she has finally understood the mission God had chosen for her: "to make Éric happy." "And she intends to keep doing so for a very long time."[15]

In 2018, the Prix Romance was awarded to *À sa rencontre* (*The Château by the River*), a novel that, in a somewhat different vein, seems to be framed as a contemporary version of *Beauty and the Beast*. To the lovelorn, Chloé Duval responds that having a romantic soul and wearing rose-tinted glasses is sometimes "the best way to see the world,"[16] and she sets out to prove it in this text that brings two resigned characters face to face with each other. Living in the Napa Valley, in California, Alexandra Dawson is in a passionless relationship, engaged to an ambitious young lawyer who neglects her by devoting all his time to his work. She doesn't dare ask more of her relationship, because she feels fragile and vulnerable and has no real resources. Behind a façade of success, her life seems empty to her. Meanwhile, Éric Lagnel works in Africa as a doctor. Having been exposed to many misfortunes, he is convinced that life is but "an endless succession of disillusionments, disappointments and drab days" and that his everyday life is only "darkness, poverty and sadness."[17]

On a business trip to France, Alexandra Dawson takes the opportunity to visit the village of Chandeniers, in the Loire region, where her great-great-great paternal grandmother, Gabrielle D'Arcy, was born. In retracing her own genealogy, she wants to get to know herself better and perhaps reconnect with her destiny. She travels to the Château of Ferté-Chandeniers. Though in ruins, the site exudes a magical and enchanting ambience. The castle seems "straight out of a fairy tale" to her. She imagines standing before sleeping beauty's, or rather, the beast's palace, when she meets the owner, Éric Lagnel. Recently orphaned, he has returned from Africa to take possession of his heritage. The Frenchman's impression on her is that of a boor whose "powerful charisma" would have been irresistible were it not for his "superior and condescending" attitude. Far from being taken aback by his insults, she responds tit for tat to his sarcastic remarks, to the point that he can only sigh in frustration with this American woman, who he accuses of being "stubborn" when she is only "determined."

It is clear that Alexandra has a barely concealed romantic soul. Her favourite book is *Jane Eyre,* her ancestor has the same family name as the hero of *Pride and Prejudice,* and she has two cats named Milady and D'Artagnan. Éric tells her, not once but twice, that "life isn't a fairy tale,"[18] but her life soon takes an unexpected turn when she discovers that she is the descendant of the last Baron of Saint-Armand, the owner of the Château of Ferté-Chandeniers. In the subsequent chapters and interspersed with her own inquiry, we learn of the breathtaking love story of her French ancestors before they emigrated to America. Gabrielle D'Arcy's diary, discovered in an old bookshop, opens a window onto the torrid passion of her great-great-great-grandparents and on a fusion of bodies that both consummates and anticipates a communion of hearts. One evening, while Alexandra is recalling erotic passages from her grandmother's diary, she is surprised to find herself thinking of Éric. She "throbbed with desire, head thrown back, eyes closed." Éric explores her body with his tongue, he "dipped over [her] navel and travelled further down, where every sensation was heightened, where [she] wanted to feel his hands, his lips, his tongue—him—the most."[19] She suddenly awakens "on the verge of eruption."

It is obvious that her feelings toward the chatelain are changing. Behind his boorish facade, Éric cannot hide his tender, loving heart. After a series of obstacles and rifts, Alexandra and Éric exchange a fiery, intense kiss, that is "raw" and "primal." She had never felt as alive as in this moment. The next day, in the delicate, light snowfall, she sees "dozens of small lanterns [trailing] a path of light through the snow, like so many miniature stars calling for [her] to follow."[20] Alexandra feels she is "in a scene from a romance, with the hero about to declare his love to his lady."[21] Éric confides he wants "all" of her. "I want your smile, your light, your humour. I want your heart. I want you, all of you."[22] He had tried in vain to hate her, to forget her. He came back to her "for all the reasons that had made [him] keep [his] distance at first: [her] light, [her] view of the world, as though through rose-tinted glasses, [her] heart as big as this planet."[23] Before he can finish, she flings her arms around his neck and kisses him "breathlessly."[24]

The conclusion of Chloé Duval's novel confirms that Alexandra is a "princess," that her meeting Éric was written in the stars, and that their story is a "fairy tale." Éric blesses this woman who has "literally" changed his life. "She appeared one day out of nowhere with her dreams and romantic ideas and upended my every certainty, overthrew my plans and opened my eyes."[25] In her presence, this disillusioned man has recovered his taste for life, the old château is transformed into a luxurious winery, and the village of Chandeniers is infused with new life, thanks to the American woman's determination. In the novel's epilogue, we are treated to a sumptuous marriage on the domain's ancestral and now resplendent land. "Drunk with happiness," dreaming of a flock of children, Éric is convinced his love will never end, because the "love of his life" has become his wife "for better and for worse, until death do us part. And beyond."[26]

One falling from Heaven, the other travelling back to the past, the two heroines of *Un cadeau du ciel* and *À sa rencontre* remind us that a woman is nothing without love. The naivety of the first and the determination of the second do not detract from their inevitable destinies, which is a quest, even without their knowing it, for love with a capital L. This love goes far beyond simple friendship, sweet harmony. True love can be recognized by the fact that a woman is driven to seek out her partner in the middle of the day to kiss him, caress him, make love to him, and open her heart to him. When a woman is attracted to a man in this way, and he is thus attracted to her in turn, she can be sure that she has found her place in the universe and, with great relief, consider herself fulfilled. "I was happy," exclaims Alexandra when she admits her passionate feelings for Éric. "At last. I knew who I was. I knew what I wanted. Everything was clear now."[27] Elina is happy with a bungalow overlooking the river, and Alexandra moves into temporary quarters while her ancestors' château is being rebuilt, but both have found true happiness in the arms of their doctors, because they know who they are and what they really want: "to make Éric happy."

Homoromance

Until recently, there were no LGBTQ+ romance novels in the Quebec French-language literary corpus that respected the three invariants of the genre. Readers interested in the subject had to make do with literature produced elsewhere.[28] The traditional romance novel, highly heteronormative, was limited to the image of a woman and a man destined to raise a family together. Anything that ventured off the beaten path of heterosexuality was considered an anomaly if not a monstrosity.[29] Things slowly began to change at the turn of the 2010s, with romance novels published in Quebec under the LGBTQ+ banner inspired by an English-language corpus already making strides.[30]

In 2013, for example, Samuel Champagne published *Recrue* (Recruit) in the Éditions de Mortagne "Tabou" collection.[31] This novel for young adults features Maxence and Thomas, who do not initially seem destined to get along. The first is an extroverted athlete, and the second is a shy and solitary dancer. Also, Maxence, who grew up in England, has been hiding his

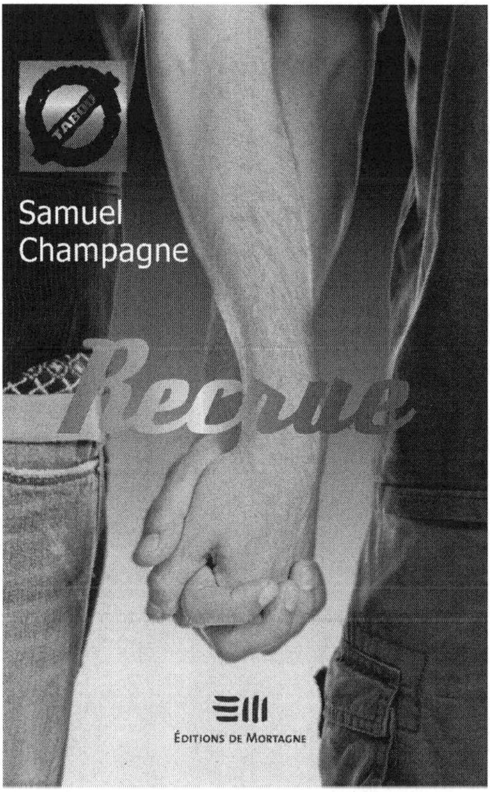

Samuel Champagne, *Recrue*, Boucherville, Éditions de Mortagne, 2013.

homosexuality since arriving in Montreal. The two boys feel attracted to each other, without being able to reveal their love. They become friends first, then confess their feelings. Through their story, a number of sensitive issues are raised, such as relationships with parents, tensions at school, and prejudices. This is why the novel does not end with the first kiss. After the "coming out," the author wanted to portray the challenges that the characters still face. But the fundamental moral of the story is, still and always, that love knows no bounds. We find numerous variations on this lesson in other LGBTQ+ books, including in the lesbian novel *La fille dans le placard* (The girl in the closet).[32]

The recent diversification of romance genre scenarios sheds light on the plasticity of different forms of love. At the same time, the authors' continually demonstrated ingenuity also—and perhaps primarily— reflects the simplicity of the pattern that the stories are based on. If the production of LGBTQ+ romance novels reveals anything, it is no doubt the extent to which the genre is capable of renewing itself while also preserving its basic structure. By affirming, for example, that the asymmetrical gendered relationship can be reinterpreted to incorporate different sociohistorical contexts, the LGBTQ+ novel does not disrupt the romance genre, but, on the contrary, confirms it. The basic framework of the romance novel indeed does not change, even if it involves a boy-meets-boy, girl-meets-girl or queer-meets-queer story. From the point of view of the feelings depicted, the characters' sexual orientation seems entirely anecdotal or incidental (one of the causes for the disjunction, for example, is the challenge of "coming out of the closet"). Apart from the characters' sexual orientation and questioning of gender identities, nothing in these novels really departs from the conventional story.

On this topic, it is revealing that the transposition of non-heteronormative scenarios in the Harlequin style is openly embraced by some authors. Cy Jung, a French author who publishes with the Québécois Homoromance Éditions,[33] admitted at the launch of one of her novels that she had "embarked on the 'lesbian pink novel' adventure" by reading "some novels from the famous Harlequin romance collection" in order to "decode their writing rules" and "note the vocabulary."[34] It seems she is not the only one to have prepared for a career publishing lesbian, gay, bi, and trans novels by imbibing the structure and style of the most hackneyed romance novels. For example, in *Au-delà du devoir* (Beyond duty) (2017), by Québécois author Judith Gagnon,[35] Kansas is sent by the government on a secret mission to kill the leader of a rebel group. She finds herself face to face with the latter's daughter, Phoenix. The two warriors from the future (the action takes place in 2060) cannot resist their feelings for one another. In a realm situated "beyond duty," their "fusional" love triumphs.

What the reader discovers, or rediscovers in the LGBTQ+ novel, is the extent to which love, transcending the old sexual taboos, is presented as being really "stronger than everything." Jérémy Lambert's contention that the reconfiguration of roles in LGBTQ+ literature cuts to the heart of the romantic dynamic as historically portrayed in the romance novel, thus modifying "in a profound way the very structure of the romantic story,"[36] seems clearly exaggerated if not misleading. Lambert claims that "if popular literature 'doesn't like homos,' this likely has less to do with moral reasons than with literary conventions."[37] This contestable hypothesis is based on the idea that by depicting individuals of the same sex, homosexual love ensures more equality in the couple, since it becomes more difficult to insinuate gender categories into the power relations between the characters. The romance novel's asymmetrical rapport between men and women (judged at best as "equal but different," since the former are from Mars and the latter, from Venus), can thus be undermined in the homosexual romance novel through the ambivalence or abolition of the domination-subjection dynamic of the couple. This implies a new role-sharing that challenges the traditional romance novel's binary structure, the "natural" asymmetry between men and women being no longer relevant to the stories of gay and lesbian couples.

Jérémy Lambert's hypothesis seems much more a reflection of a historical moment than a constant of the romance genre. There is nothing preventing power relations, which embody one of the types of disjunction in the traditional story, from being formulated in a variety of ways (age, profession, education, etc.) that are based neither on gender nor sexual orientation, or from being rerouted through new gender stereotypes in unexpected ways (under the labels of dyke, butch, lipstick, or sissy). The recent inclusion by Harlequin, a publisher always attentive to its readers' needs, of a few gay titles in its catalogue[38] suggests that if popular literature "doesn't like homos," this is primarily due to a collective attitude still oscillating between discomfort and homophobia, and not the result of certain literary imperatives. The Québécois LGBTQ+ romance novels already published show, if there was any doubt, that a good love story is a good love story, regardless of who is kissing who.

Chick lit

Parallel to more conventional forms, romantic storylines were renewed in the new millennium in the wave of different trends, including, notably, chick lit, whose popularity was propelled by the British and American success of works like *Bridget Jones's Diary* (1996) by Helen Fielding, *Confessions of a Shopaholic* (2000) by Sophie Kinsella, *The Devil Wears Prada* (2003) by Laurence Weisberger, and of course *Sex and the City* (1994) by Candace Bushnell. In Quebec, the interest for chick lit soon exploded, fuelling an important local production. Rafaële Germain was a pioneer, having published three best sellers with Éditions Libre Expression: *Soutien-gorge rose et veston noir* (2004) (*Pink Bra and Black Jacket*, 2008), *Gin tonic et concombre* (2008) (*Gin & Tonic and Cucumber*, 2009), and *Volte-face et malaises* (About-face and discomfort) (2012).[39] Inspired by these best sellers, several Québécois publishing houses now boast a chick lit author who situates well known *fabula* in very Québécois settings.[40] Éditions de Mortagne even took the opportunity to create the "Lime et citron" collection, whose program is advertised as being "refreshing, amusing and sometimes thought-provoking."[41] If, as mentioned at the outset, some of these stories do not respect the invariants of the romance genre and end, in "romantic comedy" mode, with the heroine remaining single, we can still speak of a Québécois chick lit, because many novels do replicate, in the end, the typical scenario of romance.

The expression "chick lit," referring to literature for chicks, first appeared in a volume on postfeminist fiction.[42] The volume's editors thought the name had an ironic aspect that captured the spirit of this literary genre very well. Colourful covers are one of the signature features of works published under this banner, along with images of stiletto heels, designer bags, and girly titles, making it easy to recognize the genre at a glance.[43] The cover illustration for *Gin tonic et concombre* (2012) depicts a young woman with a stick-thin figure and legs that never end being served three tiny men on a platter, presented as "beverages." Written, like the Harlequin books, from the heroine's point of view, chick lit novels privilege a first-person singular narration over a third-person perspective. By immersing the readers even more directly in the young adventure-seeking woman's mind, these fictions create an impression of authenticity that is reinforced by the inclusion of diary passages and internal monologues, along with very familiar and concrete situations, despite the dreamy element specific to romance.[44]

Most often, chick lit novels depict the tribulations of a trendy young city girl in her twenties who works in the fashion, advertising, art, or publishing industry. She is surrounded by loyal friends and often a cat, and she likes to party. She is chronically clumsy, lacks self-confidence, and has body-image issues. Single, she seems more interested in advancing her career than in meeting a lover, a position that dictates her anti-maternal rhetoric. Though not aspiring to huge professional success, she finds herself working in a job that suppresses her real potential, probably because she is subjected to the tyranny of a female boss who detests her. She appears triply unsatisfied: too unfeminine to be seductive, too awkward to rise in the ranks at work, and too angst-ridden to ever feel good about herself, the heroine describes her problems frankly and openly, with a good dose of humour and self-deprecation. At the end of the story, she has not lost as much weight as she wanted to or shaken her bad habits (notably her excessive consumption of beauty products, alcohol, and chocolate), but she has learned to accept herself in the arms of a man who finds her flaws to be part of her charm.

Aware that the search for prince charming is no longer realistic in today's world, the heroine of chick lit at first glance seems to be seeking happiness in the single life. Two factors contribute to her antiromantic stance. First, her lucidity makes it impossible to believe in fairy tales at a time when divorce rates are rising and the couple's life is consumed by the division of domestic tasks. Also, as a daughter of the feminist revolution, the heroine knows that to prove her worth she has to carve out her own path without the help of a partner to pave the way. However, no one is entirely duped by her individualist convictions, with many clearly interspersed clues recalling that, even mocked and relativized, the dream of happiness in a couple remains very alive for her. From the beginning of *Soutien-gorge rose et veston noir*, for example, the friends realize that their society reserves a "dim fate" for singles: "the ultimate symbol of success [...] It's love. If you don't succeed in love, you're a pariah."[45] In *Volte-face et malaises*, when the main character Geneviève sees her divorced mother doing Tai Chi in a park, she laments: "I said to myself that she looked happy, but... just thinking that to myself scared me ... as if in some way I was trying to convince myself that it was okay to end up like that ..."[46] Just as in the stories of the previous period, the old maids in chick lit novels cannot expect a fulfilling destiny.

The heroine's disappointments and difficulties serve to reiterate her inability to live her life alone, despite her claims to the contrary. The hero indeed often saves her from a tight spot or humiliating situation (like in a scene where, to calm her anxiety, she gets drunk on several gin and tonics and other colourful cocktails). In *Si tu t'appelles Mélancolie* (If your name is Melancholia) (2010), the heroine seems to be immersed in a crisis from the first page. Using bullet points (a favoured fictional device of this genre, which constantly interrupts the narration with different layouts to include recipes, magazine quizzes, song excerpts, emails, or doodles), the narrator makes a list of her faults:

> Dear reader, don't go thinking that my life is so simple, that I live in a fairy tale. Trust me, I don't!
> I don't have a boyfriend.
> I don't have a lover.
> I don't have an exciting career.
> I don't have (a lot) of money.
> I don't have (a lot) of sex.
> I don't have any projects that work out.
> I'm not at my ideal weight.
> I'm going to be 30 in less than a month.
> HELP![47]

We can easily surmise that by the end of her adventure, Melancholy will have crossed off everything on her list (except for the weight loss), because she will have found love and reoriented her career, implying that she gets to live in a kind of "fairy tale" after all. Many Québécois chick lit authors reserve a similar fate for their heroines and, though including details on their careers and friendships, still represent contemporary adaptations of the romance novel. After studying a sample of novels written by female Québécois authors, Corinne Gervais confirms that "most of the time, the heroine of Québécois chick lit will find her great love by the end of the story,"[48] just like in the British and American novels.[49] While certain dimensions specific to the dominant American versions (obsession with fashion and rampant consumerism, among others) are downplayed in the Québécois works, this is done without sacrificing the romantic storyline, which remains fundamental.

Whatever may be said of this literature and its long litany of clichés on "womanhood,"[50] the man is still the privileged means by which the heroine finds happiness and security. In Rafaële Germain's novels, the male characters are professionally superior to their female partners. The man, who is a rich publicist, renowned chef, emergency doctor, architect, journalist or successful writer is met with a female counterpart who is a freelance researcher or unknown author. These hierarchical differences reflect a disparity between the characters, with the woman's intrinsic fragility opposing the man's natural strength. "For the last little while," confides Chloé in *Soutien-gorge rose et veston noir*, "I'd been feeling vaguely like an imposter when I thought of Simon and me—I was a joke, a girl of many faults, someone who was irremediably ordinary. I was unstable and changeable, like a weather vane or a stream; he was solid and upright [...]."[51] Always questioning herself, insecure and flawed, the heroine has little confidence in herself.[52] In the continual introspections presented through her inner monologue, lurks a frightened person hiding behind a more confident exterior. The sweet and sensitive man she seeks must be able, above all, to demonstrate devotion, even paternalism. It seems he is there to save her from herself in a fable that, despite appearing more free from sexist stereotypes, is not unlike the romance novels of Suzanne Roy and Chloé Duval.

Interestingly, in Quebec, the figure of the boyfriend is quite often crossed with that of the father, who is depicted as reassuring and protective. Most of the time, the heroine (the "single girl") is on her own when she enters adult life, but it is precisely because of this new partial and precarious autonomy that she constantly needs advice, guidance and instruction. In the constellation of characters that surround her, the father occupies a privileged place insofar as he represents the ideal male that the heroine seeks after leaving the family home. This is one of the most illuminating observations in Gervais' research,[53] as illustrated in the following excerpt from *La vie épicée de Charlotte Lavigne* (The spicy life of Charlotte Lavigne) (2011) by Nathalie Roy, chosen from among many others. Wanting to seduce her suitor by cooking a gourmet meal using local products, the heroine imagined by Roy leaves in the middle of a storm to purchase bison meat from a producer in a remote region. She finds herself far from home and stuck in the snow, which leads to the following reflection: "It is in these moments, when I feel alone and threatened, that I think of my father. If he was here, he would have definitely braved the storm to come and get me. He would have borrowed a snow removal truck from the City of Laval, which he worked for his whole life. He would have found a way to Ulverton to come rescue his daughter, captive among the bison."[54] Passages like this show how the heroine of Québécois chick lit is no more able than the others in our corpus to be a woman by relying only on her own abilities. Her fierce desire for independence is difficult to reconcile with her attitude of being still an eternal little girl, expressed by her need for the masculine strength that her father, the only man of uncontested virility and unwavering love, represents as an archetype.

From the beginning of *Si tu t'appelles Mélancolie*, the narrator begins with the following observation, speaking of the love that still unites her parents after so many years: "My father is the strongest [...] When I think about it, I say to myself that it's actually normal that I'm single. This type of fairy tale doesn't happen twice in the same family. I think their story has contributed a lot to my illusions about love."[55] Proving her wrong on the presumed non-existence of prince charming, the story's ending also reaffirms the similarity between the father and the boyfriend. In fact, Pablo, who Melancholia meets in Mexico, saves her from drowning, just like her father had done for her mother decades earlier. Her friend Jéricho mentions this to the narrator, implying that the couple will live happily ever after, surrounded by children: "Colia! He saved you from drowning, like your father did for your mother 30 years ago. I'm the only one to have noticed this, really? Now I recognize you my friend, you have found him!"[56] The fairy tale is repeated in the same family, with the father being reincarnated in a foreign figure (many of the heroes have an exotic background, which helps mitigate the incestuous charge of their attraction), whose male strength symbolizes the possibility of the couple's happiness. Thanks to this presence, the heroine is saved from a social, existential and psychological drowning.

Conversely, and consistent with the Freudian interpretation of the Electra myth, the female characters must seek independence from their mothers to access their own femininity.[57] The typical scene involving their attempts to master the art of seduction is the moment when the heroine and her friend borrow their mothers' beauty products to try to improve their appearance, with predictably disastrous results. When Aurélie from the *Journal d'Aurélie Laflamme* (Aurélie Laflamme's diary) by chance finds her mother's sexy underwear, she is literally appalled: "I wish I had never discovered that my mother wears thongs. I think I might be traumatized."[58] Aurélie is surprised to learn that her mother also has a sex life, which places them on the same level, at a time in her life when she is looking for a man who resembles her father. As in Anglo-American chick lit, the heroine of Québécois chick lit prefers to turn to her group of girlfriends or to her boyfriend, rather than to her family, for comfort and support.

Chick lit attempts to tell a love story that takes place at a time of disillusionment and disappointment. The heroines go to sleep "every night inventing stories worthy of a Harlequin romance"[59] and try to convince themselves of the futility of these dreams, all the while clinging to the ideal of being cuddled, pampered and adored. They struggle with a contradiction. On the one hand, if they display perfect autonomy, they are renouncing the reassuring and comforting presence of a prince charming. On the other hand, if they admit to being weak and incomplete without a man by their side, they turn their backs on the advances of feminism. Most of the time, the heroine seeks to demonstrate her independence and act alone, but, deep down, she feels an intense need for protection that reduces her to the status of a child. The example of *Volte-face et malaises* (2012) illustrates this ambivalence. Geneviève's character is both "troubled" and "reassured" when she realizes that "she had long had the impression of being treated like a child by her boyfriend."[60] Unable to square the circle of emancipation and infantilization, the heroines of chick lit are plagued with doubts, tormented by the fear of not being up to the challenge of meeting contradictory demands.

In a context that requires the woman to both fulfill her own destiny and depend on a man, irony is used to play the game of love[61] while simultaneously keeping it at a distance. Chick lit can thus be understood as "a realistic parody of romance,"[62] as Stephanie Harzewski astutely observes. The authors acknowledge that, for the young generation, the quest for love has become as banal as it is ridiculous. Heir to both feminism and patriarchy, chick lit depicts heroines who know they can live without men but are not convinced they can be completely fulfilled without them. On this subject, the main character of *Soutien-gorge rose et veston noir* declares: "I'd thought (sluggishly, it's true) about what I'd become: a twenty-eight-year-old, single (irreparably, joyously and proudly single), researcher and freelance writer, living in a less-than-modern two-bedroom apartment with three cats and a recycling bin full of empty Gatorade bottles—none of these bottles, I must admit, had been consumed in relation to anything athletic."[63] This passage denies the need for love while also in the end affirming it. It shows that the aspiration to live a beautiful and great love story may well be "pathetic," but the heroines cannot suppress it without denying an apparently essential part of themselves. With the quest for Mr. Right sometimes postponed indefinitely, the female characters avoid having to choose between self-love and love for the other, a dilemma that in previous romance novels was resolved with the heroine's sacrifice in a redeeming ordeal that magically transformed the fiancé into an attentive husband.

Though the search for prince charming is long and hazardous, the heroines in our corpus eventually end up meeting him. Melancholia, who had lost hope, discovers the love of her life: "OMIGOD," she writes [...]. "I'm living a fairy tale. I don't want to wake up from it. He is by far the guy who has had the greatest effect on my life."[64] This happy ending was clearly announced by Melancholia at the beginning of the novel: "Listen, my story is like a Harlequin romance. Sensitive single girls be warned."[65] *Mademoiselle Tic Tac* (2009), by Karine Glorieux, hammers home the same sentimental message. At the beginning of the story, the fairy tale seems dead in the water, killed by the fickleness of contemporary relationships: "What? I'm going to spend my life hopping from one guy to the next? What about prince charming? And the *they lived happily ever after*? And the Patrick Swayze lookalike I dream of sharing total, conventional monogamy with? Shit. I'm screwed."[66] However, in the chapter titled "How to recognize a prince charming without a white horse," the dream is resuscitated: "This time, ignoring the general confusion, Florent kissed me passionately, like a real Harlequin romance character. Then he smiled at me, and, in a flash of astonishing clarity, I saw us in a few years, surrounded by a group of little monsters."[67]

To "recognize a prince charming without a white horse," chick lit accords a central place to sexuality. Instead of the hero deflowering the young virgin woman, as in the past, we find the inverse scenario: the hero "re-virginizes"[68] a woman who has had several more or less important and unsatisfying sexual relationships. In the arms of the man who is revealed, through this very performance, to be the love of her life, the heroine has the impression of making love "for the first time." "We made love three times that night, and every time it was more intense. [...] He knew exactly how to please me. That's when I understood that Maxou was mine. After tons of relationships, each more disappointing than the other, the man of my life had finally appeared..."[69] The heroine of fairy tales was "made" for love (and for practically nothing else, having only her innocence and beauty to go on), but she had no sexual experience. The chick lit heroine knows what she wants in bed, but her love life has only been a series of disappointments. Having encountered her "true love," she can now feel deeper affection for him than for her past boyfriends and get more pleasure from sex than from her former lovers. She now knows that love exists and what it means to be sexually satisfied in the arms of a man. Her femininity is confirmed in a complicity and sexuality that she experiences as though having sex for the first time.

Compared to the more "fleur bleue" romance novels depicting women who preserve their innocence, one cannot help reading chick lit as a kind of time-travel machine: a woman in her late-twenties to mid-thirties is seeking a man who resembles her father so she can become a little girl again and finally live the fairy tale she dreamed of as an adolescent watching romantic comedies on television. While her lovers are revealed to be "adulescents," children trapped in adults' bodies, not knowing how to commit to a serious romantic relationship and shirking their responsibilities, the heroine realizes that, despite her career aspirations, she is not really capable of being an adult either, due to an analogous emotional immaturity, a natural weakness. For her, full and complete freedom continues to depend on finding love, and love still requires a "prince" or, at least, a tall, handsome and protective man, who will allow her to be a real woman by letting her be essentially a little girl.

As in the young adult novels of the 1980s, with which many parallels can be drawn, the quest for love in chick lit is sometimes spread over several volumes, with no guarantee of success in the end. The heroine has known many romantic failures and is torn between several partners. She seems to lack skill in matters of the heart, which leads to one disappointment after the other. Love is present but so disenchanted that one can barely recognize the fairy tale at its source, which clearly sets these novels apart from the romances of Suzanne Roy and Chloé Duval. India Desjardins' novel *La mort d'une princesse* (Death of a princess) traces the disappointments of the central character, who believed in "true love" stories as a child and expected to find prince charming. Realizing that "the typical romantic comedy scenario is not in her cards,"[70] Sarah makes do with her thirty-something single status and tries to reconcile her social and professional life. She eventually realizes that love is made of compromises and the height of passion is to be found in moments of simple joy with someone who shares her everyday life. In the last pages of the novel, she arrives unannounced at Pascal's apartment door and presents herself as a jaded girl who only wants to be in a relationship with a nice person. Pascal responds that he can "deal with that." They kiss. "How long," Sarah wonders, "before I move on to the next thing? I decide to banish these thoughts and simply live in the moment. There will always be time to work out the rest later."[71]

This type of "satisfactory ending" is perfectly suited to a disillusioned readership that knows, as Lisa Leblanc sings, that "Y'en aura pas de facile" (there's no easy way).[72] The authors are aware that an exciting conclusion "with fireworks" is improbable and that it is better to avoid disappointing readers by replacing this with the pleasure of being with a simple guy, with his qualities and flaws. At the same time, the heroine does not latch on to the "first guy who comes along," still and always dreaming of finding her "true" love one day. On the back cover of *Jeune libraire cherche roman d'amour* (Young bookseller seeks romance novel) by Joanie Mailhot Poissant, the heroine classifies men according to literary categories: men, she says, are either like erotic novels, adventure novels, crimes novels or like a romance novel. There are *some* detective novels and *some* science fiction novels, but, for Mailhot Poissant, there is only *one* romance novel... "the one we are all waiting for..."

Liberated and handcuffed love

We have seen in the previous chapter how the influence of the Anglo-American romance novel tradition led to an unprecedented recognition of female sexuality at the end of the 1970s. One might have expected the uninhibited sexuality of contemporary novels to simply add a few salacious passages to an otherwise predictable story. However, one intriguing fact stands out: the sexuality depicted in numerous romantic stories is haunted by sadomasochistic tendencies. Despite the sober descriptions and clichés of the young virgin deflowered in the arms of a legitimate husband, numerous novels depict women as simultaneously chaste, chased, and chastised. But, while until the 2000s, this cocktail of aggressivity and sexuality was confined to a few more daring scenes, with the representation of sex being usually metaphorized and euphemized, the publication of *Fifty Shades of Grey* (2011) changed everything. The unprecedented success of E. L. James's trilogy (125 million copies sold worldwide in 2019) has mystified many observers, especially women, who are unsure how to reconcile this fad with the parallel desire to challenge the stereotype of the innocent and submissive woman. The spectacular popularity of the three volumes is even more enigmatic, given that the majority of readers are women (over 90 percent).[73]

This so-called new adult or new romance literature—also pejoratively dubbed "Mommy Porn"— recycles the most worn clichés about the young girl with a pure heart who instantly falls for an ultravirile man who abuses her. It is no easy task to reconcile, on the one hand, growing demands for equality between the sexes and, on the other, a literary form that re-actualizes the Cinderella myth, spicing it up with an eroticism focused on the woman being oppressed and degraded. Leaving aside other aspects of the novel for the moment, we concentrate here on the nature of this sadomasochistic premise and what it can tell us, as a story that indeed respects the invariants of the romance novel, about the representation of the couple in the contemporary novel. We are also leaving aside other dimensions of BDSM related to the discovery of the "total sexed body" and belonging to a register of kinky or extreme practices in contemporary relationships. It goes without saying that the use of the strap and other sex toys extends far beyond the framework of the romance novel.

On close inspection, the novelty of *Fifty Shades of Grey* lies neither in the style nor the story, but in the portrayal of a sadomasochism that had never been pushed so far in a work destined for the general public.[74] Beyond this, the S&M eroticism of *Fifty Shades of Grey* is rooted in a fantasy that goes back to at least 1740, the year that Samuel Richardson published *Pamela: or Virtue Rewarded*, a novel in which the heroine falls in love with a man who mistreats her and holds her captive.[75] Anastasia Steele also ends up marrying Christian Grey and bearing his child. The sadism scenes allow her to enjoy the different forms of abuse she suffers at the hands of her master, which are like challenges for her and a source of arousal for him. To a certain extent, one could argue that hardcore sex posits the partners as enemies, making the sex act itself the site of disjunction, followed by romantic conjunction: the heroine accepts being reduced to sex that only becomes love after many ordeals. From this point of view, the sadomasochism in romance novels only adds a bit of spice to a "fairy tale for adults" that incorporates a sensibility already explored in the rape saga and bodice ripper trends, as seen in Marie-Claude Bussières-Tremblay's Québécois takes on these genres.

The heroine of new adult romance novels is relegated to the status of slave, made into a pure object, degraded and humiliated to the point of being branded with an iron like an animal, and reduced to her orifices for the phallic pleasure of different men in orgies. She is completely denigrated, and yet this is the source of her pleasure.[76] The more she is abused, beaten, whipped, bound, and raped, the more she feels alive, as long as she is loved in the end. The ordeals she must undergo to attain love are channelled through the body. The sacrifice of the body complements the sacrifice of the soul, constituting the ultimate proof of love. In exchange, the woman wins the affection of a man who, previously, was unable to really open his heart. The story recounted in *Fifty Shades of Grey* quickly spawned imitations in Quebec seeking to offer new adult fiction to a readership already prepared for sex scenes. The trilogy composed of *Sous l'emprise de Monsieur Addams* (Under the spell of Mr. Addams, 2015), À la merci de Monsieur *Addams* (At the mercy of Mr. Addams, 2015), and *Dans l'ombre de Monsieur Addams* (In the shadow of Mr. Addams, 2016) by Marjorie D. Lafond and published by Éditeurs réunis, is an excellent example. The back cover description makes no attempt to hide that Lalond's novel was inspired by the success of E. L. James' bestseller: "If you liked *Fifty Shades of Grey*, you are going to love being under the spell of Mr. Addams..."[77]

Félicia Roby, a nineteen-year-old student at the Cégep de Saint-Jérôme, falls in love with Liam, her classmate in a literature course. At the beginning of the story, Félicia's virginity at her age is presented as problematic. Despite the fact that the "meeting" between Félicia and Liam is in keeping with the canonical scene of the romance novel, including the moment when the two lovers recognize each other and exchange looks,

Marjorie D. Lafond, *Sous l'emprise de Monsieur Addams*, Marieville, Les Éditeurs réunis, 2015.

we quickly realize that Félicia's true quest will be to overcome her sexual inexperience. "I'm really ashamed to admit it. I mean, I'm 19, almost 20 years old! And still a virgin… […] I feel like letting go. I want guys to drool over me at the club, to desire me intensely. It's like a calling in me. Something that has been awakened in the depths of my being. Like a necessity. I need to know "that." It's becoming urgent. It's a burden. I want a man."[78] However, a few days after having kissed the handsome Liam, Félicia is kidnapped by her boss, Gabriel Addams, a man in his 40s who is filthy rich. Depriving himself of nothing, he has built a castle for himself surrounded by water called the Citadel. There are tons of women there, brought against their will but nearly all crazy for the "Master," from whom they hope to receive favours. This gigantic harem—a fantasy that informs many romance novels, from *The Sheik* (1919) up to the contemporary works of Harlequin's "Ispahan" collection[79]—is governed by the master's entourage.

The Citadel is an environment that is not conducive to love, but this should be put in perspective. The discourse is constructed in a way that defuses potential objections on the part of readers and tempers their indignation. The space contributes to creating a phantasmagoric effect likely to awaken dreamlike impulses. The site is characterized both as a prison and a simple holiday resort. After only a few days, Félicia participates in a "spa" day, which leads her to exclaim: "Wow! The facilities are amazing! We spent an hour relaxing in the whirlpool."[80] The Citadel is not so different from a five-star hotel, being compared specifically to Quebec City's Château Frontenac. Having being assigned, as the Master's fiancée, one of the most beautiful rooms, Félicia provides a magical description of what is essentially her prison cell:

> It is as big as my entire basement. A modern decor. Everything is white, with a touch of gold, refined, immaculate. There is an impressive chandelier too. Several mirrors. A canopy-style *king* bed, draped in diaphanous white curtains. Magnificent paintings by an artist I don't know. I even have my own private bathroom. And what strikes me the most is the view. An enormous window overlooks a cliff and rough sea.[81]

What follows at the Citadel are many booze-soaked evenings during which Félicia faces perpetual female rivalry. The symbolism draws heavily on the fairy tale repertoire. The first parties Félicia attends revolve around the theme of "19th-century nobility" (a different theme is chosen every month). The captive has her make-up applied by a professional beautician (who uses Lise Watier products), wears Prada designer heels, and, above all, dons magnificent robes: "'I held my breath,' she said, looking at her reflection. 'The dress fell perfectly, like in the old Empress Sissi films that my mother loved so much. Yet in the store, nothing ever fits me. Here it seems everything is adapted to my size. Mystery!'"[82] There is also a passage in which the Master makes declarations of love surrounded by flowers in a sumptuous, moonlit garden, which rouses this comment from her: "This garden is too beautiful to be true. Like in the movies—or in my grandmother's encyclopedias of European castles."[83] The more the story advances, the more Félicia struggles to remember that she is living in a "golden prison" and that Gabriel is a "false prince charming."[84]

Against all logic, given the state of confinement required by the story, the action is transported to Greece, because the Master wants to offer his fiancée a gift. It is on a Greek island that Félicia sleeps for the first time with the man she calls, in moments of intimacy, "my darling." The latter is presented sometimes as her oppressor (because she doesn't love him), sometimes as her saviour (because he makes her orgasm). The girl who arrived a virgin at the Citadel ends by observing: "It changes my mind to let myself go in these inviting arms, to receive the caresses that bring me every time to explosive orgasms, sometimes two, or even three or four in a row. Incredible, the power of the female body! On a more positive note, my captivity will at least have contributed to the sensual and sexual discovery of my body..."[85] This disarming admission is made more acceptable by the pact that binds the two main characters and is gradually revealed. Mr. Addams is a wounded man who saw his wife and child die in a car accident twenty years earlier: Félicia is faced with the challenge of reconciling his relation to love. In return, his mission is to initiate the young girl into sexuality. The crux of the novel is centred on this double transformation: when Mr. Addams has outbursts of violence and brutality, is he not formally asking her to "make him a better man"?

The tension between desired sexuality and repressed love breeds a climate of aggression. When she first arrives at the Citadel, Félicia is warned by the other characters to keep her rebellion in check. The Master is a dangerous man, because dissidents disappear from the Citadel, in all likelihood assassinated. For those who remain, the spectre of rape is always looming. For example, the doctor who evaluates her health when she arrives at the Citadel, though aware of her virginity, decides to offer her a gift, a new product that he wants to test out. "He poured a bit of clear lotion on two of his fingers, then applied it between my legs, *there*, on the most sensitive part of my body! [...] a wave of pleasure spread through my genitals, but I felt like breaking everything around me, I felt so ashamed of what was happening, so violated in my privacy, so robbed of my freedom."[86] After this ordeal, she knows that it is only a matter of time before she will be reduced to the level of a sex object. "'Usually,' says one of Félicia's guards, 'the men refrain for a few days before one of them has a taste of you. I recommend the master himself for this.' I feel like vomiting. I don't want anyone to touch me."[87] In this context, Félicia's virginity is her most precious asset. Exceptionally, the Master "takes his time" before stealing Félicia's innocence, and her privileged status protects her from being attacked by the others. Small reward, she ends up being the sex slave of one rather than being the sex toy of all.

Sous l'emprise de Monsieur Addams recounts the heroine's almost complete loss of control over her own body. Félicia is a prisoner who feels "at the mercy" of men. "As a young Québécois woman full of ambition, I could never have imagined that one day a man could control my life like this."[88] However the domination is not based on maternity, domesticity or paid work, but her own sexuality. The woman who can be equal to the man by day (Félicia's beauty is the mirror equivalent of Mr. Addams' power) must accept being his inferior by night. To experience pleasure she must surrender. He will be her torturer; she will be his slave. At first resisting the man she detests, the woman ends by giving herself bound hand and foot to her "tyrant." She is beaten, bullied and bruised, but she revels in this aggression imposed on her, having indeed succumbed to the charms of her partner, because he is a "real male," muscular, savage, violent, tall, haughty, proud, and determined. She is suffocated with pleasure, trembling in voluptuous delight. She asks for more. At the very moment she says no, her capitulation is complete.

In *Sous l'emprise de Monsieur Addams* the sadomasochistic charge is partially defused by the fact that Félicia loves Liam and not Gabriel. She dreams of being reunited with her true love since, as a shy young girl who knew nothing of life, she has learned to discover carnal pleasure. While Liam, who is also taken prisoner on the island, tries to become erect thinking of Félicia when he sleeps with Gabriel's sister, a woman over forty years old, Félicia, who is carrying the Master's child, realizes that sexuality is not only an "animalistic" thing in the arms of her "sex God." She understands that sex is something that "is far from being just conceived for pleasure."[89] Having managed to meet Liam in secret, she confides to him: "I want to go back home, Liam. I want a real love story with the guy I love. If you only knew how happy I am in your arms."[90] They promise each other that, once freed and back in Saint-Jérôme, they will make love non-stop. In the meantime, they try to deal with the difficult consequences of their confinement, and it is with this open-ended scenario that the first volume of the trilogy ends.

The system of oppositions between the man as "hunter" and the woman as "prey" is far from having been invented by these contemporary publishing successes. Since the advent of the romance novel, the woman has established the norms and limits in the relationship, and the man has transgressed them, either physically or psychologically. Élise Salaün's studies have shown how eroticism, present in diverse forms in the Québécois novel from its beginnings, infused the mass-market literature of the 1990s, all the while reproducing unequal sexual relations.[91] On one level, the new adult trend only reveals in more crude terms something that has always informed the stories in our corpus. By eroticizing the man's domination over the woman, by making the bed, as was the case with other places (office, kitchen, car) a theatre for expressing female desire as a desire for domination,[92] new adult romance perpetuates a time-honoured trope, as old as the romance novel itself. A woman with a repressed body meets a man with a broken heart. Along the way, each undergoes a transformation. As Béatrice Damian-Gaillard has shown, the asymmetry between the heroine's and hero's resources is the very condition for the romantic collision, at the end of which the two characters will have abandoned a part of themselves to fuse in an all-encompassing love.[93] Behind the hero's dark and distant appearance hides a wounded soul only waiting to open for a woman who demonstrates her total innocence, total abnegation to him. After a confrontation that is exacerbated to the point of making one a pure torturer and the other a pure victim, the seduction takes effect, the love is revealed, and the union can be consummated.[94]

However, at this level of analysis, one still has to wonder why women readers find any satisfaction at all in new adult romance and persist in reading novels that seem so inconsistent with their presumed sexual preferences. While there is surely an element of alienation in the pleasure women derive from reading dark romance type novels, this single hypothesis cannot explain everything. Other dimensions have to be considered to understand the phenomenon. In *Sous l'emprise de Monsieur Addams,* the hero plays the role of the dominator and continually threatens the women around him with reprisals. Why does the heroine agree to bend to theses sadistic impulses?

The answer appears simple: to avoid punishment. But in giving him pleasure, in giving herself totally, entirely and freely, Félicia is doubly rewarded: not only is she able to truly know herself through the "penetrating gaze" of a so-called "superior" man, but she can also conquer her conqueror by breaking his solitude.

This dialectic is further illuminated in *Corps et âmes* (Body and soul) (2017), a novel published by the same house as the *Monsieur Addams* trilogy, modelled even more on the plot of *Fifty Shades of Grey*, and typical of new adult novels in its depiction of sexuality across the five romance story stages described by Julia Bettinotti and her team: meeting, polemical confrontation, seduction, revelation of love and union.[95] Here, in an original way, the classic scenario of polemical confrontation is expressed in the sadomasochism, in a sort of sexual variation on the victim novel. It is through the sacrifice of her body that the woman, muzzled and passive, demonstrates her power and subjugates the man she thought she detested. In other words, what changes in the BDSM of *Corps et âmes*, is that the disjunction and conjunction are integrated into the sexual relations themselves. Love had always been a war[96] that saw the conquered woman also emerge victorious. New adult fiction recognizes this and only transposes this war into the bedroom.

In *Corps et âmes* (2017), Raphaëlle Lacroix reunites with Arnaud Laflamme, a childhood friend she has passionate feelings for. He is revealed to be the guru of a sect that, like Mr. Addams' Citadel, turns its back on feminism and hierarchizes gender relations. Raphaëlle experiences exquisite pleasure in the arms of her "male" with a "divine body." He makes her orgasm like she has never orgasmed in her life. But the young woman also dominates him in her surrender to him, and clearly derives a sense of superiority in the pleasure she gives her partner: "He's at my mercy. I feel he's entirely controlled by the pleasure I am giving him, and it excites me like crazy. I feel victorious. Powerful."[97] In the sadomasochist sessions of *Corps et âmes*, the woman, as an object of desire, is both dominated and dominating. Ultimately, her submission gives her the same power that the sadist feels he has over his victim. It is thanks to her that he comes. It is entirely her doing—she is the one giving him pleasure by giving herself to him.

The BDSM practices allow the heroine to not only abandon herself to sexuality (which her moral portrayal as a young virgin would make unacceptable in normal times), the sexual relations being initially devoid of affection, but also transform the man into an instrument of her own pleasure. Through him, she can always go further in her discovery of carnal pleasure, which includes, for example, sleeping with other men or women. In the love and lust dialectic, the woman can, in other words, experience orgasm by giving in to sex without love, in the name of a love yet to be born. She allows her sexual desire to arise within her male partner's sexual desire, thus giving her submission a certain form of agency. One could argue that, in the corpus under study, the representation of sadomasochism allows the heroine to fulfill her fantasies, just like the hero does. The pain in surrendering to the sexual games triggers "new sensations, a mix of suffering and intense pleasure, of a ravaging that drives her wild" and that culminates in a "spectacular orgasm."[98]

Since sexual liberation has not liberated sex from love, since infidelity among others is still considered a betrayal by the majority of couples, regardless of their sexual orientation, BDSM makes it possible to redeem a complete sexual liberation. For the woman especially, whose sexuality is always suspect, the sex act can take place with a man who treats her as a stranger, even a whore, and who subjects her to series of "desecrations." This debasement is acceptable because it is done in the name of love, present or to come. However, over the course of the story, the happy ending is never guaranteed. Halfway through the novel *Annabel et Max*, Max, deaf to the cries and pleading of his partner, sodomizes Annabel, who had never had anal sex, with such ardour that her body "was nothing but burning pain."[99] Later, everything works out and Annabel has the "joy" of "orgasming for Max." New adult fiction nonetheless could be said to constitute one of the limits of the romance genre: porn love. It is not Harlequin with more sex, but "pure" sex with a lasting dream of love.

Dreaming of love

In the twenty-first century, Québécois readers are still devouring romance novels. They adore titles by French authors Marc Lévy and Guillaume Musso, whose best sellers are disseminated throughout the francophone world. English-language writers (Diana Gabaldon, Danielle Steel, in translation or not) are also still very popular, without forgetting Harlequin, which continues to garner a sizeable share of sales, despite a visible decline. In a globalized Québécois book market dominated by foreign authors, a number of romance novels written by local writers have nonetheless managed to stand out. What these novels have to say about romantic feelings continues to be a rich source of information for anyone seeking to understand the evolution of the romantic imaginary in Quebec.

Throughout this chapter, we have seen how different versions of the contemporary romance novel, building on the previous period, have a number of features in common. These include, on the one hand, an affirmation of the female characters' greater independence (notably in chick lit, even if this quest is not always successful), and, on the other, the emergence of a more uninhibited sexuality (especially in the new adult fiction). From one sub-genre to the other, the works of the 2000s depict a plethora of couples facing a crisis following an adulterous betrayal, as though love outside the couple could only be precarious and still demanded fidelity. While BDSM authorizes the inclusion of extremely crude passages, sometimes between strangers, sexuality in romance novels does not lead to a situation where sex can dismiss love altogether: the connection between sex and love remains important in our corpus, even in the most extreme cases.

Whether it be in the more traditional romance of Suzanne Roy and Chloé Duval or in the chick lit stories of Rafaële Germain and company, the heroines, unable to accept themselves as single or act as though it were possible to be completely "self-sufficient," ultimately experience an "irrepressible need" to be in a couple, and when they dare pretend otherwise, it is because they are lying to themselves. The female characters inspired by chick lit are certainly more independent and in charge of their destinies than Elina in *Un cadeau du ciel.* They bear no resemblance to ethereal, luminous, virginal, divine, perfect dolls. They admit from the outset to having "many faults," to being "ordinary," "instable" and "changeable,"[100] but these deficiencies are precisely a result of their obsession with love and their attention-seeking hearts. Somehow, they are too "girly,"[101] in their profound need to love and be loved. Their first challenge thus consists of finding the ideal man, even though they are not "very talented in love." Their second challenge is learning to accept themselves for who they are, though also seeking what they lack from someone else. Chick lit not only portrays career women searching for love. More fundamentally, it shows how the female characters' multiple deficiencies and problems can only be appeased by the discovery of love, even with a small "l." In these novels, the heroines' newly acquired freedom, which exposes them to the "dangers" of the world and gives rise to many questions and anxieties, ultimately serves to remind them how incomplete and deficient they are without love. At a time in their lives, the thirty-something crisis, when the first ravages of age are appearing, their unhappiness can only be relieved in the arms of a man.

The other lesson of the romance novels of the twenty-first century is that love is based on a fulfilling sex life and that a fervent sexuality needs love. This connection to carnal desire reinforces the place of love while also undermining it. Prior to the 1940s, the end goal of love was oriented toward other factors besides the couple. This love grew with the family and flourished even more with the birth of every child, and it could thus even be deferred if the passion fizzled out. The recentring of love first on the couple, then on the subjectivity of an individual seeking love but putting their personal happiness first, makes sexuality a crucial and immediate factor in the confirmation of love. Now, love is manifested by and through a sexuality that seems never more ardent than when the couples are young, both in terms of their age and the stage of their relationship. Believing that couples are incapable of reconciling love and desire for very long, the French writer Frédéric Beigbeder summarized this situation with a pithy phrase in the title of his 1997 autobiographical novel *L'amour dure trois ans* (Love lasts three years). In Quebec, this mantra appears in numerous passages in chick lit, hammering home the fear that love progressively fades with the "little not-so-glamourous things" that are part of the couple's life. In *Soutien-gorge rose et veston noir*, Daphné warns her sister Chloé about rose-tinted dreams: "I know, I know. I'm talking with my head, not my heart, blah, blah, blah… That's easy to say, Chloé. You don't have any kids, you don't have a mortgage to pay, a relationship to maintain, a family to feed. Think about it for a couple of seconds: do you really think it's possible to keep up the passion fest when you have to remind your boyfriend to pick up a bottle of April Fresh Downy?"[102] That said, if love is to be prevented from dying, the "passion fest" can never become routine nor lose steam, which condemns the couple to continually replaying the inaugural scene of their first encounters in order to love each other "like the first time."

The case of *J'ai hâte à vous* (I yearn for you) by Julie Beaulieu is exemplary of contemporary "sexlove."[103] Very popular among male and female readers in Quebec,[104] the novel recounts the epistolary relation between Amélie, a young writer in her thirties suffering from a fatal illness, and an admirer who, seeing himself in the young woman's prose, begins writing her increasingly passionate letters. The day before Amélie's death, they give in to their desires. Beaulieu's novel is interesting for its premise but also for its very subdued eroticism. The author, who had become known with a first novel describing lascivious scenes,[105] explained her choices: "Eroticism is not just penetration, a tongue in someone else's mouth. I thought that this time, it was going to be really easy for me to write the only erotic scene, because I was used to writing these, but I realized that it was the most difficult scene to write. I had to really show that eroticism was not just a fuck, a fusion of one in the other. Eroticism goes beyond all that..."[106]

There are a multitude of erotic or pornographic novels in which sexuality is completely separated from love. Since the novels in our corpus are based on the triumph of love, we cannot find, by definition, any examples of sexuality without love. In romance, the characters make love for the sake of love or, at least, seek love when they are making love. What is new, is not the physical attraction between the characters. It is the role that sexuality plays in forming the happy couple. And the reason presented in the novels for this sexlove, is that love is never as profound as when the couple has a good sex life, and inversely, that sex is never as good, never as pleasurable or orgasmic as when it unites two people who are in love. On the last pages of *Annabel et Max, adultes consentants*, Max vigorously penetrates Annabel, while she massages her clitoris with a vibrator. Completely abandoning herself to the sexual play, she is dizzied by so much intense pleasure. "She wanted more than anything to prolong this moment of pure bliss. So she did something she never dared allow herself before; she continued masturbating with the device while also making a back-and-forth movement against Max's pelvis."[107] The latter, holding back from coming, had never found his partner so womanly, so magnificent, so desirable. The coitus barely finished, he asks her to marry him. "'Yes,' she happily accepts.'"[108]

The characters in the novels of the previous decades, who were seeking ways to fully satisfy their sexuality with the love of their life, have been replaced by women and men who have sex while dreaming of love. Thus the satisfaction that accompanies a more-or-less fulfilling sex life does not completely deny the romantic quest.[109] In intimate relations, love is not yet entirely abandoned between friendship and sex.[110] In 2014, Justin Laramée asked Anne-Marie Olivier and Véronique Côté why their documentary theatre piece based on impromptu interviews was titled *Faire l'amour* (Make love), rather than *Baiser* (Fuck) or *Fourrer* (Screw). "When we asked for real fucking stories from people during the evening interviews," answered Côté, "everyone just told us love stories." When Olivier and Côté asked again: "Give us just the sex for sex," all they got back were love stories.[111] The responses of people interviewed by Olivier and Côté are consistent with what is found in the twenty-first-century romance novels that make up our corpus.

CONCLUSION

The Codes of Love

Considered the result of a simple recipe, the romance novel proposes a framework that is so fixed that it can be repeated *ad infinitum* by more-or-less talented authors: two people fall in love and are soon separated by a series of obstacles. Reunited in the end, they can finally love each other. However, as its history shows, even limited to the most rudimentary composition rules, the romance novel remains a reservoir of fantasies and regulations. It thus represents a remarkable point of departure for reflecting on the evolution of the romantic imaginary in Québécois society. Though these novels endlessly repeat the same meeting-disjunction-conjunction scenario and reproduce the worst stereotypes of the "eternal feminine," they are nonetheless filled with information on what has shaped dreams of love and, in turn, on the ways these dreams have been nurtured or repressed. Because, while presenting what love should be in each period, the romance novel reveals at the same time what it should not be, that is to say, what its social context does not fully authorize it to say. As intimate as it may be from the point of view of the characters, the love portrayed in the novels is still a complex social construction.

The history of love seen through the lens of romance novels provides an original perspective on the codification of feelings.

To briefly summarize the multiple interpretations of love in the French-Canadian, then Québécois, romance novel, we could say that while it has always been dependent on a collective fabrication, both reflecting and idealizing the realities of each epoch, it has also been continually grounded in imperatives that gave it an ancillary function, whether in relation to a continued heritage, a religious vocation, maternity, marriage, or sexuality. This "re-purposing" is masked by an image of love presented from the outset as impenetrable, unpredictable, alchemical, inalienable, and ineffable, with canon law making marriage a free act and poets proclaiming a sovereign passion that knows no laws. A female columnist wrote in 1885: "The ideal of love, where is it? It is in the freely consented union between two beings freely chosen by each other."[1] While in the postwar period, love was entirely focused on the couple, rather than being directed toward exterior goals (the homeland, religion, social milieu, motherhood), its celebration took an even more absolute turn, and nothing, it seems, could constrain it without altering its nature.

Love is believed to be a universal and invariable feeling that transcends time. It is said that love never changes, regardless of the form it takes. The liberty and intransigence of love are indeed two of the most powerful and pervasive clichés in the literature. Romance novels written in Quebec celebrate the meeting of two beings who find the mysterious reason for their happiness in their uniqueness. One can never impose their feelings on another who does not feel the same intense passion. "Love is a thing of the heart not of the mind, will and intelligence have nothing to do with it,"[2] declares the heroine of *L'épreuve* (1900) to her uncle, before adding a little later for her suitor: "Can one reason with a love that is born and blossoms without us knowing, that invades and dominates our entire life?"[3] Love is also an irresistible, irrepressible intoxication. So irresistible and irrepressible, in fact, that the impossibility of giving oneself to it body and soul condemns lovers to despair.

Without love, life has no meaning: lovers find themselves at the mercy of the one they love. Their passion can be as much a source of life as a cause of death. Transfixed by love, the suitor of *Marie-Anna la Canadienne* (1913) confides to her: "I am waiting for you to give me life or take it from me!"[4] Likewise, in *Le secret de la marquise* (1906), Hector exclaims to his fiancée: "My little darling [...], if I had to leave you, I would rather be dead!"[5]

For a long time, stories published by French-Canadian authors had little to say about love. It is rather troubling to note that, in most nineteenth-century novels, matters of the heart are rarely mentioned. When the romances in these stories are not quickly dismissed in favour of another plot line, the heroes and heroines are killed off like flies. We observe an antagonism between a romantic sentiment that revolves around the couple and the expectations of a society that seeks to contain, divert or sublimate love, if not repress it altogether. The love stories of the period are dreadfully trite because most novelists struggle to accept the disjunction, which is one of the principles of the genre. Instead, they endeavour to show how much the characters are destined for each other, without any possible failure. Either the stories present people who are happily in love, thus with no story, or who, when passion arises, are never finally reunited. Not knowing what to do with a sentiment that threatens to shatter a community founded on national traditions, religious faith, and the transmission of heritage—in other words, on the identical reproduction of the social order—authors redirect passion toward self-sacrifice or the renouncement of personal happiness. A long procession of texts that begin as love stories thus end with passion being sacrificed on the altar of family, homeland, and religion. From *Charles Guérin* (1846) to *Maria Chapdelaine* (1913), countless love stories are suppressed in the name of great sacrifices. While appearing to give full liberty to romantic feelings, the characters in these novels seem unable to commit to each other without an attachment to tradition.

During the period 1860-1920, there are nonetheless a few exceptions to the endogamy in the love stories or their sublimation in the divine. Two novels written by an English Canadian living in Montreal and almost immediately translated into French, *Le manoir de Villerai* (1860) and *Antoinette de Mirecourt* (1864), are real romance novels that transgress a social taboo of the period: the mismatch of an aristocratic man and a commoner woman, on the one hand, and a marriage between a French-Canadian woman and an Englishman, on the other. *Les Ribaud : une idylle de 37* (1898) also condones the marriage between the daughter of a Patriot and a British soldier. Even more strikingly, *Amour vainqueur* (1915) recounts a young woman's quest for success and love, ending with her moving to New York with her fabulously wealthy husband. But these stories are rare, dominated as they are by the theme of community seclusion. Even after the First World War, romance novels were still strictly monitored, and though one critic may have rightly observed in 1926 that the "'prince charmings' of farm girls and peasants are popular on the stage and in novels,"[6] it was primarily in reference to foreign works, including French serial novels, love stories and theatre, as well as American cinema.

In the 1920s, the creation of staunchly nationalist publishing houses, notably the Bibliothèque de l'Action française and Éditions Édouard Garand, lead to a clerical-nationalist reclaiming of the romance novel for its own ends. At a time when French-Canadian society still saw itself reflected in a ruralist and traditionalist image, the stories largely depict a humble life and often take place in the countryside: love is at the service of the family-religion-homeland triad. In *Un cœur fidèle* (1925), Jean is mistaken in thinking he could succeed in the United States. He retains only bitter memories of his experience, as he confides to Marie: "Nobody knows what a person endures when he has no sense of home, when he is like the wandering Jew going from place to place! I will never forget that for the rest of my life... I found it so hard, so very hard..."[7] Georgine, in *Le secret de l'orpheline* (1928), flatly refuses the advances of Mr. Hammett, because he is an Englishman: "Giving oneself to the other race is nothing less than treason: a loss for the French side, and vainglory for the English side."[8]

We detect, however, an important shift in the stories' focal point. The community is less and less the definitive criteria for the couple, whose central function seems to be increasingly oriented toward their progeny. There is no marriage without love, and no marriage without children. The ideal for every woman is to be a mother. This imperative is so strong that in *Yolande la fiancée* (1935), the main heroine, who has lost her suitor, finds a substitute marital vocation in caring for the woman who would have been her mother-in-law, along with an old aunt and her brother's children.[9] The author writes that "she divided her care and devotion between her aunt Sylvic and Madame Desruisseaux. For both of these elderly women, she would accompany them until death. Henri could reproach her for nothing. After caring for her parents, she would be there for his mother, an affectionate and devoted girl as she had promised him. Later, she would go on to share with her sister-in-law the numerous duties that a family demands."[10] Even without a husband or children, the woman is expected to be a mother. The old maids in these novels adopt nieces or orphans while thanking heaven for giving them the children they could never have.

In the postwar period, the purpose of love changes again. The basic plot of the romance novel is not altered: a young girl of exquisite beauty and unwavering virtue lives an adventure that ends either in marriage or at least with the promise or expectation of it. But the simple fact that the heroines in the novels are a little freer to circulate already reveals that the traditional community was no longer able to contain romantic relationships. Negotiations between families, marriages of convenience, unions between young men and women perceived as "brothers" and "sisters," and requiring their parents' permission to be together, sometimes under the family roof, give way to the emergence of feelings beyond the immediate family circle. The lovers are increasingly "alone in the world." In *Dernier amour*, for example, Luc, unburdened by the weight of his past, says to his wife: "there is nothing left now but the two of us, and that, that is the good life."[11] This liberation resulted in an unprecedented celebration of conjugal love in magazines, advertisements, love letters, and, of course, "dime novels."

In the 1940s and 1950s, girls and boys begin "going out" and entering the game of flirting. Women can no longer passively wait for a fiancé as in the old days. Since dating has become the only exit route from the family home, they must take every opportunity to meet a potential suitor, without whom they can forget about marriage. Marriage as the union between two families is replaced by marriage as the union between two individuals, and young people sometimes get engaged without even mentioning it to their parents, confronting the latter with a *fait accompli*. It is no longer required to submit to the parental blessing, a rite that was already in serious decline during the interwar period. In short, unions begin revolving around the intimacy of the couple, while also more clearly consummating the split between the nuclear family and the rest of society.

The real challenge for the young girl now is to make the quantum leap (because no longer mediated by her enlarged family, parish or village) between her condition as a girl and her status as a wife. Love becomes the guarantee that, once ensconced in her new home with no going back ("for better or for worse"), she will find true happiness. Her quest for a home fuses with her search for a great love. The fables suggest, however, that this quest for the perfect home is not always completely fulfilling. The modern young woman can perhaps count on having a refrigerator and washing machine, but her life is often boring. The spouses do not always manage to transform their home into a "cozy nest" and instead end up creating a hell for two. Since divorce is prohibited, women who are frustrated in the family setting have no way out. In *Souffle de passion* (1947), the heroine, married to a man who leaves her indifferent, laments her routine existence and imagines herself dying, "lying in the flowerbed, her face buried in the grass, with both hands over her ears so as not to hear the beating of her tired, wretched heart."[12] Luckily the war hero Claude returns, Marcel dies, and she can finally be happy at the end of the story.

The power imbalance between the female and male characters is at a peak here. Even as orphans, frightened victims without any support, the heroines of the previous novels had the same standing as the heroes and could always find atonement in a death that came close to making them saints or martyrs. They died gazing up to heaven with a smile on their lips. The heroines of the 1940s and 1950s are more at the mercy of the male characters. Without them, they are nothing, or worth very little, even though now for the first time they are usually gainfully employed. Their training and specialized work as typists, secretaries, and so on, is a smoke screen: these scenarios serve as a pretext for the meeting of the hero, which is the true purpose of the story. They have to rush to the altar in a society that destines single women for the convent (in contrast to the unique place of old maids in English-language novels).[13] Passion is excessively celebrated because it is the condition *sine qua non* of a girl's success. If the romance novels of this period are based so much on gendered roles, it is because they portray a quest that more directly concerns women. Between prewar endogamy and postwar autonomy, they are condemned to loving subjectively or perishing socially.

The dime novels describe the new matrimonial market in which women are immersed and how this differs from that of men. Women have to work at "being more" (more beautiful, more charming, more refined, more educated); men have to work at "having more" (more money, more prestige, more strength). *Le héros de mon cœur* (The hero of my heart) describes the life of Marie, a talented young reporter who is making her way up the professional ladder to become, in the last pages of the story, head of the reporting division of her paper. Her personality contrasts with that of her rival, the mean-spirited Miss Lindsay, who is also the boss's mistress. Daft and not very gifted, the latter is only an interchangeable object for the boss, who is very frank about this: "Oh! So the young lady is jealous! But jealous of the brains and success of colleagues. My dear, has it never occurred to you that you are here for your looks, because your pretty face is part of the office decor? And nothing else!"[14] However, Marie does not resemble her little handicapped sister Reine either. Just pretty enough and with an intelligence that has not diminished her femininity, Marie can expect success on the matrimonial market. But she better hurry up: all the young women are in the race, and they know that to make a life for themselves they have to get married and become, like one of the characters in our corpus, "Mrs. Bob Lemieux."[15]

One might have expected the romance genre to take off in the 1960s, a period finally relieved of the weight of conservative morality. We observe instead its erasure. First, the internationalization of the publishing field facilitated the penetration of major French publishers and American publishing intermediaries into the French-language Québécois market. Second, the romance novel had competition from other increasingly appealing media, like television, cinema, and photo novels. Third, the sexual revolution made love a self-sufficient sentiment (*All you need is love*), without requiring, as before, compliance with social or personal demands. Rising divorce rates and decreasing birth rates destabilized a love once based on the indissolubility of the couple. Since women no longer needed a man to make a life for themselves, the old romantic rhetoric seemed outdated and stultifying, even though it persisted in many milieus.

This is why, in the context of the Quiet Revolution, Québécois authors were late to produce the "great romance novel" that many literary critics were calling for. It wasn't until the end of the 1970s that the romance novel (in the form of the historical novel) was able to carve out a place among the books written by local authors. This renewed interest coincided with the appearance of a new codification of love, centred this time on sexuality. The English-language literary tradition had explored this avenue long before the French-language tradition, but even among the British and Americans, recognition of a sexualized love remained veiled and metaphorized until then. The publication of *The Flame and the Flower* (1972) by Woodiwiss, in the wake of the sexual revolution that shook the West, established the definitive union between love and sex in the romantic discourse.[16] In Quebec, the first book of Marie-Claude Bussières-Tremblay's *Rachel* series was published six years later.

The example of Bussières-Tremblay could have led to the development of an interesting niche market, but that same year, in 1978, the arrival of the Harlequin publishing house swept the local competition. Its success was so great that the publisher's name came to stand in for the genre in general. According to Fred Kerner, a Montreal author turned vice-president of the Canadian multinational's literary sector, "A woman doesn't enter a store to buy a romance novel by this or that author, but to buy a Harlequin romance."[17] Since none of the publisher's authors were Québécois women, and since the novels' stories did not take place in Quebec,[18] Harlequin dealt a hard blow to the production of a local romantic imaginary. The few attempts to launch Harlequin substitutes in Quebec ended in failure.

In the 1980s, the Québécois romance novel found an outlet in young adult literature, which enjoyed an unprecedented boom. The latter's resemblance to the Harlequin works lay in the idea that a fully lived life was not possible without love and that one had to be in love to make love, while making sexuality, in both a direct yet subtle way, an essential dimension of the fulfillment of passionate feelings. However, while the Harlequin works were abstract or exotic in their descriptions of places, the young adult novels were rooted in a Québécois reality, including numerous unifying cultural references and symbols (specific places, hockey, popular music, local expressions). This was not the only difference: the ironic reappropriation of stereotypes, the self-mockery and humour, the occasional use of the male character's narrative point of view, the awareness of a new serial aspect of love, and the feminist critique of machismo, all decisively distinguished this production from that of Harlequin, which continued to reproduce the clichés of the dominating man and passive, objectified woman.

In the twenty-first century, like a phoenix that refuses to die, the romance novel made new inroads into the Québécois book market. This type of romance reiterates the message that every individual's true vocation is to find love. The characters, especially the women, are presented as being helpless and lost before meeting that special someone who allows them to know who they really are, to discover the burning love in the hearts. Alexandra, in *À sa rencontre*, cries tears of joy when Éric tell her that he wants her in his life. We sense that their love story marks the real beginning of Alexandra's life, which prior to this moment had not really been lived. In the final pages before the epilogue, she muses: "Maybe it had been no coincidence that I had been the one to find Gabrielle's picture. Maybe it had been my destiny to track hers and follow it to the threshold of happiness where I stood now."[19]

Following young adult romance, chick lit seems to endorse a free love that abandons the quest for Mr. Right. Depicting young women who imbibe Manhattan cocktails and gin and tonics to forget their single status and sour-tempered (usually female) boss, these novels insist on a young woman's ability to marry her work and make it on her own. At the same time, these heroines, haunted by an inner emptiness, seem incapable of finding a balance in their lives. Their misfortunes and blunders send them the message that something, somewhere, is not quite right. In *Si tu t'appelles Mélancolie* (2010), when everything is going wrong—which happens often—the heroine "opens an umpteenth bottle of red." At university, while her Communication Studies colleagues were hoping to become great reporters, she was "dreaming," "but never really knew of what,"[20] and one senses that this indecision never really left her, whether at work or in love. By the end of the novel, after endless setbacks, she will have found a sympathetic companion who she hopes to date for "quite a long time," which seems to indicate that her self-quest is over for the time being.

In chick lit, the ideal of sacrifice, so recurrent in the traditional literature, has almost entirely disappeared. While the female characters of the past accepted self-erasure in the presence of their companions, here they affirm themselves. More often than not, they are the ones who refuse to commit, while also trying to escape the single life, a contradictory attitude that fuels their anxieties and doubts. Chick lit is thus more the story of the tribulations of a woman prey to loneliness, even in the arms of a man, than the story of a couple. Hesitating between giving up on or continuing the romantic quest, confronted with so many disappointing representatives of the male species (too young, too old, too stingy, too distant), the heroine knows that "nothing comes easy." The proliferation of qualifiers used to name romantic partners already points to a blurring of affections. While female characters before the Quiet Revolution could easily distinguish between "true" and "false" love based on the sexual relation (one only slept with one's spouse and only married for love), the contemporary heroines of chick lit realize they're caught "between girlfriends, mistresses, boyfriends, lovers, and one-night stands, fuck friends and true love."[21] Given this state of romantic chaos, a chick lit series can go from one volume to the next without providing readers any assurance of an outcome for the couple, contrary to the dime novels or Harlequin series. Love may never be born or reborn. The heroine accepts postponing finding a love that she knows in any case to be mortal.

The fragility and unpredictability of love can be seen as the price to pay for her liberty. Today, emancipated from the former social constraints weighing on the romantic encounter, love can strike any time, any place. It is no longer necessary to wait for the engagement to kiss, or to get married to make love. It is no longer indispensable to obtain the consent and support of the parents before moving in together. Officially, interdictions based on class, status or nationality no longer have a place in romantic relationships. The partner's religion has lost its importance, and Catholics are in any case less and less likely to get married at the church. Sexual orientation is no longer a taboo. Apart from incest and pedophilia, passion involves everyone, the very beauty and power of love being that it knows no bounds: mixed marriages (whatever combination) show, as Madame de Sévigné wrote, that "love is stronger than all reasons."

There are many who would now question the very necessity of love. On the one hand, porno sites and social networking platforms are replacing the bonds of fidelity and sexuality between two people. On the other hand, increased individualism makes the compromises demanded of a couple's life difficult. It looks as if the challenges of love have taken a 180-degree turn. In the past, the elites were alarmed by the idea of loving a foreigner (based on social milieu, class, religion, and nationality); today the concern is whether individuals can only love themselves. Perhaps the game of love is not worth the effort, and it would be better to stop believing in love, just as people stopped one day believing in God, rather than insisting on pursuing an illusion. "I wondered if anyone in the restaurant, or even in the whole city," muses the heroine of *Gin tonic et concombre*, "had a completely satisfying or intoxicating relationship, or if the very concept of shared true love was nothing but a huge, rather mean joke whose only purpose was to make us feel pathetic with our approximate love that all too often seemed like a compromise."[22]

If love still manages to fuel passions, drive personal quests, and inspire dreams "despite everything," it is because it is has lodged itself within contemporary sexuality. Today, it would seem unusual to say the least for a couple to declare being in love without feeling any physical attraction, as evidenced by the popularity of drugs that enhance erectile performance among men, and the colossal sums of money spent on cosmetics and plastic surgery among women. But while the characters of the successful romance novels of the 1980s share their love to achieve full sexual satisfaction, the characters in the 2000s have sex with the hope of finding love. No longer inhibited, sex has become a game that can be free from love, even though many still believe that the best sex is with the person they love. When this connection is lost—and many fear this is only a matter of time with the development of sexbots and virtual reality technologies—the quest for love will be seriously compromised.

Romance literature explores the code of sexlove to the fullest. In *Sous l'emprise de Monsieur Addams*, Félicia Roby is held captive against her will, which keeps her in the camp of the guardians of morality and virtue, because her sexual pleasure is forced out of her and she is plagued with remorse. The following citation incorporates the prohibition, transmitted from mother to daughter, of any sexual desire without love: "It has become routine for me to have orgasms with men I have no romantic feelings for. I'm ashamed. My mother would tell me that girls who are balanced and of sound mind have no need for that. What they need is the comforting arms of a good family man."[23] Far from bearing witness to a hypersexualized society, the BDSM in romance novels recounts how immoral and shameful sexuality is without love. Worse still: sex without love is inferior, superficial, insignificant and ordinary. The heroines claim to have had only disappointing sexual relations with their lovers before achieving "spectacular" orgasms in the arms of their true love. Raphaëlle, the introverted bookseller in *Corps et âmes* lets herself be tongued by her partner "until her cries of pleasure resound through the room, making both of them completely mad with the devouring passion that consumes them."[24] For the readers of this passage, there can be no doubt that Raphaëlle loves Arnaud, and that she will love him, as she says, "very deeply for the rest of [her] life."[25]

Along with the idea that it is better to love when sleeping with someone, the very recent contemporary romance novel reiterates the conviction that one can only love a single person at a time. This is hardly surprising given the genre-based definition of the romance novel, which, according to its invariants, must present the triumph of love through the story of a single couple that is reunited in the end. But a mutation has nonetheless occurred. While, prior to the 1960s, the Québécois romance novel was based on the myth of androgynous incompleteness, each person having to find their missing half, the more recent novels cannot sustain this claim without losing all credibility. The heroines and heroes are therefore portrayed as practising a serial love, faithful to one partner at a time but also able to have several romantic relationships over the course of their lives. It is thus not hard to imagine the popular Québécois romance novel one day integrating the idea of polyamory[26] and exploring scenarios that are a lot more open than those found in chick lit. It is difficult, however, to predict what the novels to come have in store for us. What new dreams will they weave for us? Will they succeed in revolutionizing our understanding of love once again? If there is one thing that the history of the romance novel in Quebec has revealed to us, it is the genre's fabulous capacity to renew itself. The past two hundred years, punctuated with stories that are always similar yet always different, suggest that the last chapter of the history of the romance novel in Quebec has yet to be written.

Acknowledgments

We would like to thank our research assistants Karol'Ann Boivin and Danielle Miller-Béland for their help in the data collection and compiling of notes. Anthony Glinoer and Adrien Rannaud kindly agreed to read a preliminary version of the manuscript and provide very generous feedback. Our research benefited from the financial support of the Social Sciences and Humanities Research Council of Canada and the Concordia University Research Chair for the Study of Québec.

Notes

Introduction: All your fine words

1. Alain Corbin, Jean-Jacques Courtine and Georges Vigarello (ed.), *Histoire des émotions, Tome 3, De la fin du XIX*[e] *siècle à nos jours*, Paris, Seuil, 2017, 620 p.
2. See in particular the work of French scholar Anne-Claire Rebreyend, *Intimités amoureuses. France, 1920-1975*, Toulouse, Presses universitaires du Mirail, 2008, 340 p.
3. Our corpus is restricted to French-language literary production. To respect the chronological usage, we use "French-Canadian" for the period prior to 1960, and "Québécois" for the period from 1960 to the present.
4. See the work of Denis Saint-Jacques, among others, "L'idéologique dans le texte," in Guy Bouchard *et al.*, *Le phénomène IXE-13*, Québec, Presses de l'Université Laval, 1984, p. 283-322, and of Marc Angenot, "Qu'est-ce que la paralittérature?" *Études littéraires*, Vol. 7, No. 1, April 1974, p. 9-22. Marc Angenot, *Le roman populaire. Recherches en paralittérature*, Montréal, Presses de l'Université du Québec, 1975, 145 p.
5. Niklas Luhmann, *Love as Passion: The Codification of Intimacy* (Cambridge, Polity, 1986). On the different sociological interpretations of love feelings, see Mihai Stelian Rusu, "Theorising Love in Sociological Thought: Classical Contributions to a Sociology of Love," *Journal of Classical Sociology*, Vol. 18, No. 1, 2018, p. 3-20.
6. Far from lessening the scornful gaze of traditional elites, the feminist revolution only changed the form of the indictment: previously suspected of filling young girls' heads with unhealthy ideas, romance novels were now castigated for their rigid conservatism. Thus, for many Quebec feminists, outraged by the rise of "Harlequin" type stories in the 1980s, "everything we want to change is in these novels." Andrée Chapleau, quoted by Jacques Marchand, "Harlequin et Colombine : l'industrie plafonne, l'amour aussi," Études littéraires, Vol. 16, No. 3, December 1983, p. 361.
7. Several articles and a few dissertations and theses, which can be found in the bibliography, have dealt with the representation of love either in specific collections, or in particular bodies of work such as bestsellers, or finally, in Quebec literature in the broad sense. Our approach owes much to these pioneering works, which will be cited throughout the chapters: the fact remains that no research to date has attempted to measure the complete evolution of the Quebec sentimental novel as

a specific genre. For an excellent synthesis of the history of love in the novel since Greek antiquity, which contains several Quebec examples, see Fabienne Claire Caland, Bertrand Rouby and Paul Bleton, *L'amour au temps du roman*, Québec, Télé-université, 2015, 232 p.

8. Serge Gagnon, *Mariage et famille au temps de Papineau*, Sainte-Foy, Les Presses de l'Université Laval, 1993, 300 p.

9. Jean-Philippe Warren (ed.), *Une histoire des sexualités au Québec au XXe siècle*, Montréal, VLB éditeur, 2012, 288 p. Gaston Desjardins, *L'amour en patience : la sexualité adolescente au Québec, 1940-1960*, Québec, Presses de l'Université du Québec, 1995, 261 p.

10. Mixing many aspects (marriage, sexuality, emotions, etc.) and piecing together numerous anecdotes in a non-academic style, the journalist Jean-Sébastien Marsan published *Histoire populaire de l'amour au Québec de la Nouvelle-France à la Révolution tranquille, Tome I, Avant 1760*, Montréal, Fides, 2019, 217 p. and *Tome 2, 1760-1860*, Montréal, Fides, 2020, 186 p.

11. To name just one title: Jean-Marie Schaeffer, *Pourquoi la fiction?*, Paris, Seuil, 1999, 346 p.

12. Janice A. Radway, *Reading the Romance: Women, Patriarchy and Popular Literature*, Chapel Hill, The University of North Carolina Press, 1991 [1984], 276 p. Helen Wood, "What *Reading the Romance* Did for Us." *European Journal of Cultural Studies*, Vol. 7, No. 2, 2004, p. 147—154. For France, read Séverine Olivier, *Le roman sentimental. Productions contemporaines et pratiques de lecture*, PhD Thesis, Brussels, Université libre de Bruxelles, 2009, 449 p.

13. A distinction is sometimes made between the romance novel (*roman d'amour* or *roman rose*), which ends well and belongs to a minor genre, and the sentimental novel (*roman sentimental*), which ends badly and has produced classics. But this dual designation obscures the fact that "we are dealing with a single genre of fictional narrative, since the same structural and thematic elements, the same obligatory motifs, and many recurring variable motifs are inscribed in the achievements." Ellen Constans, "Du roman sentimental au roman d'amour. Qu'en est-il du déclassement?" in Jacques Migozzi (dir.), *Le roman populaire en question(s)*, Limoges, Presses universitaires de Limoges, 1997, p. 349.

14. Ellen Constans, *Parlez-moi d'amour. Le roman sentimental, des romans grecs aux collections de l'an 2000*, Limoges, Presses universitaires de Limoges, 1999, 349 p.

15. *Ibid.*, p. 18.

16. Although heterosexuality is not a condition of the romance novel, Quebec LGBTQ+ novels have only recently appeared. We will address this sub-genre in the last chapter.

17. Ellen Constans, *Parlez-moi d'amour*, p. 18.

18. To use here the title of the volume edited by Julia Bettinotti, *La corrida de l'amour: le roman Harlequin*, Montréal, XYZ, 1990 [1986], 151 p.

19. George Paizis uses the same categories as Constans, under different names: first meeting, obstacle(s) and solution. George Paizis, *Love and the Novel: Contemporary Romantic Fiction and Society*, Basingstoke, Palgrave Macmillan, 1998, 212 p. Séverine Olivier takes a similar approach, reframing it around an additional stage, interposed between the disjunction and the conjunction, which she

considers essential: meeting, disjunction, internal focalization, final conjunction. The internal focalization designates the process of unveiling the thoughts of the hero and the heroine. Séverine Olivier, *Le roman sentimental. Productions contemporaines et pratiques de lecture*, PhD, Brussels, Université libre de Bruxelles, 2009, p. 49.

20. Ellen Constans, *Parlez-moi d'amour*, p. 27.

21. Suzanne Roy, *Un cadeau du ciel*, Paris, Milady, 2014, p. 294.

22. For reference works, see the *Dictionnaire des œuvres littéraires du Québec, La vie littéraire au Québec, L'histoire de l'édition littéraire au Québec.* One can also consult databases of the catalogues of several editors, created by researchers of the Groupe de recherches et d'études sur le livre au Québec and available at the following address: https://recherche.flsh.usherbrooke.ca/GRELQ/.

23. By "book" we mean any autonomous publication, detached from the periodical press, which includes the 32-page booklets published by the Éditions Police-Journal in the 1940s, 1950s and 1960s.

24. Though we accepted late editions, such as *Anne Mérival*, a novel by the journalist Anne-Marie Gleason Huguenin (Madeleine). Published in three parts in *La Revue moderne* in 1927, it was later reprinted in an electronic edition by the Bibliothèque électronique du Québec. Madeleine is the pseudonym of Anne-Marie Gleason Huguenin, *Anne Mérival*, coll. "Littérature québécoise," Vol. 713, La Bibliothèque électronique du Québec, [Online], [1927], 192 p., https://beq.ebooksgratuits.com/pdf-xpdf/Madeleine-Anne.pdf.

25. Flavien-J. Granger and Alphonse-A. Granger, "Leprohon (Madame)," *France-Canada. Bibliographie canadienne : catalogue d'un choix d'ouvrages canadiens-français, accompagné de notes bibliographiques, et préparé à l'occasion de l'Exposition universelle de 1900*, Montréal, Granger frères, 1900, p. 43.

Chapter 1: Repressed Love (1830-1860)

1. George Stephen Jones, *A Love Story From 19th Century Quebec: The Diary of George Stephen Jones*, Peterborough, Broadview Press, 1989, p. 56.

2. Serge Gagnon, *Mariage et famille au temps de Papineau*, Sainte-Foy, Presses de l'Université Laval, 1993, 300 p. For a general analysis, see Edward Shorter's classic, *The Making of the Modern Family*, New York, Basic Books, 1975, 369 p.

3. In particular, correspondence of the period could not exhibit intense or uncontrolled passions. Julie Roy, *Stratégies épistolaires et écritures féminines. Les Canadiennes à la conquête des lettres (1639-1839)*, PhD Thesis, Montréal, Université du Québec à Montréal, 2002, 868 p. Mylène Bédard, *Rhétorique et autoreprésentation : la pratique épistolaire des femmes en temps d'insurrections*, PhD Thesis, Québec, Université Laval, 2014, 413 p. Robert Blondin and Gilles LaMontagne (collab.), "Le grand amour," in *Chers nous autres. Un siècle de correspondance québécoise*, Tome 1, Montréal, VLB, 1978, p. 77-132.

4. "Bovarysm" takes its name from Flaubert's famous novel, published in 1856. "And Emma tried to find out what one meant exactly in life by the words *felicity, passion, rapture*, that had seemed to her so beautiful in books." Having taken to reading sentimental books, she had become "the mistress of all the novels, the vague 'she' of all the poetry books." Gustave Flaubert (trans. Eleanor Marx-Aveling), *Madame Bovary*, London, Collector's Library, 2003 (1857], p. 46; 324.

5. Joseph Vincent Quiblier, *Cours abrégé de belles lettres, à l'usage du Collège de Montréal*, Montréal, C. P. Leprohon, 1840, p. 174.
6. Pierre Hébert, *Censure et littérature au Québec. Le livre crucifié 1625-1919*, Montréal, Fides, 1997, 296 p. For example, to counter the influence of the Institut canadien (which kept officially prohibited works of fiction), the Sulpicians founded the Oeuvre des bons livres in 1844, a library that tended to exclude novels from its catalogue. Marcel Lajeunesse, *Les Sulpiciens et la vie culturelle à Montréal au XIXe siècle*, Montréal, Fides, 1982, 278 p.
7. See Michel Biron, François Dumont and Élisabeth Nardout-Lafarge, "Le roman contre lui-même," *Histoire de la littérature québécoise*, 2nd edition, Montréal, Boréal, 2010 [2007], p. 128-130; Philippe Rioux, *La préface de romans québécois du XIXe siècle et ses discours*, Master's Thesis, Sherbrooke, Université de Sherbrooke, 2014, 149 p.
8. François-Réal Angers, *Les révélations du crime ou Cambray et ses complices: chroniques canadiennes de 1834*, Québec, Fréchette et cie, 1837, p. 31. On this work, that lies somewhere between a novel and a collection of anecdotes, see Alex Gagnon, *La communauté du dehors. Imaginaire social et crimes célèbres au Québec (XIXe-XXe siècle)*, coll. "Socius," Montréal, Presses de l'Université de Montréal, 2016, 500 p.
9. Jacques Blais, *De l'ordre et de l'aventure. La poésie au Québec de 1934 à 1944*, coll. "Vie des lettres québécoises," Tome 14, Québec, Presses de l'Université Laval, 1975, 411 p.
10. Michel Lord, *En quête du roman gothique québécois 1837-1860*, Québec, Nuit blanche éditeur, 1994, p. 18. Robert D. Hume, "Gothic versus Romantic: A Revaluation of the Gothic Novel," *PMLA*, Vol. 84, No. 2, March 1969, p. 282-290.
11. "Contrary to a lot of European adventure novels, where love is absent or only an accessory to develop a character's dramatic role," writes Ducharme, "in Quebec, the genre essentially revolves around the motif of thwarted love as a main driver of the adventure. It is the love of fairy loves: a young man meets a young woman, is immediately smitten and [...] remains devoted to this love right up until the conclusion [...]." Nathalie Ducharme, *Espaces, personnages et société dans le roman d'aventures québécois au XIXe siècle*, PhD Thesis, Montréal, Université du Québec à Montréal, 2007, p. 285. According to Ducharme, the Québécois adventure novel finds its origins in two types of corpora: the British-American gothic and the French melodrama. In these two corpora, the love story seems essential to the unfolding of the narrative. Ducharme's revised thesis was published under the title *Le roman d'aventures au Québec, 1837-1900*, coll. "L'archive littéraire au Québec," Québec, Presses de l'Université Laval, 2019, 264 p.
12. Philippe Aubert de Gaspé fils, *L'influence d'un livre. Roman historique*, Québec, William Cowan et Fils, 1837, 122 p.
13. Joseph Doutre, *Les fiancés de 1812 : essai de littérature canadienne*, Montréal, Louis Perrault imprimeur, 1844, 493 p.
14. The first work of Canadian literature is *The History of Emily Montague* (translated into French as *Voyage dans le Canada ou Histoire de Miss Montaigu*). Published in 1769 by Frances Brooke, it recounts the story of three couples headed for marriage.

15. Philippe Aubert de Gaspé Jr., *The Influence of a Book*, trans. Claire Rothman, Montréal, Robert Davies, 1993, p. 25.
16. Philippe Aubert de Gaspé Jr., *The Influence of a Book*, 1993, p. 153.
17. On the reproduction of French serials in Québécois papers, see Frédérick Durand, *Le transfert culturel du roman-feuilleton français dans le réseau de la presse québécoise du XIXe siècle : contre-légitimation de la déviance et de l'excès dans l'imaginaire littéraire*, PhD Thesis, Trois-Rivières, Université du Québec à Trois-Rivières, 2003, 358 p. The period studied by Durand concerns that last quarter of the nineteeth century. For France, see Anne-Marie Thiesse, *Le roman du quotidien. Lecteurs et lectures populaires à la Belle Époque*, Paris, Le Chemin vert, 1984, 272 p.
18. Lukasz Marek Szkopinski, *L'œuvre romanesque de François Guillaume Ducray-Duminil*, Paris, Classiques Garnier, 2015, 298 p.
19. Kenneth Landry, "Le roman-feuilleton français dans la presse périodique québécoise à la fin du XIXe siècle : surveillance et censure de la fiction populaire," Études françaises, Vol. 36, No. 3, 2000, p. 65-80.
20. Philippe Aubert de Gaspé Jr., *The Influence of a Book*, 1993, p. 82.
21. Véronique Nahoum-Grappe, "L'échange des regards," *Terrain*, No. 30, March 1998, p. 70. Jean Rousset, *Leurs yeux se rencontrèrent. La scène de première vue dans le roman*, Paris, J. Corti, 1981, 216 p.
22. Philippe Aubert de Gaspé Jr., *The Influence of a Book*, 1993, p. 85. Similarly, in *La fille du brigand* (published in series in *Le Ménestrel* in 1844), the hero is consumed by the fire of love; if he listened to himself, he would marry the heroine "even if she were the daughter of the most wretched of all men, because she is honest, beautiful and virtuous." Eugène L'Écuyer, *La fille du brigand*, Montréal, Imprimerie Bilodeau, 1914, p. 31. Lécuyer uses the image of the spark (which serves as the title of one of the chapters) to illustrate the ravages of love, that often awaits but a first encounter to set the heart aflame.
23. Philippe Aubert de Gaspé Jr., *The Influence of a Book*, p. 87
24. Philippe Aubert de Gaspé Jr., *The Influence of a Book*, p. 153.
25. *Les fiancés de 1812* was condemned in 1848, four years after its first publication, for its romantic excesses. See L. L., "Chronique littéraire," *Mélanges religieux, politiques, commerciaux et littéraires*, Vol. 12, No. 17, 10 November 1848, p. 67 and [Anonymous], "Le chroniqueur," *Mélanges religieux, politiques, commerciaux et* littéraires, Vol. 12, No. 19, 17 November 1848, p. 74.
26. "*The Mysteries of Paris* is a learned school of private and public discipline. We invoke on this subject the testimony of the thousands who have devoured this amazing and sublime construction of the imagination. Indeed, would we be in an epoch depraved enough that the spectacle of virtue and the horrors of vice made no difference in the efforts and progress of civilization? We challenge any public man to produce as much good as has Eugène Sue with his admirable novel." Joseph Doutre, *Les fiancés de 1812*, p. xii-xiii. On the dissemination of Sue in Québec, see Yves Dostaler, *Les infortunes du roman dans le Québec du XIXe siècle*, coll. "Cahiers du Québec,"Montréal, Hurtubise HMH, 1977, 175 p.
27. Joseph Doutre, *Les fiancés de 1812*, p. 49.
28. *Ibid.*, p. 51.

29. *Ibid.*, p. 28.
30. *Ibid.*, p. 478.
31. In *L'influence d'un livre*, the description of the hero's beloved also reproduces these stereotypes: "It was during one of his long walks on this tract of land that he first saw Amélie, a girl of fifteen, with a sad, pensive smile. Amélie was a French-Canadian beauty, with long black hair that hung down to her feet and ebony eyes which made her pale face seem almost angelic. Her figure quite rivalled those of the loveliest women of southern France." Philippe Aubert de Gaspé Jr., *The Influence of a Book*, pp. 81—82.
32. Joseph Doutre, *Les fiancés de 1812*, p. 51.
33. *Ibid.*, p. 89.
34. *Ibid.*, p. 94.
35. *Ibid.*, p. 72-73.
36. *Ibid.*, p. 73.
37. *Ibid.*, p. 492.
38. *Ibid.*, p. 92.
39. *Ibid.*
40. Edmond Lareau, *Histoire de la littérature canadienne*, Montréal, John Lovell, 1874, p. 281. André Sénécal, "L'autorité du sentiment dans *Les Fiancés de 1812*," *Voix et Images*, Vol. 7, No. 1, Fall 1981, p. 169-175.
41. Joseph Doutre, *Les fiancés de 1812*, p. 198-199.
42. Niklas Luhmann, *Amour comme passion : de la codification de l'intimité*, translated from the German by A.-M. Lionnet, Paris, Aubier, 1990 [1986], 300 p.
43. Joseph Doutre, *Les fiancés de 1812*, p. 47, p. 48 and p. 308.
44. *Ibid.*, p. 101.
45. *Ibid.*, p. 93.
46. *Ibid.*, p. 73.
47. *Ibid.*, p. 45.
48. *Ibid.*, p. 308.
49. *Ibid.*, p. 96.
50. *Ibid.*, p. 59.
51. *Ibid.*, p. 309.
52. *Ibid.*, p. 104-105.
53. *Ibid.*, p. 105.
54. *Ibid.*, p. 405-406.
55. *Ibid.*, p. 49.
56. *Ibid.*
57. *Ibid.*, p. 261.
58. *Ibid.*, p. 309.
59. *Ibid.*, p. 123.
60. *Ibid.*
61. *Ibid.*, p. 123-124.
62. Elsie B. Michie, *Vulgar Question of Money: Heiresses, Materialism, and the Novel of Manners from Jane Austen to Henry James*, Baltimore, Johns Hopkins University Press, 2014, 320 p.
63. Joseph Doutre, *Les fiancés de 1812*, p. 123.
64. *Ibid.*, p. 124.

65. *Ibid.*, p. 125.
66. "This freedom to marry one's chosen love, of one's own decision and the basis of simple acts, opens the door to anarchy." Myriam Greilsammer, *L'envers du tableau. Mariage et maternité en Flandre médiévale*, Paris, Armand Colin, 1990, p. 57.
67. Jean-Louis Flandrin, *Les amours paysannes. Amour et sexualité dans les campagnes de l'ancienne France (XVIe-XIXe siècle)*, Paris, Gallimard / Julliard, 1975, 258 p.
68. Serge Gagnon, *Mariage et famille au temps de Papineau*, p. 146. For the subsequent period, see Denise Lemieux and Lucie Mercier, "Des stratégies familiales d'alliance," in *Les femmes au tournant du siècle, 1880-1940*. Âges de la vie, maternité et quotidien, Québec, Institut québécois de recherche sur la culture, 1989, p. 110-140.
69. Serge Gagnon, *Mariage et famille au temps de Papineau*, p. 146.
70. G. H. Cherrier, "Avis de l'éditeur," in Pierre-Joseph-Olivier Chauveau, *Charles Guérin*, Montréal, John Lovell, 1853, p. vi.
71. Pierre-Joseph-Olivier Chauveau, *Charles Guérin*, Montréal, John Lovell, 1853, p. 27.
72. *Ibid.*, p. 111.
73. *Ibid.*, p. 70.
74. *Ibid.*, p. 70.
75. *Ibid.*, p. 73.
76. *Ibid.*, p. 127.
77. *Ibid.*
78. *Ibid.*, p. 95.
79. Pierre Bourdieu, *La domination masculine*, coll. "Liber," Paris, Éditions du Seuil, 1998, p. 58.
80. Pierre-Joseph-Olivier Chauveau, *Charles Guérin*, p. 131.
81. *Ibid.*
82. *Ibid.*, p. 133.
83. *Ibid.*, p. 137.
84. *Ibid.*, p. 334.
85. *Ibid.*, p. 335.
86. André Sénécal, "Charles Guérin : le récit et la thèse," *Voix et Images*, Vol. 5, No. 2, 1980, p. 338.
87. Corinne Saminadayar-Perrin (ed.), "Les mystères urbains au XIXe siècle : le roman de l'histoire sociale," *Autour de Vallès*, No. 43, 2013, 255 p.
88. The historian Serge Gagnon confirms that "the richer young people are, the more their freedom of choice is subordinated to economic imperatives." *Mariage et famille au temps de Papineau*, p. 167.
89. Pierre-Joseph-Olivier Chauveau, *Charles Guérin*, p. 160.
90. This does not mean that one or the other of the protagonists never dies in the novels: see the beginning of the series "La Huronne de Lorette," by Henri-Émile Chevalier, which indeed opens with the discovery of a letter from Alfred, who is protesting the injustice of the death of his beloved and proclaiming his desire to join her: "Adieu! I cannot live without her! Since those wretched ones killed her on me, I will die also. God will give her back to me; he is less cruel than men!",

Henri-Émile Chevalier, "La Huronne de Lorette," *La Ruche littéraire et politique*, août 1854, p. 425. Republished in *La Huronne: Scènes de la Vie Canadiennes*, Paris, Michel Lévy Frères, 1861.

91. D. F***, "Fatalité," *La Ruche littéraire et politique*, November 1853, p. 583-584.

92. On the origins and evolution of this legend, see Jean Du Berger, who collected 500 versions. *Le Diable à la danse*, Québec, Presses de l'Université Laval, 2006, 248 p.

93. Philippe Aubert de Gaspé Jr., *The Influence of a Book*, p. 69.

94. Élise Salaün, *Oser Éros. L'érotisme dans le roman québécois des origines à nos jours*, Québec, Éditions Nota bene, 2010, p. 34.

95. Philippe Aubert de Gaspé Jr., *The Influence of a Book*, p. 71.

96. Philippe Aubert de Gaspé Jr., *The Influence of a Book*, p. 76.

97. Pierre Berthiaume, "L'annonce faite à Rose," *Voix et Images*, Vol. 19, No. 1, Fall 1993, p. 121-131.

98. Malvina D., "De Québec à la chute Montmorency," *La Ruche littéraire et politique*, May 1854, p. 225.

99. *Ibid.*

100. *Ibid.*, p. 226.

101. "The Romantics were enamored of death." Allan H. Pasco, *Sick Heroes. French Society and Literature in the Romantic Age, 1750-1850*, Exeter, University of Exeter Press, 1997, p. 134.

102. Numerous legends incorporating Indigenous characters can be found in nineteenth-century Québécois periodicals. They inspired stories of different lengths, but in which love is never very far off. Of note among other texts is the novel by Clara Chagnon [the pseudonym of Marie Sarah-Clarisse Chagnon], "Les fiancés d'outre-tombe," published in *La Revue canadienne* from May to July 1869. In this first feminine Québécois novel, the author revisits and expands on the narrative plot of "L'Iroquoise," an anonymous story published by Michel Bibaud in *La bibliothèque canadienne*, then in "Françoise Brunon," signed "C. V. Dupont," and published in 1848 in *Le Répertoire national* of James Huston. Guildo Rousseau traces the American origin of this plot in *La légende de l'Iroquoise. Aux sources historiques de l'imaginaire québécois*, Québec, Éditions GID, 2018, 516 p. The same scholar is working on a forthcoming, annotated version of the *Fiancés d'outre-tombe*.

103. Georges Boucher de Boucherville, *La Tour de Trafalgar* suivi de *Louise Chawinikisique*, coll. "Littérature québécoise," Vol. 125, La Bibliothèque électronique du Québec, [Online], [1835], p. 50, https://beq.ebooksgratuits.com/pdf/Boucher-Trafalgar.pdf.

104. *Ibid.*, p. 50-51.

105. *Ibid.*, p. 51.

106. *Ibid.*, p. 52.

107. *Ibid.*, p. 53.

108. Vincent Masse, "L'Amérindien 'd'un autre âge' dans la littérature québécoise au XIXe siècle," *Tangence*, Vol. 90, Summer 2009, p. 107-133. Vincent Masse, *Figures de l'Amérindien dans la littérature québécoise, 1855-1875*, Master's Thesis, Montréal, Université McGill, 2002, 146 p. Sandra Hobbs, "La représentation

ambivalente de l'Autochtone dans le roman québécois : vers une perspective postcoloniale," *International Journal of Francophone Studies*, Vol. 9, No. 3, 2006, p. 347-364.
109. Georges Boucher de Boucherville, *La Tour de Trafalgar*, p. 66.
110. *Ibid.*
111. *Ibid.*, p. 73.
112. *Ibid.*, p. 54.
113. *Ibid.*, p. 75.
114. *Ibid.*, p. 65-66.
115. Ulric-Joseph Tessier, "Emma ou l'amour malheureux. Épisode du choléra à Québec en 1832," *Le Télégraphe*, 1 and 3 May 1837, p. 1-2.
116. Ulrich-Joseph Tessier, "Emma ou l'amour malheureux. Épisode du choléra à Québec en 1832," in James Huston, *Le Répertoire national*, Vol. 2, Montréal, Lovell et Gibson, 1848, p. 28.
117. *Ibid.*, p. 29.
118. Maxime Foerster, "Différence des sexes et désordre amoureux dans la littérature romantique française," *Itinéraires*, [Online], 2014-2|2015, [n.p.], http://journals.openedition.org/itineraires/2455.
119. Henri-Émile Chevalier, *Le pirate du Saint-Laurent*, Montréal, John Lovell, 1859, p. 50.
120. Eugène L'Écuyer, *La fille du brigand*, p. 26-27.
121. "In the same way as a misalliance," writes Nathalie Ducharme, "a marriage that has not been approved by the family isolates the couple, breaks the bond between generations and jeopardizes the offspring, who are deprived of legitimacy, since the couple is always cursed and separated from their child." Nathalie Ducharme, *Espaces, personnages et société dans le roman d'aventures québécois au XIXe siècle*, p. 29.
122. Ellen Constans, *Parlez-moi d'amour. Le roman sentimental, des romans grecs aux collections de l'an 2000*, Limoges, Presses universitaires de Limoges, 1999, p. 26.

Chapter 2: Sublimated Love (1860-1920)

1. The full citation is: "Let us hasten to listen to the delightful stories of the people, before they have forgotten them, before they blush at them, and their chaste poetry, ashamed of being exposed, is covered with a veil like Eve exiled from paradise." Charles Nodier, "La légende de sœur Béatrix," *Revue de Paris*, Vol. 46, 1 October 1837, p. 280.
2. "The omnipresence of the feminine element can be partially attributed to the limited number of readers, because, while France saw a gradual sexual division of readerships of mass market literature at the end of the century—men and boys turning to adventure and women to sentimental fiction—, in Quebec, women seem to have remained from one year to the next great consumers of adventure stories." Nathalie Ducharme, *Espaces, personnages et société dans le roman d'aventures québécois au XIXe siècle*, Montréal, PhD Thesis, Université du Québec à Montréal, 2007, p. 203.
3. Joseph Marmette, *Charles et Éva. Épisode des hostilités entre le Canada et les colonies anglaises en 1690*, Chapter 8, in the *Revue canadienne*, Tome 4, 1867,

p. 341. It should be noted that this *mise en abyme* can be found in the series, published in the *Revue canadienne* as of December 1866, but was removed from the book version published by Éditions Lumen, in 1945.

4. Mary Jean Green studied the cases of Rosanna Mullins Leprohon, Laure Conan, and Adèle Bibaud, in *Women and Narrative Identity. Rewriting the Quebec National Text*, Montréal and Kingston, McGill-Queen's University Press, 2001, 197 p. Julie Roy, "Quelques écrivaines québécoises du XIXe siècle. Quand le roman historique se conjugue au féminin," *Québec français*, No. 140, Winter 2006, p. 34-36.

5. Deborah Blacklock, *Constancy in the Canadian Canon: The Reception History of Rosanna Leprohon's Antoinette de Mirecourt and William Kirby's The Golden dog*, Master's Thesis, Burnaby, Simon Fraser University, 1993, p. 11. Admitting that "this delightful writer" was "the first to charm the leisures of adolescence," Gaëtane de Montreuil (born 1867) affirms that the works of Leprohon "are known to all French Canadian readers." Gaëtane de Montreuil, "Mme Rosanna-Eleanore Leprohon," *La Canadienne*, Vol. 5, No. 2, May 1922, p. 3. A sign of her integration into French-language literature, Leprohon is included in the *Bibliographie critique du roman canadien-français, 1837-1900* published by David Hayne and Marcel Tirol (Toronto, University of Toronto Press, 1968, 144 p.).

6. See Maurice Lemire and Denis Saint-Jacques (ed.), *La vie littéraire au Québec*, t. III, *Un peuple sans histoire ni littérature, 1840-1869*, Sainte-Foy, Presses de l'Université Laval, 1996, p. 116.-117.

7. The publishers J.B. Rolland & Fils write that the success of the novel, "quite rare in the annals of the Canadian bookstore," convinced them to proceed with "a second edition of a novel that was essentially [French] Canadian in its form and in its content." "Note des éditeurs," in Rosanna Eleanor Leprohon, *Antoinette De Mirecourt ou mariage secret et chagrins cachés. Roman canadien*, Montréal, J. B. Rolland & fils, 1881, p. iii.

8. See John C. Stockdale, "Antoinette de Mirecourt," *Dictionnaire des œuvres littéraires du Québec*, Tome I, *Des origines à 1900*, Montréal, Fides, 1978, p. 34. Their interpretation adding nothing essential, we have left aside analysis of a third romance novel by Rosanna Leprohon, *Armand Durand ou la Promesse accomplie* (Montréal, Plinguet & Laplante, 1869, 315 p. and Montréal, Beauchemin et Fils, 1892, 367 p.), as well as her series "Ida Beresford or The Child of Fashion," published in French in *L'Ordre* in 1859-1860 under the title "Ida Beresford ou la Jeune Fille du grand monde," in a translation by Joseph-Édouard Lefebvre de Bellefeuille. The series is the story of a young British orphan born into "high society," but raised by a country doctor. Her godmother aspires to a "blue blood" marriage for her, but Ida prefers to marry the doctor's son.

9. *Antoinette de Mirecourt* was later adapted for the stage by Elzéar Roy and Adélard Lacasse, and presented at the Monument national in 1901, a sign of the growing place for romantic themes in the theatre repertoire at the turn of the century. Lucie Robert, *Apprivoiser la modernité théâtrale. La pièce en un acte de la Belle époque à la Crise. Anthologie*, Québec, Nota Bene, 2012, 264 p.

10. Lawrence Stone, *The Family, Sex and Marriage in England, 1500-1800*, New York, Harper & Row, 1977, 800 p. Peter Ward, *Courtship, Love, and Marriage in*

Nineteenth Century English Canada, Montréal and Kingston, McGill-Queen's University Press, 1990, 219 p.

11. It is likely that male and female readers of the period found something to guide them in their own search for a satisfying match in this literature. Green notes that, uncertain about who to differentiate between a good and a bad match, and between sincere and feigned love, nineteenth-century women took clues from romantic novels to guide them in the choice of a future husband. Katherine Sobba Green, *The Courtship Novel, 1740-1820: A Feminized Genre*, Lexington, University Press of Kentucky, 1991, p. 140-141. In English Canada, "reading novels as prescriptions for social behaviour proved a constant habit." Carole Gerson, *A Purer Taste: The Writing and Reading of Fiction in Nineteenth-Century Canada*, Toronto, University of Toronto Press, 1989, p. 26.

12. The authors of *La vie littéraire au Québec* are correct in observing that, even though the story takes place shortly after the Conquest, "this setting has very little to do with the action [...]. Totally absorbed by matters of the heart, the novelist has little interest in the political context [...]." Maurice Lemire and Denis Saint-Jacques (eds.), *La vie littéraire au Québec*, Tome 3, p. 420. The critics of the period agree with this observation. "The novel of manners is her favourite [Leprohon's]; she does not really address the historical novel. The drama itself, which she situates in an interesting historical period and in which she tells, but incidentally, the story of a historical event, is not a historical novel. She has only chosen this period, using known names, to pique the reader's curiosity and especially to study the mores and make use of the facts that these events gave rise to in social life; but the events themselves are but secondary for her book, they are not part of her plot, they are not the main interest that she seeks to elicit; in short, she does not make use of them." E. Lef. [Joseph-Edouard Lefebvre] de Bellefeuille, "*Antoinette de Mirecourt : or, secret marrying and secret sorrowing. A Canadian Tale.* By Mrs Leprohon, 369 p., in-12, John Lovell, $1,00.," *Revue canadienne*, Vol. 1, No. 7, July 1864, p. 442-443.

13. Rosanna Mullins Leprohon, *The Manor House of de Villerai, A Tale of Canada Under the French Dominion*, ed. Andrea Cabajsky, Peterborough, Broadview Editions, 2015 (1859), p. 173.

14. *Ibid.*, p. 47.

15. *Ibid.*, p. 54.

16. *Ibid.*, p. 157.

17. *Ibid.*, p. 191.

18. *Ibid.*, p. 207.

19. Hannah More, *Strictures on the Modern System of Female Education, With a View of the Principles and Conduct Prevalent Among Women of Rank and Fortune*, London, T. Cadell Jun. & W. Davies, 1799, Vol. 1 p. 4.

20. Mrs. Leprohon, *The Manor House of de Villerai*, p. 201.

21. Geneviève Bernier, *La figure mythique des amants maudits ou Le couple mixte dans le roman historique québécois de 1864 à aujourd'hui*, Master's Thesis, Sherbrooke, Université de Sherbrooke, 2015, 145 p. The political context is suitable for a novel that celebrates the rapprochement between "the two founding nations of the country," leading up to the adoption of a federal pact, in 1867. Carl Murphy,

"The Marriage Metaphor in Nineteenth-Century English Canadian Fiction," *Studies in Canadian Literature*, Vol. 13, No. 1, Winter 1988, p. 1-19.

22. In our corpus, only Leprohon's novels portray the rite, still common among the Montreal bourgeoisie in the interwar period, that consisted in the high society young girl making her "debut" on the matrimonial market by participating in the public social events of her milieu. Denise Girard, "Les débuts dans la jeunesse bourgeoise montréalaise (1920-1940)," in Gérard Bouchard and Martine Ségalen (eds.), *Une langue, deux cultures. Rites et symboles en France et au Québec*, Sainte-Foy/Paris, Presses de l'Université Laval/La Découverte, 1997, p. 249-263.

23. Mrs. Leprohon, *Antoinette de Mirecourt; or, Secret Marrying and Secret Sorrowing. A Canadian Tale.* Montreal: John Lovell, p. 39.

24. *Ibid.*, p. 68.

25. *Ibid.*, p. 72.

26. *Ibid.*, p. 82.

27. *Ibid.*, p. 128.

28. Francis R. Hart, "The Spaces of Privacy: Jane Austen," *Nineteenth-Century Fiction*, Vol. 30, No. 3, December 1975, p. 305-333.

29. Mrs. Leprohon, *Antoinette de Mirecourt*, p. 144.

30. *Ibid.*, p. 265.

31. *Ibid.* p. 266.

32. *Ibid.*, p. 189.

33. *Ibid.*, p. 145.

34. *Ibid.*, p. 178.

35. *Ibid.*, p. 250.

36. *Ibid.*, p. 299.

37. *Ibid.*, p. 326.

38. In *Peut-on être heureux sans se marier?* (Un célibataire [the pseudonym of Victorien de Saussy], Montréal, [n.p.], circa 1890, 14 p.), the author responds in the negative.

39. With the relative exception, as we have seen, of Joseph Doutre in *Les fiancés de 1812*, the autonomy left to the heroine in relation to the father's choice is strictly limited.

40. Five years after her death, her husband wrote: "I am still the same, lamenting the loss of this 'Rosanna' who charmed my existence over 30 years. I will be going to join her soon, because my health leaves something to be desired." Cited by John C. Stockdale, "Antoinette de Mirecourt," *Dictionnaire des œuvres littéraires du Québec*, Tome I, *Des origines à 1900*, Montréal, Fides, 1978, p. 34.

41. E. Lef. [Joseph-Edouard Lefebvre] de Bellefeuille, "*Antoinette de Mirecourt: or, secret marrying and secret sorrowing. A Canadian Tale.* By Mrs Leprohon, 369 p., in-12, John Lovell, $1,00.," p. 443.

42. *Ibid.*, p. 444.

43. *Ibid.*

44. *Ibid.* An identical critique was formulated by an anonymous author in "Bibliographie. *Antoinette de Mirecourt*," *L'Ordre*, 12 December 1864, p. 2.

45. Ernest Choquette, *Les Ribaud : une idylle de 37*, Montréal, Eusèbe Senécal & Cie, 1898, p. 143.

46. *Ibid.*, p. 166-167.
47. "Love is an essential part of woman's existence: it is the great motive of her life. [...]. For the woman, love is the great reality to which everything is related and around which everything is concentrated." [Anonymous], *Le guide des amoureux et des gens du monde. L'amour, la cour, le mariage*, Montréal, C.O. Beauchemin & Fils, 1898, p. 4.
48. Ernest Choquette, *Les Ribaud*, p. 172.
49. Maria Pilar Cuder-Dominguez, "Negotiations of Gender and Nationhood in Early Canadian Literature," *International Journal of Canadian Studies*, No. 18, 1998, p. 115-132. The secondary characters are less subject to this rule.
50. Ernest Choquette, *Les Ribaud*, p. 182.
51. *Ibid.*, p. 183.
52. *Ibid.*, p. 184.
53. *Ibid.*, p. 196.
54. *Ibid.*, p. 260.
55. The novel demonstrates, according to one critic, that love "knows no limitations of race." [Anonymous], "Romance of Canadian history," *The Quebec Chronicle*, 27 October 1898, p. 2.
56. Ernest Choquette, *Les Ribaud*, p. 265.
57. It is no doubt because the moral of *Les Ribaud* goes so against the discourse of the era that the parish priest intervenes in the narration: it is one of the rare examples in our corpus, where the priest plays a central role. In remaking the history of the romance novel, one might think that the Catholic church does not exist in Quebec, except to provide a place for the heroines to pray.
58. Louis Dantin, "Deux drames de M. Ernest Choquette : Madeleine — La Bouée," *Essais critiques*, Tome 1, coll. "Bibliothèque du Nouveau Monde," Montréal, Presses de l'Université de Montréal, 2002 [1928], p. 320-327.
59. *Ibid.*, p. 325.
60. *Ibid.*, p. 326.
61. *Ibid.*
62. *Ibid.*
63. *Ibid.*
64. *Ibid.*
65. *Ibid.*
66. Ernest Choquette, *Claude Paysan*, Montréal, la Cie d'impression et de gravures Bishop, 1899, p. 75.
67. Ernest Choquette, *La terre*, Montréal, la Maison de librairie Beauchemin, 1916, p. 43.
68. *Ibid.*
69. René Hardy, *Contrôle social et mutation de la culture religieuse au Québec, 1830-1930*, Montréal, Boréal, 1999, 284 p.
70. Patricia Smart, *De Marie de l'Incarnation à Nelly Arcan. Se dire, se faire par l'écriture intime*, Montréal, Boréal, 2014, 430 p.
71. As the authors of *La vie littéraire* call it. Denis Saint-Jacques and Lucie Robert (eds.), *La vie littéraire au Québec*, Tome VI, *Le nationaliste, l'individualiste et le marchand, 1919-1933*, Québec, Presses de l'Université Laval, 2010, 748 p.

72. Laure Conan [the pseudonym of Félicité Angers], *Un amour vrai*, Montréal, Leprohon & Leprohon, 1879, p. 29.
73. As Christine Hudon notes: "In the sermons, periodicals or pious books, the woman resembles an angel in the home. Through her piety, modesty and devotion, she forms consciences, edifying her husband and children. She helps them earn their salvation or, on the contrary, opens the doors of hell to them." Christine Hudon, "Des dames chrétiennes. La spiritualité des catholiques québécoises au XIXe siècle," *Revue d'histoire de l'Amérique française*, Vol. 49, No. 2, Fall 1995, p. 177.
74. Laure Conan [the pseudonym of Félicité Angers], *Un amour vrai*, p. 38.
75. *Ibid.*, p. 37.
76. *Ibid.*, p. 50.
77. *Ibid.*, p. 60. On Jesus as spouse and lover, see Claude-Marie Gagnon, "Autobiographie religieuse et roman sentimental québécois," Études littéraires, Vol. 16, No. 3, 1983, p. 441-462.
78. See, among others, an issue of *Voix et Images*, co-edited by Mylène Bédard, Virginie Fournier, Ariane Gibeau, and Adrien Rannaud: "Contemporanéités d'*Angéline de Montbrun* et de Laure Conan," Vol. 44, No. 1, Fall 2018, p. 7-180. See in particular in this issue, Liliana Rizzuto, "Un roman 'né dans sa propre négation' : l'articulation du littéraire et du religieux dans *Angéline de Montbrun* de Laure Conan," *Voix et Images*, Vol. 44, No. 1, Fall 2018, p. 27-38.
79. Laure Conan [the pseudonym of Félicité Angers], *Angéline de Montbrun: A Psychological Romance of Quebec*, trans. Yves Brunelle, Toronto, University of Toronto Press, 1974, p. 72.
80. Laure Conan [the pseudonym of Félicité Angers], *Un amour vrai*, p. 7. "Some are known to have their hearts reduced to ashes." Laure Conan [pseudonym of Félicité Angers], *Angéline de Montbrun*, p. 49.
81. Jacques Cotnam, "*Angéline de Montbrun*: un cas patent de masochisme moral," *Journal of Canadian Fiction*, Vol. 2, No. 3, Summer 1973, p. 152-160.
82. Laure Conan [the pseudonym of Félicité Angers], *Angéline de Montbrun: A Psychological Romance of Quebec*, p. 136.
83. *Ibid.*, p. 75.
84. *Ibid.*, p. 103-104.
85. *Ibid.*, p. 77.
86. E. D. Blodgett and Claudine Potvin (eds.), *Relire Angéline de Montbrun au tournant du siècle*, coll. "Convergences," Québec, Nota bene, 2006, 458 p. An enduring popular theory read in *Angéline de Montbrun* the story of an incestuous relationship. François Gallays, "Angéline de Montbrun : reflets et redoublements. L'infra-textuel," *Incidences*, Vol. 4, No. 1, January-April, 1980, p. 51-66.
87. Laure Conan [the pseudonym of Félicité Angers], *Angéline de Montbrun: A Psychological Romance of Quebec* p. 77.
88. Madeleine Gagnon-Mahony, "*Angéline de Montbrun* : le mensonge historique et la subversion de la métaphore blanche," *Voix et images du pays*, Vol. 5, No. 1, 1972, p. 64. Patricia Smart, "*Angéline de Montbrun* ou la chute dans l'écriture," Écrire dans la maison du père : l'émergence du féminin dans la tradition littéraire du Québec, coll. "Littérature d'Amérique," Montréal, Éditions Québec/Amérique, 1990 [1988], p. 39-86.

89. According to the theory of Sister Jean-de-l'Immaculée, "Angéline de Montbrun," in Paul Wyczynski (ed.), *Le roman canadien-français*, Archives des lettres canadiennes, Tome 3, Montréal/Paris, Fides, 1964, p. 105-122.
90. Laure Conan [the pseudonym of Félicité Angers], *Angéline de Montbrun: A Psychological Romance of Quebec*, p. 97
91. *Ibid.*, p. 112
92. Mary Jean Green, "Laure Conan and Madame de La Fayette: Rewriting the Female Plot," *Essays on Canadian Writing*, No. 34, Spring 1987, p. 50-62.
93. Madame de La Fayette, *La princesse de Clèves et autres romans*, Paris, Gallimard, 1972, p. 306.
94. Laure Conan [the pseudonym of Félicité Angers], *Angéline de Montbrun: A Psychological Romance of Quebec*, p. 31. One should only love "a man of character, dignity, refinement," but "all that seems very rare," p. 61.
95. *Ibid.*, p. 74. Angéline's attachment to her father is illuminated here by the fact that "ordinarily one loves one's children more than one is loved by them." Knowing that she is perfectly loved by her father, Angéline can return his love and there is a "boundless attachment" between them that is not possible between spouses who have been married for a long time. *Ibid.*, p. 27.
96. *Ibid.*, p. 66. "Ah! You can be sure that in blessing the union of spouses, the blood of Christ does not ensure the immortality of love, and whatever we do, resignation remains always the great difficulty, as it is the great duty," p. 168-169.
97. *Ibid.*, p. 100. These words are pronounced by her friend Mina Darville, but they apply perfectly to Angéline.
98. *Ibid.*, p. 87.
99. Lori Saint-Martin, "Mina Darville : roman inédit," *Voix et Images*, Vol. 44, No. 1, Fall 2018, p. 105-116.
100. Laure Conan [the pseudonym of Félicité Angers], *Angéline de Montbrun: A Psychological Romance of Quebec*, p. 100.
101. *Ibid.*, p. 169.
102. Lucie Joubert and Annette Hayward (eds.), *La vieille fille : lectures d'un personnage*, Montréal, Triptyque, 2000, 181 p.
103. Emma Liggins, *Odd women? Spinsters, Lesbians and Widows in British Women's Fiction, 1850s-1930s*, Manchester, Manchester University Press, 2014, 275 p.
104. Laure Conan [the pseudonym of Félicité Angers], *Angéline de Montbrun*, p. 285. Writing to Félicité Angers barely a few months before the publication of *Un amour vrai*, her friend and counsellor Sister Catherine-Aurélie-du-Précieux-Sang confided to the writer: "Yes, we love Jesus, my dear Félicité, we only love Jesus by saying to all that is not him: stay away from me, pasture of death... you are not my God... you are not life!" Sister Catherine-Aurélie-du-Précieux-Sang to Félicité Angers, 21 January 1879, in Laure Conan [the pseudonym of Félicité Angers], *J'ai tant de sujets de désespoir. Correspondance, 1878-1924*, Montréal, Les Éditions Varia, 2002, p. 77.
105. Louis Gérenval, *Entre l'amour et le devoir*, Montréal, Imprimerie Bilaudeau, 1912, p. 32.
106. Laure Conan [the pseudonym of Félicité Angers], *Angéline de Montbrun: A Psychological Romance of Quebec*, p. 26.

107. Mary Jean Corbett, *Family Likeness: Sex, Marriage, and Incest from Jane Austen to Virginia Woolf*, Ithaca, Cornell University Press, 2008, 264 p.
108. Adèle Bibaud, *Les fiancés de St-Eustache*, Montréal, [n.p.], 1910, p. 57.
109. *Ibid.*, p. 77.
110. *Ibid.*, p. 161.
111. *Ibid.*, p. 163.
112. Allan H. Pasco, *Sick Heroes. French Society and Literature in the Romantic Age, 1750-1850*, Exeter, University of Exeter Press, 1997, p. 114.
113. "Typically, consanguineous incest is reserved for the Gothic novel, which exploits it to elicit a sense of horror, and for pornography, which depends to a large degree upon the infraction of conventions, rules, and laws. Unless the incest will be averted by revelation, general literature seldom does more than hint at incestuous yearnings. When incest rises to the surface and takes on major importance, it is between those related by adoption. Almost always it is between those raised together from childhood." Allan H. Pasco, *Sick Heroes*, p. 122.
114. Peter L. Thorslev, "Incest as Romantic Symbol," *Comparative Literature Studies*, Vol. 2, No. 1, 1965, p. 41-58.
115. "For romantic writers, sibling attachment fuses with sexual desire to constitute an idealized erotic love, yet death disrupts or closely follows upon the consummation of that love." *Alan Richardson*, "Rethinking Romantic Incest: Human Universals, Literary Representation, and the Biology of Mind," *New Literary History*, Vol. 31, No. 3, Summer 2000, p. 555.
116. Our observation is based on the reference to incest in the literature. Real incest is clearly a complex phenomenon, founded on the power relations within the family. Marie-Aimée Cliche, "Un secret bien gardé : l'inceste dans la société traditionnelle québécoise, 1858-1938," *Revue d'histoire de l'Amérique française*, Vol. 50, No. 2, Fall 1996, p. 201-226.
117. Adèle Bibaud, Le secret de la marquise *et* Un homme d'honneur, *suivi des* Poésies canadiennes *de Michel Bibaud*, Montréal, Imprimerie P. H. Dalaire, 1906, p. 10.
118. Édouard Duquet, *Pierre et Amélie*, Québec, J.-N. Duquet, 1866, p. 16.
119. *Ibid.*, p. 15.
120. Paul-Émile Prévost, *L'épreuve*, Montréal, Alph. Pelletier, 1900, p. 6.
121. *Ibid.*
122. Nathalie Ducharme, *Espaces, personnages et société dans le roman d'aventures québécois au XIXe siècle*, p. 309.
123. Louis Hémon, *Maria Chapdelaine*, trans. Alan Brown. Montreal: Tundra Books, 1989, 119. "This may be why," speculates the author of *Maria Chapdelaine* (1913), "they [the French Canadian peasants] avoid for the most part using highly charged words, preferring to say "friendship" for "love," "annoyance" for "pain," so as to keep the joys and sorrows of the heart in their proper place alongside other concerns of greater practical importance, such as their daily work, harvesting, or a life of greater ease in the future" (*ibid.* 119).
124. Mary Jean Green, *Women & Narrative Identity. Rewriting the Quebec National Text*, Montréal, McGill-Queen's University Press, 2001, 197 p. Nicole Deschamps, "*Maria Chapdelaine*, roman de Louis Hémon," in Maurice Lemire

(ed.), *Dictionnaire des œuvres littéraires du Québec*, Tome 2, *1900-1939*, Montréal, Fides, 1980, p. 663-673.

125. Louis Hémon, *Maria Chapdelaine*, trans. Alan Brown, p. 187

126. Revealingly, one of the heroine's cousins who had been courted by two men, both spending their Sundays at the house, ends up choosing the one she likes less. "'I liked both of them,' she confessed to Maria, "and I really think I liked Zotique the best. But he went off for the drive on Saint-Maurice River and wasn't due back till summer. That was when Roméo asked the question, and I said yes. I like him too." *Ibid.*, p. 84. Contrary to the Americans with their flirting and the French with their courtship, French Canadians barely knew their partners when they got engaged, even when they were neighbours or cousins. "People got married to strangers," confirms the historian Marie-Josée Huot. Marie-Josée Huot, *Les pratiques rituelles entourant le mariage dans les régions du Saguenay et de Charlevoix*, mémoire de maîtrise, Chicoutimi, Université du Québec à Chicoutimi, 1991, p. 49. Love, though considered a foundation of marriage, did not appear to be essential to the initial relations between the future spouses, who might at first enjoy just a close friendship or simple reciprocal trust. Martine Tremblay, *Le mariage dans la vallée du Haut-Richelieu au XXe siècle. Ritualité et distinction sociale*, coll. "Géographie historique," Sainte-Foy, Presses de l'Université Laval, 2001, p. 59.

127. Colette [the pseudonym of Édouardine Lesage], "Un roman nouveau. *Marie-Anna la Canadienne*," *La Presse*, 26 July 1913, p. 2.

128. Floris Bluther [the pseudonym of Fernand Baboulène], *Marie-Anna, la Canadienne*, Québec, [n.p.], 1913, p. 7 and p. 15.

129. *Ibid.*, p. 9.

130. *Ibid.*, p. 15.

131. *Ibid.*, p. 30.

132. *Ibid.*, p. 76.

133. *Ibid.*, p. 77.

134. *Ibid.*

135. *Ibid.*, p. 121.

136. *Ibid.*, p. 212.

137. *Ibid.*, p. 112.

138. *Ibid.*, p. 170-171.

139. *Ibid.*, p. 283.

140. *Ibid.*, p. 283.

141. *Ibid.*, p. 177.

142. *Ibid.*, p. 227.

143. *Ibid.*, p. 286.

144. *Ibid.*, p. 298-299.

145. *Ibid.*, p. 302.

146. Jean de La Malbaie, "Causerie littéraire. *Marie-Anna la Canadienne* par Floris Bluther," *Le Devoir*, 30 August 1913, p. 1.

147. Referring to *Martyr de l'amour*, by Pierre Zaccone, a Québécois critic says that "those who have loved and suffered will relive in reading it [...] the happiness of these incomparable moments that we remember for life, when we loved to suffer because

we were suffering from loving." [Anonymous], "Un nouveau roman," *Le Canada Français*, 30 March 1894, p. 1. A series written by a French author titled *Amour vainqueur* was published in *La Presse* in 1895. Abandoned for "lack of copies," it was re-issued in booklet form by Éditions Leprohon & Leprohon. Jules de Gastyne, *Amour vainqueur*, Montréal, Leprohon & Leprohon, 1896.

148. Micheline Tremblay, "Une auteure subversive? Virginie Dussault (1891-1969)," *Revue du Nouvel-Ontario*, No. 27, 2002, p. 93-122. Micheline Tremblay, "Présentation," in Virginie Dussault, *Amour vainqueur*, coll. "Voix retrouvées," Ottawa, Éditions David, 2003, p. 13-37.

149. While certain passages of the novel seem to have autobiographical sources, Dussault's real biography deviates from her fiction. Born in Guigues, Virginie Dussault (1891-1969) studied in English in 1910 at the Ursuline Sisters of Chatham convent (Ontario) then, in 1912, at the École normale de Trois-Rivières at the Monastère des Ursulines. She settled in Montreal for a while before leaving to teach in Bonnyville, Alberta, in 1915. She no doubt dreamed, like the heroine in her novel, of renouncing a career in teaching, which "did not make it possible to become rich, teaching being barely sufficient for a young girl to live well" (Virginie Dussault, *Amour vainqueur*, Montréal, Imprimerie J.-R. Constantineau, 1915, p. 44). Dussault however married an Italian immigrant, Angelo Petosa, in 1920, and returned to live with him in her village in 1922 to pursue her teaching career.

150. Virginie Dussault, *Amour vainqueur*, p. 22.

151. *Ibid.*, p. 157.

152. *Ibid.*, p. 163.

153. *Ibid.*, p. 12.

154. *Ibid.*, p. 80.

155. *Ibid.*, p. 52.

156. With the exception of the moment when Ninie is attacked by Harry on Mount Royal. It would appear that this concession was made to allow for the heroic scene in which Rogers arrives out of nowhere as a veritable saviour: "She had her head resting on his shoulder, her face and arms all swollen and bloody, her clothes dirty and torn, pale as death, stammering only a few words: my liberator!" *Ibid.*, p. 112.

157. *Ibid.*, p. 80.

158. *Ibid.*, p. 77.

159. *Ibid.*, p. 13.

160. *Ibid.*, p. 41.

161. *Ibid.*, p. 50.

162. *Ibid.*, p. 45.

163. *Ibid.*, p. 79.

164. *Ibid.*, p. 82.

165. *Ibid.*, p. 79.

166. Guildo Rousseau, *L'image des États-Unis dans la littérature québécoise (1775-1930)*, Sherbrooke, Éditions Naaman, 1981, 456 p.

167. Virginie Dussault, *Amour vainqueur*, p. 125. Openness to the world of the "Survenant" will also pique the interest of the community thirty years later, in Germaine Guèvremont's *Le Survenant* (1945): "Every evening since the Stranger's arrival, the kitchen filled up with what became a pleasant little gathering. [...]

Curious to hear what the Stranger had to tell about the great world, the dwellers on the Inlet began to frequent the Beauchemin house." Germaine Guèvremont, *The Outlander*, trans. Eric Sutton, New York, McGraw-Hill, 1950, p. 25.
168. Virginie Dussault, *Amour vainqueur*, p. 131.
169. *Ibid.*, p. 87.
170. *Ibid.*, p. 85.
171. *Ibid.*
172. *Ibid.*, p. 76.
173. *Ibid.*, p. 109.
174. *Ibid.*, p. 115.
175. Denis Saint-Jacques and Maurice Lemire (eds.), *La vie littéraire au Québec*, Tome 5, *Sois fidèle à ta Laurentie, 1895-1918*, Québec, Presses de l'Université Laval, 2005, p. 409.
176. [Anonymous], *Guide des amants : considérations sur l'amour et le mariage suivies de pensées sur les femmes, lettres d'amour, déclarations, aveux, reproches, ruptures, réconciliations, billets d'invitation pour dîners et soirées, du langage des fleurs, langage du mouchoir et d'un choix de poésies pour albums, etc.*, Montréal, [n.p.], 1889, p. 7.
177. "No one can avoid the empire of love other than by violating their nature, by violently breaking the ties that bind them to other beings. God, who wanted to place this law, this instinct, this duty, among the most inviolable, made love under the protection of pleasure, he made what nature commands us the occasion for the most tender sentiments of the heart." *Ibid.*, p. 1.

Chapter 3: Domesticated Love (1920-1940)

1. Ellen Constans, *Parlez-moi d'amour. Le roman sentimental, des romans grecs aux collections de l'an 2000*, Limoges, Presses universitaires de Limoges, 1999, p. 172.
2. Marsha Vanderford Doyle, "The Rhetoric of Romance: A Fantasy Theme Analysis of Barbara Cartland Novels," *Southern Speech Communication Journal*, Vol. 51, No. 1, 1985, p. 24-48.
3. Denis Saint-Jacques and Marie-José des Rivières, "Le magazine canadien-français : un média américain?," *Mens*, Vol. 12, No. 2, Spring 2012, p. 17-36. Marie-José des Rivières and Denis Saint-Jacques, "Révolution, conversion et disparition. La littérature de fiction dans la presse d'information générale," *COnTEXTES*, [Online], No. 11, 2012, [n.p.], https://doi.org/10.4000/contextes.5365.
4. [Anonymous], "Dans notre prochaine édition," *La Revue moderne*, October 1927, p. 8.
5. [Anonymous], "Notre feuilleton," *Le Devoir*, 4 April 1913, p. 1.
6. [Anonymous], "La vie des livres," *Le Canada*, 31 May 1943, p. 5. In 1946, in a letter to Charles Holmes, Bernard Valiquette writes: "There is a very high demand for novels by Berthe Bernage, Delly, Magali, which are not subject to any condemnation." Cited by Claude-Marie Gagnon, "La censure au Québec," *Voix et Images*, Vol. 9, No. 1, 1983, p. 113.
7. Marc Fortin, "D'un vendredi à l'autre," *L'Avenir du nord*, 27 May 1949, p. 3.
8. Jacques Michon (ed.), *Histoire de l'édition littéraire au Québec au XX*[e] *siècle*, Vol. 2, *Le temps des éditeurs : 1940-1959*, Montréal, Fides, 2004, p. 289.

9. For example, Myrto Gauthier, born in 1923 and herself behind the romance novel *La dame de Sahib* (1947), has the name of Delly's character. See also Georges Seltzer, "Rénald Savoie : un prénom de roman et un grand amoureux des voyages," *Ici Radio-Canada*, Vol. 2, No. 19, 4 au 10 May 1968, p. 6.
10. Ellen Constans, "Le roman catholique et B.C.-B.G.; bien penser pour bien écrire," *Ouvrières des lettres*, coll. "Mediatextes," Limoges, Presses universitaires de Limoges, 2007, p. 101-130.
11. The elites continually condemned young girls wanting to meet a movie star, rather than seeking the company of a neighbour or childhood friend, who were of course not very rich, but hard-working. [Anonymous], "Vous qui attendez le prince charmant," *La Patrie*, 1 December 1920, p. 1. The author of the article is not entirely wrong, as confirmed in the informant testimonies collected by Denise Girard, *Différenciation sociale et rituels du mariage : les Montréalais francophones, 1925-1940*, PhD Thesis, Québec, Université Laval, 1998, p. 84.
12. Pie XI, "Encyclique Casti Connubii : sur le mariage chrétien," *Le Saint-Siège*, [Online], [1930], https://w2.vatican.va/content/pius-xi/fr/encyclicals/documents/hf_p-xi_enc_19301231_casti-connubii.html.
13. Organizations like the Association catholique de la jeunesse canadienne-française (A.C.J.C.), the Association sociale catholique (A.S.C.) and the Œuvre de la presse catholique, were established to promote morally acceptable readings. Dominique Marquis, "Un nouveau combat pour l'Église : la presse catholique d'information, 1907-1940," Études d'histoire religieuse, Vol. 68, 2002, p. 73-88. Pascale Ryan, *Penser la nation. La Ligue d'action nationale 1917-1960*, Montréal, Leméac, 2006, 328 p.
14. Pierre Hébert, with the collaboration of Patrick Nicol, *Censure et littérature au Québec. Le livre crucifié 1625-1919*, Montréal, Fides, 1997, p. 159.
15. Delly, *Esclave... ou reine?*, coll. "Classiques du 20e siècle," Vol. 100, La Bibliothèque électronique du Québec, [Online], [1910], p. 243, https://beq.ebooksgratuits.com/classiques/Delly-esclave.pdf.
16. *Ibid.*, p. 246.
17. Delly, *Cœurs ennemis*, Vol. II, *Orietta*, coll. "Les romans pour tous," Montréal, Variétés, 1943, p. 240. Les éditions Variétés started publishing Delly with this work, making the most of the absence of French publishers during the Second World War. Between 1940 and 1950, three Québécois publishers published fifty-seven novels by Delly.
18. Ellen Constans, *Parlez-moi d'amour*, p. 233.
19. Pierre Hébert, with the collaboration of Patrick Nicol, *Censure et littérature au Québec*, 296 p. Pierre Hébert and Élise Salaün, *Censure et littérature au Québec: des vieux couvents au plaisir de vivre (1920-1959)*, Montréal, Fides, 2004, 252 p.
20. In 1917, an article in the *Progrès du Golfe* of Rimouski turned this sad reality into a rule of life: "The art of happiness in conjugal life can be resumed in three words: suffer and endure." [Anonymous], "La vie conjugale," *Le Progrès du Golfe*, 25 May 1917, p. 4.
21. Casanova's expression is used by a few Québécois commentators, but, it goes without saying, with a very different intention than the famous Venetian adventurer's.

22. Ubald Paquin, *La mystérieuse inconnue* : roman canadien inédit, coll. "Le Roman canadien," Montréal, Éditions Édouard Garand, 1929, p. 25.
23. Madame Elphège Croff [the pseudonym of Marie-Anne Perreault], *La petite maîtresse d'école : roman canadien inédit*, coll. "Le Roman canadien," No. 57, Montréal, Éditions Édouard Garand, 1929, 46 p.
24. François Provençal, *Fleur lointaine* : roman canadien inédit, coll. "Le Roman canadien," No. 27, Montréal, Éditions Édouard Garand, 1926, p. 26.
25. Matthieu Letourneux makes the same observations for serial romance novels published during the same period in France, by Ferenczi. In these stories, "it is less love than marriage, as the guarantee of social stability, that is foregrounded. When the man saves the woman from poverty or deprivation, she often feels more gratitude than passion, and the stories end not on love, but on the promise of a love to come, born of conjugality." See Matthieu Letourneux, "Amour, couture et prostitution, Discours social, écriture féminine et sérialité dans 'Le Petit roman' de Ferenczi," *L'Ull Critic*, No. 17-18, 2014, p. 225-226.
26. Roch Hurtubise, *L'amour, le soi et la société. Sociologie de la connaissance amoureuse dans les correspondances québécoises (1860-1988)*, PhD Thesis, Montréal, Université de Montréal, 1989, p. 190-191.
27. Blanche Lamontagne-Beauregard, *Un cœur fidèle: roman canadien*, Montréal, Bibliothèque de l'Action française, 1924, p. 121.
28. Madame Elphège Croff [the pseudonym of Marie-Anne Perreault], *Celle qui revient*, coll. "Littérature québécoise," Bibliothèque électronique du Québec, [Online], [1930], p. 133, http://beq.ebooksgratuits.com/pdf/Perreault-revient.pdf.
29. Blanche Lamontagne-Beauregard, *Un cœur fidèle*, p. 176.
30. Denise Lemieux, "La famille dans la littérature : 'Restons chez nous,'" *Une culture de la nostalgie. L'enfant dans le roman québécois de ses origines à nos jours*, Montréal, Boréal Express, 1984, p. 17-57. Corrie Scott, *De Groulx à Laferrière. Un parcours de la race dans la littérature québécoise*, Montréal, XYZ éditeur, 2014, 245 p.
31. Marie-Rose Turcot, *Un de Jasper : roman*, coll. "Les romans," Montréal, Éditions Albert Lévesque, 1933, p. 38.
32 On this subject, see Daniel Chartier, "Désirer un ''Sauvage': la figure de l'Amérindien dans le roman *Mon sauvage* (1938) de Laure Berthiaume-Denault," *Voix et Images*, Vol. 39, No. 2, Winter 2014, p. 69-84.
33. Frédéric Monneyron, *L'écriture de la jalousie*, Grenoble, Ellug, 1997, p. 8.
34. Ringuet, *Thirty Acres*, trans. Felix and Dorothea Walter, Toronto, McClelland and Stewart, [1940] 2009, p. 8.
35. One could say of the novel what Lucie Robert says of poetry. "The feminine poetry of the 1930s presents a sublimated romantic relationship. [...] This poetry identifies the object of feminine desire with two institutions, religion and art, even though, in both cases, the institution refers back to a masculine figure," Lucie Robert, "D'*Angéline de Montbrun* à *La chair décevante*. La naissance d'une parole féminine autonome dans la littérature québécoise," *Études littéraires*, Vol. 20, No. 1, 1987, p. 105.
36. Adrien Rannaud, *De l'amour et de l'audace. Femmes et roman au Québec dans les années 1930*, Montréal, PUM, 2018, 336 p.

37. Out of all of Canada's ethnic groups, Catholic francophones have the lowest rate of mixed unions, even among those living in very ethnically diverse urban centres. Danielle Gauvreau and Patricia Thornton, "Marrying 'the Other': Trends and Determinants of Culturally Mixed Marriages in Québec, 1880-1940," *Canadian Ethnic Studies*, Vol. 47, No. 3, 2015, p. 111-141.
38. This observation corroborates some testimonies of the period. A woman born in 1914 speaking of her husband says: "For us, by taking each other as husband and wife, it obviously wasn't a question of love at first sight, but a reasonable and logical choice in the circumstances, given the neighbourhood that shaped our experience and a community of like-minded people [...]. We were made for each other... so also for marrying each other." Though she was born in 1914, her testimony could also apply to the previous period. Annette Lachance Dallaire, *De l'orphelinat au centre d'accueil*, Montréal, P. Dottini, 1986, p. 101. Colette Moreux, *Douceville en Québec : la modernisation d'une tradition*, Montréal, Presses de l'Université de Montréal, 1982, 454 p. This attitude recalls the old French Canadian saying:"Marie-toi à ta porte avec gens de ta sorte" (Marry at your door with people of your sort).
39. Jacques Michon (ed.), *Histoire de l'édition littéraire au Québec*, Vol. 1, *La naissance de l'éditeur : 1900-1939*, Montréal, Fides, 1999, p. 313.
40. *Ibid.* It is difficult to have an accurate picture of the readership. In a 1928 contest that thousands of people participated in, there were 100 winners: 39 men and 61 women (30 of the latter not married). It is possible that these proportions are representatives, but this remains hypothetical.
41. Gérard Malchelosse, "Les Éditions Garand, leur mission, leurs œuvres," *La Vie canadienne*, No.8, supplement published after Jean Féron, *Le patriote : grand roman canadien historique inédit*, coll. "Le Roman canadien," Vol. 24, Montréal, Éditions Édouard Garand, 1926, p. 66.
42. In her thesis, Caroline Loranger demonstrated the generic hybridity of these texts, partially inherited from their connection to the periodical press. Caroline Loranger, *Imaginaires du "roman canadien" : discours sur le genre romanesque et pratiques d'écriture au Québec (1919-1939)*, PhD Thesis, Montréal, Université de Montréal, 2019, p. 183-240.
43. The characters' recreational activities never deviate from the codes of decorum. Dancing, for example, is exceptionally tolerated in only one situation: the celebration of a marriage, ceding at the same time to another regionalist imperative—respect for traditions. Otherwise, dancing is clearly designated "the prerogative of frivolous people..." It is even the source of disjunction in *L'enjôleuse*, since Marielle, who is a member of the Enfants de Marie, has promised to never dance. Before starting his laborer's job in the city, Marc congratulates her on this choice, but things change when he begins taking a liking to urban pleasures. Having returned to his village for a marriage, he tries to get Marielle to renege on her promise: "Come on, you think all the girls who dance are bad girls? [...] You've let the nuns fool you, those days are over now..." It is that same night that Marc, rejected, breaks Marielle's heart by dancing with Cécile, the "charmer," who convinces him to come live with her in the city. Madame Elphège Croff, *L'enjôleuse*, Montréal, Édouard Garand, 1928, p. 11. As a corollary, the heroines are pious very pious. Georgine, in *Le secret de l'orpheline*, goes to church "almost

everyday at noon," to "recite her rosary, to ask for light and courage." Andrée Jarret [the pseudonym of Cécile Beauregard], *Le secret de l'orpheline : roman canadien*, coll. "Le Roman canadien," Vol. 52, Montréal, Éditions Édouard Garand, 1928, p. 33.

44. Madame Graveline, *Le triomphe de l'amour : roman canadien inédit*, coll." Le Roman canadien," No. 58, Montréal, Éditions Édouard Garand, 1929, p. 24.

45. *Ibid.*

46. Only three heroines in the corpus of the period (in *Sœur ou fiancée*, *L'amour trompé*, and *Amour moderne*, none of which were published by Éditions Édouard Garand), wanting to remain faithful to their beloved, succumb to the temptation of the convent. But again, in these novels, the final reunion of the lovers is nonetheless respected because, learning the news, the heroes either hasten to also leave the world and also join a monastery, or spend the rest of their lives crying over their lost love.

47. It should be noted that this work is one of our rare "regionalist" novels to depict only bourgeois characters living in the city. It nonetheless conveys the clerico-nationalist values of the 1920s through the patriotic flourishes it contains, formulated by the male character Gérard Sautet, an ardent defender of national literature.

48. Antonin Proulx, *Le cœur est le maître*, Montréal, Éditions Édouard Garand, 1930, p. 30.

49. *Ibid.*, p. 44.

50. *Ibid.*, p. 67.

51. Madame Elphège Croff [the pseudonym of Marie-Anne Perreault], *L'enjôleuse*, p. 10.

52. *Ibid.*

53. Captivated by Laure's beauty, Alexandre in *À deux* (1937) rejects Lucille: "He had tried to see Lucille more often, but now he found her insignificant. He found her too skinny, too short [...]." Laetitia Filion, À deux, [s.l.], [n.p.], 1937, p. 13. The severity with which Alexandre criticizes, over several pages, Lucille's outfits, judging them too tight, too dark, too pale, reveal the hero's superficiality as much as the heroine's fear of being supplanted by a rival: "Alexandre had requested a white dress, as he would have requested a black dress. What he desired was to see Lucille nicely attired, so he could better compare her to the other. He hadn't thought, she neither, that being blond, but very pale, white would not flatter her." Laetitia Filion, À deux, p. 16. Alexandre only returns to Lucille on the rebound, since a relationship with Laure, who is revealed to be his half-sister, is no longer possible.

54. Andrée Jarret [the pseudonym of Cécile Beauregard], *La dame de Chambly : roman canadien*, coll. "Le Roman canadien," Montréal, Éditions Édouard Garand, 1925, p. 82-83.

55. *Ibid.*, p. 10.

56. *Ibid.*, p. 107. The moral is even more implacable in a novel that is not part of our corpus, *Ma cousine Mandine*, written by Napoléon-Magloire Mathé (coll. "Le Roman canadien," Montréal, Éditions Édouard Garand, 1928 [1923], 147 p.). A young girl who lives in a rural village seduces a civil servant named Jules. Ignoring her parents' objection, she moves with him to Ottawa. Mandine, wasteful and

fickle, cheats on her husband with a Scotsman. Jules turns to drink and ends up committing suicide. Having lost everything and full of regrets and remorse, Mandine returns to live with her parents. She gets remarried with a young man who, like a true French Canadian, decides to stay and live in his village.

57. François Provençal, *Fleur lointaine*, p. 16.

58. *Ibid.*

59. *Ibid.*

60. *La Revue moderne* teaches that "the true vocation of a woman is to be a wife and mother. Nature has blessed her with these important functions, and she can achieve nothing in this life that surpasses this dignity." Cousine Avette, "En causant — la véritable vocation de la femme," *La Revue moderne*, Vol. 15, No. 12, October 1934, p. 37. "If the object of your affection does not have a feeling for domestic duty," warns *Le Guide des amoureux* to men, "one would do well to abandon the relation." [Anonymous], *Le guide des amoureux et des gens du monde. L'amour, la cour, le mariage*, Montréal, C.O. Beauchemin & Fils, 1898, p. 31.

61. Blanche Lamontagne-Beauregard, *Un cœur fidèle*, p. 73.

62. *Ibid.*, p. 153.

63. Ellen Constans, "Du bon chic-bon genre dans un mauvais genre : le roman d'amour de Delly," dans Julia Bettinotti and Pascale Noizet (eds.), *Guimauve et fleurs d'oranger. Delly*, coll. "Études paralittéraires," Québec, Nuit blanche éditeur, 1995, p. 110.

64. Blanche Lamontagne-Beauregard, *Un cœur fidèle*, p. 23-24.

65. *Ibid.*, p. 57.

66. *Ibid.*, p. 103.

67. *Ibid.*, p. 35-36.

68. *Ibid.*, p. 100-101.

69. *Ibid.*, p. 145.

70. *Ibid.*, p. 103-104.

71. *Ibid.*, p. 120-121.

72. *Ibid.*, p. 121.

73. *Ibid.*, p. 175.

74. We find a very similar scenario in *Le médaillon fatal* (1924), by Andrée Jarret [the pseudonym of Cécile Beauregard], in which Blandine must first marry a good man, but who is not her true love, but is able to reunite with Maurice after her husband dies.

75. *Ibid.*, p. 135.

76. *Ibid.*, p. 136.

77. *Ibid.*, p. 136-137.

78. *Ibid.*, p. 163.

79. *Ibid.*, p. 106.

80. Maurice Lemire, "*Un cœur fidèle*," in Maurice Lemire (ed.), *Dictionnaire des œuvres littéraires du Québec*, Tome 2, *1900-1939*, 2nd revised and updated edition, Montréal, Fides, 1987 [1980], p. 1106.

81. Blanche Lamontagne-Beauregard, *Un cœur fidèle*, p. 100.

82. *Ibid.*, p. 82.

83. *Ibid.*

84. *Ibid.*, p. 82-83.

85. *Ibid.*, p. 86.
86. *Ibid.*, p. 89.
87. *Ibid.*, p. 176.
88. David Décarie, "L'évolution du roman urbain (1934-1945) : du roman bourgeois au roman du peuple," *Voix et Images*, Vol. 41, No. 2, Winter 2016, p. 27.
89. Denise Girard, *Mariage et classes sociales. Les Montréalais francophones entre les deux guerres*, Sainte-Foy, Éditions de l'IQRC, 2000, 203 p.
90. Marie-Rose Turcot, *Nicolette Auclair*, Montréal-New York, Les éditions du Mercure, 1930, 179 p.
91. Dr E. A. René de Cotret, *Les voies de l'amour*, Montréal, [n.p.], 1931, p. 129.
92. *Ibid.*, p. 152.
93. *Ibid.*, p. 153.
94. *Ibid.*, p. 152.
95. *Ibid.*
96. *Ibid.*
97. *Ibid.*, p. 153.
98. One hero stands out from this gallery of affluent men: Alexandre Daubouge, in *À deux* (1937), is a travelling salesman specializing in lady's hats.
99. J.-Wilfrid Pion, *Ce que peut l'amour : roman de mœurs canadiennes*, Laprairie, Chez l'auteur, 1943, 345 p.
100. See the works of Denis Saint-Jacques and Marie-José Des Rivières and on the subject of this novel, notably in *Chercher fortune à Montréal. Anthologie*, coll. "Alias Poche," Montréal, Éditions Alias, 2014, 270 p., and Denis Saint-Jacques and Marie-José Des Rivières, "Le féminisme problématique d'un roman d'amour, *Anne Mérival*," *Recherches féministes*, Vol. 24, No. 1, 2011, p. 61-76.
101. Madeleine [the pseudonym of Anne-Marie Gleason Huguenin], *Anne Mérival*, coll. "Littérature québécoise," Vol. 713, La Bibliothèque électronique du Québec, [Online], [1927], p. 189, https://beq.ebooksgratuits.com/pdf-xpdf/Madeleine-Anne.pdf.
102. *Ibid.*, p. 84.
103. *Ibid.*, p. 27.
104. Julia Hallam, "Nursing an Image: The Sue Barton Career Novels," in Sarah Sceats and Gail Cunningham (eds.), *Image and Power: Women in Fiction in the Twentieth Century*, London (NY), Longman, 1996, p. 91-102.
105. According to sociologist Philippe Garigue, who conducted one of the first studies on the subject in the 1950s, "the attitude of French Canadians toward the question of love and relations between the sexes directly stems from their cultural orientation toward the family. The family being conceived primarily as a "universe of rules," it is therefore in their relations as father and mother, husband and wife, etc. that the notion of love and relationships between the sexes is situated." Philippe Garigue, *La vie familiale des Canadiens français*, Montréal, Presses de l'Université de Montréal, 1962, p. 89. In such a universe, the children are the natural extension of love, that is to say, not only the fruit of love but love "made flesh."
106. Albertine Laperle-Bernier, *Le château des illusions*, Montréal, Published by the author, 1949, 188 p.
107. See the answers to the survey on the reasons for marrying conducted by Luc Aubry in *La Revue moderne* in 1926-1927, which are often centred on the idea that

the wife is, through and in love, the slave of her husband. Luc Aubry, Chroniques "À la conquête du bonheur!" et "La Nouvelle enquête de Luc Aubry," *La Revue moderne*, June 1926-July 1927.

108. Laetitia Filion, *Yolande la fiancée*, Lévis, Imprimerie Le Quotidien, 1935, p. 69. Filion's novels are a hymn to a love that is impossible and sacrificed. In *Amour moderne* (Beauceville, l'Éclaireur, 1939, p. 142), the heroine realizes that "human love can never satisfy her" and enters the convent, while her love, inconsolable, hides away at the Oka Abbey.

109. Bonne Amie, "Ce que Luc Aubry veut savoir... Quel est votre auteur favori?" *La Revue moderne*, November 1927, p. 43. We cannot refrain from citing the title of a romantic collection of the French publisher Tallandier, published between 1939 and 1942: "Pour oublier la vie" ("So as to forget life!")! See Anne Simonin, "'Parlez-moi d'amour': la littérature rose et l'oubli du quotidien (1939-1942)?" *Contemporary French Civilization*, Vol. 23, No. 2, Summer-Fall 1999, 289-308.

110. [Anonymous], "Un enlèvement," *Le Jour*, 9 December 1944, p. 7. A. Giroux, "Amour tenace," *Culture*, Vol. 7, No. 1, March 1946, p. 118. Jean Luce, "Littérature canadienne 1948. Le romancier est obligé de respecter la morale, soutient Adrienne Maillet," *La Presse*, 27 November 1948, p. 34. The ads present her as an "author" who "knows how to maintain the interest found in the most popular works of her French sisters, the most famous novelists for young girls." "Vient de paraître : *Amour tenace* par Adrienne Maillet," *Revue dominicaine*, Vol. 51, Tome 2, October 1945, p. 13.

111. Yveline Baticle, "Delly : autopsie du roman rose," *Communication et langages*, No. 61, 3rd quarter 1984, p. 7786.

112. Cynthia Lemieux, *L'œuvre romanesque d'Adrienne Maillet : une production sentimentale bourgeoise dans un monde en plein changement (1937-1954)*, Master's Thesis, Sherbrooke, Université de Sherbrooke, 2014, 94 p.

113. "I don't know why," says a character in *Peuvent-elles garder un secret ?*, "when an old maid gets involved in raising a child, I always assume it is hers." Adrienne Maillet, *Peuvent-elles garder un secret?*, Montréal, [n.p.], 1937, p. 192.

114. The plot of *Peuvent-elles garder un secret ?* is based on the fact that Yolande's sister, seduced by her sister's fiancé, dies giving birth in a convent. The child is adopted by a nun who leaves the cloister. In *Trop tard* (1942), the heroine refuses to get married, because she fears the pain of childbirth. An operation for appendicitis renders her sterile. She then bitterly regrets her decision to not have children. She breaks off her affair with Merlin, because he is "suffering too much in a home without children" and the presence of a child is "necessary for the attachment between spouses." Adrienne Maillet, *Trop tard*, Montréal, [n.p.], 1942, p. 185 and p. 189. She enters the convent and "her children will be the children of others." In *Un enlèvement* (1944), Françoise begins a relation outside of marriage with Marc Sandoux, who marries someone else. Having become pregnant, the unwed mother places her child with the nursery, hoping to take her back. Marc illegally adopts his daughter. Françoise marries the president of an aviation company she works for. Her husband agrees to adopt her daughter, who she has kidnapped thanks to a ruse. In *De gré ou de force* (1948), Monique gets remarried with Luc upon the death of her husband who had left for the war. When—miracle!—the latter returns, she is pregnant and her second marriage is declared void according to Church law. Her legal husband must agree to adopt the child she is carrying.

Finally, in *L'ombre sur le bonheur* (1951), a haughty mother-in-law reconciles with her daughter-in-law from a working-class background when she learns that she will soon be a grandmother. She takes on the role of godmother.

115. Lise Queffélec, "Héroïne et martyre : la figure de la femme dans le roman sentimental de la fin du XIXe siècle," in *Trames. Le roman sentimental, Actes du colloque international des 14-15-16 mars 1989*, Limoges, Presses universitaires de Limoges, 1990, p. 253-261.

116. Anne Martine Parent, "Un ver dans le fruit, révolte féministe dans *Trop tard* (1942) d'Adrienne Maillet," in François Ouellet (ed.), *Décliner l'intériorité. Le roman psychologique des années 1940-1950 au Québec*, Québec, Nota bene, 2011, p. 105-119.

117. Adrienne Maillet, *L'oncle des jumeaux Pomponnelle*, Montréal, Éditions de l'Action canadienne-française, 1939, 249 p.

118. Adrienne Maillet, *Amour tenace*, Montréal/Ottawa, Éditions du Lévrier, 1945, 200 p.

119. We find other examples of unfaithful husbands, including Michel in *Les voies de l'amour* (1931), Richard Tellier in *Un de Jasper* (1933), and Paul Noizeux in *L'amour trompé* (1937).

120. Albertine Laperle-Bernier, *Dans la nuit sombre*, Montréal, Les Éditions Modèles, 1942, p. 22.

121. *Ibid.*, p. 240.

122. Albertine Laperle-Bernier, *La voix de l'âme*, Montréal, Les Editions Modèles, 1944, p. 21.

123. *Ibid.*

124. *Ibid.*, p. 27.

125. *Ibid.*, p. 101.

126. *Ibid.*, p. 106.

127. *Ibid.*, p. 184.

128. *Ibid.*, p. 185-186.

129. André Tilly, "Albertine Laperle-Bernier—'Le Château des illusions.' Roman. Montréal. 1949. 18.5 cm. 192 pages," *Revue dominicaine*, February 1950, p. 127.

130. Albertine Laperle-Bernier, *Le château des illusions*, p. 179.

131. *Ibid.*, p. 186-187.

132. Léonce Cantin, "*Dans la nuit sombre* et autres romans d'Albertine Laperle-Bernier," in Maurice Lemire (ed.), *Dictionnaire des œuvres littéraires du Québec*, Tome 3, *1940-1959*, Montréal, Fides, 1995 [1982], p. 260.

133. *Ibid.*

134. In 1929, the life expectancy for women in Quebec was 55, and, for men, 53.

135. "The heroines of novels in the 1930s relegate the figures of God and their beloved to the background, thus assuming their full autonomy and emancipation. The different ends recount an alienation and privation that are the necessary and paradoxical conditions for the emergence and proclamation of a different voice. "On the margins of life," the women in novels are also "on the margins" of something, subjectivized by this unstable position, and refusing the annihilation of their being by establishing themselves as autonomous subjects." Adrien Rannaud, *De l'amour et de l'audace. Femmes et roman au Québec dans les années 1930*, Montréal, Presses de l'Université de Montréal, 2018, p. 299.

136. In *Yolande la fiancée* (1935), Yolande's father is worried about his daughter's future and is preparing her entry into the world: "You have to consider accepting a few invitations. Next summer, I will take care of this, even if it means sending you and your mother on a more-or-less prolonged vacation on a fashionable beach. We don't have the right to become disinterested in your future." Laetitia Filion, *Yolande la fiancée*, p. 132.

137. "In the period from 1920 to 1940, rituals aimed to break the young people's dependence, whether the parents liked it or not. Very quickly, almost without transition, the marriage would take place. In certain cases, the rites cut to the essential: a religious ceremony, a toast raised to the health of the newlyweds, and the immediate departure for the honeymoon. The predominant element was the urgency felt by the newlyweds to establish their space of intimacy." Martine Tremblay, *Le mariage dans la vallée du Haut-Richelieu au XXe siècle. Ritualité et distinction sociale*, coll. "Géographie historique," Sainte-Foy, Presses de l'Université Laval, 2001, p. 222.

138. Roch Hurtubise, *L'amour, le soi et la société*, p. 213.

Chapter 4: Celebrated Love (1940-1965)

1. Gaston Desjardins, *L'amour en patience : la sexualité adolescente au Québec, 1940-1960*, Québec, Presses de l'Université du Québec, 1995, 261 p. Written by Father Gérard Petit and launched in 1941, the collection "Face au mariage" published by Éditions Fides, and whose print run surpassed a million copies in 1962, included twenty-three novels of thirty-two pages, with enticing titles like *Mon fiancé, Ai-je le droit de plaire?* or *Le flirt*. It was also in 1944 that Éditions Novalis in Ottawa published the first *Cours de préparation au mariage*, which set a precedent and was quickly translated into sixteen languages. See Jacques Michon, *Fides. La grande aventure éditoriale du père Paul-Aimé Martin*, Montréal, Fides, 1998, 387 p.

2. Marcel-Marie Desmarais, *La clinique du cœur*, Vol. 1, Montréal, Éditions du Lévrier, 1957, p. 30. The books by Father Desmarais appealed to a very large public. The famous *L'amour à l'âge atomique* (1950) reached a circulation of 132,000 copies, and *Le cœur et ses trésors*, 150,000 copies. Broadcast on the radio starting in 1955, his chronicles *La clinique du cœur* were printed in *La Presse*, then published in ten volumes by Éditions du Lévrier, with a print run reaching 600,000 copies. See Marie-Pier Luneau, "L'amour au temps de la Révolution tranquille. Le père Marcel-Marie Desmarais, médecin du cœur," Études d›histoire religieuse, Vol. 75, 2009, p. 69-88.

Marcel-Marie Desmarais, *La clinique du cœur*, p. 30.

3. Jocelyne Mathieu, *"Le Bulletin des agriculteurs* : pour vous mesdames : l'empreinte d'Alice Ber (1938-1979)," *Les Cahiers des dix*, No. 60, 2006, p. 277-292.

4. Gérard Tessier, *Face à l'imprimé obscène. Plaidoyer en faveur d'une littérature saine*, Montréal, Les éditions de la Feuille d'Érable, 1955, p. 56.

5. According to a correspondent of the *Bulletin des agriculteurs*: "I'm 17 years old; I really like reading, especially romance novels; it is a real passion." Blondine Affligée, "Le courrier d'Alice Ber. Trop de romanesque dans les pensées amène le déséquilibre de l'âme," *Le Bulletin des agriculteurs*, October 1940, p. 66.

6. Cited by Gérard Tessier, *Face à l'imprimé obscène. Plaidoyer en faveur d'une littérature saine*, p. 59.
7. François Hébert, *La littérature populaire en fascicules au Québec*, Tome 1, Québec, Les Éditions GID, 2012, p. 13.
8. Denis Saint-Jacques *et al.*, *Femmes de rêve au travail. Les femmes et le travail dans les productions écrites de grande consommation au Québec, de 1945 à aujourd'hui*, Québec, Éditions Nota bene, 1998, p. 21.
9. Jacques Michon (ed.), *Histoire de l'édition littéraire au Québec au XXe siècle*, Vol. 2, *Le temps des éditeurs : 1940-1959*, Montréal, Fides, 2004, p. 296. Table 2 in Michon's work provides a panorama of popular serial fiction from 1940 to 1966. *Ibid.*, p. 298-302.
10. Marc-Adélard Tremblay and Gérald Fortin, *Les comportements économiques de la famille salariée du Québec*, Québec, Presses de l'Université Laval, 1964, 405 p. Jean-Pierre Charland and Jacques Saint-Pierre, "Le pouvoir d'achat des travailleurs, 1929-1960 : quelques éléments d'évaluation," *Recherches sociographiques*, Vol. 30, No. 2, 1989, p. 199-227.
11. Luc Côté and Jean-Guy Daigle, *Publicité de masse et masse publicitaire : le marché québécois des années 1920 aux années 1960*, Ottawa, Presses de l'Université d'Ottawa, 1999, p. 104. Sébastien Couvrette, "La classe moyenne se met en scène : la publicité des quotidiens montréalais comme discours de classe, 1920-1970," *Recherches sociographiques*, Vol. 53, No. 3, September-December 2012, p. 605.
12. Danielle Gauvreau and Benoît Laplante, "Baby-boom et déclin de la fécondité : l'évolution paradoxale de la fécondité durant les années 1950 au Québec," *Bulletin d'histoire politique*, Vol. 24, No. 1, Fall 2015, p. 46.
13. Albert Colangelo, "Le bonheur et l'amour," *Le Mouvement ouvrier*, 1945, p. 42.
14. Chantal Savoie, "La chanson à succès dans les années 1940. Une modernité culturelle par acclamation?" *Globe*, Vol. 15, No. 1-2, 2012, p. 161-182.
15. *Ibid.*
16. Jeanne Zéphire, *La Fille sans nom*, coll. "Roman d'amour mensuel," Montréal, Éditions Police-Journal, [n.d.], 32 p.
17. Caroline Barrett, *La femme et la société dans la littérature sentimentale populaire québécoise 1940-1960*, Master's Thesis, Québec, Université Laval, 1979, p. 19.
18. Jean Vernois, *La belle Mathilde*, coll. "Roman d'amour," Montréal, Éditions Police-Journal, 1957, p. 29.
19. Mimi Estival, *Ivresse de Noël*, coll. "Les plus belles histoires d'amour," Montréal, Éditions Police-Journal, [n.d.], p. 32.
20. The study conducted by Sylvie Provost confirmed that the readership of serial romance novels published in the 1940s and 1950s was primarily composed of women, in general young adults. See Sylvie Provost, "Avez-vous déjà lu IXE-13, Albert Brien, Guy Verchères...?" Études littéraires, Vol. 15, No. 2, August 1982, p. 133-164.
21. Yves Pérou, "Du mariage obligatoire au mariage facultatif," in Victor Piché and Céline Le Bourdais (eds.), *La démographie québécoise. Enjeux du XXIe siècle*, Montréal, Presses de l'Université de Montréal, 2003, p. 110-143.
22. One of the characters in *Marie-Louise des Champs* (1947), by Pierre de Grandpré, spelled it out: "Deep down, we are all preoccupied with the same thing:

the future; but for young girls, the future is a husband, whereas for us it is... a situation." Pierre de Grandpré, *Marie-Louise des Champs : roman*, Montréal, Fides, 1948, p. 60.

23. See the possible statuses of female characters in fiction according to Isabelle Boisclair, "Laure Clouet, femme de personne," in Lucie Joubert and Annette Hayward (eds.), *La vieille fille. Lectures d'un personnage*, Montréal, Triptyque, 2000, p. 87.

24. Patricia Smart, Écrire dans la maison du père, coll. "Littérature d'Amérique," Montréal, Éditions Québec-Amérique, 1988, 337 p.

25. Adèle Lauzon, "La femme est-elle exploitée ?" *Cité libre*, No. 17, June 1957, p. 44.

26. Betty Friedan, *The Feminine Mystique*, New York, W.W. Norton & Company, 1963, p. 15.

27. Pol Delval, *Tes désirs sont des ordres, ma chérie*, Berthierville, Éditions Irène, [n.d.], 32 p.

28. Making this sociological reality a dimension of the "eternal feminine," one author wrote in 1969: "the woman's entire psychological apparatus is centred on love. Among men, on the contrary, other interests manifest themselves just as powerfully if not more so: his profession, the economy, politics. It is the drama that plays out in so many households, where the wife insists on pursuing the impossible dream of the eternal feminine, polarizing all of her partner's vital energies, making him a prisoner of her love and her home." Jules-Bernard Gingras, "Au chapitre de l'amour et de l'intelligence," *L'Action nationale*, December 1969, p. 351.

29. Surveyed on what interested her the most in the romance novels of the period in 1958, a twenty-year-old female reader responded: "The love story that unfolded as I thought it would and ended well." Anonymous reader born in 1938 in Saint-Augustin, "Sondage auprès des lectrices de romans sentimentaux en fascicules," conducted by email by Marie-Pier Luneau and Jean-Philippe Warren, 2 December 2020.

30. Jacques Beauchamp-Forget, who wrote dime novels in the 1940s for Éditions Fleur de Lys, summed up the formula: "The novel is divided into four episodes called, 'chapters,' of five pages each. The first three episodes end on a question mark, like in a soap opera. The first chapter presents two of the three main characters and specifies the time and place of the story. To spice up the action as quickly as possible, the third character appears at the beginning of the second chapter. In the third, it is the drama 'in all its horror.' The plot is resolved in the second half of the fourth chapter: two of the three characters find happiness and..." [Anonymous], "Témoignage d'un ex-marchand de prose qui manqua de sens pratique," *Québec français*, 27, 1977, p. 48.

31. As Jean L'Archevêque records: "This worked pretty well at the time, but always with the continual struggle on the part of the Church. We didn't feel at ease." Interview by Jean L'Archevêque with Michel René, projet Liquefasc, Département des littératures, Université Laval, May 1979. Bernard Bourgeois, from Éditions Bernard, confirms this: "I have to say in passing that the clergy put me on trial every 15 days [...]. I was censored by the clergy. Then the clergy would complain to the attorney general or the provincial police." Telephone interview by Bernard

Bourgeois with Michel René, 1 May 1979. The two interviews are cited by Claude-Marie Gagnon, "La censure au Québec," *Voix et Images*, Vol. 9, No. 1, Fall 1983, p. 116.

32. [Anonymous], "Amour et aventure," *Le Front ouvrier*, 17 May 1947, p. 6.

33. On this subject, see Marie-Pier Luneau and Jean-Philippe Warren, "Ce que le roman catholique fait au roman sentimental : le cas de la collection 'Amour et aventure,'" *COnTEXTES*, [Online], No. 23, 4 April 2019, http://journals.openedition.org/contextes/7903.

34. Caroline Barrett and Michel René, "Littérature de masse au Québec," *The French Review*, Vol. 53, No. 6, May 1980, p. 872-879.

35. [Anonymous], "Les romans Lanthier à la portée de tous," *La Tribune*, 30 November 1945, Cahier 2, p. 8. Les Éditions Lanthier affirm that, since 1942, their total print run reached over a million copies.

36. We sometimes find a familiar toponymy in the stories (Sainte-Catherine Street, Jean-Talon Market, Dorval Airport, Saint-Hyacinthe, Noranda, Anse du Havre-Aubert, etc.), and some dialogues are riddled with anglicisms ("hood," "tougher," "cutter"), Canadianisms ("boghei," "robine," "feu sauvage," "radoub," "ouâguines"), or popular expressions: these features combine local colour and charm, adding a touch of authenticity to the stories while varying the composition of the dialogues.

37. The prospect of reading 878 novels being unfeasible, we settled on analyzing fifty novels. In any case, it would have been ineffective to proceed with a separate analysis of each novel in the series, as one would for a classic work, by considering it independently of other publications; not only would we quickly see an effect of saturation after reading a handful of works, but, more importantly, the significance of these stories is only revealed in the analysis of their seriality, which gives rise to new readings.

38. We know that Michelle Thériault, Yves Thériault, Pierre Daignault, and Alexandre Huot, notably, wrote extensively for Éditions Police-Journal. The editor-in-chief of *Police journal*, the Éditions Police-Journal magazine, boasted in 1946, of counting among its contributors a writer who belonged to the Académie canadienne-française and two recipients of the Prix David. Cited by François Hébert, *La littérature populaire en fascicules au Québec*, p. 31. For the collector François Hébert, the identity of the authors remains, given the scarcity of archives, one of the great blind spots of research on Québécois serial romance novels. *Ibid.*, p. 51. On the question of pseudonyms, see Karol'Ann Boivin and Marie-Pier Luneau, "Qu'ont en commun Mimi Estival, Roxanne d'Avril et Georgette Mars? Auctorialité et roman sentimental québécois de l'après-guerre (1944-1965)," in Ruth Panofsky (ed.), *Authorship in Canadian Literature*, forthcoming.

39. Pierre Saurel, the pseudonym of Pierre Daignault, author of nearly 2000 stories, mainly adventure and spy novels, "officially" wrote a dozen romance novels, no doubt to encourage the migration of a male readership to the romance novel.

40. Our analysis corroborates an observation already made by the authors of *Femmes de rêve au travail*, which is that, in the postwar period, "the economic sphere was abundantly thematized in diverse ways in the love story." These scholars estimate that around 11.5 percent of the "Roman d'amour" collection published

by Éditions Police-Journal portray the heroine's financial autonomy, attributable either to an inheritance, a personal initiative or being drawn to an adventurous lifestyle. Denis Saint-Jacques *et al.*, *Femmes de rêve au travail*, p. 47-48.
41. Francine Barry, *Le travail de la femme au Québec. L'évolution de 1940 à 1970*, Montréal, Presses de l'Université du Québec, 1977, 80 p.
42. Rita Lebrun, *Le roman d'une garde-malade*, Montréal, Éditions Police-Journal, 1955, p. 30.
43. Betty Forest, *Souffle de passion*, coll. "Roman d'amour," Montréal, Éditions Police-Journal, 1947, p. 7.
44. *Ibid.*, p. 3.
45. *Ibid.*, p. 6.
46. *Ibid.*, p. 10.
47. "Of course she would love to! Especially for one reason: Ruth could not go without him, because she still hadn't received that hoped-for raise, and in her current situation, she didn't have enough pocket money to allow herself this luxury very often." *Ibid.*, p. 11.
48. *Ibid.*, p. 13.
49. *Ibid.*, p. 11.
50. *Ibid.*, p. 15.
51. *Ibid.*, p. 16.
52. *Ibid.*, p. 17.
53. *Ibid.*, p. 2.
54. Marc Angenot, "Qu'est-ce que la paralittérature?" *Études littéraires*, Vol. 7, No. 1, April 1974, p. 21.
55. Martine Tremblay, *Le mariage dans la vallée du Haut-Richelieu au XX*[e] *siècle. Ritualité et distinction sociale*, coll. "Géographie historique," Sainte-Foy, Presses de l'Université Laval, 2001, p. 59. The same was true in Montreal: Daniel Fournier, "Consanguinité et sociabilité dans la zone de Montréal au début du siècle," *Recherches sociographiques*, Vol. 24, No. 3, 1983, p. 307-323.
56. Denyse Baillargeon, *Ménagères au temps de la Crise*, Montréal, Éditions du remue-ménage, 1991, 311 p. Denise Girard, *Mariage et classes sociales. Les Montréalais francophones entre les deux guerres*, Sainte-Foy, Éditions de l'IQRC, 2000, p. 46. Peggy Roquigny, "La danse pour tout un chacun : pratiques différenciées d'un loisir commercial à Montréal pendant l'entre-deux-guerres," *Mens*, Vol. 16, No. 1, Fall 2015, p. 21-61. Denise Lemieux, "Lieux de socialité de la jeunesse et changements socio-culturels dans la formation des couples (1880-1949)," in Roger Levasseur (ed.), *De la sociabilité. Spécificité et mutations*, Montréal, Boréal Express, 1990, p. 137-152.
57. "It is no longer said that the young woman 'receives' a young man, but rather that she 'goes out,' with him. In many circumstances, they go out alone for a drive [...], or they go alone to the theatre, to a restaurant, or to a club or dance hall." Moïse Roy, "Les fréquentations," *Nos cours*, Vol. 8, No. 9, 1946, p. 2.
58. [Anonymous], "L'adolescent ouvrier et ses loisirs," *Prêtre aujourd'hui*, Vol. 12, No. 6, June-July 1962, p. 230.
59. [Anonymous], "Les problèmes de vie sentimentale des étudiants canadiens," *Cahiers d'action catholique*, No. 154, June-July-August 1953, p. 315. Martine Côté and

Madeleine Gauthier, "À propos des péchés d'amour," *Cap-aux-Diamants*, No. 55, Fall 1998, p. 18-21. For France, see Anne-Claire Rebreyend, *Intimités amoureuses. France, 1920-1975*, Toulouse, Presses universitaires du Mirail, 2008, p. 146.

60. Paul Verchères, *Le plus beau cadeau*, coll. "Roman d'amour," Montréal, Éditions Police-Journal, 1949, p. 6.

61. Paul Verchères, "[Préface]," *Le plus beau cadeau*, p. 2.

62. "I admit [...] that the laws of marriage, both from a civil and religious point of view, are extremely severe, and this is why people have to reflect on it a lot longer before making a lifelong commitment. Because it is a proven fact that if all those who, in the name of love at first sight or all-consuming love, put the rope around their neck thought twice about it, the aftermath of disappointments would be a lot less considerable." Pascale France, "Le courrier de Pascale France," *Le Soleil*, 1 July 1945, p. 4.

63. [Anonymous], *Le doux pays des amants*, Montréal, Éditions Police-Journal, 1954, p. 14.

64. *Ibid.*, p. 18.

65. *Ibid.*, p. 16.

66. Pol Delval, *Hasard ou destinée*, Berthierville, Éditions Irène, [n.d.], p. 12.

67. *Ibid.*, p. 19.

68. *Ibid.*, p. 21.

69. *Ibid.*, p. 22.

70. *Ibid.*, p. 28.

71. *Ibid.*, p. 29.

72. *Ibid.*

73. "Gabriel Normand was big and tall. He measured over six feet. Next to him, Colette appeared even smaller than in reality because the contrast was so great. Yet she felt safe with him." Jeanne Zéphire, *Mon beau soldat*, coll. "Roman d'amour," Montréal, Éditions Police-Journal, 1952, p. 22.

74. Jeanne Zéphire, *L'amoureux de Noranda*, coll. "Roman d'amour," Montréal, Éditions Police Journal, 1961 [1951], p. 8.

75. *Ibid.*, p. 31.

76. Only two novels dating before 1940 in our corpus shed light on sexual relations prior to marriage: *Les Voies de l'amour* (1931) and *Entre neuf et onze heures* (1939). Though, in the first of these two works, the narrator only recounts the retrospectively very timid emotions inspired in him by Lucille, the young girl from the boarding house where he lived while studying medicine. Dr. E. A. René de Cotret, *Les voies de l'amour*, Montréal, [n.p.], 1931, 311 p. Wolfred Nelson, *Entre neuf et onze heures*, Montréal, Published by the author, 1936, 159 p.

77. Véronique Ostiguy, *Dire sans dire : censure et affirmation du désir dans* Désespoir de vieille fille *de Thérèse Tardif (1943) et* Orage sur mon corps *d'André Béland (1944)*, Master's Thesis, Montréal, Université du Québec à Montréal, 2010, 101 p. Also of interest is Élise Salaün, *Oser Éros. L'érotisme dans le roman québécois des origines à nos jours*, Québec, Éditions Nota bene, 2010, 398 p. The researcher's descriptions of classical Eros and romantic Eros largely correspond to what we found in the romantic novels of the nineteenth century and early twentieth century. After this, the increasingly explicit representations of eroticism in Québécois

novels no longer correspond with our findings, since, as Ellen Constans observes, "the flesh has its reasons that the heart does not know." Thus in the romance novel, "the heart and happiness are placed higher than the body, its desires and pleasures": as soon as eroticism takes up too much space, the romance novel gives way to the erotic novel. Ellen Constans, *Parlez-moi d'amour. Le roman sentimental, des romans grecs aux collections de l'an 2000*, Limoges, Presses universitaires de Limoges, 1999, p. 29.

78. Jeanne Zéphire, *Mon beau soldat*, p. 12.

79. Gaston Desjardins, *L'amour en patience*, p. 168.

80. Voir Jeanne Zéphire, *Marjolaine, la garce*, coll. "Roman d'amour," Montréal, Éditions Police-Journal, 1951, 31 p.

81. Voir Paul Verchères, *La fille-mère*, coll. "Roman d'amour," Montréal, Éditions Police-Journal, 1950, 32 p. and Jacques Marinier, *Un mariage blanc*, coll. "Mon roman d'amour," Montréal, Éditions Police-Journal, 1958, 32 p.

82. Jean Bretigny, *Le survenant amoureux*, coll. "Mon roman d'amour," Montréal, Éditions Police-Journal, 1958, p. 18-19.

83. Jeanne Zéphire, *Mon beau soldat*, p. 25.

84. Jeanne Zéphire, *Au diable les hommes!*, coll. "Roman d'amour," Montréal, Éditions Police-Journal, 1952, p. 1.

85. "You know for us," recalls a woman, "as young girls, that was our goal, it was to get married. When we got into our 20s, it was to find a husband. But it wasn't like today. It wasn't the girl who made the first move. It was the man. That meant finding a man without it being too obvious. It was frowned upon to show it." Cited by Denise Girard, *Différenciation sociale et rituels du mariage : les Montréalais francophones, 1925-1940*, PhD Thesis, Québec, Université Laval, 1998, p. 72.

86. Mimi Estivale, *Au bord de la faute*, coll. "Grand roman d'amour," Montréal, Éditions Police-Journal, 1947, p. 16.

87. *Ibid.*

88. *Ibid.*, p. 20.

89. *Ibid.*, p. 7.

90. *Ibid.*, p. 19.

91. *Ibid.*

92. *Ibid.*

93. *Ibid.*, p. 22.

94. *Ibid.*, p. 23-24.

95. *Ibid.*, p. 24.

96. *Ibid.*

97. *Ibid.*, p. 26.

98. *Ibid.*, p. 27.

99. *Ibid.*

100. *Ibid.*, p. 28.

101. *Ibid.*

102. *Ibid.*

103. She says, for example: "Sometimes, I confess without shame, I would have the impulse to jump in the river." *Ibid.*, p. 16. This comes up again in the following two pages, to the point that the heroine elaborates a veritable introspection on

her suicidal tendencies: "It is perhaps out of habit that I spoke of suicide [...]. The idea of water makes me think of suicide [...], because when I had already suffered great disappointments and the idea of suicide came to me, it was the river that I thought of..." *Ibid.*, p. 18.

104. *Ibid.*, p. 31.

105. *Ibid.*, p. 23.

106. *Ibid.*, p. 30.

107. It is often observed that a large proportion of Québécois women entered the job market in the 1940s and 1950s. It is important to note, however, that the majority of these women were single, contrary to what was happening elsewhere in Canada. "Quebec is a highly industrialized province, and a higher proportion of workers than for the rest of Canada; however, the proportion of married women working outside the home is well below the national average." Ministère du travail du Canada, *La femme canadienne au travail*, Ottawa, Le Ministère, 1957, p. 21. The incompatibility of marriage and a professional career for woman still prevailed in the immediate postwar period. "The norm of career interruption was uniformly shared, and, in general, the idea of postponing childbearing was not yet thought of." Denise Lemieux and Lucie Mercier, "La formation du couple et ses rituels : l'analyse des changements de la période 1950-1980, à travers les récits de vie," *Comprendre la famille: Actes du 1st symposium québécois de recherche sur la famille*, coll. "Comprendre la famille," Montréal, Presses de l'Université du Québec, 1992, p. 61. Francine Barry, *Le travail de la femme au Québec*, p. 20.

108. Note that the series read predominantly by men conveyed a different moral. In "Les Aventures étranges de l'Agent IXE-13," Gisèle Tuboeuf "deeply" loves Jean Thibault, "the ace of Canadian spies," and intends to prove her passion through steadfast fidelity. In issue 585, published in 1959, ten years after the launch of the series, the one known under the code name T-4 finally marries him, despite the resistance of Jean, who doesn't want to live an ordered and sedentary life. Conjugal life nonetheless leaves Gisèle unsatisfied. The woman accustomed to thrilling adventures finds life as a housewife too idle, solitary, and boring. What should have been a "little paradise" turns out to be domestic confinement. Her child having died, killed by the communists, she returns to her work in the secret service. Jean, for his part, had never stopped living a life far from home. The second and third series depict a single hero having erotic adventures with countless partners. Marie-José des Rivières, *La représentation de la femme dans la roman populaire "Les Aventures étranges de l'agent IXE-13, l'as des espions canadiens," de Pierre Saurel*, Master's Thesis, Université Laval, 1978, 122 f. Marie-José des Rivières and Claude-Marie Gagnon, "Résumé du corpus," Études littéraires, Vol. 12, No. 2, August 1979, p. 137—142. See also Madeleine Godin, "La place du cœur chez Diane la belle aventurière," *Études littéraires*, Vol. 16, No. 3, December 1983, p. 429-440.

109. See the letters sent to Jean Despréz [the pseudonym of Laurette Larocque], who ran the love advice column in *Photo-journal* (1955-1960).

110. [Anonymous], *Le doux pays des amants*, p. 31.

111. Ronald Vernes, *Le dernier baiser*, coll. "Roman d'amour," Montréal, Éditions Police-Journal, [1956], p. 7.

112. The secondary female characters, however, can be single: widows and independent women are there to help the heroine find a husband.
113. [Anonymous], *Le Roman d'une orpheline*, Montréal, Éditions Police-Journal, 1946, p. 31-32.
114. *Ibid.*, p. 32.
115. Jeanne Zéphire, *Au diable les hommes!* p. 6.
116. Jacques Régent, *Dernier amour*, coll. "Roman d'amour," Montréal, Éditions Police-Journal, 1947, p. 6.
117. *Ibid.*, p. 12-13.
118. *Ibid.*, p. 13.
119. *Ibid.*, p. 14.
120. *Ibid.*, p. 15.
121. *Ibid.*, p. 16.
122. *Ibid.*, p. 16-17.
123. *Ibid.*, p. 25.
124. *Ibid.*, p. 29.
125. Pierre Valdel, *Mère et fille rivales*, coll. "Roman d'amour," Berthierville, Éditions Irène, 1953, p. 11.
126. *Ibid.*, p. 26.
127. [Anonymous], *Le courage de l'amour*, coll. "Roman d'amour," Montréal, Éditions Police-Journal, 1947, p. 29.
128. *Ibid.*, p. 30.
129. Jacques Régent, *Dernier amour*, p. 21.
130. *Ibid.*
131. "My father attacked me and not always to ask me for money. He was vicious and wanted to force me to commit abominable acts with him." Paul de Varennes, *Ma vertu compromise*, Montréal, Éditions Populaires, [n. d.], p. 1.
132. Gil du Parc, *L'enfant de la misère*, Berthierville, Les Éditions Georges Couture, [between 1940 and 1949], p. 5.
133. Mimi Estival, *Nuit divine*, coll. "Roman d'amour," Montréal, Éditions Police-Journal, 1949, p. 26.
134. Michele Pierre, *Cendrillon et son beau prince*, coll. "Roman d'amour," Montréal, Éditions Police-Journal, 1954, p. 30.
135. *Ibid.*, p. 21-22.
136. *Ibid.*, p. 21.
137. The Americanization of French-Canadian culture can be seen in the details. Upon his return from the war, Gabriel, in *Mon beau soldat*, has nothing more urgent to do than go eat "a couple of good hamburgers." Colette adds a condition: "with french fries and a Coke." The couple meets at a "restaurant called LE HAMBURGER SUPRÊME." Jeanne Zéphire, *Mon beau soldat*, p. 22-23. As a sign of its undeniable conquest, American food even invaded distant rural regions. In *Le survenant amoureux*, Gertrude asks Philémon Boisvert, a guy she finds handsome like a "hero in a cowboy movie": "Do you like strawberries and cream in your Corn Flakes?" Jean Bretigny, *Le survenant amoureux*, p. 10.
138. On the relationships between Americanness and Québécois literature, see the works of Jean Morency, in particular, *La littérature québécoise dans le contexte américain. Études et explorations*, Québec, Nota bene, 2012, 180 p.

139. In this, they also resemble their dime novel counterparts in other genres, notably, the series starring IXE-13, which, concealing the strong Québécois francophone opposition to mandatory conscription, celebrates personal success and courage. "IXE-13 is the hero of a fictive desire for military participation in current events that take place in what he refers himself to as the "free world," a dynamic and positive hero who no longer resembles the uptight and continually humiliated defender of traditional values." Denis Saint-Jacques, "L'idéologique dans le texte," in Guy Bouchard *et al.*, *Le phénomène IXE-13*, Québec, Presses de l'Université Laval, 1984, p. 296.
140. Mimi Estival, *Nuit divine*, p. 3.
141. Caroline Bergeron, *"En vacances... en voiture... en Pontiac!" Les représentations de genre à travers les loisirs dans la* Revue moderne *et* Châtelaine, *1945-1969*, Master's Thesis, Montréal, Université de Montréal, 2014, 111 p.
142. Mimi Estival, *Nuit divine*, p. 20.
143. *Ibid.*, p. 8.
144. *Ibid.*, p. 9.
145. *Ibid.*, p. 16.
146. *Ibid.*
147. *Ibid.*, p. 25.
148. This conjugal misery lasts into the 1970s. Édith Manseau, *La presse du cœur : un indicateur culturel*, Master's Thesis, Trois-Rivières, Université du Québec à Trois-Rivières, 1985, 137 p.
149. Marie-Josée, "Le courrier de Marie-Josée," *La Terre de chez nous*, 3 janvier 1968, p. 13, cited by Édith Manseau, *La presse du cœur : un indicateur culturel*, p. 108. Luc Bellerive, *Problèmes conjugaux et divorce dans les courriers du cœur de la fin des années soixante au début des années quatre-vingt*, Master's Thesis, Trois-Rivières, Université du Québec à Trois-Rivières, 1996, 147 p. Marie-José Des Rivières, *Châtelaine et la littérature (1960-1975)*, Montréal, L'Hexagone, 1992, p. 133-148. Serge Gagnon, "Confession, courrier du cœur et révolution sexuelle," in Manon Brunet and Serge Gagnon (eds.), *Discours et pratiques de l'intime*, Québec, Institut québécois de recherche sur la culture, 1993, p. 71-93.
150. In 1954, a woman is astounded by the changes in couple relationships. After recounting that one of her granddaughters has become engaged to a man who doesn't care to know whether she is good at cooking and cleaning, hoping only that she will be happy, the eighty-two-year-old woman continues: "My God, how everything has changed!... When I was young, we didn't get married for comfort, nor to be happy. We got married to fulfill our duties, and no one spoke of separation or divorce, like today. The husband was the master. When there were hard times, we got through them, and the wife would never dare blame her husband, even if he wasn't working or was wasting money. The priest themselves told us to endure, that it earned us merit. [...] In my time, a woman would never have even said anything if her husband had beat her. My daughter thinks I'm behind the times, and my granddaughter laughs out loud when I talk to her about all this." Une Vieille Maman, "Le courrier d'Odette," *Chic*, Vol. 1, No. 1, 7 février 1954, p. 5.
151. Jeanne Zéphire, *Mon beau soldat*, p. 28.
152. Mimi Estivale, *Au bord de la faute*, p. 25.

153. According to Bourdieu, instead of asking whether disinterestedness and generosity are possible, it is better to question "the means that have to be implemented in order to create universes in which, as in gift economies, agents and groups would have an interest in disinterestedness and generosity..." Pierre Bourdieu, *Pascalian Meditations*, trans. Richard Nice, Cambridge, Polity Press, 2000, p. 201-202.
154. Though some of Gabrielle Roy's first novellas are "l'eau de rose" stories. See, for example, "Cendrillon '40," *La Revue moderne*, Vol. 21, No. 10, February 1940, p. 8-9 and p. 41-42.
155. For a general overview of sentiments in Roy's work, see Pierrette Daviau, *Passion et désenchantement. Une étude sémiotique de l'amour et des couples dans l'œuvre de Gabrielle Roy*, Montréal, Fides, 1993, 198 p.
156. See Pierre Popovic, "Le différend des cultures et des savoirs dans l'incipit de *Bonheur d'occasion*," in MarieAndrée Beaudet, "Bonheur d'occasion" *au pluriel. Lectures et approches critiques*, Québec, Nota bene, 1999, p. 15-61.
157. Gabrielle Roy, *The Tin Flute*, trans. Hannah Josephson, New York, Reynal and Hitchcock, 1947. P. 17.
158. *Ibid.*, p. 314.
159. *Ibid.*, p. 220.
160. Gabrielle Roy has already admitted that the idea for her novel came to her during "a night of solitude." "I think it is from this very solitude that the character of Florentine came to me, half springtime, half misery, a young girl desperately needing love." Gabrielle Roy, "Ma rencontre avec les gens de Saint-Henri," *Les Cahiers franco-canadiens de l'Ouest*, Vol. 8, No. 2, 1996, p. 278.

Chapter 5: Serial Love (1965 to 2000)

1. Monique Bosco, *L'isolement dans le roman canadien-français*, PhD Thesis, Montréal, Université de Montréal, 1953, p. 8. Jean Le Moyne, "La femme et la civilisation canadienne-française," *Cité libre*, No. 17, June 1957, p. 33. Reprinted in *Convergences*, coll. "Nénuphar," Montréal, Fides, 1992, p. 96. Claire Martin, "Notre roman, image de notre milieu," *Revue dominicaine*, July-August 1960, p. 18-24. André Renaud, "L'héroïne du roman canadien et l'expérience de l'amour," in Paul Wyczynski, Bernard Julien, Jean Ménard and Réjean Robidoux (eds.), *Archives des lettres canadiennes*, Tome 3, *Le roman canadien-français. Évolution-Témoignages-Bibliographie*, Montréal, Fides, 1964, p. 183-196. Michel Van Schendel, "L'amour dans la littérature canadienne-française," *Recherches sociographiques*, Vol. 5, No. 1-2, 1964, p. 155. Paul Gay, *Du sentiment de l'amour dans le roman canadien-français contemporain (1952-1962)*, Master's Thesis, Ottawa, University of Ottawa, 1964, 259 p.
2. This gap between the literature "qui se fait" (that is made) (to give a nod to Gilles Marcotte, who, in his 1962 classic *Une littérature qui se fait. Essais critiques sur la littérature canadienne-française*, does not devote a line to romantic literature) and the academic and media discourse on the latter, would only grow over the years and reach a staggering distance in the 1980s, with the emergence of the best-seller phenomenon. See notably Denis Saint-Jacques, Jacques Lemieux, Claude Martin and Vincent Nadeau, *Ces livres que vous avez aimés. Les best-sellers au Québec de 1970 à aujourd'hui*, Québec, Nuit Blanche, 1994, 223 p.

3. [Anonymous, "Pénurie de romans 'romanesques.' Prix du roman d'amour reporté à l'an prochain." *La Presse*, 7 April 1960, p. 10.
4. Catherine Rihoit, *Regards de femmes*, Paris, Presses de la Renaissance, 1984, p. 247. Jacques Migozzi, "Postface. Mauvais genres et bons livres : ce n'est qu'un début, continuons le débat," in Loïc Artiaga (ed.), *Le roman populaire*, Paris, Autrement, 2008, p. 157-167. France saw the disappearance of the sentimental collections created in the 1920s. See the periodization proposed by Yves-Olivier Martin, *Histoire du roman populaire en France : de 1840-1980*, Paris, Albin Michel, 1980, 301 p.
5. A fourth hypothesis proposed that we were witnessing a sophistication of readers' literary tastes. According to Claire Roy, the "little romance novel of our youth became less popular when more substantial works became available on bookstore and library shelves." Claire Roy, "Propos délibérés. Nos amis les livres," *Le Nouvelliste*, 15 November 1971, p. 4. This explanation seems unconvincing given the resurgence of the romance novel at the end of the 1970s.
6. [Anonymous], *Pas d'argent, pas d'amour!*, Montréal, Éditions Police-Journal, 1959, 2nd inside cover page.
7. For example the Angélique series: *Angélique, marquise des anges* (1964), *Merveilleuse Angélique* (1965), *Angélique et le roy* (1966), starring Michèle Mercier, based on the historical novels of Anne and Serge Golon (15 million copies sold worldwide in 1965). Martine R.-Corrivault, "Pierrette Daigle, hôtesse du Tour cycliste. Elle rêve comme toutes les jeunes filles de son âge," *Le Soleil*, 16 August 1966, p. 9.
8. Anne-Lise Louise Josiane Feral, *Genre and Gender in Translation: The Poetological and Ideological Rewriting of Heroine-Centred and Women-Oriented Fiction*, PhD Thesis, Edinburgh, University of Edinburgh, 2009, p. 83.
9. Anne-Marie Dardigna, *La presse "féminine." Fonction idéologique*, Paris, François Maspero, 1978, p. 216. Extremely popular in Catholic-influenced Latin countries, photo novels did not see wide circulation in Protestant-majority countries, where comics dominated. Michelle Nolan, *Love on the Racks: A History of American Romance Comics*, Jefferson, McFarland & Company, 2008, 229 p.
10. Pamela Regis, *A Natural History of the Romance Novel*, Philadelphia, University of Pennsylvania Press, 2003, 224 p.
11. Jean Pastureau, "Le bel ailleurs, le bon hier," in Paul Bleton (ed.), *Amours, aventures et mystères, ou les romans qu'on ne peut pas lâcher*, Québec, Nota bene, 1998, p. 48-61.
12. Robert Turgeon, *Analyse du marché de l'édition de livres au Québec*, Master's Thesis, Montréal, École des hautes études commerciales, 1984, 154 f. Jean-Paul Baillargeon, "Les livres québécois en langue française au Québec face aux livres de France," *Communication. Information Médias Théories*, Vol. 12, No. 2, Fall 1991, p. 190-217.
13. Affected by this disinterest, the Cercle du livre romanesque—which incorporated French romance novels— showed signs of fizzling out before discontinuing the publication of new titles as of 1969. L'Agence Marc et Yves, which, from 1964 to 1968, published two French novelists, Magda Contino and Claude Jaunière, gradually turned to erotic literature.
14. Renée Legris, *Histoire des genres dramatiques à la radio québécoise : sketch, radioroman, radiothéâtre, 1923-2008*, Québec, Septentrion, 2011, 512 p.

15. Jocelyne Valois and Denise Lemieux, *Familles et changements socio-économiques*, Mont-Joli, Bureau d'aménagement de l'est du Québec, 1965, p. 164.
16. *Ibid.*, p. 218.
17. A 1973 report on the distribution of periodicals and paperback books in Quebec by the Ministère des Affaires culturelles explained the declining popularity of dime novels as due to the advent of television. *Rapport sur la distribution des périodiques et du livre de poche au Québec*, Québec, Ministère des Affaires culturelles, January 1973, p. 4.
18. Jocelyne Valois and Denise Lemieux, *Familles et changements socio-économiques*, p. 217. In France, the photo novels were considered partially responsible for the demise of romance collections in the postwar period. Daniel Compère, *Les romans populaires*, coll. "Les fondamentaux de la Sorbonne nouvelle," Paris, Presses Sorbonne nouvelle, 2012, p. 104.
19. Émilia Lacroix, "La femme ouvrière d'aujourd'hui," *Le Mouvement ouvrier*, Montréal, Les Éditions de la L.O.C., 1960, p. 131. It is estimated that in the 1960s one in three people read photo novels in France. Évelyne Sullerot, *La presse féminine*, coll. "Kiosque," Paris, Armand Colin, 1966, p. 93-94.
20. Céline Légaré, "Les Québécoises achètent un demi-million de photos-romans par mois," *La Patrie*, 24 September 1967, p. 23.
21. R. H. R., "L'école, l'amour et le reste," *Photo-journal*, 3 February 1965, p. 26.
22. Régis Tremblay, "Le photo-roman, 'junkfood' d'un million de Québécois," *Le Soleil*, 28 March 1981, p. C1.
23. "Toi ma folie," cited by Sylvette Giet, *"Nous deux," 1947-1997 : apprendre la langue du cœur*, Paris, Vrin, 1997, p. 10-11.
24. Évelyne Sullerot, *La presse féminine*, p. 93-94.
25. "The photo novels of Reynald Longpré, ex-actor turned photographer, were very popular with the Québécois public." Edmond Côté and Paul-Émile Beaulne, "Télé-radio-potins," *Télé-radiomonde*, 9 January 1965, p. 24.
26. See the ad on page 36 of issue 5 of *Amour digeste* (no date, circa 1965). Our efforts to find copies of these photo novels were in vain. A summary of the story of "Simple et candide" can be found in [Anonymous], "Simple et candide," *Le guide*, Vol. 35, 11 June 1964, p. 17.
27. [Anonymous], "Le bruit de la ville. Scénariste," *Le Devoir*, 4 December 1964, p. 6.
28. R. H.-R., "L'école, l'amour et le reste," p. 26.
29. [Anonyme], "La photo choc de la semaine," *Télé-radiomonde*, 5 December 1964, p. 3.
30. Thurston proposes a list of 30 possible structural oppositions. The only ones the female readers of Harlequin novels (interviewed by Thurston) did not perceive as different between the heroes and heroines were: interesting/uninteresting and unreasonable/sensible. The largest gap was between the heroine's inexperience and the hero's experience. Carol Thurston, *The Romance Revolution: Erotic Novels for Women and the Quest for a New Sexual Identity*, Urbana, University of Illinois Press, 1987, p. 84.
31. Philippe Sohet, "Le photo-roman : ces archétypes que nous aimons," *Antennes*, No. 20, 1980, p. 36-43.
32. [Anonymous], *Le correspondant impossible*, Montréal, Phototek, circa 1969.

33. *Ibid.*
34. Ellen Constans, "Cri du cœur, cri du corps dans les romans de Delly," in Julia Bettinotti and Pascale Noizet (ed.), *Guimauve et fleurs d'oranger. Delly*, coll. "Études paralittéraires," Québec, Nuit blanche éditeur, 1995, p. 117-136.
35. It is understood that when the Leprohon bookstore in Montreal sold the work *L'art de faire l'amour* in 1897, it had a different meaning than the one it has acquired today! "The act of courting girls has different names; one says: "courting her, going out with her, making love to her." Sister Marie-Ursule, *Civilisation traditionnelle des Lavalois*, coll. "Les archives de folklore nos 5-6," Québec, Presses de l'Université Laval, 1951, p. 122.
36. Except for the secondary characters: the heroine's rival, often a seductress of foreign origin, competes with her by using her lustful body and erotic drives.
37. Anne-Marie Lugan-Dardigna, "Presse du cœur et roman rose : la quête de l'amour vrai ou comment se trouver un maître," in Didier Coste and Michel Zéraffa (ed.), *Le récit amoureux*, Seyssel, Éditions Champ Vallon, 1984, p. 293.
38. *Ibid.*
39. Over half (54 percent) of the one hundred American novels published between 1972 and 1985 in Thurston's sample include rape scenes. Carol Thurston, *The Romance Revolution*, p. 78.
40. Ad for Éditions Sélect published in *Le Devoir*, 24 November 1979, Supplement 1, p. 18.
41. Julia Bettinotti, "*Tendre Rachel* et autres romans de Marie-Claude Bussières-Tremblay," in Gilles Dorion (ed.), *Dictionnaire des œuvres littéraires du Québec*, Tome 6, *1960-1969*, Montréal, Fides, 1984, p. 784.
42. Marie-Claude Bussières-Tremblay, *Tendre Rachel*, Montréal, Presses Sélect, 1978, p. 65.
43. *Ibid.*, p. 161.
44. *Ibid.*, p. 162.
45. Another character maintains that nothing is as important for a woman than "virility in all its power." *Ibid.*, p. 141.
46. *Ibid.*, p. 200.
47. *Ibid.*, p. 187.
48. *Ibid.*, p. 38.
49. *Ibid.*, p. 79. In Canada, "marital rape" only became a criminal act in 1983.
50. *Ibid.*, p. 240.
51. Sarah Frantz Lyons and Eric Murphy Selinger, "Strange Stirrings, Strange Yearnings: *The Flame and the Flower, Sweet Savage Love*, and the Lost Diversities of Blockbuster Historical Romance," in Eric Murphy Selinger and William A. Gleason (eds.), *Romance Fiction and American Culture: Love as the Practice of Freedom?*, New York, Routledge, 2016, p. 89-110.
52. Marie-Claude Bussières-Tremblay, *Suis ton destin*, Montréal, Presses Sélect, 1980, p. 122.
53. *Ibid.*, p. 41.
54. *Ibid.*, p. 133.
55. *Ibid.*, p. 181.
56. *Ibid.*, p. 202.
57. *Ibid.*, p. 220.

58. Micheline Perron, *Une biche pour le tigre*, Montréal, Presses Sélect, 1980 [1979], 169 p.
59. *Ibid.*, p. 7.
60. *Ibid.*, p. 16.
61. *Ibid.*, p. 22.
62. *Ibid.*, p. 112.
63. Yves Bernier, "Beaucoup d'imagination et de talents dans ces 'Bozé-jeunnnes,'"*Le Soleil*, 2 March 1981, p. B5. We know that in France in 1980, the collections specializing in what was pejoratively called "guimauve" (sappy) were very successful. Françoise Helgorsky, "Harlequin ou la quête du grand amour," *Communication & Langages*, Vol. 63, 1985, p. 83-98.
64. In 1977, J'ai Lu became her exclusive publisher. At the start, J'ai Lu was publishing two to four books per year by the British author; in 1979, it increased the pace to two per month, to meet the demand. Already in 1980, 200 titles by Cartland were translated into French. Ads for her books began appearing in Québécois media at the same time. Magali Bigey, "Romances en séries : amour toujours et marketing," *Le Temps des Médias*, Vol. 2, No. 19, 2012, p. 87-100.
65. Archana Rampure, "Harlequin a bâti un empire," in Carole Gerson and Jacques Michon (eds.), *Histoire du livre et de l'imprimé au Canada*, Vol. 3, *de 1918 à 1980*, Montréal, Presses de l'université de Montréal, 2007, p. 199. Québécois publishers responded by turning to rejacketing or by translating English titles. For example, the publication in paperback format of the "Marie-France" collection by the mysterious "Éditions des 2 rives" located in Iberville should not fool us: the eight titles published were only reissues of some of the thirty works already published in the "Cristal" collection at Plon. As for the collection "Cœur-à-cœur," romance novels intended for young adults published by Éditions Héritage from 1982 to 1998, it was limited to translating works already published in English. See Joanie Corbin, "La représentation de l'adolescente dans une collection de romans à grande diffusion," *Mémoires du livre / Studies in Book Culture*, [En ligne], Vol. 1, No. 1, 2009, [n.p.], https://www.erudit.org/en/journals/memoires/2009-v1-n1-memoires3559/038640ar/.
66. Harlequin novels from the period 1958-1962 were translated into French in Quebec and partly adapted for the local market. Though the language tends to adhere to a standard French, Québécois orality comes through in the dialogues when the protagonists encounter characters of modest backgrounds. Likewise, though geographical names usually remained unchanged, no doubt to preserve a part of the exoticism apt to spark readers' imaginations, the names of characters are sometimes translated. On the "Garde-Malades" collection published by the Agence Marc et Yves, which used the same themes as the first Harlequin novels published in Quebec, see Julia Bettinotti and Chantal Savoie, "À chacune son M.D. et les malades seront bien gardés," in Paul Bleton (ed.), *Armes, larmes, charmes...*, Québec, Nuit Blanche éditeur, 1995, p. 233-253.
67. Founded in 1949, in Winnipeg, the Harlequin publishing house began specializing in romance as of 1957. It distributed the catalogue of the British publishing house Mills and Boon, before buying this company in 1971. In 1975, it was incorporated into Torstar. The creation of an affiliate company in the Netherlands

in 1975 was followed by subsidiaries in many other countries in the world and translations into a dozen languages, allowing it to increase sales by more than 40 percent annually between 1975 and 1980. For an analysis of the history of Harlequin in Canada, see Margaret Ann Jensen, *Women and Romantic Fiction: A Case Study of Harlequin Enterprises, Romances, and Readers*, PhD Thesis, Hamilton, McMaster University, 1980, 404 p.

68. Jacques Benoit, "Harlequin, le géant du roman d'amour. Au Québec, des ventes à faire rêver...," *La Presse*, 13 October 1981, p. A6. [Anonymous]. "Une entente Hachette-Harlequin laisse entrevoir un réseau mondial du livre," *La Presse*, 16 February 1985, p. F-2. In France, as of 1982, Éditions Harlequin was selling thirty million books per year. Françoise Helgorsky, "Harlequin ou la quête du grand amour," p. 83.

69. Margaret Ann Jensen, *Love's $weet Return: The Harlequin Story*, Toronto, Women's Educational Press, 1984, 188 p. Joseph McAleer, *Passion's Fortune: The Story of Mills and Boon*, New York, Oxford University Press, 1999, 322 p.

70. Jay Dixon, *The Romance Fiction of Mills & Boon, 1909-1990s*, Philadelphia, UCL Press, 1999, 218 p.

71. Jennifer McKnight-Trontz, *The Look of Love: The Art of the Popular Romance Novel*, Princeton, Princeton Architectural Press, 2002, 144 p. An Goris, "Hidden Codes of Love: The Materiality of the Category Romance Novel," *Belphégor*, Vol. 13, No. 1, 2015, [n.p.].

72. John Markert shows with the help of quantitative tables not only the replacement of "sweet romance" stories by "bodice rippers," but also the explosion ù of the number of titles starting in 1975. John Markert, *Publishing Romance: The History of an Industry, 1940s to the Present*, McFarland & Co., 2016, p. 45.

73. Monique Van de Velde, head of marketing of collections published in languages other than English, cited by Jacques Marchand, "Harlequin et Colombine : l'industrie plafonne, l'amour aussi," Études littéraires, Vol. 16, No. 3, décembre 1983, p. 353.

74. Maïca Sanconie, "'Tout un monde d'évasion' : adapter les romans sentimentaux pour un lectorat français," *Meta*, Vol. 55, No. 4, 2010, p. 732-751.

75. See Julia Bettinotti (ed.), *La corrida de l'amour : le roman Harlequin*, Montréal, XYZ, 1990 [1986], 151 p.

76. Cited by Séverine Olivier, *Le roman sentimental. Productions contemporaines et pratiques de lecture*, PhD Thesis, Bruxelles, Université libre de Bruxelles, 2009, p. 136. Contemporary translations of chick lit from English into French are just as marked by "modesty" and fantasy. See Anne-Lise Louise Josiane Feral, *Genre and Gender in Translation*, 306 p.

77. George Paizis, "Category Romances. Translation, Realism and Myth," *The Translator*, Vol. 4, No. 1, 1998, p. 1-24.

78. Louise Leblanc, *37 1/2 AA*, série "Quinze/prose entière," Montréal, Quinze, 1983, 199 p.

79. Jacques Benoit, "Harlequin, le géant du roman d'amour. On ne vend pas des romans mais une marque," *La Presse*, 15 October 1981, p. A6. Stéphane Baillargeon, "L'empire rose bonbon," *Le Devoir*, 20-21 February 1993, p. D1. Robert

Brasseur, client service coordinator at Éclair, Harlequin's distributor, cited by Jacques Benoit, "Harlequin, le géant du roman d'amour. Au Québec, des ventes à faire rêver…," *La Presse*, 13 October 1981, p. A6.

80. "Even though Quebec does not represent two percent of its global sales, five market studies are conducted each year, including some by Compton, a New York advertising firm." Jacques Benoit, "Harlequin, le géant du roman d'amour. On ne vend pas des romans mais une marque."

81. Pierre Vennat, "Harlequin aura de la concurrence au Québec," *La Presse*, 15 December 1991, C4.

82. Élaine Sinclair, *L'espace d'un été*, Laval, Éditions Cyrano, 1992, 186 p. Élaine Sinclair, *Patrouille de nuit*, Laval, Éditions Cyrano, 1992, 145 p. *L'espace d'un été* was written by Brisson. The name of the person who wrote *Patrouille de nuit* is unknown.

83. Élaine Sinclair, *Patrouille de nuit*, p. 85.

84. *Ibid.*, p. 145.

85. Élaine Sinclair, *L'espace d'un été*, p. 170.

86. Dominique Paupardin, "L'amour, intelligent et de qualité," *La Presse*, 8 March 1998, p. B2.

87. Francine Beaudoin, "Que serait la littérature sans Soucy?" *La Voix de l'Est*, 30 May 1998, p. 55.

88. *Ibid.*

89. Soucy cited by Dominique Paupardin, "L'amour, intelligent et de qualité," p. B2.

90. *Ibid.*

91. He entertained the idea of writing one of the volumes of his collection himself "during vacation." The story follows the tribulations of a gardener hired by a septuagenarian millionaire, whose wife, daughter and housekeeper "are somewhat tantalized by the handsome newcomer…" Francine Beaudoin, "Que serait la littérature sans Soucy?"

92. Béatrice Côté, *Le cœur prisonnier*, Montréal, VLB éditeur, 1998, p. 257.

93. Michele Brabant, *Le rêve de Justine*, Montréal, VLB éditeur, 1998, p. 237.

94. *Ibid.*, p. 256.

95. Cited by Margo Nobert, "Le titre comme séduction dans le roman Harlequin : une lecture sociosémiotique," *Études littéraires*, Vol. 16, No. 3, 1983, p. 388.

96. See the brief history of the publisher Tallandier on the Bibliopoche website. "Éditions Tallandier," *Bibliopoche.com. Tous les livres au format poche*, [Online], [n.d.], https://www.bibliopoche.com/editeur/Tallandier/171.html.

97. Annick Capelle, "Harlequin Romances in Western Europe: The Cultural Interactions of Romantic Literature," in John Dean and Jean-Paul Gabilliet (eds.), *European Readings of American Popular Culture*, London, Greenwood Press, 1996, p. 91-100.

98. On the trajectory and success of André Mathieu, see Marie-Pier Luneau, "Le redéploiement des genres populaires," in Jacques Michon (ed.), *Histoire de l'édition littéraire au Québec*, Vol. 3, *La bataille du livre, 1960-2000*, Montréal, Fides, 2010, p. 277-281.

99. Françoise Lepage (ed.), *La littérature pour la jeunesse, 1970-2000*, Montréal, Fides, 2003, 352 p.

100. This remark also applies to the historical novel, which often sees love stories woven in. For example, *Les filles de Caleb* (1985, 1986 and 2003), by Arlette Cousture, is not a romance novel as we define but still gives an important place to the burning passion between Émilie Bordeleau and Ovila Pronovost.
101. Danielle Thaller, "Les collections de romans pour adolescentes et adolescents : évolution et nouvelles conventions," Éducation et francophonie. Revue scientifique virtuelle, ACELF, Association canadienne d'éducation de langue française, Vol. 24, No. 1 and 2, 1996, [n.p.]. See also Jacques Michon (ed.), *Histoire de l'édition littéraire au Québec au XXe siècle*, Vol. 3, *La bataille du livre, 1960-2000*, Montréal, Fides, 2010, p. 213-250.
102. In 1994, 77 percent of girls and 19 percent of boys in high school consumed romance novels. "Les choix des livres," in Monique Lebrun (ed.), *Les pratiques de lecture des adolescents québécois*, Sainte-Foy, Multimondes, 2004, p. 45-70.
103. Claire Le Brun, "Éducation sentimentale et œil du narrateur : le cas de Raymond Plante," *Cahiers de la recherche en éducation*, Vol. 7, No. 1, 2000, p. 113-130. For an in-depth analysis of the novel, see Dominique Demers, "François Gougeon, le dernier des raisins," in Dominique Demers, with the collaboration of Paul Bleton, *Du petit poucet au dernier des raisins. Introduction à la littérature jeunesse*, Montréal, Québec / Amérique, 1994, p. 229-244.
104. Raymond Plante, *The Big Loser*, trans. Alan Brown. Toronto: McClelland and Stewart, 1989, p. 12.
105. *Ibid.*, p. 20.
106. *Ibid.*, p. 14.
107. *Ibid.*, p. 51.
108. Bertrand Gauthier, *Une chanson pour Gabriella*, Montréal, Éditions La courte échelle, 1990, p. 8.
109. *Ibid.*
110. *Ibid.*, p. 50.
111. *Ibid.*, p. 41.
112. *Ibid.*
113. *Ibid.*, p. 42.
114. *Ibid.*, p. 58.
115. *Ibid.*, p. 75.
116. *Ibid.*, p. 110111.
117. *Ibid.*, p. 48.
118. *Ibid.*, p. 92.
119. *Ibid.*, p. 124.
120. *Ibid.*, p. 149.
121. Ginette Anfousse, *Les vacances de Rosalie*, Montréal, Éditions La Courte échelle, 1990, p. 66.
122. *Ibid.*, p. 88.
123. *Ibid.*
124. Marie Fradette, "Le roman québécois pour adolescentes depuis 1940 jusqu'aux années 2000 : pour une littérature garde-fou," *Lurelu*, Vol. 30, No. 1, Spring-Summer 2007, p. 15.
125. Bertrand Gauthier, *Une chanson pour Gabriella*, p. 95.

126. Julia Bettinotti (ed.), *La corrida de l'amour*, p. 90.
127. [Anonymous], "1973-75, la commune?" *Mainmise*, No. 46, April 1975, p. 14.
128. Jean-Claude Kaufmann, *Sex@mour*, Paris, Armand Colin, 2010, 213 p.
129. [Anonymous], "Je l'aimais tant," *Les plus belles histoires d'amour*, No. 9, Montréal, Éditions Police-Journal, [n.d.], p. 59.
130. Jodi McAlister, "'That Complete Fusion of Spirit as Well as Body': Heroines, Heroes, Desire and Compulsory Demisexuality in the Harlequin Mills & Boon Romance Novel," *Australasian Journal of Popular Culture*, Vol. 3, No. 3, September 2014, p. 299-310.

Chapter 6: Love Despite Everything (since 2000)

1. *Harlequin*, [Online], [n.d.], www.harlequin.fr.
2. See *Les Éditeurs réunis. La fureur de lire*, [Online], [n.d.], http://lesediteursreunis.com/catalogue-grand-public/7/romans-pour-elles.html?page=5.
3. [In collaboration], *Romances d'aujourd'hui : une anthologie de romance contemporaine*, Montréal, Éditions Laska, 2014, 205 p.
4. *Divaromance. Je lis comme une diva* [Online], [n.d.], http://editionsdivaromance.fr/prix-de-la-meilleure-romance/.
5. Chloé Duval, "Biographie," Chloé *Duval. Auteure de romance*, [Online], [n.d.], http://chloeduval.ca/biographie/.
6. Suzanne Roy, *Un cadeau du ciel*, Paris, Milady, 2014, p. 168.
7. *Ibid.*, p. 182.
8. *Ibid.*, p. 235.
9. *Ibid.*, p. 227.
10. *Ibid.*
11. *Ibid.*, p. 76.
12. *Ibid.*, p. 222.
13. *Ibid*, p. 290.
14. *Ibid*, p. 294.
15. *Ibid.*
16. Chloé Duval, *The Château by the River*, trans. Domitille Vimal du Monteil. New York, Lyrical Press, 2018, p. 334.
17. *Ibid.*, p. 333.
18. *Ibid.*, p. 49 and p. 77.
19. Chloé Duval, *The Château by the River*, trans. Domitille Vimal du Monteil. New York, Lyrical Press, 2018, p. 234.
20. *Ibid.*, p. 327.
21. *Ibid.*, p. 328.
22. *Ibid.*
23. *Ibid.*
24. *Ibid*
25. *Ibid.*, p. 333.
26. *Ibid.*, p. 335.
27. *Ibid.*, p. 266.
28. See, among others, Muriel Fortier, "Les lesbian pulps, un instrument de conscientisation," in Irène Demczuk and Frank W. Remiggi (eds.), *Sortir de l'ombre.*

Histoires des communautés lesbienne et gaie de Montréal, coll. "Des hommes et des femmes en changement," Montréal, VLB éditeur, 1998, p. 27-52.

29. In the 1960s, a title like *Jeannot, l'efféminé* (*Jeannot, the Effeminate*), published in series by Éditions Police-Journal, spoke for itself. Jeanne Zéphire, *Jeannot, l'efféminé*, Montréal, Éditions Police-Journal, 1962, 32 p.

30. Kacey Whalen, *A Consumption of Gay Men: Navigating the Shifting Boundaries of M/M Romantic Readership*, Master's Thesis, Chicago, DePaul University, 2017, 83 p.

31. Samuel Champagne, *Recrue*, coll. "Tabou," Boucherville, Éditions de Mortagne, 2013, 286 p.

32. Chantal Brunette, *La fille dans le placard*, 2 Vol., Montréal, Libre expression, Vol. 1, 2016, 288 p.; Vol. 2, 2016, 320 p.

33. Founded in 2015 in Montreal's gay village, the publishing house predominantly distributed French writers.

34. Anaïs Paquin, "Interview de Cy Jung pour 'Piste Rose,'" *HR Éditions. Publications d'homoromances*, [Online], 26 juillet 2017, https://homoromance-editions.com/interviews/interview-de-cy-jung-pour-piste-rose.html.

35. Judith Gagnon, *Au-delà du devoir*, Longueuil, Homoromance, 2017, 272 p.

36. Jérémy Lambert, "Le roman sentimental gay francophone," *Revue critique de fixxion française contemporaine*, No. 12, 2016, p. 25.

37. *Ibid.*

38. At the beginning of the 2010s, the giant Harlequin began integrating homosexual novels into its collections. See Elio Iannacci, "What Women Want: Gay Male Romance Novels," *The Globe and Mail*, [Online], 11 February 2011, https://www.theglobeandmail.com/life/relationships/what-women-want-gay-male-romance-novels/article565992/.

39. Kim Renaud-Venne, *Représentations féminines, identités génériques et familiarité socioculturelle : les stratégies d'écriture dans les romans de Rafaële Germain*, Master's Thesis, Montréal, Université du Québec à Montréal, 2016, 108 p.

40. "When I'd gone through all the translations of chick lit available in the bookstores," confides India Desjardins, "I had the idea of writing my novel. I said to myself it would be good to see this type of heroine in a Québécois context." India Desjardins, cited by Marie-Claude Fortin, "Romans de filles!" *La Presse*, 16 January 2005, cahier Arts et spectacles, p. 1. Marie-Pier Luneau, "Georgia, Mia, India... clones de Bridget? Spécificités culturelles et stratégies éditoriales dans la 'chick-lit' pour adolescentes au Québec," in Jean Foucault, Michel Manson and Luc Pinhas (eds.), *L'édition de jeunesse francophone face à la mondialisation*, Paris, L'Harmattan, 2009, p. 175-187.

41. "Catalogue," *Éditions de Mortagne*, [Online], [n.d.], https://editionsdemortagne.com.

42. Cris Mazza and Jeffrey DeShell (eds.), *Chick Lit: Postfeminist Fiction*, Normal (IL), FC2, 1995, 205 p.

43. Françoise Hache-Bissette, "La *chick lit* : romance du XXIe siècle?" *Le Temps des médias*, No. 19, Fall 2012, p. 101.

44. "My stories are situated in Quebec, the characters' views are really from Quebec, but it's also a different world, far from the realities of real life. We are in romance, a dream world, don't forget. If I'd spent time making

the story faithful to the pure and raw reality of our society, it might have not been possible to speak of romance..." Marie Potvin, cited in Clément Solym, "Des héros infaillibles, pour une Romance venue du Québec," *Actua-Litté*, [Online], [n.d.], https://actualitte.com/article/40103/reportages/des-heros-infaillibles-pour-une-romance-venue-du-quebec.

45. Rafaële Germain, *Pink Bra and Black Jacket*, trans. Dawn M. Cornelio. Toronto, McArthur and Company, 2010, p. 17.

46. Rafaële Germain, *Volte-face et malaises*, Montréal, Libre Expression, 2012, p. 115

47. Mélanie Leblanc, *Si tu t'appelles Mélancolie*, Boucherville, Éditions de Mortagne, 2010, p. 7-8.

48. Corinne Gervais, *"Pour moi, un homme, c'est papa" : représentations de l'amoureux dans la* chick lit *québécoise*, Master's Thesis, Sherbrooke, Université de Sherbrooke, 2015, p. 50.

49. "The world of work in chick lit is thus essentially window dressing: a backdrop to the real business of finding love." Juliette Wells, "Mothers of Chick Lit? Women Writers, Readers and Literary History," in Mallory Young and Suzanne Ferriss (eds.), *Chick Lit: The New Woman's Fiction*, New York, Routledge, 2006, p. 55.

50. To cite just one example, we note the regrettable *Danger! Femmes en SPM*, which reveals the extremely reductive character of certain stories: "Besides the mood swings," observes the summary on the publisher's website, "sugar cravings and other compulsions, their premenstrual syndrome is also responsible for memorable mistakes." Catherine Bourgault, *Danger! Femmes en SPM*, Boucherville, Éditions de Mortagne, 2016, 336 p.

51. Rafaële Germain, *Pink Bra and Black Jacket*, trans. Dawn M. Cornelio. Toronto, McArthur and Company, 2010, p. 202.

52. Séverine Olivier, "La *chick lit* ou les mémoires d'une jeune femme 'dérangée,'" *Belphégor*, [Online], Vol. 6, No. 2, June 2007, [n.p.], http://etc.dal.ca/belphegor/vol6_no2/articles/06_02_oliv_chic_fr.html.

53. Corinne Gervais, "'Pour moi, un homme, c'est papa.'"

54. Nathalie Roy, *La vie épicée de Charlotte Lavigne, Tome 1, Piment de Cayenne et pouding chômeur*, Montréal, Libre expression, 2011, p. 63.

55. Mélanie Leblanc, *Si tu t'appelles Mélancolie*, p. 11.

56. *Ibid.*, p. 307.

57. This attitude had already been noted for the young adult novel of the 1990s. Daniela Di Cecco, *Entres femmes et jeunes filles. Le roman pour adolescentes en France et au Québec*, Montréal, Les Éditions du remue-ménage, 2000, p. 94.

58. India Desjardins, *Le journal d'Aurélie Laflamme, Tome I. Extraterrestre... ou presque!*, Montréal, Les Intouchables, 2006, p. 162.

59. Rafaële Germain, *Volte-face et malaises*, Montréal, Libre expression, 2012, p. 189.

60. *Ibid.*, p. 240-241.

61. Catherine d'Anjou, "*Chick lit* : l'ironie comme prise de parole métaféministe dans *Soutien-gorge rose et veston noir, Gin tonique et concombre* et *Volte-face et malaises* de Rafaële Germain," Master's Thesis, Québec, Université Laval, 2018, 139 p.

62. Stephanie Harzewski, *Chick lit and Postfeminism*, Charlottesville, University of Virginia Press, 2011, p. 25-26.

63. Rafaële Germain, *Pink Bra and Black Jacket,* p. 9.
64. Mélanie Leblanc, *Si tu t'appelles Mélancolie,* p. 107.
65. *Ibid.,* p. 282.
66. Karine Glorieux, *Mademoiselle Tic Tac. Tome 1 — Le manège amoureux,* Montréal, Québec / Amérique, 2009, p. 15.
67. *Ibid.,* p. 335.
68. "Interestingly, whatever their degree of sexual experience, heroines are frequently 're-virginised' in the narrative when it comes to the encounter with their hero." Rosalind Gill and Elena Herdieckerhoff, "Rewriting the Romance: New Feminities in Chicklit?" *Feminist Media Studies,* Vol. 6, No. 4, 2006, p. 494.
69. Nathalie Roy, *La vie épicée de Charlotte Lavigne,* p. 137.
70. India Desjardins, *La mort d'une princesse,* Montréal, Éditions de l'Homme, 2017, back cover.
71. *Ibid.,* p. 283.
72. " I can't stand hearing about Disney fairy tales / The prince Charming is a moron / And the princess is a little bitch / There's no easy way." Lisa LeBlanc, "Aujourd'hui, ma vie c'est d'la marde" (Today, my life is shit), *Lisa LeBlanc,* Montréal, Bonsound, 2012, CD. "There's no easy way. [...] my love life is [...] shit": is also the beginning of the novel by Alexandra Larochelle, *Des papillons pis de la gravité,* Montréal, Libre Expression, 2015, 184 p. It also recalls the book *Ma vie amoureuse de marde* (*My shitty love life*), by Anne-Marie Dupras, in collaboration with Annie Deschamps, *Ma vie amoureuse de marde,* Montréal, Éditions de l'Homme, 2014, 200 p.
73. See the interesting analysis of the phenomenon proposed by Eva Illouz in *Hard Romance. Cinquante nuances de Grey et nous,* trans. F. Joly, Paris, Seuil, 2014, 153 p.
74. *Histoire d'O* by Pauline Réage (1954) was not intended for a mass market. Pauline Réage, *Histoire d'O,* Paris, Chez Jean-Jacques Pauvert, 1954, 247 p. Note that with its stories of vampires, "bit lit" preceded "new adult" fiction by a few years.
75. Anne K. Kaler, "Conventions of Captivity in Romance Novels," in Anne K. Kaler and Rosemary E. Johnson Kurek (eds.), *Romantic Conventions,* Bowling Green (OH), Bowling Green State University Popular Press, 1999, p. 86-99.
76. Susan Sontag refers to this an "ascent through degradation." Susan Sontag, "The Pornographic Imagination," *The Partisan Review,* Vol. 34, No. 2, Spring 1967, p. 181-212.
77. Marjorie D. Lafond, *Sous l'emprise de Monsieur Addams,* Montréal, Les Éditeurs réunis, 2015, back cover.
78. *Ibid.,* p. 37-38.
79. The novel by British author Edith Maude Hull, *Le Sheik* (1919), recounts the abduction and rape, in Algeria, of the icy Lady Diana Mayo by the implacable Sheik Ahmed Ben Hassan. Emily A. Haddad, "Bound to Love: Captivity in Harlequin Sheikh novels," in Sally Goade (ed.), *Empowerment versus Oppression: Twenty First Century Views of Popular Romance Novels,* Cambridge, Cambridge Scholars Publishing, 2007, p. 42-64.
80. Marjorie D. Lafond, *Sous l'emprise de Monsieur Addams,* p. 164.
81. *Ibid.,* p. 100-101.
82. *Ibid.,* p. 118.

83. *Ibid.*, p. 129.
84. *Ibid.*, p. 150.
85. *Ibid.*, p. 344.
86. *Ibid.*, p. 112.
87. *Ibid.*, p. 87.
88. *Ibid.*, p. 383.
89. *Ibid.*, p. 428.
90. *Ibid.*, p. 253.
91. Élise Salaün, *Oser Éros. L'érotisme dans le roman québécois des origines à nos jours*, Québec, Éditions Nota bene, 2010, p. 345.
92. Examining the motives for this romantic structure is not part of our analysis. Different hypotheses have been proposed. In the 1980s, the most common one was based on a psychoanalytical approach. Jessica Benjamin, *The Bonds of Love. Psychoanalysis, Feminism, and the Problem of Domination*, New York, Pantheon Books, 1988, 304 p. Sarah Frantz Lyons and Eric Murphy Selinger suggest that this literature can be read as negotiating greater sexual freedom for women in a phallocentric political context. "Strange Stirrings, Strange Yearnings: The Flame and the Flower, Sweet Savage Love, and the Lost Diversities of Blockbuster Historical Romance," in Eric Murphy Selinger and William A. Gleason (eds.), *Romance Fiction and American Culture: Love as the Practice of Freedom?*, New York, Routledge, 2016, p. 89-110.
93. "The woman stops repressing her femininity, her fear of the man (his virility) and accepts conforming to a heterosexual sexuality; the man becomes open to feelings and resigns himself to monogamy." Béatrice Damian-Gaillard, "Les romans sentimentaux des collections Harlequin: quelle(s) figures de l'amoureux? Quel(s) modèle(s) de relation(s) amoureuse(s)?" *Questions de communication*, No. 20, 2011, p. 324.
94. Carol Thurston, *The Romance Revolution. Erotic Novels for Women and the Quest for a New Sexual Identity*, Urbana, University of Illinois Press, 1987, p. 78-79.
95. Julia Bettinotti (ed.), *La corrida de l'amour : le roman Harlequin*, Montréal, XYZ, 1990 [1986], p. 69.
96. Hélène Bédard-Cazabon, Julia Bettinotti and Christiane Provost, "Harlequin : quand l'amour est une guerre," Études littéraires, Vol. 16, No. 3, December 1983, p. 399-427.
97. Marjorie D. Lafond, *Corps et âmes*, Saint-Jean-sur-Richelieu, Les Éditeurs réunis, 2017, p. 217.
98. Sonia Alain, *Annabel et Max, adultes consentants*, Marieville, Les Éditeurs réunis, 2016, p. 220.
99. *Ibid.*, p. 222.
100. Rafaële Germain, *Pink Bra and Black Jacket*, p. 202.
101. Rafaële Germain, *Pink Bra and Black Jacket*, p. 75.
102. Rafaële Germain, *Pink Bra and Black Jacket*, p. 51.
103. Julie Beaulieu, *J'ai hâte à vous*, Chicoutimi, Éditions JCL, 2008, 200 p.
104. *J'ai hâte à vous* fait was on the list of favourite books based on a poll conducted by *La Presse*, in 2010. Catherine Schlager, "Les plus beaux romans d'amour," *La Presse*, [Online], 12 February 2010, https://www.lapresse.ca/arts/livres/201002/11/01-948691-les-plus-beaux-romans-damour.php.

105. Julie Beaulieu, *Un peu après minuit*, Montréal, Lanctôt, 2006, 152 p.
106. Jean-Luc Doumont, "*J'ai hâte à vous* de Julie Beaulieu + entrevue," *Made in Québec. Au coeur de l'actualité littéraire québécoise*, [Online], 3 November 2008, https://madeinquebec.wordpress.com/2008/11/03/jai-hte-vous-de-julie-beaulieu-entrevue/.
107. Sonia Alain, *Annabel et Max*, p. 410.
108. *Ibid.*, p. 412.
109. Régine Atzenhoffer, "Du roman sentimental à la littérature féminine érotique contemporaine," *Germanica*, No. 55, 2014, p. 211-227.
110. Céline Morin, "Du romantisme à la relation pure? Les amours des héroïnes de séries américaines depuis 1950," *Le Temps des médias*, Vol. 2, No. 19, 2012, p. 159-171.
111. Anne-Marie Olivier, "Entretien," *Faire l'amour*, coll. "Pièces," No. 1, Montréal, Atelier 10, 2014, p. 109.

Conclusion: The Codes of Love

1. Maud, "Chronique," *Le Journal du dimanche. Revue littéraire, artistique et de modes*, Vol. 2, No. 7, 14 February 1885, p. 50.
2. Paul-Émile Prévost, *L'épreuve*, Montréal, Alph. Pelletier, 1900, p. 69.
3. *Ibid.*, p. 106.
4. Floris Bluther [the pseudonym of Fernand Baboulène], *Marie-Anna la Canadienne*, Québec, [n.p.], 1913, p. 153.
5. Adèle Bibaud, Le secret de la marquise *et* Un homme d'honneur, *suivi des* Poésies canadiennes de Michel Bibaud, Montréal, Imprimerie P. H. Dalaire, 1906, p. 33.
6. R. Leoni, "La musique à Montréal," *La Lyre*, Vol. 4, No. 45, October 1926, p. 28.
7. Blanche Lamontagne-Beauregard, *Un cœur fidèle : roman canadien*, Montréal, Bibliothèque de l'Action française, 1924, p. 185.
8. Andrée Jarret [the pseudonym of Cécile Beauregard], *Le secret de l'orpheline*, coll. "Le Roman canadien," Vol. 52, Montréal, Éditions Édouard Garand, 1928, p. 25.
9. Laetitia Filion, *Yolande la fiancée*, [Lévis], [Imprimerie Le Quotidien], 1935, p. 188.
10. *Ibid.*
11. Jacques Régent, *Dernier amour*, coll. "Roman d'amour," Montréal, Éditions Police-Journal, 1947, p. 30.
12. *Ibid.*, p. 17.
13. Laura L. Doan, *Old Maids to Radical Spinsters: Unmarried Women in the Twentieth-century Novel*, Champaign (IL), University of Illinois Press, 1991, 285 p. Maroula Joannou, "'Nothing is Impracticable for a Single, Middle-Aged Woman with an Income of her Own': The Spinster in Women's Fiction of the 1920s," in Sybil Oldfield (ed.), *This Working-Day World: Women's Lives and Culture(s) in Britain, 1914-1945*, London, Taylor & Francis, 1994, p. 175-191.
14. Paul Guy, *Le héros de mon cœur*, coll. "Roman d'amour," Montréal, Éditions Police-Journal, 1958, p. 10.
15. "Quatre longs jours avant de devenir Madame Bob Lemieux." Maguy Lambert, *Trois belles filles*, Montréal, Éditions Police-Journal, [1958], p. 3.

16. Carol Thurston, *The Romance Revolution. Erotic Novels for Women and the Quest for a New Sexual Identity*, Urbana, University of Illinois Press, 1987, p. 16-32.
17. Jacques Benoit, "Harlequin, le géant du roman d'amour. On ne vend pas des romans mais une marque," *La Presse*, 15 October 1981, p. A6.
18. In 2001, out of 1500 authors, only a dozen were Canadian, even though the offices of the parent company were located in Toronto. Stéphanie Bérubé, "Harlequin, plus sexy et plus branché. Donna Hayes, la nouvelle PDG, part à la conquête des jeunes," *La Presse*, 14 October 2001, p. B1. Just a few titles in the Harlequin catalogue make references to Canada, for example, Sally Carr, *Escapade au Canada*, coll. "Azur," No. 1716, Toronto, Harlequin, 1997, 150 p.
19. Chloé Duval, *The Château by the River*, trans. Domitille Vimal du Monteil. New York, Lyrical Press, 2018, p. 330.
20. Mélanie Leblanc, *Si tu t'appelles Mélancolie*, Boucherville, Éditions de Mortagne, 2010, p. 29.
21. Rafaële Germain, *Gin & Tonic and Cucumber*, trans. Dawn M. Cornelio, Toronto, McArthur and Company, 2009, p. 334.
22. *Ibid.*, p. 13.
23. Marjorie D. Lafond, *Sous l'emprise de Monsieur Addams*, Montréal, Les Éditeurs réunis, 2015, p. 214.
24. Marjorie D. Lafond, *Corps et âmes*, Saint-Jean-sur-Richelieu, Les Éditeurs réunis, 2017, p. 338.
25. *Ibid.*, p. 344.
26. Marie-Pier Boisvert, *Partenariats pluriels : le polyamour dans trois romans québécois, suivi de* Au 5e, roman d'amours, Master's Thesis, Sherbrooke, Université de Sherbrooke, 2015, 193 p.

MIX
Paper
FSC® C100212

Printed by Imprimerie Gauvin
Gatineau, Québec